CAMBRIDGE TEXTS IN THE
HISTORY OF PHILOSOPHY

MOSES MENDELSSOHN

Philosophical Writings

CAMBRIDGE TEXTS IN THE HISTORY OF PHILOSOPHY

Series editors
KARL AMERIKS
Professor of Philosophy at the University of Notre Dame
DESMOND M. CLARKE
Professor of Philosophy at University College Cork

The main objective of Cambridge Texts in the History of Philosophy is to expand the range, variety and quality of texts in the history of philosophy which are available in English. The series includes texts by familiar names (such as Descartes and Kant) and also by less well-known authors. Wherever possible, texts are published in complete and unabridged form, and translations are specially commissioned for the series. Each volume contains a critical introduction together with a guide to further reading and any necessary glossaries and textual apparatus. The volumes are designed for student use at undergraduate and postgraduate level and will be of interest not only to students of philosophy, but also to a wider audience of readers in the history of science, the history of theology and the history of ideas.

For a list of titles published in the series, please see end of book.

MOSES MENDELSSOHN

Philosophical Writings

TRANSLATED AND EDITED BY

DANIEL O. DAHLSTROM

Boston University

CAMBRIDGE
UNIVERSITY PRESS

Published by the Press Syndicate of the University of Cambridge
The Pitt Building, Trumpington Street, Cambridge CB2 1RP
40 West 20th Street, New York NY 10011–4211, USA
10 Stamford Road, Oakleigh, Melbourne 3166, Australia

© Cambridge University Press 1997

First published 1997

Printed in the United Kingdom at the University Press, Cambridge

A catalogue record for this book is available from the British Library

Library of Congress cataloguing in publication data applied for

ISBN 0 521 57383 1 hardback
ISBN 0 521 57477 3 paperback

CE

On the ability to know, the ability to feel, and the ability to desire

Contents

Acknowledgments

A number of individuals have been of enormous help to me in producing this translation of Mendelssohn's essays. For their criticisms, suggestions, help in locating eighteenth-century texts, and proofreading, I would like to thank Abraham Anderson, Arnd Bohm, Conrad Cahill, Eugenie Schleberger Dahlstrom, Christopher Doss, Anthony Dowler, Knud Haakonssen, John Kelly, Anton Losinger, Michael O'Neill, Patricia Pintado, Irmgard Scherer, Mary Troxell, and Kevin White. I am also grateful to Hilary Gaskin and Lindeth Vasey of Cambridge University Press for the patience they showed me and to Karl Ameriks for suggesting the project and encouraging me to complete it.

Introduction

Moses Mendelssohn, one of the most gifted and intriguing figures of the German Enlightenment, first published his *Philosophical Writings* in 1761, and in a revised edition in 1771. Only one essay ("Rhapsody") was newly written; the others, dating back to 1754, had already established his reputation as a thoughtful and effective writer on a variety of issues of pressing concern to his contemporaries. In the *Philosophical Writings* the reader will find: an explanation of the various sorts and sources of pleasure, a nuanced defense of Leibniz's theodicy and conception of freedom, an examination of the ethics of suicide, an account of the "mixed sentiments" so central to the tragic genre, a hypothesis about weakness of will, an elaboration of the main principles and types of art, a definition of sublimity and analysis of its basic forms, and, lastly, a brief tract on probability theory, aimed at rebutting Hume's skepticism.

Despite its rich range of themes, Mendelssohn's collection of six youthful essays does not lack for unity. Their common purpose is to demonstrate the continuing viability of a metaphysical framework shaped by Leibniz and Christian Wolff, especially for a topic – the nature and variety of sentiments – often neglected by that metaphysical tradition and treated with greater sensitivity by English and French authors. "Sentiment" stands here for an emotionally and hedonically charged human knowledge or awareness by way of the senses, one that can be "perfect or complete" when its object is something beautiful. In the Wolffian tradition, *cognitio sensitiva* is an inferior variant of cognition, the subject of an "empirical psychology" that is a division of a metaphysically grounded epistemology. Wolff himself admitted, however, that his system lacked a sustained treatment of this topic in regard to the arts, thereby opening the door for the work of Johann Christian Gottsched, Johann Jacob Bodmer, and Johann Jacob Breitinger, and, most famously, Alexander Baumgarten. Much of Mendelssohn's *Philosophical Writings* can be read as yet another contribution to this project.

Included with the *Philosophical Writings* is Mendelssohn's prize winning essay of 1763, "On evidence in the metaphysical sciences," of which Lewis White Beck has written: "No other single work gives so perspicuous a presentation of the Leibniz–Wolffian tradition."[1] Because of their historical significance for developments in the German Enlightenment, two short pieces – "On the ability to know, the ability to feel, and the ability to desire" (1776) and "What does 'to enlighten' mean?" (1784) – have also been included in the present volume. Moving beyond both Baumgarten's single-faculty (cognitive) theory and Johann Georg Sulzer's dual-faculty (cognitive and affective) theory, "On the ability" is a harbinger of theories developed by Johann Nicolaus Tetens and Kant. The final essay, which preceded by four months Kant's article on the same topic, is important for its identification of enlightenment (*Aufklärung*) and culture (*Cultur*) as complementary sides of education (*Bildung*), but perhaps even more so for its contention that the enlightenment of human beings and the enlightenment of citizens can be in conflict with one another.[2]

Mendelssohn's beginnings

The son of Mendel Heymann, a Torah scribe, and Bela Rachel Sara, Moses Mendelssohn entered the world on 6 September 1729 in the Dessau ghetto (Germany). As a youth, under the tutelage of the learned Rabbi David Fränkel, Mendelssohn studied the Bible and the Talmud and was introduced to Moses Maimonides's adaptation of Muslim Aristotelianism to the Jewish tradition. At the age of fourteen,

---

[1] *Early German Philosophy: Kant and his Predecessors* (Cambridge, Mass., Harvard University Press, 1969), p. 332. There is some warrant for the inclusion of the prize essay in the present volume since Mendelssohn contemplated publishing a revised version in the 1771 edition of the *Philosophical Writings*.

[2] Kant's essay "Reply to the question: what is enlightenment?" was completed before he had the opportunity to read Mendelssohn's piece. On the possibility of a conflict between the virtue of a good human being and that of a good citizen, see Aristotle, *Politics*, Bk. III, ch. 4.

Mendelssohn followed Fränkel to Berlin. There his appreciation of Jewish medieval philosophy was profoundly enriched by his close relationship with the noted Maimonides scholar, Israel Samoscz. But two friends and mentors, Abraham Kisch and Aaron Solomon Gumperz, also opened up entirely new worlds to the precocious young man. Kisch gave Mendelssohn his first lessons in Latin, and through Gumperz, who helped him with French and English, Mendelssohn became acquainted with members of the Royal Academy of Sciences. More significantly, perhaps, Gumperz provided Mendelssohn with an important example of a Jewish intellectual capable of reaching out to other movements of European thought without forfeiting his own roots. During this period Mendelssohn developed an uncommon familiarity with the classic and modern texts that formed the horizon for the issues debated among his Christian colleagues. Mendelssohn's contemporaries could hardly have appreciated the unique blend of linguistic competences and knowledge of the history of diverse theological and philosophical traditions, including medieval Aristotelianism, that he was able to bring to this study. When Mendelssohn began to hit his stride in the essays contained in the present volume, he was able to make remarkably competent use of works by Sophocles and Plato, Horace and Virgil, Jean Baptiste Du Bos and Voltaire, Locke and Shaftesbury, Leibniz and Wolff (to name only a few of the authors cited by Mendelssohn from the four languages mentioned).

Through Gumperz, Mendelssohn made Gotthold Ephraim Lessing's acquaintance in 1754. Mendelssohn's senior by eight months, Lessing would become a lifelong friend and occasional collaborator (see their "Pope, A Metaphysician!" in 1755) and immortalize Mendelssohn as the model for the religious tolerance and good will of the protagonist in the dramatic poem *Nathan the Wise* (*Nathan der Weise*, 1779). For twenty-five years, until shortly before Lessing's death in 1781, the two would correspond with one another, leaving behind, among other things, a remarkable debate about the significance and import of the tragic genre.

The essays in the "Philosophical Writings"

Metaphysics, not literary theory, was the principal subject of discussion between Lessing and Mendelssohn during the early years of their friendship. Lessing initiated Mendelssohn into the public world of letters by publishing Mendelssohn's *Dialogues* (probably with some improvements of Mendelssohn's still halting command of German). Later revised (over Lessing's objections) and published in *Philosophical Writings*, the *Dialogues* is noteworthy for its critical and qualified endorsement of Leibniz's theodicy. The first two dialogues revive the argument that Leibniz's formulation of his metaphysics is seriously indebted to Spinoza's thought.[3] Mendelssohn argues not only that Spinoza articulated the basic notion of a preestablished harmony in advance of Leibniz, but that even his errors in denying divine and human freedom contributed essentially to Leibniz's ability to articulate the compatibility of freedom with the preestablished harmony. (Mendelssohn concludes the first dialogue by noting that Leibniz, "not merely the greatest, but also the most careful philosopher," did not acknowledge his debt for prudential reasons; p. 104.) In the third dialogue, after dismissing Voltaire's trivial criticisms of Leibniz's view that this is the best possible world, Mendelssohn notes some lingering difficulties with the doctrine. For example, in order for the divine intellect to choose to create this world as the best possible world, the possibility of this world must have presented itself as a definite whole to the divine intellect, even if this world is, indeed, infinite in some respects. However, if this supposedly best possible world is limited in some measure, then it is not clear why a more perfect world is not possible. As long as this possibility obtains, it is also not clear how God could ever have had a sufficient reason to choose this world. Though this difficulty remains unresolved in Mendelssohn's eyes, he does not consider it debilitating for the Leibnizian doctrine that this is the best possible world. Once God's existence and wisdom are countenanced, he contends, the conclusion that this is the best possible world is inevitable. The fourth dialogue presents Wolff's defense of Leibniz's doctrine of the identity of indiscernibles in the face of criticisms advanced by Voltaire and, more recently, André Pierre Le Guay Prémontval.

The response to Prémontval's recent publications points to an important historical dimension of the *Dialogues*. In its essay contests of 1747 and 1751, with Maupertuis as president, the Royal Academy had awarded prizes to essays that criticized the Leibnizian doctrine of monads and its alleged determinism. By taking issue with Prémontval and

---

[3] See Alexander Altmann, *Moses Mendelssohn: A Biographical Study* (University, Alabama, University of Alabama Press, 1973), p. 52.

advancing a qualified endorsement of Leibnizian–Wolffian metaphysics in the *Dialogues*, Mendelssohn is countering an antispeculative tendency in the Royal Academy that was prominent among its French members.[4]

In early 1755 Mendelssohn became friends with Friedrich Nicolai who introduced him to Berlin's literary and scientific circles, in particular, the exclusive "Scholars' Coffee House." The essay "On probability" was first presented to this club. Nicolai was instrumental in, as Mendelssohn put it in a letter to Lessing, his "infidelity" to metaphysics and attempt to become a *bel esprit*.[5] Indeed, it was Nicolai's "Treatise on Tragedy" (1756) that prompted the memorable correspondence between Lessing and Mendelssohn on the tragic genre. For over two decades beginning in 1757 (until their friendship began to wane in later years), Nicolai would enlist Mendelssohn's help in producing three successive journals: *Bibliothek der schönen Wissenschaften und der freyen Künste* (*Library of Fine Sciences and Free Arts*; twenty-one articles by Mendelssohn appear in the four volumes of 1757–58, two of which resurface in the *Philosophical Writings*), *Briefe, die neueste Literatur betreffend* (1759–65; Mendelssohn composed over 112 of the *Letters Concerning the Latest Literature*, which contained critical reviews), and *Allgemeine deutsche Bibliothek* (*General German Library*; only occasional short reviews by Mendelssohn between 1765 and 1775).

Nicolai clearly provided Mendelssohn with an important vehicle and stimulus, but he was already moving in this direction, as evidenced by his second publication, the letters "On sentiments," the first and longest essay in the *Philosophical Writings*. Yet, this exchange of letters, loosely modelled on the Third Earl of Shaftesbury's *The Moralists, A Philosophical Rhapsody* (1709), also belies or at least qualifies Mendelssohn's remark about his infidelity to metaphysics. For the entire account of sentiments is framed by epistemological and psychological considera-

---

[4]   As a Jew, Mendelssohn never gained entry into the Academy though it, acting on a resolution moved by Sulzer, did propose his name in 1771, only to be vetoed by the king; for details, see Altmann, *A Biographical Study*, pp. 264–5 and 801–2. Forming part of the horizon for the issue discussed in the *Dialogues* is the argument made against Leibniz's account of divine freedom by Christian August Crusius (1715–75) in *Sketch of Necessary Truths of Reason* (*Entwurf der notwendigen Vernunft-Wahrheiten*) (Leipzig, 1745) which also contains a criticism of Wolff's attempts to model philosophy on mathematics.

[5]   See the "Jubilee edition" of Mendelssohn's works, vol. 11, Letter 27, p. 55: "Madam Metaphysics may forgive me. She asserts that friendship rests on the identity of inclinations, and I find that, on the contrary, identity of inclinations may, in reverse, rest on friendship." For full information about the "Jubilee edition," see Further reading. Cf. also Altmann, *A Biographical Study*, p. 66. According to Altmann (p. 65), Mendelssohn met Nicolai in early 1755.

tions which are themselves rooted in broader metaphysical conceptions of the nature of things and their perfection.

Thus the letters commence with an appeal to Baumgarten's definition of beauty as an indistinct representation of a perfection.[6] On the basis of this definition, the youthful and Epicurean-minded Euphranor contends that pleasure and rational analysis, like beauty and truth, are incompatible. The older Theocles responds by noting that what is wholly obscure (a whole without parts) is just as incompatible with pleasure and the experience of beauty as something wholly distinct (parts without a whole). Pleasure, Theocles submits, involves a clear but indistinct representation of a whole, and rational analysis of the parts can prepare the way for this satisfying perception of the whole. Moreover, rational analysis and insight into a harmony existing among the parts afford a kind of pleasure even when they do not, as in the case of God or sheer intellectual activity, lead to a clear and distinct representation of things.

Theocles accordingly distinguishes between the pleasure of sensuous perfection and that of intellectual perfection. The former is the pleasure of beauty in the sense of a unity of a multiplicity of things, capable of being taken in at a single clear but indistinct glance.[7] In other words, the

---

6   Alexander Baumgarten, *Aesthetica* (Frankfurt an der Oder, 1750), Pt. I, Section 1, §14, p. 6: "Aesthetices finis est perfectio cognitionis sensitivae, qua talis, haec autem est pulchritudo, et cavenda eiusdem, qua talis, imperfectio, haec autem est deformitas" ("The end of aesthetics is the perfection of sensuous cognition which, however, as such is beauty. To be avoided is the imperfection of sensuous cognition, which, however, as such is deformity"). Cf. Baumgarten's, *Metaphysica*, 7th edn. (Halle and Magdeburg, 1779), Part I, ch. 1, Section VII, §94, p. 26: "Si plura simul sumta unius rationem sufficientem constituunt, *consentiunt* (*übereinstimmen*), consensus ipse est *perfectio* (*Vollkommenheit*), et unum, in quod consentitur, *ratio perfectionis determinans* (focus perfectionis)" ("If many things, taken at the same time, constitute the sufficient reason for some one thing, they *agree* (*übereinstimmen* [=harmonize]); this agreement is the perfection (*Vollkommenheit* [=perfection or completeness]) and that one thing, in which there is this agreement is the *determining reason for the perfection* (the focus of the perfection)"). A representation is indistinct if the parts or multiplicity that it represents are not distinguished or delineated. Colors and sounds, for examples, are indistinct representations because they cannot be broken down into discrete parts or, in other words, analyzed into more basic components. Hence, they are also indefinable. See note 9. Alexander Baumgarten (1714–62) disciple of Wolff, is best known for giving the field of aesthetics its name with his *Aesthetica*, and was held in high esteem by Kant.

7   Sulzer is Mendelssohn's apparent source for the definition of beauty as, objectively, a unity of a multiplicity of things and, subjectively, a clear but indistinct representation. The explication of this clear representation in terms of the ease with which a whole of things is perceived (cognized) was taken over by Sulzer from Louis Jean Levesque de Pouilly's *Théorie des sentiments agréables* (Paris, 1747). For a discussion of Mendelssohn's early critical consideration of Sulzer's position, see Altmann, *A Biographical Study*, pp. 56–7.

beautiful object is experienced as a whole (therein lies the perfection of sensuous cognition), but it affords too many features for them all to be perceived distinctly. Conversely, for something to be beautiful, its parts cannot be so uniform as not to be perceived nor so diverse that no unity can be detected. While the pleasure we take in beauty thus rests upon the limitations of the human soul, the pleasure of intellectual perfection is based upon "a positive power of our soul," namely, an ability to grasp the purposive harmony of a multiplicity of things (p. 24). Moreover, inasmuch as these levels of pleasure (beauty and truth) are distinguished as different kinds of perfection of the same inherent cognitive capacity, there is a natural propensity towards them as goods. Theocles thus adds that pleasure and willing differ "only to a degree" (p. 29).

Euphranor is willing to concede that reason is not a killjoy, but he still contests the notion that "the basis of all pleasure is to be found either in perfection or in beauty" (p. 35). Euphranor raises two counterexamples to Theocles' thesis. In the first place, there are some typical cases ("love and wine") where, instead of regarding something as "pleasurable" because of its goodness, we call it "good" or "perfect" because of the sheer sensuous pleasure it affords us. In the second place, human beings often take a strange sort of pleasure in the representation of what are not mere imperfections, but utterly terrifying or ghastly sights ("vertigo-inducing heights" and "bloody slaughters"; p. 36). Without naming it as such, Euphranor has introduced the subject of the sublime.

Theocles responds by conceding that sensuous pleasures for the most part have more power over the soul than intellectual forms of enjoyment and that some sources of pleasure seem to be anything but perfections. But he is not willing to relinquish his basic principle that pleasure in all its forms corresponds to the representation of some perfection. An improvement in the state of one's body (typically, the achievement of some harmony among its parts) produces pleasure prior to thought. The soul then comes along and, without being able to oversee all this distinctly, will nevertheless have an obscure but lively *"representation of the perfection of its body"* (p. 46).

At this point, the account in the letters of the kinds and sources of pleasure is practically complete. There are three kinds of pleasure: sensuous pleasure, the pleasure of beauty, and intellectual pleasure. The sources of the pleasures are, respectively, some improvement in the condition of our bodies, some unity (sameness) among a multiplicity of parts or things, and some harmony in such a multiplicity.[8] The three kinds of pleasure correspond roughly to the threefold division of the most basic ways of cognizing (entertaining, representing) things, namely, obscurely, clearly, and distinctly. This division, the cornerstone of rationalist epistemology and psychology, is based upon levels of distinguishability. We are aware of something only *obscurely* when our perception of it and its makeup is not sufficient to enable us distinguish it from other things. Something is cognized *clearly but confusedly* when it is perceived as a definite whole (a unity of a multiplicity of things) and, hence, distinguishable from other wholes and reidentifiable, even though the things that make it up as a whole are not distinguished. Something is cognized *distinctly* (and not just clearly) when the things that make it up as a whole are distinguished, thereby allowing it to be defined.[9]

Left unaddressed by Theocles' account of the kinds and sources of pleasure is the second counterexample mentioned by Euphranor, namely, the example of so-called "mixed sentiments" or the pleasure that people take in the sight of something painful, terrifying, or ghastly.[10] Theocles turns to this lingering issue in the conclusion to the letters. He distinguishes between cases where sympathy is not involved (the tightrope artist) or even suppressed (gladiatorial bouts), and those where sympathy is aroused (tragic drama). In the former cases, we delight in someone's skill, and, in the latter, we feel affection for

---

[8] While all arts draw in one way or another upon these three sources according to Theocles, he claims that music alone draws on all three at once; see the Eleventh letter.

[9] Alternatively: something is entertained (thought, cognized, or represented) *confusedly* when its features are represented or perceived but not distinguished. Something is entertained *distinctly* when those features are distinguished. If the features are so dimly perceived that it is not possible to distinguish what is confusedly represented from other things, then it is represented *obscurely*. Cf. Baumgarten, *Metaphysica*, Pt. III, ch. 1: Psychologia Empirica, §510, p. 175: "Quaedam distincte, quaedam confuse cogito. Confuse aliquid cogitans, eius notas non distinguit, repraesentat tamen, seu percipit. Nam si notas confuse repraesentati distingueret, quae confuse repraesentat, distincte cogitaret: si prorsus non perciperet notas confuse cogitati, per eas confuse perceptum non distinguere valeret ab aliis. Ergo confuse quid cogitans quaedam obscure repraesentat" ("I think some things distinctly, some things confusedly. Thinking something confusedly, one does not distinguish its marks but nevertheless represents or perceives them. For if one would distinguish the marks of what is confusedly represented, one would think them distinctly; if one would not perceive straightaway the marks of what is thought confusedly, one would not have the power to distinguish what was confusedly perceived through them from other things"). Cf. ibid., §521, p. 180: "*Repraesentatio* non distincta *sensitiva* vocatur" ("A nondistinct *representation* is called *sensuous*").

[10] Another issue raised by Euphranor (see the Ninth letter) is the question of the justifiability of suicide. The bulk of the final three letters (Thirteenth–Fifteenth) are devoted to refuting arguments that there are conditions under which suicide is permissible. Cf. also Alexander Altmann, *Moses Mendelssohns Frühschriften zur Metaphysik* (Tübingen, Mohr, 1969), pp. 138–183.

someone because of his virtue or innocence, qualities magnified by the misfortune facing him. Thus, in each case a perfection, the skillfulness or the quality of the person arousing our sympathy, remains the source of the pleasure we feel.

Six years after the publication of the letters on sentiments, Mendelssohn revises his conception of mixed sentiments in "Rhapsody, or additions to the Letters on sentiments." Much as Kant does later, he distinguishes between the existence of an object and the act of representing or entertaining it, noting that, even if we would rather that the object did not exist, we can still prefer having the representation of it to not having it.

> Each individual representation stands in a twofold relation. It is related, at once, to the matter before it as its object (of which it is a picture or copy) and then to the soul or the thinking subject (of which it constitutes a determination). As a determination of the soul, many a representation can have something pleasant about it although, as a picture of the object, it is accompanied by disapproval and a feeling of repugnance. Thus, we must indeed take care not to mix or confuse these two relations, the objective and the subjective, with one another. (p. 132)

By sorting out these two relations, Mendelssohn solves what would otherwise be a problem for the theory that pleasure is always directed at or based upon some perfection. In the case of something terrifying or ghastly, the perfection that yields the pleasure is not in the object but in the subject. In other words, the recognition of the imperfection in the object is a perfection or, as Mendelssohn also puts it, "an affirmative determination of the soul" (p. 133).[11]

This explanation of the pleasure of mixed sentiments is valid, Mendelssohn adds, only as long as the object and the act can be distinguished. If the object is our own pain or misfortune or that of someone with whom we genuinely identify, then the distinction collapses and, with it, the pleasure. The peculiar advantage of the artistic medium lies precisely in its ability to sustain this distinction. Art is able to render the most terrifying or unjust events pleasant by imitating them in some medium (stage, canvas, marble) that both

---

[11] In acknowledging this revision, Mendelssohn concedes that his criticism, in the letters on sentiments, of Du Bos' explanation of these mixed sentiments must be retracted: see pp. 136–7).

moderates the painfulness of the object and elevates the pleasure yielded by the affirmation of the subject's ability to recognize what is terrifying or unjust for what it is. In the case of the tragic genre, the situation is more complicated, to be sure. But in Mendelssohn's eyes, it nonetheless confirms this basic account of the pleasure afforded by mixed sentiments. Tragedy, he maintains, is based upon sympathy, "a mixed sentiment composed of love for an object and discontent at its misfortune" (pp. 141–2).[12] That love for the object involves two perfections, one on the part of the object and one on the part of the subject, each a source of pleasure that is enhanced by the pain and misfortune (imperfection) befalling the tragic hero.

The sheer immensity of certain things or properties presents yet another wrinkle on the theory of mixed sentiments outlined above. In these cases the imperfection lies, not in the object as such, but in the subject, where it is joined, of course, with some perfection insofar as the experience is pleasurable.

> The unfathomable world of the sea, a far-reaching plain, the innumerable legions of stars, the eternity of time, every height and depth that exhausts us, a great genius, great virtues that we admire but cannot attain; who can look upon these things without trembling? Who can continue to feast his eyes upon them without experiencing a pleasant sort of dizziness? This sentiment is composed of gratification, and its opposite. The magnitude of the object affords us gratification but our inability to comprehend its boundaries adds a certain degree of bitterness to this gratification, making it all the more alluring. (pp. 144–5)

This theory of mixed sentiments leads to a further emendation of the account of pleasure in the letters on sentiments. Inasmuch as the soul's activity of representing things, even imperfections, constitutes a pleasure-inducing perfection of it, so its experience of pleasure cannot be that of a spectator, merely appreciating the improved condition of the body (as "On sentiments" suggested was the case for the most basic sorts of pleasures). Rather, the soul's pleasure must also stem from the reality that is added to it by "the harmonious engagement and exercise of the powers of sentiment and desire" (p. 140). This observation points to the importance of educating our sentiments.

---

[12] This definition of tragedy is presented as a direct challenge to standard views that tragedy is based upon sentiments of terror and sympathy or fear and sympathy; cf. p. 142.

We are called in this life not only to improve our powers of understanding and willing, but also to educate feeling by means of sentient knowledge and to raise the obscure impulses of the soul to a higher perfection by means of sensuous pleasures. When we neglect the latter, we act as contrary to the intentions of the creator as when we neglect the former. We only make ourselves miserable when we lack a sense of proportion, preferring the trivial to the important, the lesser perfection to the higher one, the passing moment to the lasting future. (p. 140)

The theory of mixed sentiments was initially developed to explain the special instances of pleasures, such as those afforded by the tragic genre and immense objects, that clearly involve some sort of imperfection and displeasure. But the finitude of human nature insures that mixed sentiments are not special instances, but in fact the rule, to which there is no exception. This consideration provides Mendelssohn with yet another opportunity to challenge Maupertuis and, in the process, elaborate the ethical import of mixed sentiments. In particular, the theory of mixed sentiments provides him with the means of contesting Maupertuis' project of computing sentiments in order to arrive at a so-called "sum of happiness," as though there were quantifiable units of sheer pleasure, and displeasure in every case diminished the sum of pleasure (see p. 148). Mendelssohn attributes this project to the revival of a refined Epicureanism that attempts to reduce the human being's highest good to pleasant sentiment rather than, "with the Stoics, looking for it in a state of harmony with nature or, with the modern philosophers, looking for it in the original drive for perfection" (p. 150). Mendelssohn accordingly adds that, while pleasant sentiments have a place in practical ethics, they have no place in theoretical ethics. "Perfection and not pleasant sentiment," he insists, "must be called 'the supreme ground of all free actions,' that is to say, 'the *highest good* '" (p. 151).[13]

Mendelssohn concludes "Rhapsody" by proposing a hypothesis to solve the problem of human evil or, as it might also be called, weakness

---

[13] Mendelssohn's claim that perfection is the basis of ethics is rooted in a wider theological and metaphysical conception of perfection: cf. "The essence of God consists in perfection; it is the plan of creation, the source of all natural and supernatural events, the goal of all our desires and wishes, the guiding principle of our actions and omissions; it is the supreme principle in ethics, in politics, and in the arts and sciences of pleasure" (p. 154). This opposition to modern Epicureanism, even while Mendelssohn affirms the practical necessity of refined sentiments for ethics, is iterated in "On the main principles of the fine arts" and in the final section of "On evidence in metaphysical sciences" (pp. 169–91 and 295–306).

of will (p. 158). "According to this hypothesis, one could thus say that the effective force of impulses is (1) proportional to the magnitude of the good that they strive for, (2) proportional to the magnitude of our insight, and (3) inversely proportional to the time required to consider this good" (p. 160). This proportion, he submits, explains how emotions ("nothing but indistinct representations, arising simultaneously in the mind, of some considerable good or evil") can be more powerful than rational insight into (a distinct concept of) some good (p. 161). The emotion "defeats" reason when the goods obscurely perceived by the emotion outnumber the goods distinctly perceived and/or when those emotional goods are perceived more rapidly than the rational goods (even though the former are perceived less distinctly and surely than the latter). One implication that Mendelssohn draws from this consideration is the vital importance of proficiencies or perfected habits, capacities to perform certain actions so speedily that we are no longer conscious of everything that we are doing in the process.

The next essay in *Philosophical Writings*, "On the main principles of the fine arts and sciences," returns, as its title suggests, to the ancient issue of the relation between painting and poetry, epitomized by Horace's line: *Ut poesis pictura.*[14] "Fine sciences," it bears noting, refers to writing that is fine or, more literally, beautiful (*schön*). By addressing this problem, Mendelssohn is taking issue with Charles Batteux, though Francis Hutcheson's *An Inquiry into the Original of Our Ideas of Beauty and Virtue* (London, 1725) also becomes the object of explicit criticism. Batteux, the author of *Les beaux arts réduits à un même principe* in 1746 (translated into German by Johann Elias Schlegel in 1751), defended the traditional principle that the essence of all arts consists in the imitation of nature. Mendelssohn agrees with the attempt to locate a single principle but he rejects the notion that it is to be found in the difference between art and nature. Instead, after noting that nature is quite pleasing when it is not imitated, he asks what the beauties of nature and of art have in common, in relation to the human soul, that accounts for their being so pleasing to it. Rejecting an appeal to God's will as well as Hutcheson's attempt to invoke an aesthetic sense (in

---

[14] "Poetry is like painting." Cf. the Greek lyric poet Simonides of Keos' formulation of the thesis: "poema loquens pictura, pictura tacitum poema"; for a brief overview of the history of this issue, especially among Mendelssohn's contemporaries and immediate forerunners in Europe, see Armand Nivelle, *Kunst- und Dichtungstheorien zwischen Aufklärung und Klassik*, 2nd, expanded edn. (Berlin and New York, de Gruyter, 1971), pp. 115–17.

Mendelssohn's view they are equivalent), Mendelssohn once again elaborates the basic theory that beauty is the perfection of a sensuous cognition, an awareness or knowledge that is not obscure, but indistinct. However, amplifying a point broached in earlier writings, he also stresses the underlying connection between desire and the pleasure of beauty as well as the mediating potential of beauty based on that connection. Every sentiment, Mendelssohn observes (and here the term "sensation" would be an even more appropriate translation), involves a degree of satisfaction or dissatisfaction, respectively corresponding to some perfection or its opposite, on the one hand, as well as to a love of the former and an abhorrence of the latter, on the other. To be sure, there is, as noted earlier, an intellectual pleasure in knowing something distinctly. But, according to Mendelssohn, this capacity to know something in all its distinctness can set in motion the soul's capacity to desire only by transforming that object of distinct knowledge into something beautiful. This claim plainly foreshadows the difference, later formulated by Mendelssohn, among the faculties of cognition, sentiment, and desire, but it also confirms their underlying complementarity. As the very perfection of sensuous cognition, beauty and, by implication, the arts have a mediating role to perform between what a person knows and what he or she desires (p. 169).

From the basic account of beauty as a form of pleasurable sentiment, Mendelssohn derives his main principle for fine arts and sciences. "We have now found the universal means of pleasing our soul, namely, the *sensuously perfect representation*. And since the final purpose of the fine arts is to please, we can presuppose the following principle as indubitable: the essence of the fine arts and sciences consists in an artful, sensuously perfect representation or in a sensuous perfection represented by art" (pp. 172–3). This sensuously perfect, i.e., beautiful representation is, Mendelssohn recalls, possible even where the object of the representation is neither good nor beautiful in nature. When, for example, the paradigm in nature is not beautiful, we delight in the imitation both for the artistry and for the realization that it is only an imitation. Indeed, in an obvious concession to Batteux and the tradition he represents, Mendelssohn notes the necessity of imitation in art and the advantage over nature that accrues to art precisely because it consists in imitation. The artist is not hampered, as nature is, by the need to pursue any purpose higher than beauty. This advantage, Mendelssohn adds, explains why study of the ancients can be more useful than study of nature. The ancients have already performed the necessary abstraction and idealization.

Mendelssohn does not pretend to have worked out an entire system of the arts. But the second half of "On the main principles" does contain a division of the fine arts and sciences, which turns on a difference between natural and arbitrary signs.

> They [the signs] are natural if the combination of the sign with the subject matter signified is grounded in the very properties of what is designated. The passions are, by virtue of their nature, connected with certain movements in our limbs as well as with certain sounds and gestures. Hence, anyone who expresses an emotion by means of the sounds, gestures, and movements appropriate to it, makes use of natural signs. Those signs, on the other hand, that by their very nature have nothing in common with the designated subject matter, but have nonetheless been arbitrarily assumed as signs for it, are called "arbitrary." The articulated sounds of all languages, the letters, the hieroglyphic signs of the ancients, and some allegorical images, which can rightly be counted among the latter, are of this type. (pp. 177–8)

On the basis of this division, Mendelssohn presents the following breakdown of "fine sciences" and "fine arts":

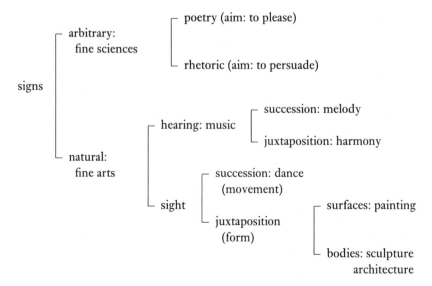

The fine sciences can express everything of which we can have a clear concept, while the fine arts are more limited. At the same time Mendelssohn acknowledges that these borders quite naturally "often blur into one another" (p. 181). "On the main principles" accordingly concludes with a discussion of the ways the arts may borrow from each other (e.g., in the painter's use of allegories) and even be combined with one another (e.g., in opera).

The theory of mixed sentiments in "Rhapsody," outlined above, is based in part upon an earlier and more extended account of the sublime in the penultimate essay of the *Philosophical Writings*. The explicit aim of the essay, entitled "On the sublime and naive in the fine sciences," is to define the sublime. Mendelssohn moves toward a definition in three steps: first, he contrasts the enormous and the immense with the beautiful, then he identifies two forms of immensity, and finally he locates the sublime as a kind of immensity. The difference between the beautiful and the enormous is the difference between something with definite boundaries that can be taken in by the senses all at once and something that oversteps those boundaries. When something is so enormous that it defies any attempt to experience it as a definite whole, it is immense (p. 193). The pleasure we derive from such immensities is mixed since they are immense or enormous relative to an imperfection on our part, a limited cognitive facility. Art, Mendelssohn adds, has a particular means of arousing this mixed sentiment, namely, through uniform and frequent repetitions at equal spatial or temporal intervals (for example, a straight corridor of pillars in architecture or monotone repetitions in music) where we are unable to perceive any symmetry or order that would indicate the end of the repetition.

Not unlike Kant's later distinction between the mathematically and the dynamically sublime, Mendelssohn distinguishes two sorts of immensity, the immensity of extended and of non-extended ("intensive") magnitudes, though he clearly shows a preference for the latter. "Power, genius, virtue have their unextended immensity that likewise arouses a spine-tingling sentiment but has the advantage of not ending, through tedious uniformity, in satiation and even disgust, as generally happens in the case of the extended immensity" (p. 194). In general, something that is intensively enormous or immense is said to be strong and when that strength is a matter of a perfection, it is said to be sublime. Hence, as the following chart illustrates, Mendelssohn defines the sublime in terms of the immense as a subspecies of the latter.

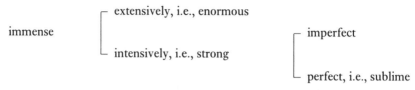

immense

extensively, i.e., enormous

intensively, i.e., strong

imperfect

perfect, i.e., sublime

The mixed sentiment produced by the sublime is awe, an awe at a perfection that, because of its immensity, goes beyond our customary expectations or conceptions of it. With these general considerations of the sublime in hand, Mendelssohn defines the sublime in art as a sensuously perfect representation of something immense, capable of inspiring awe.[15]

This definition is somewhat misleading, since Mendelssohn delineates two types of sublimity, depending upon whether the awe is directed at the object represented (including human sensibilities and character) or the manner of representation. He acknowledges the relativity of the latter type of sublimity but maintains that sublime objects "must be pleasing to everyone everywhere" (p. 218). He discusses each type of sublimity with a view towards addressing the question of the degree of embellishment that can be countenanced by each type. Since Longinus was concerned primarily with this second type of sublimity ("genius"), Mendelssohn devotes more space to the question of what constitutes a sublime object. He notes that the awe directed at the sublime object is such that it cannot be said either to follow from any particular conception or to be directed (via the imagination) at any particular conception. Nor is this awe to be confused with any other sort of emotion such as love or sympathy. Such observations, it bears recalling, prefigure important features of Kant's aesthetics, for example, his insistence on the disinterestedness of aesthetic judgments, on their nondeductibility from any concept of taste, and on the indeterminacy of the concepts involved in the free play between imagination and understanding.

Mendelssohn concludes this essay with a consideration of the sort of naive expressions that are particularly well-suited to represent the first

---

[15] Mendelssohn observes that, since "the enormous is for the outer sense precisely what the sublime is for the inner sense" (p. 196), art often is able to present the former as a means of preparing the way for a depiction of the latter.

type of sublimity. An expression or representation is naive if the manner of expression or representation is simple and uncontrived but what is expressed or represented is sublime (p. 229). Speaking of the naivete of a face, which has served painters and sculptors so well, Mendelssohn remarks that "it is always something not sought, something unsophisticated in the outer appearance that unintentionally betrays an inner splendidness" (p. 226). So, too, grace ("sublime beauty in movement") is bound up with the naive expression by revealing "the stirrings of the heart" in an unforced manner (p. 226).[16]

The prize essay

With the exception of the *Dialogues*, Mendelssohn's essays in the *Philosophical Writings* and many contributions to the *Bibliothek der schönen Wissenschaften* attest to the fact that the first five years of Mendelssohn's public life as a writer were principally devoted to issues at the crossroads of aesthetics and psychology, criticism and epistemology. By no means, however, did he lose interest in metaphysics. Nor would it have been possible for him to lose interest in a discipline whose very nature and integrity had been, as noted earlier, a matter of such public dispute within the Royal Prussian Academy of Sciences.

In 1761 the *Classe de philosophie spéculative* of the Royal Academy announced an essay contest for the year 1763 on the question: "Whether metaphysical truths in general, and the first principles of natural theology and morality in particular, are susceptible of the same evidence as mathematical truths; and in case they are not, what is the nature of their certitude; which degree can it attain; and whether this degree is sufficient to impart conviction?"[17] The very formulation of the question may seem to put the metaphysician on the defensive. Maupertuis' term as president of the Royal Academy ended in 1756 but not before he issued an answer to the question with his "Examen philosophique de la preuve de l'existence de Dieu employée dans l'Essai de Cosmologie."[18]

---

[16] Mendelssohn also acknowledges another kind of naivete in which an expression simply reveals something unintentionally and what is revealed is foolish or dangerous (in such cases the naive is said to be, respectively, "ridiculous" or "tragic"): see pp. 231–2).

[17] Adolf Harnack, *Geschichte der Königlich preußischen Akademie der Wissenschaften zu Berlin* (Berlin, Reichsdruckerei, 1900), vol. 2, pp. 306–7.

[18] *Histoire de l'Académie Royale des Sciences et Belle-Lettres*, Année 1756 (Berlin, 1758), pp. 389–424.

In this essay Maupertuis argues that there is evidence and agreement only in the case of mathematical sciences because these sciences' objects (number and extension) alone admit of addition and subtraction. Computing with qualities, he contends, is possible only to the extent that their effects can be related to numbers or extension. When Mendelssohn mentions in the Introduction that many a discerning mind rejects the first principles of metaphysics, he no doubt has Maupertuis in mind.

Nevertheless, Maupertuis died in 1759 and the question raised by the Royal Academy, far from denying the existence of metaphysical truths, simply inquires whether they are capable of the same sort of evidence as mathematics. Moreover, Sulzer, a Wolffian, was head of the "Classe de philosophie spéculative" and Mendelssohn's essay was in fact awarded the prize (over, among others, Kant's entry, *Inquiry Concerning the Distinctiveness of the Principles of Natural Theology and Morals*, though the Royal Academy showed its high regard for Kant's piece by publishing it together with Mendelssohn's).[19] Hence, there is little reason to think that the question was motivated by some anti-metaphysical bias or that, as Leo Strauss maintains, Maupertuis was the main object of Mendelssohn's essay.[20] The question seems to stem instead from a debate over the Wolffian view that philosophy and mathematics share a common method, derived from logic. Wolff's views on method had been challenged by Crusius for some time, and the issue had recently resurfaced in Lambert's essay on the "Criterion of Truth."[21]

Mendelssohn ultimately endorses the Wolffian view but in a highly qualified fashion. In fact, he begins by acknowledging that metaphysics has not been provided with the same degree of evidence as mathematics has. He notes, however, that there is more than one kind or level of mathematical evidence. The truths of geometry are not more certain but they are more "perspicuous" than those of differential calculus. Hence,

---

[19] In the first vote, the essays by Mendelssohn and Kant each received twenty votes. In the end, however, Sulzer and the others decided to award the prize to Mendelssohn's essay but declared publicly before the Assembly that Kant's essay "approached [the prizewinning essay] as much as possible and merited the highest praise." See Strauss's introduction to the prize essay in the Jubilee edition, vol. 2, p. xlvi.

[20] Ibid., pp. xlvii–xlviii.

[21] Christian Wolff, *Philosophia Rationalis sive Logica* in *Gesammelte Werke*, ed. Jean Ecole (Hildesheim and New York, Olms, 1983), vol. 1.2, Pt. I, §139, pp. 69–71; Crusius, *Wege zur Gewißheit und Zuverläßigkeit der menschlichen Erkenntnis* (Leipzig, 1747; Hildesheim, Olms, 1964); Johann Heinrich Lambert, *Criterium Veritatis* (1761), in *Kant-Studien*, Ergänzungsheft 36, ed. K. Bopp (Berlin, Reuther & Reichard, 1915), pp. 1–63.

doing justice to the Academy's question requires that metaphysical evidence be compared and contrasted with the kinds of mathematical evidence afforded by geometry as well as by calculus. Mendelssohn accordingly sets out to prove that metaphysical truths are, like the basic principles of the infinitesimal calculus, "capable, to be sure, of the same certainty but not the same perspicuity as geometrical truths" (p. 255). The term "perspicuity" (*Faßlichkeit, perspicuitas*) is borrowed from Baumgarten, who used it to signify the transparency of some whole, that is to say, a complex of parts that we are capable, through the use of the imagination, of comprehending.[22] Mendelssohn's point is that metaphysics is no less certain than calculus but, like it, lacks the transparency and thus the imaginative resources available to geometry. What insures certainty in both mathematics and metaphysics is, according to Mendelssohn, a common method, namely, analysis. The mathematician as well as the metaphysician proceeds by unpacking and rendering distinct what is confused in a given concept, be it a static or non-static quantity (extension or temporal measurement) or a quality of things (pp. 257, 271). In both cases, the certainty of the analysis is based upon the underlying identity of the content of some clear but indistinct perception or concept of something and the content of the distinct conception of it, afforded by analysis.[23]

While insisting on this sameness in method, Mendelssohn, like the mature Leibniz, acknowledges a "basic difference" between the content of mathematics and that of metaphysics (p. 269). Mathematics is a science of quantities, metaphysics a science of qualities.[24] But even this

[22] Baumgarten, *Metaphysica*, 8th edn. (Halle and Magdeburg, 1779; reprint Hildesheim, Olms, 1963), §531, pp. 184–6: "Utraque claritas est *perspicuitas*. Hinc perspicuitas vel est vivida, vel intellectualis, vel utraque" ("Each clarity is a perspicuity. Hence, perspicuity is either vivid or intellectual or both"). In a footnote Baumgarten identifies "perspicuitas" with "Faßlichkeit."

[23] Mendelssohn initiates his account of analysis by discussing its apparently paradigmatic employment in geometry. But even with respect to geometry, his construal of analytic method is highly problematic. In the first place, it is not clear how geometric truths are derivable from the mere concept of extension. If, however, some limit to extension or figure is meant, the method seems plainly to be, at bottom, synthetic. In the second place, Mendelssohn identifies inferences as analyses, although the process of inferring or syllogizing is traditionally understood to be synthetic (involving a combination of theses). On the ambiguities besetting Mendelssohn's account of analysis, see Altmann, *Frühschriften*, pp. 271–6.

[24] Alexander Baumgarten, *Acroasis logica* (Halle and Magdeburg, 1761) in Christian Wolff, *Gesammelte Schriften*, ed. Jean Ecole et al. (Hildesheim and New York, Olms, 1973), Section III, vol. 5, §1, p. 1: "Philosophia est scientia qualitatum in rebus sine fide cognoscendum" ("Philosophy is the science of qualities in things insofar as those qualities are to be known without faith").

difference in content, Mendelssohn emphasizes, points to a basic kinship. For quantity and quality (at least in the case of finite things) are reciprocally necessary and distinguishable only by abstraction. This kinship, he adds, becomes even more profound with the possibility of a science of non-extended (intensive) magnitudes, applicable not only to the degrees of such things as velocity, warmth, light, and so on, but also "to the value of things, to their possibility, actuality, perfection, and beauty, to the degree of truth, certainty, distinctness, and inner efficacy of our knowledge, to the goods of moral actions, and so forth. For all these degrees are true quantities and thus capable of measurement and respective comparison" (p. 261).[25]

Yet, given the sameness in metaphysics' and mathematics' method, the reciprocal nature of their subject matters, and the potential of a *mathesis intensorum* for an even more profound connection, why does metaphysics remain less perspicuous than mathematics? Mendelssohn gives three reasons: first, the lack of the sort of "essential signs" one finds in mathematics (signs that "essentially agree with the nature of thoughts and the connections among them"; (p. 272); second, the wholistic character of qualities ("bound up with one another so exactly that one cannot define any of them clearly without an adequate insight into the others"; p. 273); and third (and most important), the demand placed on the metaphysician of not merely assuming the possibility or phenomenal character, but also establishing the actual existence of the subject of his or her inferences.[26]

---

[25] According to Mendelssohn, such a science has yet to be developed because a way of distinctly construing the limits of intensive magnitudes remains to be discovered and because there is a lack of nonarbitrary signs in this domain. It is true, he concedes, that in arithmetic and algebra, as opposed to geometry, it is necessary to learn some arbitrary signs, but these, he insists, are only a few, and the composite signs, formulas, and equations are in the same configuration as the thoughts.

[26] All that mathematics, by contrast, requires is the testimony of the senses ("some tangled concept") that, for example, we have a triangle rather than a square in front of us from which a set of propositions can be derived. The mathematician demands, in other words, no more than is conceded by skeptics and idealists alike, namely, a difference between constant and variable appearances. Yet while the mathematician can thus prescind from questions of existence, the metaphysician cannot.

In addition to these reasons based upon the nature of the subject matter of metaphysics, Mendelssohn adds other reasons for the less perspicuous character of metaphysical evidence. Metaphysics is also handicapped by the fact that it is of such consequence for life and its basic concepts so customary that it has to contend with many more deep-seated prejudices than mathematics does. There is a substantial difference of opinion about the importance of these additional reasons. For Leo Strauss they are central to what he sees as Mendelssohn's attempt in the essay to give a new, more limited sense to Wolffian metaphysics. To Altmann, on the

We have Descartes to thank, according to Mendelssohn, for showing the metaphysician the two means of making the transition from the concepts of something to its existence, namely, the "cogito, ergo sum" and the inference from the possibility of a necessary being to its actuality. The third section of the prize essay contains Mendelssohn's attempt, as he puts it, "to give an easier rendition" of that proof of God's existence (p. 281).[27] That easier rendition begins with a consideration of why something does *not* exist, namely, either because it is impossible, that is to say, it contains a contradiction (and, hence, is indeterminable) or because it is contingent, that is to say, its existence is not intrinsic to it, but rather a "mode" of it, based upon the existence of something else (and, hence, it is indeterminate). The most perfect being, by definition, contains all affirmative determinations ("realities") and no negation or limitation.[28] Hence, it is not impossible (contradictory things cannot be said of it). Nor can a perfect being be contingent; it cannot be based upon the existence of something else. Since the perfect being is neither impossible nor merely possible, it must exist.[29]

The fourth and final section of the prize essay – completed, according to Mendelssohn, "amidst a thousand distractions" during his honeymoon – is concerned with the sort of evidence to be found in ethics.[30] Like geometry and theology, ethics is distinguished by Mendelssohn into a theoretical part and an applied or edifying part. In order to demonstrate that theoretical ethics is capable of as high a degree of certainty as these other disciplines, Mendelssohn offers a posteriori, a priori, and theological proofs for the first principle of theoretical ethics, namely, the natural obligation to make oneself and

---

other hand, the passage containing these differences is relatively unimportant. Cf. Jubilee edition, vol. 2,, pp. XLVIII–XLIX and Altmann, *Frühschriften*, p. 304.

[27] Theology can also prove God's existence by beginning with the cogito, a method that is, in Mendelssohn's words, "indisputably the easiest" (p. 281). He also praises the edifying, if less certain proofs from beauty, order, and purpose. Theology is also capable, like pure geometry, of analyzing its subject matter in a purely formal manner, that is, as mere possibilities, quite apart from the question of their existence.

[28] On this basis, Mendelssohn excludes extension, movement, and color from "realities" and regards them as mere phenomena. The "actual" or "true" realities are not extended but simple, and can have no other basic property than "representing" cf. pp. 290–1.

[29] The Third section of the prize essay also contains another version of this proof that leads to some illuminating observations on indeterminate and determinate (true or false) propositions as well as on the ontological implications of the principle of sufficient reason, especially in regard to a distinction between moral and physical necessity.

[30] Strauss's introduction in Jubilee edition, vol. 2, p. xlvi.

others, in the proper proportion, as perfect as one can.[31] All the duties to God, others, and oneself can be derived from this first principle. Proofs in ethics are, Mendelssohn admits, less perspicuous than those given in metaphysics or natural theology but only because ethics is founded upon metaphysics.

Matters, however, are quite different when it comes to applied ethics. Given the plethora of circumstances, contingencies, unforeseen consequences, and potential conflicts among duties, it is the rule rather than the exception that a practical syllogism in particular cases contains one or more premises that are not simply derived from theoretical ethics. As a result, the conclusion of such a syllogism must be less than certain. In such cases, an inner feeling, a combination of conscience and a sense for the truth (*bon sens*), must take the place of reason.[32] This inner feeling is a proficiency or virtue (and not simply a moral sense), the result of constant practice, that has a far greater effect on our desires than "the most distinct rational inferences" do (p. 303).

Mendelssohn concludes the final section of the prize essay by indicating four "means of maintaining the harmony of the lower powers of the soul with reason" or, as he also puts it, the ways of bringing about "an enduring and constant readiness for virtue" (pp. 305–6). In order for the principles of ethics to to have the proper effect, it is important [1] to accumulate as many compelling and persuasive reasons to abide by them as possible. In addition, the principles of ethics "must be [2] enlivened by *examples*, [3] supported by the force of *pleasant sentiment*, [4] kept constantly effective by *practice*, and finally transformed into a *proficiency*. Then there emerges the conviction of the heart that is our ultimate and most eminent purpose in ethics" (p. 306).

---

[31] "If philosophy mainly is a science of the constitution of things in general, then moral philosophy in particular is nothing else but the science of the constitution of a being with free will insofar as it has a free will" (p. 300). The a priori proof is based upon a consideration of a being of intelligence and hence free will. Thus, Mendelssohn derives moral philosophy (as Kant does later) from the concept of a being endowed with free will. For such a being, it bears noting, perfection is the basis of choice and pleasure and not vice versa. One chooses *sub ratione boni, non voluptatis* ("On the basis of the good, not of pleasure"). On an ambiguity in Mendelssohn's account of this point, see Alexander Altmann, *Frühschriften*, pp. 359–60.

[32] According to Strauss, this move by Mendelssohn represents a fundamental departure from the Wolffian conception of a *cognitio viva* that must have the certainty of mathematics; see Jubilee edition, vol. 2,, pp. l–lii and Altmann, *A Biographical Study*, p. 128.

Chronology

Hamburg; begins close friendship with Thomas Abbt in May; anonymously publishes *Philosophical Writings*, containing his major previous efforts in German as well as the newly written "Rhapsody or additions to the letters on sentiments"; becomes manager of the Bernhard firm

1762   Marriage to Fromet Gugenheim

1763   Awarded prize by the Royal Academy of Sciences for "On evidence in metaphysical sciences"; birth of daughter Sara, 29 May

1764   Publication of *On Evidence in Metaphysical Sciences*; death of Sara, on 15 April; birth of daughter Brendel, 24 October

1766   Birth of son Hayyim, 19 February (d. 3 April) death of father Mendel (Menahem) Heymann, 10 May; death of Abbt, 3 November

1767   Birth of daughter Reikel, 18 July; publication of *Phaedo: or On the Immortality of the Soul, In Three Dialogues*

1768   Completion of Hebrew commentary on *Ecclesiastes*; after Isaac Bernhard's death on 21 April, takes over comanagement of firm with his widow

1769   Birth of son Mendel Abraham, January; Lavater publishes his translation of Charles Bonnet's *The Philosophical Palingenesis, or Ideas on the Past State and on the Future State of the Living Being*, with an introduction dedicating the translation to Mendelssohn and challenging him either to refute or to embrace the arguments made for Christianity in the book; publication of *Letter to Lavater* in December

1770   Lavater controversy grows: Lavater's *Reply* and Mendelssohn's *Epilogue* are published before Easter; birth of son Joseph, 8 August

1771   Second edition of *Philosophical Writings* published; onset of illness (nervous debility); honored by Jewish community of Berlin; denied membership in Royal Academy

1774   Begins to translate the Pentateuch, first five books of the Tora, into German

1775   Birth of daughter Yente, August; death of son Mendel, September

1776   Entry in notebook "On the ability to know, the ability to feel, and the ability to desire"; birth of son Abraham 10 December

1777   Pays visit to Johann Georg Hamann and Kant in Königsberg; third edition of *Philosophical Writings* appears; successfully intervenes on behalf of Jewish community of Dresden to prevent expulsion of needy

1778   Birth of daughter Sisa, 8 June, (d. 15 September)

1780   Publishes translation of Genesis

1781   Publishes translation of Exodus in the spring and Leviticus in the summer; death of Lessing, 15 February; Kant arranges to have a copy of the newly published *Critique of Pure Reason* sent to Mendelssohn; takes over management of firm upon the death of Frau Bernhard

1782   Birth of son Nathan, 7 January; advance printing of complete Pentateuch edition in December; Friedrich Heinrich Jacobi's *Something That Lessing Said* appears, leading to controversy over Lessing's "Spinozism"

1783   Publication of Pentateuch edition in spring and Psalms translation and *Jerusalem or On Religious Power and Judaism* in May

1784   Publication of *On the Question: What Does "To Enlighten" Mean?* in September

1785   Publication of *Morning Hours or Lectures on the Existence of God* in early summer; in September Jacobi's *On the Doctrine of Spinoza in Letters to Mr. Moses Mendelssohn* appears; catches a severe cold while delivering on foot his final work (*To the Friends of Lessing: An Appendix to Mr. Jacobi's Correspondence on the Doctrine of Spinoza*) to his friend and publisher, Christian Friedrich Voβ on 31 December

1786   Dies on 4 January; publication of *To the Friends of Lessing* on 24 January

Further reading

The most complete study in English of Mendelssohn's life and all aspects of his work is the masterly work by Alexander Altmann, *Moses Mendelssohn: A Biographical Study* (University, Alabama, University of Alabama Press, 1973). Mendelssohn's place in eighteenth-century German philosophy is elaborated by Lewis White Beck in *Early German Philosophy: Kant and his Predecessors* (Cambridge, Mass., Harvard University Press, 1969). Allan Arkush, a student of Altmann, has also examined Mendelssohn's work in the context of the Enlightenment in *Moses Mendelssohn and the Enlightenment* (Albany, N.Y., SUNY Press, 1994), which contains an extensive bibliography. The mature Mendelssohn's difficulties with Jacobi are reviewed in Frederick C. Beiser's *The Fate of Reason* (Cambridge, Mass., Harvard University Press, 1987) and George di Giovanni's edition of Friedrich Heinrich Jacobi, *The Main Philosophical Writings and the Novel Allwill* (Montreal and Kingston, McGill-Queen's University Press, 1994). Other useful treatments of Mendelssohn's thought can be found in Henry Allison's *Lessing and the Enlightenment: His Philosophy of Religion and its Relation to Eighteenth Century Thought* (Ann Arbor, University of Michigan Press, 1966) and Paul Guyer's *Kant and the Experience of Freedom: Essays on Aesthetics and Morality* (Cambridge and New York, Cambridge University Press, 1993).

The introductions by Friedrich Bamberger and Leo Strauss to Volumes 1, 2, and 3.1 of Moses Mendelssohn's Jubilee edition are extremely valuable, as are the extensive notes to these volumes., which were published as part of *Moses Mendelssohn Gesammelte Schriften Jubiläumsausgabe*, introduction and notes by F. Bamberger, H. Borodianski, S. Rawidowicz, B. Strauss, and L. Strauss and ed. I. Elbogen, J. Guttmann, and E. Mittwock, by Akademie publishing house in Berlin from 1929 to 1938 (called here the "Jubilee edition"). The entire edition, encompassing Volumes 1, 2, 3.1, 7, 11, 14, and 16, has been reprinted and continued under the editorship of Alexander Altmann (Stuttgart, Frommann, 1971). Otto Best has prefixed a useful introduction to his collection of Mendelssohn's aesthetic writings: *Ästhetische Schriften in Auswahl* (Darmstadt, Wissenschaftliche Buchgesellschaft, 1974).

Altmann was undoubtedly the foremost contemporary student of Mendelssohn's works. His collection of essays on a variety of themes in Mendelssohn's corpus, *Die trostvolle Aufklärung: Studien zur Metaphysik und politischen Theorie Moses Mendelssohns* (Stuttgart and Bad Canstatt, Frommann, 1982), should be consulted. Several of the essays in the present volume are examined in great detail in Altmann's *Moses Mendelssohns Frühschriften zur Metaphysik* (Tübingen, Mohr, 1969). The meaning and import of Mendelssohn's aesthetic writings for the development of eighteenth-century German aesthetics are perceptively treated in Hermann Cohen's *Kants Begründung der Aesthetik* (Berlin, F. Dümmler, 1889) and Armand Nivelle's *Kunst- und Dichtungstheorien zwischen Aufklärung und Klassik*, 2nd, expanded edn. (Berlin and New York, de Gruyter, 1971).

Note on texts and translation

Sources of the translation

Translations of the first six essays are presented here in the same sequence as in *Philosophical Writings* (*Philosophische Schriften*). The two essays of Part I originally appeared as separate publications: *Philosophische Gespräche* (Berlin, Voβ, 1755) and *Über die Empfindungen* (Berlin, Voβ, 1755). The only notable oddity is that Mendelssohn reversed the chronological order in Part I by placing "On sentiments" first. As noted earlier, for Part II "Rhapsody" was newly written; the other three essays appeared originally as follows: "Betrachtungen über die Quellen und die Verbindungen der schönen Künste und Wissenschaften," *Bibliothek der schönen Wissenschaften und der freyen Künste*, I, 2 (Leipzig, Dyck, 1757), pp. 231–68 (renamed "Über die Hauptgrundsätze der schönen Künste und Wissenschaften" ["On the main principles of fine arts and sciences"] in *Philosophische Schriften*); "Betrachtungen über das Erhabene und das Naive in den schönen Wissenschaften," *Bibliothek der schönen Wissenschaften und der freyen Künste*, 2, 2 (Leipzig, Dyck, 1758), pp. 229–67 (renamed "Über das Erhabene und Naive in den schönen Wissenschaften" ["On the sublime and naive in the fine sciences"] in *Philosophische Schriften*); and "Gedanken von der Wahrscheinlichkeit," *Vermischte Abhandlungen und Urtheile über das Neueste aus Gelehrsamkeit* (Berlin, Voβ, 1756), pp. 3–26 (renamed "Über die Wahrscheinlichkeit" ["On Probability"] in *Philosophische Schriften*).

Philosophische Schriften was published in Berlin by Christian Friedrich Voβ in 1761, and a revised edition in 1771. According to the editors of the Jubilee edition, only changes in spelling and punctuation are to be found in a subsequent edition of 1777, again by Voβ. The work was also published in Vienna in 1783.[1] The present translation is based upon the 1771 "improved edition" (*Verbesserte Auflage*),[2] which was reprinted in *Schriften zur Philosophie und Ästhetik I*, ed. Fritz Bamberger, vol. 1 of *Gesammelte Schriften* Jubilee edition (Berlin, 1929; reprinted Stuttgart and Bad Canstatt, Frommann, 1971), pp. 229–515. This volume "Jubilee edition" also contains the original essays as they first appeared in print. Some of the 1771 essays can also be found in *Ästhetische Schriften in Auswahl*, ed. Otto F. Best (Darmstadt, Wissenschaftliche Buchgesellschaft, 1974). The introductions and notes to these editions have been consulted extensively in the preparation of the present volume.

Mendelssohn's prizewinning essay of 1763 was published the following year as *Abhandlung über die Evidenz in Metaphysischen Wissenschaften* (Berlin, Harde and Spener, 1764), pp. 1–66. The critical edition is in *Schriften zur Philosophie und Ästhetik II*, Jubilee edition, ed. by Fritz Bamberger and Leo Strauss (Berlin, 1931; reprinted Stuttgart, Frommann, 1972), vol. 2, pp. 267–330.

The penultimate essay, the unpublished notes from June 1776, entitled "Über das Erkenntnis-, das Empfindungs- und das Begehrungsvermögen," is in vol. 3.1, Jubilee edition, ed. Fritz Bamberger and Leo Strauss (Berlin, 1932; reprinted Stuttgart, Frommann, 1972), pp. 276–77. The final essay, "Über die Frage: Was heißt aufklären?", was first delivered as a lecture on 16 May 1784 to the " Berlin Wednesday Society," an exclusive and secret society also known as the "Friends of the Enlightenment," and was published in September in the *Berlinische Monatschrift*. This translation is based upon the text in *Gesammelte Schriften*, ed. G. B. Mendelssohn (Leipzig, Brockhaus, 1843), vol. 3, pp. 399–403.

Notes on the translation

Empfindung is translated as "sentiment" rather than "sensation" chiefly because the former alone has the emotive and conative connotations that Mendelssohn attaches to *Empfindung*. Moreover, the German word is

---

[1] See the editors' notes on the various editions of Mendelssohn's early works in the Jubilee edition, vol. 1, pp. 541–2, and also Moses Mendelssohn, *Philosophische Schriften* (Vienna, J. T. Edlen von Trattnern, 1783).

[2] The most revisions were made to the essay "On the sublime and naive in the fine sciences"; see Jubilee edition, vol. 1, pp. 231–2.

equivalent to the use of "sentiment" by the eighteenth-century English authors cited by Mendelssohn as well as to "sentimens" by the French authors cited. The term "feeling" is the translation for *Gefühl*.

Some explanation is also in order for translating *sinnlich* as "sensuous," especially where *sinnlich* modifies *Erkenntnis* (cognition) and such terms as "sentient," "sensible," "sensate," or even "by way of the senses/sensations" might seem more appropriate inasmuch as they lack the hedonic connotations of "sensuous." That hedonic character, however, is precisely what needs to be retained to capture Mendelssohn's sense. Beauty is, for him as for Baumgarten, the perfection of *sinnliche Erkenntnis* (or "sensitiva cognitio," as Baumgarten puts it), indicating a continuum among levels of *sinniche Erkenntnis*. While clearly involving sensation, each level of this cognition or awareness, from the experience of beauty to the faintest sensation, is a matter of desire or aversion, need or frustration, and thus pleasure or pain. This emotive and conative dimension is not adequately conveyed by terms such as "sensed" or "sentient." "Sensuous" is not perfectly suitable, to be sure, since there can be painful *sinnliche Erkenntnis* and the term "sensuous" is now associated primarily with pleasure. However, it is central to Mendelssohn's view, rooted as it is in Leibniz's and Wolff's conceptions of the soul, that every activity of the soul in some way affirms it and, to that extent, is pleasurable. The painful, moreover, is an imperfection that is only understandable by reference to the perfection.

Another word, the translation of which may seem surprising, is *entwickeln*. Mendelssohn's use plays in important ways on the root *wickeln* (to wrap or pack), that would not be conveyed by the standard translation of *entwickeln* as "develop." For this reason, *entwickeln* is generally translated "unpack," but it is translated as "disentangle" where *entwickeln* is contrasted with *eingewickelt* ("tangled up").

Mendelssohn uses the terms *Größe* and *Quantität* in roughly equivalent fashion in the prize essay. For example, he both identifies *Größe* as the object of mathematics and defines mathematics as *scientia quantitatum*. However, *Größe* is translated "magnitude" to keep its use distinct from that of "quantity" since Mendelssohn principally employs *Größe* and not *Quantität* to introduce the concept of the sublime.

The term "perspicuity" is used to translate *Faßlichkeit* in keeping with the Latin term *perspicuitas*, the meaning of which is taken over by Mendelssohn from Baumgarten (see p. xxv, n. 22).

Mendelssohn employs the following set of often parallel terms: *Vergnügen–Mißvergnügen, Wohlgefallen–Mißfallen,* and *Lust–Unlust.* In order to keep them apart, the first and most-frequent pair is usually translated "pleasure–displeasure," the second "satisfaction–dissatisfaction," and the third, "gratification–lack of gratification" (or "discontent"). Only at the end of "On sentiments" does Mendelssohn appear to distinguish "the soul's pleasure from sensuous gratification" (*Vergnügen der Seele von der sinnlichen Lust*) (p. 71).

"Awe" and, occasionally, "awe and admiration" have been employed as translations for *Bewunderung,* the state of someone encountering something sublime. The term "amazement" is reserved for *Verwunderung* (which Mendelssohn explicitly distinguishes from *Bewunderung*) (p. 198).

All translations of Latin and French quotations in the notes are original though efforts have been made to identify standard translations in most cases of the Latin texts. Also, every effort has been made to identify with full documentation the editions available to Mendelssohn.

Occasionally Mendelssohn breaks off one chain of thought and starts another, separating them merely with an ellipsis (e.g. p. 61). Thus, an ellipsis does not indicate anything has been omitted. The numbered footnotes are the editor's. Mendelssohn is the author of the footnotes marked by asterisks and of all the lettered notes to "On sentiments" (pp. 76–95).

Philosophical writings

Preface[1]

Diogenes once saw the citizens of Corinth busy with enormous war preparations and, in order not to be the only indolent soul in the city, he rolled his peaceful barrel up and down the streets. Since history does not report that this action caused the cynic's earthen house to fall apart, Menage* quite cleverly shows in how many ways the great tenant of the barrel could have avoided this misfortune. – I find myself in circumstances similar to Diogenes', with the difference that he, out of cynical stubbornness, did not want to serve the state, while I cannot. He rolled an earthen barrel with great care while I am letting little philosophical compositions be reissued.

The letters "On sentiments" and the "Dialogues," which together make up the first part of the following writings, were published separately at another time, and the second, third, and fourth essays of the second part have appeared in various periodicals. Still, the reader to whom it is important will notice some alterations and additions that are not trivial. The first essay of the second part has never appeared publicly, however, and contains assorted remarks about various philosophical matters which I did not know how else to name but as "Rhapsody or additions to the Letters on sentiments."

The content of the latter consists in some observations about the nature of mixed sentiments that are composed of pleasure and displeasure and about the astonishing power of their effect on the soul. Then I come to

---

* See Bayle's article on Diogenes in his Dictionary.[2]

[1] To the first edition of *Philosophische Schriften* (1761).
[2] See Gilles Ménage, *Aegidii Menagii Miscellanea* (Paris, 1652).

3

the *summum bonum* [highest good], refute the purified Epicureanism that has found many friends since the time of Gassendi,[3] and defend the basic principle of perfection that is considered suspicious by some philosophers. I take the opportunity to observe more closely the main source of all ethical actions; I consider the power of obscure sentiments over the capacity to desire, the effect of habit and practice, the nature of the soul's proficiencies, and venture a hypothesis for determining more precisely the moving forces of the impulses of our soul. This hypothesis appears to me to explain an array of strange phenomena in the spiritual world so easily and so naturally that I wish for nothing so much as to see it tested by a thorough mind. Finally, I show the priceless and indispensable utility of the fine sciences in ethics.

The content of the remaining essays is to be gathered from their titles. But in the case of the fourth essay, "On probability," I find it necessary to remind readers that my intention has in no way been to elaborate a theory of probability but instead to take the opportunity to shed some light on two important truths on the basis of the few well-known principles of probability. My intention was, namely,

1. to defend the correctness of all our experimental inferences against the objections of the English philosopher, David Hume, and
2. to prove the Leibnizian proposition that all voluntary decisions already have their definite certainty in advance.

I believe that I have demonstrated this in an irrefutable manner and, to be sure, independently of all systems and opinions, merely on the basis of universally assumed principles.

A final word about the presentation in this little volume. I acknowledge that no presentation is better suited to purely speculative investigations than a rigorously systematic one. But I did not trust my ability or proficiency at connecting my thoughts constantly in such a rigorous order.[4]

In the present, second edition various changes have appeared indispensable. The notes to the letters "On sentiments" have grown considerably and in them some objections to the thoughts about suicide,

---

[3] Pierre Gassendi (1592–1655), critic of Aristotelian philosophy and ardent defender of Epicurus, is perhaps best known for his objections to Descartes' *Meditations on First Philosophy*.
[4] The remainder of this preface was inserted at the end of the original preface in the second, improved edition of 1771, upon which this translation is based.

expressed in the letters, have been answered. In particular, the splendid prize essay by the court chaplain, Mr. Cochius, contained a philosophical thought for the possibility of the wish to be destroyed and that thought deserved to be scrutinized.[5] It was necessary for the third dialogue, on the best world and creation in time, to be completely reworked.

In the first essay of the second part, the doctrine of mixed sentiments has been further elaborated, cast in better light, and applied to several particular examples and phenomena from common life. Some reasons, surfacing in this context, for the limits of aesthetic deception can be of great use in the theory of fine arts and sciences. How far the artist can push his illusion appears not to have been investigated yet, though there must evidently be limits where it ceases to be pleasant, where the imitation, as one would say, becomes all too natural. I flatter myself with having given some reasons by means of which these limits to the use of art can be determined with some accuracy.

The essay on the sublime and naive sustained the most alterations and additions. I show, first, the difference between the sublime, enormous, and strong, consider the effects of them which come close to the dreadful and terrible, and thus, to this extent, are akin to one another. By this means it can be understood why the sublime would usually be accompanied and reinforced by the terrible. The definition of the naive, which seemed to correspond only to the mode of expression in the fine sciences, has also been applied to what is naive in character and to what is naive in art and, lastly, the effect of the naive has been described in somewhat more detail. I owe various remarks as well as some well-chosen examples to the Dutch translator of this little volume. The translation was published in 1769 at the expense of the editor and without mention of his name.[6] But as I see from a private correspondence that I had the pleasure of receiving a few days ago from the same individual, it is Mr. van Goens, professor of history and fine sciences at Utrecht, who took the trouble of translating this essay into Dutch and making it pleasant for his countrymen by additions and notes.

[5] Leonhard Cochius's "Untersuchungen über die Neigungen" won the prize in 1767 and appeared in 1769.
[6] *Verhandeling over het verhevene en naive in de fraeje wetenschappen uit het Hoogduitsch von Moses Mendelszoon*, tr. Ryklof Michael Van Goens (Utrecht, 1769; 3rd edn. 1775).

5

I am not inclined to add any more parts to this collection of philosophical writings if the approval of the public encourages me to devote my spare hours more to the tedious work of revising than to the pleasure of reading and thinking.

Part I

On sentiments

Theocles, an English philosopher who inherited the name of that dear enthusiast known to us from the Earl of Shaftesbury's *The Moralists*,[1] had left his homeland some time ago. The mixture of seductive imagination and French frivolity, peddled as metaphysics by so many of his countrymen, was so starkly at odds with his proclivity for rigor and fundamentals that he made the decision to renounce his fatherland, his tranquility, and his friends' embrace in order to search for a people that treasures *accurate* thinking more than *free* thinking. Germany seemed to him to hold out the promise of such a people. He read the immortal writings with which our countrymen have enriched the learned world in the past century, and people say that the soberness, indeed, the very dullness for which they are reproached by some petty critics, was one of the things that drove him to become acquainted with this nation. He went from school to school, and, in the guise of a curious soul simply passing through, he had the pleasure of attending all the gatherings of learned societies anonymously. He is supposed to have been more than a little astonished, however, by the specious and careless manner of our present philosophers. He apparently wrote his friends back in England that his hopes were betrayed and that even in Germany the philosophical dilettante had gotten the upper hand. Only here and there, he

---

[1]   Anthony Ashley Cooper, Third Earl of Shaftesbury (1671–1713) – author of *The Moralists, A Philosophical Rhapsody* (London, 1709), published as Treatise V of his *Characteristics of Men, Manners, Opinions, Times* (London, 1711) – initiates a tradition of construing human nature as endowed with a "moral sense" within a divinely instituted and purposely organic harmony. In the dialogue *The Moralists*, Theocles (the name appropriated by Mendelssohn here) elaborates an optimistic and theistic system.

7

noted, do some upright philosophers live, as it were, in obscurity; yet they scarcely dare to raise their heads and perhaps ultimately they, too, would have to give way to the mainstream.

During his stay at *** he became friends with some young members of the nobility who were completely suited to his tastes. He was most impressed with a young man among them from the house of ***, who will appear under the name *Euphranor* in what follows. Because of his fondness for this young man he stayed for some time in a little place on the S***. The young man would often visit Theocles' lonely abode where, in peace and quiet, they would devote hours to friendship and contemplation. When the youth had to take leave of his friend, they would continue their discussions by correspondence.

By chance the following letters which they exchanged about the nature of pleasure fell into my hands and I could not resist the slight betrayal of confidence by making them known to the world.

The Editor [Mendelssohn]

Mendelssohn's *Philosophische Schriften*

First letter

Euphranor to Theocles

All too careful analysis of the beautiful disrupts the pleasure. Its conflict with the sensation of surprise. Confirmed by the example of the beloved, the virtuoso, and friends.

This is already the fourth evening that I have spent without Theocles' embrace, and the memory of the unspeakable pleasure that I enjoyed in his company transforms my busiest hours into boredom. I am not as idle here as you might think. Necessary obligations rob me of most of the hours of the day. I call every occupation a necessary obligation if it conflicts with our inclination. To me even the noisy pleasure, the bustling throng at the court, to which I have been banned by my position, deserves this name. It is true, I revere the prerogatives of my youthful age, I am fond of things that bring joy; but only the quiet joys that I enjoy in the small circle of my friends. The grandiose edifice of that gilded society seems to me more barren than Theocles' isolation. Now I am free of the burdensome turmoil; now I am able to throw myself into the arms of the muses and contemplation. How lucky I would be, if I could throw myself into the arms of my friend! And how inconsolable I would be if Theocles' friendly letters did not soothe my longing for his presence.

Only yesterday I received a correspondence from you, the content of which should give me material for reflection today. How often have I unfolded the letter, read it, and folded it back together! This important letter deserves all my attention; for its content promises to have an influence on your entire life. You pride yourself on having unravelled the concepts of the nature of pleasure and you are delighted to have succeeded in delving searchingly into the depths of sentiments. Not that you would want to grab some fame because of your discoveries! No, you are much more taken by the hope of becoming master of your sentiments through this insight and binding them to the scales of reason. "The more familiar I become with the nature of pleasure," you say, "the less I should be deceived by the ghouls, the genuine will o' the wisps that lead the human race out of one swamp into the other and then mock its naivete." – You invite me to similar observations and promise to open your thoughts to me as soon as I have prepared myself for them by my own deliberation. Dearest friend! Have you even considered what danger your undertaking involves? There have been savants who have named reason the killjoy of our pleasure. I do not consider it anything of the sort; but it certainly becomes a killjoy when it broods over the origin of pleasure. Our happiness depends upon enjoyment and enjoyment depends upon the swift sentiment with which each beauty surprises our senses. Unhappy are those whom reason has hardened against the onset of such a surprise. The gratification disappears if we try to clarify our feeling too carefully.

Countless examples which confirm this truth present themselves to me. If you are smitten the moment you catch sight of someone beautiful, countless attractions conspire to make you fall for her. The symmetrical shape of her arms and legs, the dazzling glow of her face, her fiery eyes and eloquent features harmonize with one another in a pleasant confusion and take command of your soul. Thank this confusion, that it does not leave you time to disentangle it. Suppose you put yourself on guard to concentrate, not on those fiery eyes, but on the constitution of the fluids in the eye and not on those ravishing looks but on a slight movement of the facial muscles. At that very moment your pleasure would perish and you would have, instead of a sweet rapture, a set of arid truths.

Those who read the immortal works of ancient writers only for the sake of analyzing them and assembling rhetorical figures are to be pitied. They are like students of insects, who gather the dried-up remains of worms. They look for and find the rules of eloquence, they become legislators in the fine sciences, but they no longer feel the beauties that they commend to us. Their feeling is transformed into a logical inference.

Even friendship, the mother of the sublimest pleasure, runs the risk of this danger if one weighs too precisely and exclusively the merits that constitute the value of a friend. Feeling fuses the souls of friends together into a single I, and reflection splits them back into I and you. A loving feeling conceals the weak side of a friend, and reflection makes it visible. Moreover, even if a friend's merits have greater weight on the scales of reason, the fire still dies out and the love falls back into rational respect. – I tremble when I think of it. How can you, my dearest friend, do this? If, despite the reasons that I have given, you insist on pursuing your project, if you do not want to feel without thinking, then I am in danger of embracing in you a lukewarm friend. No, Theocles! If you cherish my peace of mind (and you certainly do), then rid me of these distressing cares. Give up your brooding meditations, or save them for the frigid age that knows no sentiments. I beg you, I entreat you to do this.

Mendelssohn's *Philosophische Schriften*

Second letter

Euphranor to Theocles

The obscure feeling enhances our happiness. The emotion vanishes when all concepts become distinct. To what extent reason ought to mix in our amusements. System of a youthful ethics.

My previous letter is still unanswered. Theocles leaves me with the uneasiness I felt after his last letter. What am I supposed to think of this? Was my sad hunch on target? Or is your style like that of callous hussies who take wicked pleasure in torturing their lovers with jealous thoughts? But perhaps neither of these. Perhaps it is only that you wanted to leave yourself time to evaluate my reasons in order either to accept or to reject them. If this is the case, then allow me here to give you several reasons to consider before you decide.

We would be unhappy if all our sentiments were all at once elucidated and made into clear and distinct representations. *Beauty rests*, in the opinion of every philosopher, *on the indistinct representation of a perfection*. Gratification and joy, indeed, quiet satisfaction itself, are accompanied in the body by a sweet rush in the bloodstream and by assorted pleasant motions in the limbs, without which we would be almost indifferent to them. This lovely motion is a daughter of the emotion, and the emotion is of necessity joined with an undeveloped representation. So inseparable is the feeling, so inseparable is the obscure representation from our happiness.

If we want to quell the storm of an unpleasant passion, reason commands us to reflect on the causes of our displeasure and to clarify the concepts. Only out of these dark clouds does the violent storm arise, and the furor of the passion vanishes as soon as it becomes sunny in our soul. But is the makeup of things different for pleasant sentiments? By no means! They have the very same fate. As soon as we think, we no longer feel. The emotion vanishes as soon as concepts are elucidated.

If you are concerned about your happiness, let reason select the object of your pleasure. Without it you could choose blindly or deceive yourself in your choice. Do not trust the attractions which it condemns.

Embrace only those things which it calls good. In fact, let it prescribe the measure and aim of your enjoyment. When, however, it has procured the bride, it must modestly give way, in order not to disturb you in your enjoyment by some inconsiderate impertinence.

Not in vain did the good creator combine a charm with this obscure feeling; not in vain did he put the capacity of animating this feeling in every beauty. Reason alone can make no one happy (that is, no one who is not mere reason). We are supposed to feel, enjoy, and be happy.

This, my dearest Theocles, is the system of my youthful ethics, the model of my way of life. Nature has blessed your manly years with a tender feeling. Exert your powers to make it more sensitive. It is the source of your happiness. If you can, make the feeling of beauty more lively, but guard against transforming it into barren truths. What a difference between the two claims: "this object is beautiful" and "this object is true"!

Mendelssohn's *Philosophische Schriften*

Third letter

Theocles to Euphranor

Why neither fully distinct nor fully obscure concepts are compatible with the feeling of beauty. Clarity of the representation enhances the pleasure. Necessary preparations for the enjoyment of a pleasure. Explanation of a passage in Aristotle's Poetics. *Considerations of the structure of the world from two diverse viewpoints.*

It was not coy arrogance that caused me to leave you to your jealous cares. No, noble youth! Call it an act of revenge which your immature fear had earned. If I wanted to get rid of all my annoyance with your distrusting behavior, then it was necessary for me to exact this sort of revenge from you without hesitating. Now, however, that the amends that I have procured have satisfied me, I am in a position to refute your reasons in unrelenting fashion.

It is a well-established truth that no distinct concept is compatible with the feeling of beauty. The reason for this is our limited soul's inability to grasp a multiplicity distinctly all at once. If the soul wants to think distinctly, it must withdraw its attention from the whole and reflect upon one part of the object after another. But it is also a well-established truth that no completely obscure concept is compatible with the feeling of beauty since, in its obscurity, the multiplicity of the object is as it were concealed. Hence, all concepts of beauty must be comprised within the boundaries of clarity if we are to perceive a multiplicity without tedious reflecting. Indeed, there is still more; the expansively clearer the representation of a beautiful object, the more ardent the pleasure that springs from it. An expansively clearer representation contains a richer multiplicity, more relations opposite one another. Sheer sources of gratification!

Listen, now, my noble young man, to how I prepare myself to enjoy something pleasurable. I contemplate the object of the pleasure, I reflect upon all sides of it, and strive to grasp them distinctly. Then I direct my attention at the general connection among them; I swing from the parts to the whole. The particular distinct concepts recede as it were back into the shadows. They all work on me but they work in such a state of equilibrium and proportion to one another that the whole alone radiates from them, and my thinking about it has not broken up the manifold, but only made it easier to grasp.

The wise Stagirite ascribes to each beauty specific limits with respect to its size and maintains that it no longer deserves this designation if it either oversteps or does not reach those limits. His interpreters have found enormous difficulties in this regard. On the basis of this principle the entire world, they concluded, must cease to be beautiful, and who is willing to make this claim?

But this immense universe is not a visibly beautiful object, as far as we are concerned. Nothing deserves this title that does not present itself clearly to the senses all at once. To be sure, what is immense, exhausting the limits of our winged imagination as it does, has its own particular charm which often surpasses the pleasure of measured beauty. However, we only call the structure of the world *beautiful* in the proper sense of the term when the imagination orders its chief parts in as splendid a symmetry as that of the order that reason and perception teach us that they possess outside us. Thus, one only perceives the general proportions of the parts of the world to the whole. The size that is immense (and that the senses, therefore, cannot take the measure of) diminishes in the imagination and retreats into the limitations of a beauty that is suited to our powers.

The imagination is able to confine the smallest and the largest object to the appropriate limits by extending the parts as far as possible or drawing them together until we are able to grasp the requisite manifold all at once. An animal several kilometers in height or a mite undetectable by the keenest eye can become beautiful objects in the imagination; how often has their organic structure delighted the nature lover. Yet Aristotle has denied them the designation "a visible beauty" because our shortsighted eye cannot grasp the manifold limbs of the monstrous animal all at once nor can it even grasp that mite which is simply too minute. For dramatic writers this truth is uncommonly important.[a]

The contemplation of the structure of the world thus remains an inexhaustible source of pleasure for the philosopher. It sweetens his lonely hours, it fills his soul with the sublimest sentiments, withdrawing his thoughts from the dust of the earth and bringing them nearer to the throne of divinity. Because of his contemplations he must perhaps dispense with honor, sensual ecstasy, and riches; for him they are but dust upon which he treads with his feet. Preoccupied like Archimedes, he says to the persecutors who stand behind him with their swords drawn: *Whatever you do, don't mess up my circle!* But how must he prepare himself for this fullness of pleasure? Well, my dear young man, here is the way to true pleasure! Apply my doctrine to the beauty of nature in general. It is the worthiest example that can establish a doctrine. Learn from this how useful it is for the sentiment of the whole if we have previously considered all its parts to the point where they are distinct.

Apply the doctrine! I say. If you were ignorant of the miraculous arrangement of all the heavenly bodies, if you were unaware that an immense chain of entities inhabits each planet, unaware that from the center of the structure of each world a gentle stream of light and life fans out on all sides, if you knew nothing of all these important truths, I say, and you then became certain only of the general combination of heavenly bodies, their positions, sizes, and distances, certain only of the skeleton as it were of the Copernican system of the world, this knowledge would, to be sure, please you but not be fulfilling, would not satisfy your entire soul. The impoverished state of the multiplicity of things would leave behind astonishing gaps in the concept of the whole, and the harmony which ought to delight you would amount to a few laws of nature, on the basis of which the heavenly bodies are conducted in their orbits. Now, then, recall everything that you know of the individual parts of the world. Consider the lifeless stone, the nature of which appears to be weight and color, and the plant, in the structure of which there is a detectable order and purpose; consider the worm whose entire world is a leaf and the human being whom the entire earth encloses in all too narrow spaces; in short, think of all that the eyes alone, the telescope, reason, and the senses have made known about the world. Weigh the reasons why the conjecture becomes more than probable that all heavenly bodies have a similar constitution, the reasons that cause us to see our system of world multiplied in myriads of fixed stars and our habitations here below multiplied in countless spheres that revolve around those fixed stars in luminous rotations; ascend the chain which binds all entities to the throne of the divinity; then in bold flight swing over to the universal proportion of all these parts to the immeasurable whole. What heavenly rapture will suddenly surprise you!

In the numbing ecstasy you will scarcely be able to maintain your composure. Whence this infinite difference? What ennobled your feeling and allowed your pleasure to grow by such leaps and bounds? Confess! Is it not the distinct perception of all the parts, which in the latter case happened prior to the sensation of the whole? Did consideration of the parts disrupt the gratification which springs from the perception of the whole? Oh, no! Instead, it prepared you for that. You gave the appropriate fullness to the pleasure that springs from the beauty of the whole because you brought to light a greater manifold, each element of which takes part in the determination of that whole.

Mendelssohn's *Philosophische Schriften*

Fourth letter

Theocles to Euphranor

In the moment of enjoyment all individual concepts are obscured. Application to poets. To musicians. The basis for pleasure must be sought in the positive power of our soul. But not in its limitation. A new thought on the origin of the pleasure. Objection to it.

My motto is: *choose, feel, reflect, and enjoy. Choose*: among the objects that surround you, permit yourself such as are beneficial to your sojourn. *Feel* them: outfit yourself with intuitive concepts and judgments about their constitution. *Reflect*: entertain individual parts distinctly, and weigh their relations and connections relative to one another and to the whole. Then *enjoy*: direct your attention to the object itself. Guard against thinking about the makeup of individual parts at this moment. Allow the capacities of your soul to prevail. Through the intuiting of the whole the parts will lose their bright colors, but they will leave traces behind them which illuminate the concept of the whole and lend a greater liveliness to the pleasure which arises from this.

In the moment of enjoyment, however, it is necessary that no particular concept remains distinct. As long as we still lug ourselves around among earthly things, our soul is still too limited to grasp a multiplicity distinctly all at once. Had poets considered this adequately, we would have fewer epochs which do justice to the most stringent rules and yet fail so thoroughly to fulfill the purpose of pleasing. This is a remark which many have used, though incorrectly, to get people to waver in their respect for the rules. The rules are preparations by means of which the poet should be putting himself and the object to be worked over into a state where the beauties are shown in their most flattering light. As *preparations* they can be enormously useful to the virtuoso, but in the heat of the work itself they must not disturb him. As soon as he takes a step toward the work, the theme and nothing but the theme must be the dominant idea in his soul. At this moment he must take care not to have his rules all too distinctly before his eyes. They are not supposed to put a rein on his imagination, but rather are supposed to show it the way only from a distance and to call it back when it is in danger of losing itself. Then they can set the lesser genius to the side of the greater genius and teach the poet what his spirit was perhaps too small to discover.

Even musicians could be spared disgrace and humiliation if they would never let this important remark out of their eyes. As far as the agreeableness of their melodies is concerned, it is known that musicians put greater stock in the judgment of a merely practiced ear than in the judgment of masters in music. The latter never want to conceal their expertise in the art. They take note of nothing but the rule-governed quality of a melody; they are on the lookout for some serendipitous combination of the most discordant sounds. Before their very eyes, gently stirring beauties slip by, unnoticed.

Yet from all this can the implication be drawn that an obscure feeling is the mother of all happy sentiments? No! Were this the case, then providence would have distributed its goods quite unfairly. It would have entitled entities of a higher sort to complain bitterly: "You have burdened us with your curse, in that you have imparted to us enlightened minds. We conceive everything more distinctly than the entities that are beneath us; what a miserable privilege that hides the paths to gratification from us! We lack the obscure sentiments, the source of pleasure, with which the lower entities are richly endowed."

Or do we want to overthrow the order of things? Should entities that cling most to the senses ascend to the highest steps of the creation, should angels stand lower than human beings, should human beings stand lower than irrational animals? Oh, no! It is only our weakness that makes the obscure sentiment a necessary companion of happiness because the distinctness and wealth of concepts do not find enough room next to one another in the human soul. Yet, insofar as it is an *obscure* feeling, it brings with it nothing agreeable. And entities capable of grasping a greater multiplicity distinctly are all the happier, since the objects can work on them with mightier charm.

I have said that it would be unfair to providence to look to the obscure sentiment for the essential basis of all pleasure. I could have specified this claim more precisely. Regarded as a determination of the mind and cut off from its fleshy companion, from sensual rapture, the pure gratification of the soul must be grounded in the positive powers of our soul and not in its incapacity, not in the limitation of these original powers.

Indeed, there is still more. The inclination to perfection must be a property of all thinking entities and of God himself to the supreme degree. This thesis has been challenged by a modern philosopher whose thoughts, nevertheless, deserve our attention. The difficulty which he took it upon himself to resolve, is this. We learn from experience that the soul would rather have than not have the representation of perfection and rather not have than have the representation of imperfection. Why this? In what essential determination of our soul is this property grounded?[b] Our writer took pains to untie this knot in roughly the following manner.

> "The essence of the soul," he says, "consists in a power of representing the world to itself; thus it must constantly strive to produce concepts. It must, accordingly, long for objects which provide it with an array of concepts, and it must find them pleasing.
>
> "These concepts must seem to it not overly complicated; otherwise it despairs of its capacity ever to be able to grasp them. If, then, an object appears to enable the soul to unravel the array of representations which the soul encounters in it and to do so with less trouble and effort, it must draw the soul to it in extraordinary fashion.
>
> "Perfection does this. In it one encounters a multiplicity that is in harmony and refers to a unity. The multiplicity promises the soul something that will occupy its attention and engage its efforts. The soul finds a set of representations which for a time are able to sustain its needs as an original power. But the unity in the multiplicity also promises the soul a way of easing the attentiveness and effort demanded by that multiplicity. It will be able to survey all the manifold concepts as it were from a single viewpoint; it will not cost it any particular trouble to grasp them all. Thus, the soul must long for a perfect object and find the representation of it pleasing." Thus far our writer.[1]

---

[1]   According to Fritz Bamberger, in his introduction to volume 1 of the Jubilee edition (pp. xxix–xxx, 608–9), the "philosophical writer" is Johann Georg Sulzer, author of *Theorie der angenehmen und unangenehmen Empfindungen* (Berlin, 1762), originally published as "Recherche sur l'origine des sentiments agréables et désagréables" in *Histoire (Mémoires) de l'académie royale des sciences et belle-lettres* (1751), although the quotation is not at all literal. Sulzer (1720–79), Swiss student of Bodmer and Breitinger, leading figure in the Royal Academy, and friend of Mendelssohn and Friedrich Nicolai, achieved renown for his writings on aesthetics and psychology. (For the "Jubilee edition," see Further reading.)

If this manner of explanation were correct, then our fondness for the unity in a multiplicity would be a testament to our weakness. For if we did not find the mere multiplicity all too tiresome, if we did not require some way of easing the attention and effort we expend upon it, the mere multiplicity would afford us more gratification than if it were limited by some unity. But then why does the wise creator, whom the thought of all possible worlds cannot tire for an instant, prefer what is perfect and complete to a mere multiplicity?

Mendelssohn's *Philosophische Schriften*

Fifth letter

Theocles to Euphranor

Beauty presupposes unity in a multiplicity. The pleasure that arises from this rests upon the limitation of the powers of our soul. Such does not take place in God. Perfection demands not unity but rather harmony of the multiplicity. The pleasure that arises from this is grounded in the positive power of our soul. God possesses it in the highest degree.

My dear young man, you are not answering! Good! I take the silence as a sign of your approval and proceed with my reflections. Up until now we have considered all objects of pleasure under the form of beauty. Young people are accustomed to ascribe all their gratification to beauty. But now it is time to distinguish the boundaries of perfection and beauty, and show both in their true form. Here are the rocks on which the philosopher founders, the philosopher, that is, whom I refuted in my last letter. He wanted to draw to the side of perfection what is true for beauty alone.

The distinction is obvious, Euphranor! The sameness, the oneness in a multiplicity of features is a property of the beautiful object. They must exhibit an order or otherwise a perfection which appeals to the senses and, indeed, does so effortlessly. If we want to feel a beauty, then our soul wishes to enjoy with ease. The senses are supposed to be enthralled and from them the gratification ought to extend to idle reason.

The draft of a building is beautiful if the proportion in the parts and their variations are easy to grasp. Gothic taste can be faulted for, among other reasons, casting a multiplicity of features into an order that is far too complicated.

A dance in which the dancers weave too much back and forth through one another displeases because the various movements and lines, indicated on the floor, cannot be effortlessly untangled from one another. Even sounds are musical only when the vibrations in the air maintain a simple proportion to one another.

What follows from this? That the pleasure afforded by sensuous beauty, the unity in a multiplicity, is to be ascribed merely to our inability. We tire when our senses are supposed to unpack an all-too-complicated order. Entities endowed with acuter senses necessarily find in our beauties a disgusting uniformity, and what tires us can secure them gratification. He who all at once looks over everything possible must thoroughly spurn the unity in the multiplicity. – Spurn? And so the creator has no liking for the beautiful? He does not even prefer it to the ugly? No, I maintain, and nature, work of his hands, should bear me witness. The creator has covered only the external shape of things with sensuous beauty. These things are determined to have an alluring effect on the senses of other creations. The beauty of the human form, the pleasant colors, the sinuous features that are enchanting in their expressions, are only impressed upon the outer shell. They go no further than our senses reach. Beneath the skin ugly forms lie hidden. All the parts of the vascular system are tangled up in one another without *ostensible* order; the intestines maintain a balance relative to one another, but no proportion, no sensuous relations; sheer multiplicity, nowhere unity; sheer activity, nowhere is the activity simple. How much the creator would have failed at his purpose, if his purpose had been nothing but beauty!

But, no! I come to you, the heavenly most splendid perfection! Not as the senses grasp you, but as reason conceives you! The truly ultimate purpose of creation! God's counsel! I would be giving away your divinity if I intended to grant you only what, for limited entities, are superior qualities. No! Your excellences also please the infinite. You preserve multiplicity, but no uniformity in those manifold things; there is nothing simple about the activity. You leave these slighter enhancements over to your sensuous emulator, beauty, which may permit itself to descend to the level of earth's frail inhabitants. You, however, demand rational cohesion, agreement, perspicacity. On the basis of a common final purpose it should be comprehensible why things in all their multiplicity are next to one another in one way rather than another. You preserve not simply representations, but rather representations combined and grounded in one another. In your determinations nothing must be superfluous, nothing dissonant, nothing missing. In such features the philosopher recognizes your divinity, mother of heavenly love!

And he must beware of confusing this heavenly *Venus* with the earthly, namely, with *beauty*.[c] The latter rests upon limitation, inability, but the enjoyment of the harmony of a multiplicity of things or features is based upon a positive power of our soul. If it is natural for entities which have a power of representing to yearn for representations, then it is also proper for rational entities to strive for the sort of representations that are grounded in one another. Disordered concepts, dissonances, contradictions conflict as much with nature and the original need of all thinking entities as does the lack, the complete termination of all representations. Herein lies the powerful attraction of perfection for all minds, and to the extent that a positive power is elevated above its limitation, the pleasure of the intellectual perfection is far and away superior to pleasure of the sensuous perfection or, as we earthly creatures call it, the pleasure of *beauty*.[d]

The difference is easy to comprehend. If you observe two dwarf trees in your fruit garden and pay heed to the branches which ascend in circular order, you then appreciate the sensuous beauty of the trees. Its appearance pleases you, and your sensuous feeling is excited. A type of perfection is, to be sure, bound up with this beauty since, given the general design of beauty, a reason may be given why the branches are aligned just so. But the purpose of the order is to delight the senses through a simple proportion, and the perfection depends upon beauty.

Think, now, of the genuine perfection of trees. Consider these leaves, these branches, these buds here, those blossoms there; what sort of common *final purpose* binds them together? In what connection do they stand to the tree and, through it, to the whole of things? Here your soul will become intoxicated from the ecstasy, here you will attain intuitive knowledge of an authentic perfection, a pleasure that depends not on your weakness, but on the rational striving for representations grounded in one another.

Since, now, it is certain that God can permit nothing without sufficient reason, God, too, enjoys representations grounded in one another, that is to say, God, too, enjoys perfection. Nature continues to be my witness. The ugliest shapes cloaked by human skin, the innermost, tiniest parts of creation, where no eye penetrates, do not cease to be perfect in the sense of being complete; in their reciprocal harmony with one another, they do not cease to contribute as much to the general final purpose as they can, they endure without fail neither excess nor deficiency. Everything in nature aims at *one* purpose, everything is grounded in it, everything is complete.

24

Mendelssohn's *Philosophische Schriften*

Sixth letter

Theocles to Euphranor

Ungrounded complaints against reason. Against metaphysical considerations. Illegitimate dominance of the economy over speculative philosophy. Use of the latter is extolled. Comparison of pleasure *with* wanting.

Since ancient times, to be sure, there have been learned individuals (I cannot call them "philosophers") who have considered reason to be the killjoy of our pleasure. Even today this frivolous spirit appears to be spreading from France to all cultured peoples. Yet those who think in this manner have never been acquainted with reason. They have bestowed the honorific title of reason on a product of their perverted imagination, a helpless ghost. They have prayed to this imaginary house-idol, and when he refused them his help, they tore down his sanctuary, in keeping with the custom of the ancient servants of idols, heaping insults and contempt on the deaf divinity.

No one who is acquainted with genuine reason and travels down its roads can doubt either the usefulness or the fullness of the pleasure that flows from its source. Solitary metaphysical meditations may seem ever so fruitless, so useless to the obtuseness of some learned people. They are completely unable to speak the language of a person of conviction, or their heart is as perverted as their manner of thinking.

I have never been able to read without astonishment, or rather without a kind of pity, the arrogant declaration of that Frenchman[*] who holds Reaumur's preoccupation with discovering a way to cleanse wallpaper of moths in higher esteem than Leibniz's efforts to reflect on the system of the best world or Bernoulli's attempts to plumb the

---

[*] Pluche.[1]

[1] Noël-Antoine Pluche, *Spectacle de la nature ou Entretiens sur les particularités de l'histoire naturelle, qui ont paru les plus propres à rendre les jeunes-gens curieux, & à leur former l'esprit* (Paris, 1732), preface to vol. 1.

depths in algebraic computations.[2] Is it not at all important to survey the most remote magnitudes and forces of nature, to improve our soul, and, as it were, to elevate our existence to a higher level? What is more important to a human being? If his childish finery and his rugs are eaten away by worms, or if his creator acts irrationally and blasphemers are right to rebuke the divinity?

If the endeavor of the so-called alchemists were also not in vain, if they actually discovered the secret of refining common ore into gold, their pride would still be forever ridiculous, the pride, namely, with which they deem the discovery of this secret the purpose of philosophy and the most dignified occupation of all wise men. Why, then, do the learned men of our time not turn red when they proclaim that the agricultural expert who can teach how to keep wheat pure is "the only true philosopher" and act as though wisdom itself had come home to us the moment some country squire's innovation appears to provide the solution? Does this occur out of pity for the selfish world? Oh, the learned have never flattered in a way more demeaning than they do now!

As long as a human being lacks the means of living respectably and well in society, the wise individuals who discovered these means and deigned to teach people how to nourish and appropriately clothe themselves deserve praise. Now, in an age of prosperity, we have means enough and almost too much. The outer man is more than taken care of. We are able to help ourselves to the means that have been discovered in all previous centuries. Nature always remains exactly the same. But the inner man is never adequately cultivated. In each century new members of the human race enter the scene of life. They all must work and work tirelessly to better themselves. They all must busy themselves with dignified thoughts and banish tormenting doubt from their hearts. This need is far more pressing, noble, and appropriate to our lofty station than the desire for a luxurious life. If it is true that the good life consists in peace of mind, then the contemplation of truth presents a broader field for the good life, a richer source of happiness, than all the economical means that human beings dream up to improve their situation.

---

[2]   One of the famed Swiss family of mathematicians, probably Johann Bernoulli (1667–1748), who made major contributions to the early development of differential and integral calculus, or his son Daniel Bernoulli (1700–82), discoverer of the Bernoulli principle in his *Hydrodynamics* (Paris, 1738). René-Antoine Ferchault Réaumur (1683–1757) was, by contrast, more of an applied scientist, accomplished in several fields, especially metallurgy and entymology.

These thoughts are not merely the fruits of some hypercritical act of reflection, in which the heart does not participate. No! what I am saying is what I feel, I speak from a conviction that is very much alive.

Ask our friend, the *British Eudoxus** who is delivering this letter to you. He knows how near I once came to being completely ruined. My feet wandered from the blessed path of truth. Like hellish furies, cruel doubts about providence tortured me; indeed, I can confess, without skittishness, that they were doubts about the existence of God and the blessedness of virtue. At that point I was prepared to give rein to all vile desires. I was in danger, like someone drunk, of reeling into the wretched abyss into which the slaves of vice slide ever more deeply with every passing hour. Come here, you who despise genuine wisdom! Come here, you superficial thinkers, who consider every profound consideration nonsense! Save a soul from the avenging ruin! Summon all the powers of your soul! Give counsel! What was to be done? Should I strangle the emerging doubt in its birth? By what means? By means of belief? Miserable me! I tried belief but can the heart believe if the soul doubts?

Perhaps those who have fortified themselves with carelessness are sufficiently guaranteed against the onslaughts of reason and can force their hearts into a moronic submissiveness. But was I capable of making myself so lucky or rather so unlucky, of making myself into a slave? For what slavery is harder than the slavery of a heart that leads reason into chains?

You are dumbfounded? The talkativeness that decides everything is suddenly gone. The illusions that you presented as reasons have dissolved like mist into the air and you leave me to my grief? Thanks be to those true guides who have guided me back to true knowledge and to virtue. Thanks to you, Locke and Wolff! To you, immortal Leibniz! I erect an eternal monument to you in my heart. Without your help I would have been lost forever. I have never made your acquaintance, but in my solitary hours I implored your immortal writings for help, writings which remain to this day unread by the wider world, and it was they which steered me on the sure path to genuine philosophy, to knowledge of my very self and my origin. In my soul your writings have planted the holy truths on which my happiness is based; they have inspired me.

---

* People named him so especially because of his patriotic spirit.

How astonished Eudoxus was when, after a year's absence, he perceived such a great change of heart in me. How he joked about my whimsical decision to leave the fields of my fatherland in order to visit the German schools of philosophy. He called my conversion the transformation of a free spirit into a fanatic. But he ultimately appreciated my fanaticism; he paid a great deal of attention to the history of my heart and even decided to be my travel companion for a time.

Indeed, is there any more suitable guide for the human heart than being convinced of these truths? In my soul there is a propensity which I share with all thinking beings, in a certain sense with God, the propensity for completeness and perfection. If we all were properly acquainted with ourselves and the objects of our pleasure, then each choice would coincide with the divine choice, the choice of every rational entity would be directed at the very same object. And should I choose blindly? Should I select for myself objects without asking myself: are they also in keeping with your propensity for completeness and perfection? Are they in agreement with a rational entity's genuine needs? How could they if they only had the appearance of being complete and perfect and were like flattering courtiers who, under the false pretense of friendship, lie in wait for the demise of a naive prince?

There lies in me an irresistible drive towards completeness and perfection, a yearning for concepts that are grounded in one another, and this need of my soul, despite its magnificent vocation, is supposed to be implanted in me to be at the service of sordid desires? I am supposed to distance myself from the source of all completeness and perfection, from God, and, at odds with what is satisfying to me, build on my stupid conceit?

Who is so perverted that he is not affected by these compelling reasons, these motives like a flash of lightning? And how much must the innermost core of a wicked individual quiver if that person has enough power over himself to take these deliberations into consideration?

Here you have a foretaste, dearest Euphranor, of the usefulness, of the blessed delight that reflecting on our sentiments can afford us. To be sure, it is only for those whose hearts participate in their deliberations, who think only to establish an eternal accord between heart and reason. Small minds who devote themselves to philosophy not for its own sake, but for the sake of a venal profit cannot possibly find this divine tranquillity within them. From them come only crass complaints about the uselessness of metaphysical brooding.

Until now I have only weighed the pure pleasure, only the delight that arises in the soul in the act of intuitively knowing the completeness of some perfection. I have separated from it what transpires meanwhile in the body, the play of the nerves, the rush of blood, the movement of the limbs which accompany all pleasure here below. Pleasure, as I have laid it out before your eyes, is different from willing, but only to a degree. The will, too, has at bottom some good, a genuine or apparent improvement of our situation, which determines our choice. The desiring that is bound up with each pleasure is different from willing proper only to a degree.

The essential elements, which are inseparable from both, consist

> In the consideration of the object, its multiple parts, and their combination.
> Following the consideration is the judgment, "this object is good."
> Following the judgment is the desire or the mind's effort to realize such a representation or maintain it.

From the instant that we decide, however, these concepts reside in our soul. But they reside there as *being felt themselves*, as intuitive *knowledge of the matter*, enclosed in general boundaries, and transformed into *knowledge possessed by means of signs*, not recognized by us again unless we attend to them. Each sentiment leads to a wide perspective, the objects of which, considered individually, are not easily regarded as such. Since impulses spring from assembled sentiments, an appropriately greater gathering of spirit and exertion of attention are required to assign the constitutive parts, within the purview of distinct knowledge, their appropriate positions and distance from one another.

Mendelssohn's *Philosophische Schriften*

Seventh letter

Theocles to Euphranor

Critics of providence. Their last recourse to an objection to the connection of things. Invalidated, on the basis of the identity of things. On the basis of their powers. On the basis of the capacity of our soul. On the basis of the concept of an entire world.

If the entire *life* of each of us is nothing but *representing* and *willing*, then human beings' thoughts contain at every moment the following rational inference:

> We long for what is good.
> This object is good;
> Hence we must long for it.

Fools and wise men, the virtuous and the villainous, God and human beings agree on the first premise. It is grounded in the nature of each thinking entity and cannot be doubted by the most intractable individual.

Only in the minor premise do they diverge in endless ways. Just as the degrees of knowledge, the limitations of the capacity to represent, vary, so the judgments about the goodness of an object depart from one another.

God himself, I have said, can only delight in what is good, what is perfect. Blindness has seldom dared to go so far as to doubt this truth. But have people also always grasped the consequences of this great truth in its full scope?

The most perfect entity must delight in such events that are grounded in one another, on the basis of which the wisest order shines forth. If one grasps this principle, Euphranor, then providence is justified, and those simpletons who constantly permit themselves to complain bitterly about the organization of the world are put to shame. After lengthy, arduous battles it has finally been demonstrated satisfactorily to the most rational critics of providence that this world, even as imperfect as it appears, could still be the most perfect combination of contingent things; that not the slightest improvement could be taken up in it, nor the slightest evil torn from that combination without, given the course of nature, setting up a far greater evil in the whole. Yet this wise combination itself is a stumbling block for them.

> "Cruel creator!" they cry out. "The proclamation of your wisdom was the source of our misery. You have interwoven in the world countless evils and why? Merely in order not to break the beautiful order, merely in order not to destroy the work of your wisdom, the combination of things?"

Let us allow one of these rash minds to explain himself:

> "I acknowledge," he can say, "that beings could never be created in an absolutely perfect way. Indeed, I ultimately concede that, if it were necessary for there to be a combination of things, perhaps the very best has actually come about. Yet to what end is there this combination? If it has come to be by God (and people acknowledge that it was in his power), why did he not remove every evil in the world through a miracle? Would countless other evils have resulted from this? Then he ought to have anticipated these by means of miracles. Would greater goods have been left out? Miracles could have produced them. What can an omnipotent being not do? Would the world have ceased to be a mirror of divine wisdom? What a pathetic evasion! What's the point? The creatures would have been happy and, you inscrutable one, merely out of goodness you should have called these things into existence."

Yet even if it be supposed, I would answer him, that you would have a right to demand all sorts of possibilities from the almighty, do you also consider how your demand is to be put into effect? Every evil that a rational creature can run up against consists in the representation of an imperfection.[e] And so God, by means of miracles, is supposed to have removed all representations of imperfections?

> "Of course."

And if, on the basis of the condition of my body in the world (since all my thoughts are directed at it), the result is that I will entertain an imperfection at this instant, then the divine almighty is supposed to transport me suddenly to a more blessed condition?

> "I see nothing absurd in this."

31

This altered condition would not have been allowed to be grounded in my present one?

"Why this?"

Set no goal to your demands. In order to remove every means of justification from the creator, demand miracle after miracle, a world full of miracles, bound together by no plan, no connection, but in agreement, as you believe, for the best intention. Say, for example, the creator ought to have miraculously improved, with each passing moment, the fragile constitution of my body and the imperfect condition of my soul. Even where you leave matters with only a few miracles, the following point still stands: they would, given the course of nature, have brought astonishing disorders in their wake.

> "Why a course of nature? It may be the case that not a single condition is grounded in what went before it."

Oh! Then say instead that at each passing moment God is supposed to destroy soul and body, and create something else. Consider it carefully: your demand obviously moves in the direction of this absurdity. As long as the alterations of one thing are connected with another, it can reveal itself under a thousand different shapes and yet always remain exactly the same thing. The same insect becomes in various transformations a worm, a larva, and a beetle; the same plant was seed, becomes a bud, and sprouts up into a tree.

Why? In each condition lay the basic formation of the developing shape. In the worm already, indeed, in the egg itself was the image of the future beetle and, wrapped up in the seed, the mature tree was to be found. Cancel the connection among these metamorphoses. Let the bud, that was determined to grow up into a sprout, be transformed suddenly into a beetle through some miracle. The almighty is also capable of this. Would not the plant here cease to be, and is not a new entity created? And does this not happen because the condition of the plant is in no way connected with that of the beetle?

What else are you demanding? In order to let the soul represent no imperfection, with every passing moment God is supposed to fashion new entities and annihilate the previous ones? For he would annihilate them, if the condition into which he transports them were not connected at all with the foregoing condition.

If my opponent presses to the extreme his tendency to contradict others, what can he say against this? Perhaps that it would have been better to let beings live happily for only an instant than to let them live on for almost a century? What a shallow distortion! Was this point of our dispute? Oh, no! Our adversary wanted all entities to live on and to let them live on happily through cancellation of the connection in the world. To demand its annihilation is another foolishness, the speciousness of which has been so often and so well covered up.

There is still more! Along with the universal connection among things, people cancel the powers of all beings, they cancel the beings themselves. A contingent power whose limitations are not determined can effect nothing, and a power that can *effect* nothing *is* not. Yet by what means are powers determined in the world other than by the interdependence of things? Is an immediate divine will supposed to determine them? In this case God would have had to have done everything, the creatures would not have been able to effect anything, and where would their powers remain? In what would their essences consist?[f]

Indeed, all the capacities of our soul would have to cease. Memory, insight into the future, and capacity to infer. On what do these capacities rest more than on the combination of our concepts, the foregoing ones with the present ones, and the latter with the future ones? If one cancels the combination, how can those concepts persist?

Such great disorders if only a single thinking being were actual! Should there be more than one, the confusion will be even greater. Each one would have to represent to himself another world. In this visible universe the representations of all rational beings together constitute a single whole, a world, because they are grounded in one another. In our fable-like presupposition, however, there would have to be just as many worlds as representations. With each passing moment the scene changes. For each soul in turn a new world. – No! No world at all? Disorder! No entities, no representations! Utter contradictions!

Mendelssohn's *Philosophische Schriften*

Eighth letter

Euphranor to Theocles

Some pleasures are not based upon sensuous or intellectual perfection. There are also sensuous gratifications which are far removed from all concepts of perfection. There are also amusements which appear to rest on imperfections.

Day breaks, a day that for a long time was dedicated completely to you. I anticipated it. Here I sit alone in the grotto that you called your favorite and wait for the invigorating eye of the world. What a magnificent entrance! With what splendor do the heralds of the dawning majesty appear! And how beautifully this fiery form alternates with the stern visage of the tawny night! I do not know whether anyone but a youth would be capable of feeling all these beauties. If my confreres knew what kind of gratification streams from every side into a youthful heart, how little enjoyment they would find in the military exercises which are being staged outside the city today and on account of which they have left me to my solitude. – Yet thanks to their agitated predilection for the nature of war I am able to devote the day to my Theocles and to myself.

The few hours that society leaves me room for on a daily basis disappear all too unnoticeably. Time is required for me to be able to collect myself within myself and prepare for the reflection and peace of mind, without which one does not have an overview of the full sweep of the thoughts of a Theocles.

It is generally believed that solitude is something only for a maturer age and unsuited for passionate youth. But one errs if one believes this. The sentiments of beauty are the prerogatives of youth, and tranquillity is just as useful to fine feelings as it is to contemplation. Those who have spread this false report must have immersed themselves in ignoble sentiments, sentiments that dishonor humanity. They may have their reasons for fleeing the self-examination into which tranquillity invites us and for plunging into the crowded throng. They must have let the noise outshout the voice beckoning them back, perhaps too late, to more noble amusements. Yet what age is free of such blemishes? This brood likes to mix most among young men merely because only very few of them have enough sense to distinguish the outer appearance of a wild joy from that of a youthful cheerfulness.

I had erred, Theocles, when I regarded the contemplation of the origin of pleasure as something that disturbs our joys. How much your letters convinced me of the opposite! I would perhaps have trusted your reasons even less, had experience not come to their aid. I feel the beauties of this splendid region doubled; every vista smiles back at me, twice as comely as before, from the time that your reflections led me on the trail to the properly constituted pleasure.

To be sure, if I stretch out on the lawn with nature in full view in order to allow the rapture to stream down upon me from all sides, then no clear concept appears reconcilable with my dulled feelings. The mass of images intoxicates my senses, and, in this moment, my entire life is nothing but sentiment. However, the mere view of nature cannot always produce these fiery sentiments. Contemplation must take its place and procure the return of these exhilarating moments which I would not exchange for a throne.

If, however, you believe that the basis of all pleasure is to be found either in perfection or in beauty, then forgive me, Theocles! For I cannot agree with you.

You may call it vanity or pride, Theocles! But whenever the talk is of sentiments, youth must be consulted. Taste in an older person can be ruined by manly earnestness, incessant reflection, and some preconceived scholastic opinion. For us, however, feeling, the gift of heaven, is unfalsified. If you trust no sentiment other than your own, then hearken back to the years of your own youth. What pleased you then must have been indisputably a genuine object of pleasure.

Hearken back to the years of your youth! At that time, when you saw the wine glistening in the glass and the fetching look of a beauty drew your attention to her, you often longed to enjoy both of them. You regarded the enjoyment as something good, beyond dispute. But on what basis? In this rapture lies neither a multitude of concepts nor proportions nor even relations to some common final purpose; neither an undertaking nor ease in the undertaking. We joked about that philosopher who wanted to find a multiplicity and unity of concepts even in these sensuous delights.[1] At a banquet, friendly conversations

---

[1] Mendelssohn is referring again to Sulzer; see p. 20, note 1.

are supposed to be the basis of our pleasure and, in the enjoyment of love, I know not what moral beauties.

And yet Theocles does not deny that at times he longed for these delights. Without doubt, the memory of the pleasure that love and wine afforded you at another time must be the reason why you now regard their enjoyment as a good, as a perfection. If this, however, is the case, then your entire edifice falls apart. For did you not say that the sensuous or intellectual perfection of a thing is the reason why we would find pleasure in the entertainment of it? – These examples prove the opposite. The pleasure which certain objects afford us is the reason why we call them "perfect" or "complete."[g]

Yet even this cannot be valid in every case. Believe me, my friend! Human beings are so peculiar in their delights that often they take pleasure in what ought to arouse their sorrow; indeed, even in the very instant that it arouses their sorrow.

That rocky cliff which juts outward above the river rushing by presents a grisly sight. The vertigo-inducing heights, the deceptive fear of falling, and the plunge to the depths below that those pieces of rock hanging over the edge appear to threaten – all this often forces us to avert our agitated gaze from it. Yet, after a quick recovery, we direct our eyes again to this fearful object. The grisly sight pleases. Whence this peculiar satisfaction?

"Nature is beautiful," answer some of its venerators. "Even its little disorders, its apparent ugliness, enhance its attractiveness." What insight! One would scarcely forgive a young man in love for spouting such flattery to his belle.

Why have my pals forsaken me today? Why do they wander around among weapons and heroes? The imitation of battle and arming for it, the preparation for bloody slaughters, the throng, the uproar, and the work by the members gratify them. Should not the recollection of our foolishness, indeed, what am I saying, should not the recollection of our bloodthirsty frenzy horrify them instead?

You yourself, Theocles, how often have you doted on the painting that shines in my father's cabinet, not far from the entrance? It is a ship that, having battled long enough with storm and waves, is finally sinking. Still, the hearty sailors attempt with their last ounce of strength to save it. They stand covered by the white foam of the waves and inspire one another to keep on working. But in vain! The storm presently unleashes a towering wave upon them, leading them to a certain death. They see it and grow pale, and the useless rudders drop from their feeble hands. And this sight pleases you, Theocles? You call this beautiful? – It is true, you admire the hand of the master that knew how to imitate nature so splendidly. But was this all? Confess, Theocles! You would have doted on it even less if the danger had not been simulated at the point where it was greatest. It is no longer the beautiful nature; no, it is the fearful, the terrifying nature. And you find it enjoyable? Should you not instead be downcast by the recollection that human beings are subjected to such unfortunate events? How does this rhyme with your theory?

Consider the matter carefully, Theocles! Let us suppose that at every instant we remembered that our fear was an artistic deception. In that case this consoling recollection can, to be sure, lessen our pain but the object itself cannot for that reason afford any gratification. In spite of this consolation, we continue to be dejected and saddened, and this dejectedness, this sadness has for us an unspeakable allure. A young man with the most cheerful disposition lays aside his joy and celebrates the poet who possesses the wicked skill of making him cry.

Mendelssohn's *Philosophische Schriften*

Ninth letter

Euphranor to Theocles

Ungrounded complaints against providence. Suicide can lead anyone into temptation. Religion cannot move us to this. An Englishman's reasons for permitting this. Reasons borrowed from the stage.

Have there actually been, as you say,* dimwits who have found much to censure in the ordering of things in this world? And was it possible for them to argue so stubbornly for this aberration? No, Theocles! Their hearts could never be convinced by the impudent censure that came across their lips. For let us suppose that they felt what they complained about, that they were actually beset with every sort of misfortune, that their bodies were sick and their souls oppressed by a thousand torments. Why would they have doubled their misfortune themselves by combining their sadness with complaints, their grief with despair, and their pain with gnawing worry? Could people who fancied themselves wise act so foolishly?

Yet if, in the days of torment, they find a kind of comfort in their griping, if breaking out into complaints about their creator can, even for only a moment, draw their souls back from the present pains and lead them to sullen, but less tortuous thoughts, then one can permit these poor unfortunates their consolation. Their complaints are loud sighs of someone full of anxiety and fear, sighs that pierce our hearts but procure him some relief. They are proof of the goodness of the creator whose right hand heals even while his left hand wounds. – But now that the storm is past, would you want to make your curses known to posterity? Would you want to immortalize in writings the nonsense that poured out from you, as it were, in the heat of fever? Why? What motivates you to place your misfortune and unhappiness before the eyes of fellow human beings who dream of happiness? – Do you find pleasure (I trust you as having the most praiseworthy intentions) in having your fellow human beings think precisely as you do? – Pleasure!

---

* See the Seventh letter.

So you find that? Oh, confess it! Human beings are created for gratification, but you find gratification in complaining.

Still, have not some unfortunate souls robbed themselves of life out of despair? What a horrible thought! I would scarcely have thought it, did we not have so much sad experience of it; that is to say, experience of people who appear to have done this more out of conviction than out of rage. It is true! In the few years that I have lived on earth, I have never been able to grasp the possibility of this utter despair. I have considered death among a thousand diverse figures, but it never presented itself to me as a goal of our wishes, something towards which we should be hurrying. Yet perhaps I have my temperament to thank for this love of life. The blood of youth, now rolling in my veins, animates me incessantly to cheerfulness and renders precious every moment that the creator has deemed for me here below. Youth is like the dawning of a spring morning. Everything is alive, a nimble fire pervades every being, and no one who is awake sinks into the arms of sleep before the appointed time. The ever-working nature encourages creatures to life and labor. As soon, however, as the night waltzes its dark veil around the horizon and the busy hand of nature becomes concealed before our eyes, one sees the most enormous swarm longing for the succor of sleep. Consciousness becomes a heavy burden to them. They wish, for a time, not to feel that they are. They wish for this rather than the experience of the emptiness that spreads out from nature to their souls or, even more unfortunately, the worries and cares that wander into their souls, awakening in them as night falls.

I am terrified, Theocles! If my age is supposed to become like the evening of these unfortunate souls, if my even-tempered cheerfulness should disappear with my youth, if it were possible that discouragement, indifference, and worry could in time weave their way into my life, is there ample basis for the inference that I must then long for that sleep? What will reason counsel me if my temperament abandons me?

And can I doubt that it will abandon me, someone who would certainly not have had such gloomy thoughts today if the sky had not suddenly become covered with clouds? Now the region is brightening up again; fields and meadows regain their laughing faces, and now I myself chuckle over my untimely melancholy.

How happy Eudoxus will be if he reads this passage. He is someone who wishes every young man happiness the moment that some occasion for melancholy makes its appearance. There he is now, ambling up and down in the arbor. How cheerful he is! As steady as they are, his sensibilities must not be so dependent upon the weather since the gloomy sky appears to have cheered him up. Without interrupting him, I will continue with my melancholy thoughts.

There have been some philosophers who have wanted to burden religion with giving us reasons for justifying suicide.[1] The battle over self-preservation, they say, becomes easier if we see ourselves confronted with a future of sheer happiness. Who would not gladly shorten his path and double his steps, if he is hurrying towards the goal of all his wishes? – Is this charge not absurd?

Only the most lively conviction regarding the truths of religion and our own innocence can make the expectation of future happiness certain. Yet how can this conviction exist together with the most unrestrained despair? Can the person who promises himself the reward be the person who is vanquished in the fight? After the concepts of religion, nothing else but patience and trust in God can pave the way to happiness. Should earthly misfortunes affect that person more deeply than the children of the world whom religion has brought peace and tranquillity?

Lindamour wanted recently to uphold the honor, within society, of Blount, the philosopher who committed suicide.[2] He endeavored to establish the impunity of this wild deed, independently of religion. His capricious thoughts appeared so unusual to me that I believe that I have remembered everything he said.

"If the existence of someone tortured," he says, "is combined with so many torments that he can never hope for a return to the greater world, never hope for a reconciliation with its glistening wares, self-annihilation deserves neither to be deemed punishable in nature nor to be called an assault on divine rights. The preservation of ourselves is not a law so universal as some faint-hearted philosophers would imagine it to be. It

---

[1] See John Donne's *Biathanos: A declaration of that paradox, or thesis, that self-homicide is not so naturally sin that it may never be otherwise. Wherein the nature, and the extent of all those laws, which seem to be violated by this act, are diligently surveyed* (London, 1644). Cf. a modern-spelling edn. with introduction and commentary by Michael Rudnick and M. Pabst Battin (New York, Garland, 1982).

[2] "Lindamour" is Charles Gildon's pseudonym in *Miscellaneous Works* (London, 1695) where he defended the suicide of the English writer, Charles Blount (*Miscellaneous Letters and Essays*, published with *The Impartial Critic* by John Dennis, preface by Arthur Freeman; New York; Garland, 1973).

is rather an inference from a far more original law that the creator has joined with our thinking *selves*, namely, from *the pursuit of what is good*. As long as we are compatible with the world, we can promise ourselves peace and the satisfaction it brings; in other words, as long as that holds, these two needs aim at a single ultimate purpose. Our self-preservation succeeds in what it does and can, without error, be regarded as the sole motivation of all human actions. However, if we are not able to look upon our future existence without horror, if each instant threatens us with disgust and indifference, hatred of ourselves, and inner turmoil, then a conflict between these two needs arises, and our instinct for self-preservation is defeated. That more original law, the pursuit of what is good, and its inseparable companion, the avoidance of a greater evil, maintain their rights alone and autocratically. They press for our suffering to be cut short, for liberation from a miserable captivity, for the flight from a world that has become too much of a burden.

"Let us suppose that we were destined for no future glory, that our existence would end with the present life. What does one thereby gain against one's hatred of oneself? – *Death*, people say, *is a complete annihilation; of all possible evils it is the greatest and must necessarily lose in the comparison.* Oh, no, as far as our thinking self is concerned, the greatest evil, if we do not feel it, is far more desirable than a condition of consciousness in which evil outweighs the little good that there is. An algebraist would compare the good in his life with positive quantities, the evil with negative ones, and death with zero. If in the mixture of good and evil, after reckoning them relative to one another, a positive quantity remains, then the condition is to be wished for rather than death. If they cancel each other out, then the condition is comparable to zero. If a negative quantity remains, what prevents someone from preferring zero to it?

"*The voice of friendship, his country, and all of society call him back to life.* But what can friends, what can a country, what can all of human society expect from someone in misery who, as long as he lives, will bury himself in his troubles and no longer take part in society? He has played out his role; he is a limb that has died off and can be separated from the whole. Commiserate with him, you who are his friends! But at the same time thank him for sparing you the vexing situation of embracing a friend whose only remaining feeling is one of pain.

"*Still, he dares an assault on divine rights. He is a servant of his creator and cannot retract his obedience to him.* By what means has God attained this splendid right over him? Has God given him existence as a gift? He seeks to relieve himself of precisely this gift that has become an unbearable burden. And where is the convincing argument that his action is at odds with the divine will?

"We all consider it permissible to allow a limb to be removed from us if, according to the doctors, it will be a source of unspeakable pains for the rest of our lives. Do you call this an assault on divine rights? Certainly not! For God has lent us the freedom of turning every affliction away from us and of preferring the theft of a limb to the constant pain of its mutilation. Yet is this limb not as much a part of the human being as the human being is a part of the whole?"

He wanted to continue, but it was time for the meeting to break up. We looked soberly at one another, emptied our glasses, and silently took leave of one another.

I implore you, Theocles! Consider this English philosopher's reasons and test them against your theory of sentiments. Your friend will be greatly indebted to you if you will reveal your thoughts on this enigmatic matter. For my part, I confess that I cannot free myself from this conundrum. On the one hand, Lindamour does not appear to be completely right; on the other hand, suicide does not appear to be as much in conflict with the nature of human beings as one might believe. For heaven's sake, how would someone on the stage be able to bring tears to the eyes of the audience, if he were a man of vice in every thinkable circumstance and despicable in every possible scenario? A piece of villainy can arouse disgust, repugnance, and horror but no sympathy, no social stirring, no pleasantly painful sentiment which is the prerogative of suffering virtue alone.

Orosmann and *Mellefont* would have less share of our sympathy which *Zayre* and *Sara* alone appear to deserve.[3] The former have, at least in part, brought our ill will upon themselves. Their lack of virtue appears to have set the stage for the misfortune that we lament in the person of the beloved in each case. Yet now their contrite hearts feel a thousand-fold the sufferings that cost us only easy tears. Now we see them,

---

[3] In Voltaire's *Zaire*, first staged in Paris in 1732, the Sultan Orosman mistakenly kills Zaire out of jealous rage, only to kill himself after he learns that she in fact loved him and that his jealousy was completely unfounded. In Gotthold Ephraim Lessing's *Miss Sara Sampson*, first staged in Berlin in 1755, Mellefont commits suicide after learning that his spurned mistress, Marwood, had killed his beloved Sara.

petrified, looking at the corpse of their beloved. They break out into a wail of regret, full of despair, and plunge the dagger into their oppressed breasts. They are gone! At that moment all ill will towards their recklessness disappears. A melancholy sympathy suddenly surprises us and we melt into tears. Whence this unusual transformation? Nothing but a suicide at this point has placed the dubious character of this person in its proper light and sealed their goodness. Our cursing has been transformed into well-wishing, our grief into affection, and our ill will into sympathy. Can a piece of villainy do this? Can this be accomplished by an act that is always supposed to be an abomination to the human race?

Mendelssohn's *Philosophische Schriften*

Tenth letter

Theocles to Euphranor

The source of the pleasure is to be found as much in the soul as in the body. These diverse entities must have something in common, from which this common effect springs. The sensuous gratifications afford our soul an obscure representation of the perfection of the body. All pleasure is grounded in the representation of a sensuous or intellectual perfection.

It so happens, my friend, that you anticipated me. I was just about to direct my thoughts to the matter of sensuous gratification with the aim of untying the confusing knots that most philosophers have either simply cut or left completely untouched.

Some have presented our soul as the sole subject of all pleasure. They have sensuous gratifications emerge from the obscure representation of some perfection. However, for the most part the gratifications of the senses have more power over the soul than intellectual forms of pleasure do. What explains this? Why are the obscure representations more active than the distinct ones? And who should be so bold as to suppose the opposite? Finally, this having been conceded, are there not sensuous gratifications which are utterly incompatible with any representation of perfection? Euphranor has brought this objection forth so emphatically that it is not necessary to corroborate it any further.*

Others ascribed to the spirit too small a share in our pleasure, and they encountered even greater difficulties. As they put it, the source of all pleasure lies in the body, in the intoxication of the senses, in a certain movement and attraction of the nerves which preoccupies them without tiring them. But can it be denied? Is there no pleasure that lies in the intellectual representation of some perfection? In the knowledge of God? In the knowledge of any truth? In the fulfillment of our duties? Is the spirit, independently of the body, incapable of any pleasure? Were this the case, then all yearning, all longing for the good, our self-

---

* See the Eighth letter.

determinations, indeed, the original power of our thinking being would fall by the side. What then would be left of us?

On the basis of these contrary views, some have put together a third possibility and attempted to find the source of our pleasure in both, that is to say, in soul and body at once. Should diverse causes, however, produce similar effects, then they must have something in common, from which such an effect springs. What do soul and body have in common such that both can be causes of pleasure?

The following consideration, Euphranor, will lead you to the truth.

The anatomists of the human body have taught us that the nerve vessels intersect so delicately in thousands of labyrinthine paths that, within the entire structure, everything is connected with one thing and one thing is connected with everything else. The degree of tension is harmoniously communicated from nerve to nerve, and an alteration never occurs in one part that does not have an influence, to some extent, on the whole. Those with an understanding of art call this harmonious tension the "tone."

If a limb or part of the human body is then stimulated ever so gently by a sensuous object, the effect reproduces itself from that point to the most distant limb. All vessels are ordered into a wholesome tension, the harmonious tone that furthers the human body's activity and is conducive to its survival. After the enjoyment of some measured rapture, the play of vital movements of every sort proceeds more freely and lively. Wholesome perspiration, the human body's dew, wells up in a continuous stream and at this moment, according to Sanctorius, produces the greatest wonders.[1] This is undeniable testimony that, after enjoying some sensuous rapture, the body feels well and a harmonious tone is produced in it.

All these effects proceed from some wonderful mechanical instinct before the part of the human being that thinks intermingles in that play of vital movements.

There can be no doubt of this. The enjoyment of love and wine, a cool breeze in the muggy heat of summer, a gentle warmth when your limbs are frozen: do these not have an immediate effect on the nerves? Do they need the help of your thoughts to induce perspiring, to set vital spirits in motion, and to keep limbs active?

---

[1] Santorio Santorio, *De statica medicina* (Paris, 1725).

Call, now, upon the observer of your bodily actions, call upon the soul. How will it behave? It will become aware of what condition is more comfortable for its true spouse, its body, the condition, namely, that seems to promise the body a longer life and a more active and effective reality. But the soul will never be able to oversee distinctly and lucidly the astonishing intermingling of vessels and their diverse tensions. From within, it will feel an improvement, a transition to a perfection, but it will grasp only in an obscure way how this improvement arose. Put all this together: it will arrive at an *indistinct but lively representation of the perfection of its body*; reason enough, according to our theory, to explain the origin of a pleasure.[h]

Yet how? If every sensuous pleasure is connected with the concept of a perfection, "then will all gratifications of the flesh be praiseworthy? Does that mean that someone who abandons himself to its allures without making any choices and distinctions acts virtuously?"

By no means! Every sensuous rapture agrees in this alone, that the present moment of savoring it is combined with the feeling of an improved state of the body. Yet the consequences of this can be terrifying. Once the sweet savoring is over, many a base rapture can gnaw away at the bones of its venerators and consume all vital spirits. Thus certain poisons please the palate with their sweetness and yet bring death in their wake.

This is the madness of the libertine; he does not hear the voice of the future and its stern warnings. The present is a siren that lulls him to sleep with her sweet but deadly fare. She conceals its gruesome consequences for an instant behind the scenes, as it were. Yet, sooner or later it will most certainly appear and play out its sinister role. The human being who arms himself with the weapons of reason against this seductress acts wisely and only trusts her when no future contradicts her.

As the executioner of our life, sensuous pain has no other alarms than the present sensuous consciousness of an imperfection in the body. If the parts of the nerves, which are supposed to be joined in a natural way, are torn from their connection or stretched with such force that there is the threat of a tear, then the sad effects of this extend to the entire organic edifice.[i] The tone is altered, it expresses itself as a dissonance or friction in every nerve; vital movements are either languid or in complete uproar. The nerves announce this disorder to

46

the brain without delay. What can the soul at this instant perceive other than the obscure feeling that is the sum of a thousand individual sensations, the feeling of some imperfection that threatens the body with its demise?[k]

Mendelssohn's *Philosophische Schriften*

Eleventh letter

Theocles to Euphranor

Threefold source of pleasure. Musical art affords us all three sorts. All senses have their harmonies. Lack in the case of the modern invention of a clavier of colors. Passing thought on how they can be improved.

We are finally far enough along to have discovered three sources of pleasure and to have set their otherwise confused boundaries apart from one another. We have uncovered *sameness in multiplicity* or beauty,* *harmony in multiplicity* or intellectual perfection,** and finally the *improved condition of the state of our body* or sensuous gratification.† All the fine arts draw from this sanctuary that refreshing potion by means of which they quench the soul's thirst for pleasure. How the muses must rejuvenate us, they who draw upon diverse sources in full measure and pour them out over us in a pleasant combination! Divine art of music! You are the only one that surprises us with all three of these pleasures! What sweet confusion of perfection, sensuous gratification, and beauty! The imitations of human passions; the artful combination of discordant tones: sources of perfection! The simple proportions within oscillations, the symmetry in the relations of the parts to one another and to the whole; the way it occupies the powers of the spirit in doubting, surmising, and predicting: sources of beauty! The tension of the vessels of the nerves harmonizing with every chord: a source of sensuous gratification!¹ All these delights offer their hands to one another as sisters and vie for our favor in competition with one another. Are people still surprised at the magical power of harmony? Can it strike us as strange that its pleasing qualities work on minds with an attraction so powerful that it tames people who are crude and unmannered, calms those who are in a rage, and brings joy to those who are sad?

Heaven allots you so much, indeed, several more delights, you grumbling mortals! It remains up to you; you can make your dwelling here below into a paradise and each harmless feeling into a pleasure.

---

* See the Fifth letter.　** Ibid.　† See the Tenth letter.

Doubt not, Euphranor! For each sense there is a predetermined type of harmony which is perhaps connected with an ecstasy no less than the harmony of sounds is. The predisposition for this lies in our feeling. All that has been missing are providential minds who, through their intimacy with the secrets of nature, might have explored these new ways to happiness and made visible the tracks that are strewn with flowers.

Perhaps our grandchildren will have delighted in this discovery of the soul. For those of us who are now alive, smell and taste (in the strict sense of the term) are nothing but sources of sensuous gratification. Only an obscure feeling of an improved condition of our body makes them into objects of pleasure. In the many sorts of combinations of them we perceive neither beauty nor perfection. Yet who will deny the probability that these concepts lie in those senses? Or the possibility that those who come after us will find these concepts in them?

Among all the sensuous parts of the body, the eyes have the oldest and most proper claims as much on our knowledge as on our happiness. Someone who is blind must dispense with far more goods of the soul than someone who is born deaf. The eyes sense things more distinctly, more sharply, and in a greater expanse than does the ear. And who would have thought it? In the last century people have scarcely begun to track down a harmony among colors. What people in painting knew of the harmony of colors, rested on mere experiences and was much too much obscured by the peculiar beauties of painting. For this discovery the human race is obliged to you, great Newton, and century upon century must reserve for you this immortal fame.[1]

Yet people have not been so fortunate as to elevate this harmony of colors to their true level and make it the mother of as many delights as the harmony of sounds. The clavier of colors appears to promise more than it in fact accomplishes.[2] I grant it the harmonious combination and

---

[1] For Newton's thoughts on a harmony of colors, see *Optics, or treatise of the reflections, refractions, inflections and colours of light* (London, 1704; 2nd edn., 1717) in *Opera quae exstant omnia*, with commentary by Samuel Horsley, vol. 4 (London, 1782; reprint Stuttgart and Bad Cannstatt, Frommann, 1964), p. 221: "May not the harmony and discord of colors, arise from the proportions of the vibrations propagated through the fibres of the Optick nerves into the brain; as the harmony and discord of sounds arise from the proportions of the vibrations of the air?"

[2] The "clavecin des couleurs" was invented by P. Louis-Bertrand Castel; see *L'optique des couleurs, fondée sur les simples observations & tournée sur tout à la pratique de la peinture, de la teinture & des autres artes coloristes* (Paris, 1740). "Clavier" refers here to a proposed instrument that would present an array of colors and their possible combinations, similar to the way in which a piano presents sounds.

alternation of colors, the source of sensuous beauty. Sensuous rapture, the improvement of the state of our body, can also hardly be denied it. It is extremely probable that the neural parts of the eye and their harmonious tensions can be altered by colors in precisely the same way that the vessels of hearing can be altered by sounds. That the impressions of sight spread out to the entire structure of the nerves as quickly and forcefully as do the impressions of hearing is not so certain as yet, to be sure. But one also cannot deny it with certainty. Yet what about the source of perfection, the imitation of human actions and passions? Can a melody of colors bless us with this pleasure? The passions are naturally expressed by certain sounds, and thus they can be brought back to memory by the imitation of sounds. But what passion has the slightest relation with a color?

There is still more: colors cannot be represented without spaces, and spaces cannot be represented without figures. Either they must all be allowed, within a definite space, to play off a single figure, or, along with the diverse colors, diverse figures must follow upon one another. But has a harmony of sizes yet been found? Does anyone know how to provide a unity in multiplicity for the diverse figures represented by the changing colors? If this does not happen, then either the disharmony or the uniformity of the figures must disturb the gratification with which, if I may so put it, the pleasing sounding colors promise to delight us.

But should it not be possible to combine with the harmony of colors the line of *beauty* or *charm* that affords a thousandfold pleasure in painting?

In Germany people are acquainted with the line of waves that our Hogarth has established for painters as the genuine line of beauty.[*] And charm? Perhaps it would not be improper for it to be defined as the *beauty of the true or apparent motion*. The visages and gestures of people that become charming through the beauty in their movements, these provide an example of the former; by contrast, the flame-like or, in Hogarth's terms, the serpentine lines which always appear to imitate a motion provide an example of the latter.[m] Could one not let a mixture of melodic colors move in the direction of one of these lines? Could one not, for the sake of pleasing the eye all the more, combine various sorts of lines, in the forms of waves and flames, with one another?[n]

This is a fleeting thought which I myself do not know how to realize and perhaps it is even impossible ever to carry out the idea. In that case may it have the same fate as those economical suggestions which fill up many a learned page despite the fact that they have just as little chance to be carried out.

* William Hogarth, *Analysis of Beauty.*[3]

[3] (London, 1753; reprint London, Scholar Press Limited, 1974), ch. 9, "Of composition with the waving-line" and ch. 10, "Of compositions with the serpentine-line," pp. 48–67; (It was translated into German in 1754.)

Mendelssohn's *Philosophische Schriften*

Twelfth letter

Theocles to Euphranor

In organic nature all events which are connected with one another can arise reciprocally, one from the other. Origin of the pleasant emotion. Through sensuous gratification, the body substitutes for the descent into pleasure which is caused by the obscurity of concepts. A measurement-artist's pleasure.

In the wondrous structure of the human body, causes and effects are so interconnected with one another that they often exchange roles, the effects coming first and the causes springing from them. Tried and true experiences have led those who understand medicines to this great maxim of nature and thus taught them to proceed cautiously in making judgments about complicated illnesses. Two tormented individuals can feel the exact same pains and have the same complaints, and yet it is always possible that the source of the chalice of sufferings poured out over them is different. What in one case is a consequence of the agony can in another case be its cause. For even illness, even disorders in organic nature, proceed according to certain general laws, according to a reciprocal connection of causes and effects which commonly aim at the great purpose of creation.

If nature has prescribed this law everywhere as a principle, then nowhere does it appear to have deviated less from this principle than in the connection between the brain, the container of life and sentiment, and all other parts of the body.

This truth can be verified by countless experiences.

Each disruption in the nervous vessels is accompanied by disorder in the brain, just as the slightest weakness in the brain expresses itself in the entire neural network.

If a movement in the limbs brings with it or in its aftermath a representation in the brain, then alternately this representation in turn, if it happens first, endeavors to bring about that movement.

The attentive observation of the torture administered to a criminal can produce certain twitchings in the corresponding limbs of the spectators, certain illusions of similar pains which indisputably would be like the pains of the tortured individual if the representation of them were sufficiently stirring.

In a dream, when sentiments sleep and images have complete control, one sees that, at the instigation of these images, all the movements (or at least the attempts to make them) arise in the limbs, movements which, in the normal course of sentiments, would proceed first and cause the internal representations.

All these examples teach you, my dear young man, that *each individual event in organic nature could be at one time the cause, at another time the effect, of one and the same change.*

If now it is true, in addition, that each sensuous rapture, each improved condition of the state of our body, fills the soul with the sensuous representation of a perfection,* then every sensuous representation must also, in turn, bring with it some well-being of the body, a kind of sensuous rapture.

And in this way a pleasant *emotion* emerges. It expresses itself by means of the same sorts of effects as sensuous rapture does. However, they diverge from one another in their causes. That sensuous rapture begins in the parts of the body by virtue of the effect of external objects and extends from there to the brain. The emotion, on the other hand, arises in the brain itself. The representation of a *spiritual* perfection, the memory of some previously enjoyed sensuous gratification, and the imagination (which makes us remember a thousand other pleasant sentiments on this occasion) arrange the fibers of the brain into an appropriate tone, employing them without fatiguing them. The brain communicates this harmonious tension to the nerves of the other parts of the body and the body becomes comfortable; the human being acquires a pleasant emotion.**

Hence the welling up of the bloodstream! Hence the manifold movements of the limbs which you notice in a state of emotion![†] Admire the goodness of our universal father towards his ungrateful sons! The soul would be blessed with even greater ecstasy if its concepts of perfection were perfectly distinct. But it would be impossible for its concepts of perfection to be so. Wisdom combined with necessity, Plato says, has created the world.[1] The soul of the human being was, as far as its

---

* See the Tenth letter.   ** Ibid.   † See the Second letter.

[1]   Probably a reference to *Timaeus* 48a.

intrinsic essence is concerned, incapable of the most perfect distinctness. Each instance of knowledge of the same would have had to have been mixed with the sensuous; that is to say, it would have had to be dependent upon some earthly entity that is connected with the soul and sets specific limits to its knowledge as well as to the pleasure that springs from it. And look! the earthly entity, the heavy body itself, is a new source of gratification. In every case of a representation of some perfection, it favors us with the concept of its own well-being and to some extent replaces the nonsense that sensuousness has set up in the system of our pleasures.

The profound mathematician who excavates the most hidden truths improves his soul. But the senses take no part in the joy as long as he proceeds laboriously from truth to truth. In this sequence of his reflections one distinct concept gives way to another. Sheer work! Sheer troublesome work!

If, however, he thinks all at once over the chain of inferences that he worked through, if he calculates how the truths might be assembled in the best order, segment by segment, and how one flows from all the rest and all the rest from one, what fullness of sensuous gratification must then stream from his brain over his entire body! His representation will cease to be distinct; it is not possible for him to look over the entire chain all at once with complete sobriety. But the astonishing multiplicity effecting the most beautiful order animates every fiber of his brain in a splendid concord. It energizes the play of all the nerves; the mathematician swims in rapture.

Mendelssohn's *Philosophische Schriften*

Thirteenth letter

Theocles to Euphranor

Lindamour's defense of suicide is examined. The point of contention is appropriately qualified, and it is proven that individuals involved in the most infamous cases of suicide can hope for nothing from this decision. The stage has its particular morality. Suicide is ethically good on stage, but not in life.

I was just at the high point of my impassioned meditation, as you would call it, when I saw our Eudoxus in the distance. Oh, how pleasantly the evening passed between us and how we longed for your company! The subject of our conversation was Lindamour's reasons for suicide, and we argued until midnight before we were able to come to some agreement about this question that has been so long a matter of dispute. With his usual passion, Eudoxus defended this madness that has broken out in our country. His burning zeal for the honor of England often influences his way of thinking. Without detriment to the truth, he wished to be able to defend a prejudice that has attained, as it were, the status of a citizen's right. I opposed him in every possible way, and these are the reasons which I employed against him.

Let us suppose the question is, should a person be frightened away from suicide by the fear of being buried in disgrace or be motivated to it by the hope of being divinized by posterity? If that is the question, then reason's answer is: neither. Orthodox believers may regard this action as a way of being transported into another world, while for disbelievers it is simply an annihilation of our existence. But in both cases the inner legitimacy of the action does not depend upon how people in the future will treat my corpse or the empty echo of my reputation. If the action is legitimate, then the wild rabble may stomp my corpse into dust forever. If it is not legitimate, what attraction can it have for me to be applauded in the loudest possible way by an entire world that comes after me?

Whoever allows himself to be deterred from putting an end to his life voluntarily out of fear of some ignominious revenge, is similar to the dimwit who was dissuaded from the firm resolution of drowning himself because he remembered that cold water could be harmful to his body's fragile constitution. And then there is the person who does not worry about the inner goodness of his action and sacrifices his life merely for the hope of fame later. At bottom this sort of person is guilty of the same sort of foolishness as the libertine who appears to be exactly his opposite. He sacrifices himself for the sake of happiness, but he cannot promise himself any more happiness than the present joy of flattering himself. After death, if he denies immortality, he must expect a complete annihilation. If he does not deny immortality, then he must expect the utmost scorn that is reserved for every fame after death not based upon genuine virtue. What, then, spurs him on to this horrific deed? The momentary idea: "I will be divinized; a thousand tongues will spread my fame." Thus what counts for him is the thrill of the moment, a thrill that disappears from him in an instant, and this thrill counts more than a thousand more noble goods which perhaps awaited him in the future. The same sort of lack of substance that one finds in the frailest libertine!*

> Thus, the real point of contention must be this: is suicide permitted and can someone who is virtuous commit it?

Allow me to give the defenders of suicide one more qualification to consider.

The virulence of the passion that torments the person who has resolved to commit suicide can exact from us some sympathy for his tragic fate, but lend no weight to the permissibility of his action. What is supposed to sweep away the burden of the evil deed that he has committed? "Has passion overcome his reason?" What else but the tyranny of passions over reason does one call vice? Is vice itself, then, supposed to serve as one of its excuses? Murder would then be allowed if it happens in the sudden heat of a provoked anger, and Phaedra's culpable love would have to cease to be a vice, because she was consumed with the most intense passion.[1]

---

* See the Tenth letter.

[1] According to Greek mythology, Phaedra falls in love with her stepson, Hippolytus. After he rejects her, she falsely accuses him of assaulting her, a charge that results in his death, followed by her confession and suicide.

Now that it has been qualified even more narrowly, the point of contention thus amounts to this: "Can reason ever counsel a human being to commit suicide?"

Let us suppose that reason counsels it. Then a sober deliberation must make it perfectly clear to us that all the goods of this earth will be lost to us for eternity, and there must be, at the very least, no probability that either reflection or time will be able to overcome an impression that is torturing us. It is necessary for us to have diffused the black mist that arises from the slime of passion and contemplated the objects simply and uninterruptedly. And is life still supposed to disgust us? Are our eyes still going to behold more misery than good? Is there anyone who committed suicide who was in such circumstances? Or will any hapless mortal ever sigh in such torments?

You see, my noble young man! I have been generous to the defenders of suicide. I have good naturedly allowed to stand as an excuse their inability, in their deliberations, to suppress a painful thought when they are certain of the latter as far as the future is concerned. A stricter teacher of morals will have a great deal more to object to here!

But let this be granted. Then the case presupposed by the point of contention, as we have conceived it, remains almost impossible. Consider Blount who was deceived in the hope of love, Sidney who was afraid of having killed his beloved through infidelity,[2] and Mellefont who was supposed to have provided the actual occasion for this through his villainy. Assuming the question in dispute were resolved, none of these figures can hope for reasons that might excuse them.

If you have ever loved, Euphranor, then you are able to put yourself completely in the miserable position of this person who has despaired. Feel all the humiliation of the deceived lover, the regret of someone unfaithful, and the full swath of the seducer's terrible horror. Still more! Let them all descend in an awful mix on a single head. What then? Is that miserable soul left with no other consolation than poison and the dagger? Even if, at that very moment, the impenitent seals his breast off from every source of consolation, if reason, friendship, all of nature, and the divinity itself now preach to deaf ears, won't time strew the wholesome dust of forgetfulness over his wounds? Won't the future

---

[2] Sidney is the protagonist of Jean Baptiste Louis Gresset's comedy, *Sidney ou le suicide* (Paris, 1745).

completely change him and transport him to a sphere of peaceful sentiments in which he will regard the present storm from afar? Let it be supposed that he denies providence, denies God's goodness which guides everything – Euphranor, it is true! – to what is best for us. Does he have such impoverished concepts of the nature of our sentiments that he believes that the thunder, now rolling over his head, would roar in his ears without stopping? And reason is supposed to convince him of this? Oh, no! Passion, the darkest sort of passion, has obscured his sight, encircling it like a fog. And if he still appears sober enough to reflect on the dagger in his hand, on his decision, then do not let the appearance deceive you. It is the wild, stubborn silence of someone who hates himself, the pinnacle of all rage which reason bans even further than the fuming of the wildest despair; for such despair more often boils over in words without foaming up to the awful deed itself.

You are mistaken, noble youth, if you believe that suicide seals the moral goodness of a character. It does not seal moral goodness at all. The stage has its own ethos. In life nothing is ethically good that is not grounded in our perfection. On the stage, on the other hand, everything that is grounded in powerful passions is good. The purpose of the tragedy is to arouse passion, and the darkest vice that leads to this final purpose is welcome on stage. Thus, even suicide is good from a theatrical point of view. The subsequent remorse of an Orosman and the pangs of conscience of a Mellefont would have seemed to afflict them only faintly if they had not convinced us of the opposite by making the most shocking decision.

Herein lies a major part of the art in the poetry of the theater. For the play to please, the poet must carefully conceal the conflict between genuine ethical life and that of the theater. Have someone, at the moment when the seducer of Sir Sampson's daughter stabs himself, shout the following words out to him: "What are you doing, you rogue? Are you willing to do penance for your vices?" At that moment the morality of the theater would disappear, along with the playwright's ultimate purpose. Held up to the mirror of genuine ethical life, our sympathy, that hardly began to stir, would turn into disgust.

Mendelssohn's *Philosophische Schriften*

Fourteenth letter

Theocles to Euphranor

Lindamour's comparison of sentiments with quantities is rebutted. On the basis of our soul's nature it is proven that suicide is impermissible, even without the aid of a revelation, if we assume that our soul is destroyed when we die.

Even if the almost impossible case presupposed by the dispute were to occur, reason still has grounds to dispute the permissibility of suicide. Lindamour, it bears recalling, compared *lack of consciousness* or utter annihilation with *zero* and consciousness of an imperfection with a negative quantity.[*] Either he must have advanced this comparison only in jest, or he allowed the surface appearance of a similarity to deceive him. What is a negative quantity? A contrived word that mathematicians have assumed in order to indicate an actual quantity by which another quantity must be reduced.

The negative is to be distinguished from the positive, not by any means in regard to quantity, but in regard to the reduction which is to be calculated with this quantity. The latter is supposed to be subtracted, the former added.[°] Hence, if Lindamour says that the negative quantity is less than zero, then he must be thinking either of nothing or of this: the addition of a negative quantity to an actual one, or, more precisely, the subtraction of a positive quantity equal to it from another positive quantity leaves less than if zero is added to the quantity. But does any of this have even the slightest bearing on our case?[P]

Someone who in days of agony longs for a timely sleep could perhaps make use of Lindamour's simile. He hopes to wake up again to days in which he is more blessed. His existence will cheer him up. His overdue perfection will be present, the actual quantity to which the negative quantity and zero must be added if what remains is to be suitably calculated. But the individual committing suicide who prefers annihilation (I speak with the unbeliever since, by your admission, his

---

[*] See the Ninth letter.

conception exculpates suicide the most), the individual who prefers the annihilation of himself, I say, to an imperfect condition cancels the quantity to which the calculation refers. To what is the negative quantity, to what is the zero to be added? To the perfection of his individual person? It will no longer exist. To the perfection of the whole? Oh, no, the obligation to the whole was certainly not the reason which drove him to suicide!

And how could it have been? Can an entity that has been created maintain: "My existence proves to be an imperfection for the whole?" By what means has the shortsighted individual arrived at this knowledge of what is best for *the whole*?

All other inferences of this zealous patriot are no less fraudulent. Nothing is more absurd than a sanction for suicide, an *ethical capacity* to prefer death, if it is annihilation, to life. Merit, choice, freedom, all these concepts vanish as soon as a decision is to be made between being and nonbeing.

I would like to take this opportunity to convey to you the entire exchange which Eudoxus and I had concerning Lindamour's most important conclusions.

> "Let's suppose," he said, "that I gave up Lindamour's simile of positive and negative quantities. The main matter remains untouched. No doubt: 'There can be circumstances in which annihilation, a state of not-being-conscious is to be wished for over consciousness of a thousand deficiencies.' What can be said in objection to this?"

This, I answered, that the entire thought vanishes the moment one analyzes it.

> "The proof . . ."

Is very easy. Merely answer a few questions which I will frame. "Do you believe that the soul or, in my countrymen's parlance, our *thinking self* could make a decision without reason, as it were, merely to show the resoluteness of its freedom?"

> "Certainly not. Without compelling reasons the power of our soul remains forever indeterminate. If, on the other hand, no reason lies in the matter itself, the most trivial detail can take the place of an important reason."[q]

Indeed! Everything that we want will *be better* to a certain extent, or at least it will have to appear better to us than what we do not want. Or do you find some more precise formulation to express this concept?

"None, to tell the truth! For *to be better* and *to prefer* are equivalent to one another. I *prefer* something to something else because I consider it *better*."

Must even death, if we would prefer it to life, appear to us to be *better* than this?

"Of course!"

But what does it mean *to be better*? Does it mean anything other than advancing our good, being conducive to our perfection? For everything which contributes something to our perfection is *good*.

"I note your cunning, you crafty Socrates! You believe that you have already ensnared me with your tricky questions. If I leave things here with a monosyllabic 'yes,' the next question will certainly be: 'Can death contribute something to our perfection?' But look! I untie your knots. What is *better* is either what advances our perfection or what (note well, Theocles!) frees us from a greater imperfection. Hence, I can very well say that death . . ."

Not so fast, Eudoxus, not so fast! We want to analyze our concepts as far as we can. What is perfection? Have you come across a definition of it anywhere?

"It is, as is taught in the schools, the harmony of a multiplicity."

Good! This definition is as fruitful as it is correct. But *harmony of a multiplicity* appears to presuppose *a composition of diverse things*, and this definition would accordingly apply more to the perfection of something composite than to that of simple entities. It is true that in the case of simple entities one meets with representations that remain diverse, with diverse alterations which harmonize as much with one another as with the objects they mirror and, the more they harmonize, the more perfect they are. But do you find no definition which could be suited more naturally to simple things?

"I truly find none."

Then follow me; I'll lead you to one. If a soul can represent to itself more matters than another soul can and if it can represent a matter to itself more distinctly and with less trouble than another soul can and retain it longer, is it not more perfect?

"Indisputably!"

Or, in short, a soul is more perfect if it possesses a greater power of representation.

"Indeed, so it appears."

The perfection of a soul consists then in the degree of its power of representation or, what is the equivalent, the degree of its actuality (reality)?^{r}

"Incomparably, Theocles! For the essence of the soul consists simply in its power of representation."

Therefore, what expands the boundaries of our actuality, of our power of representation or prevents its greater limitation (I have understood your recourse, Eudoxus!) makes us more perfect.

"Indeed!"

Therefore, it is also *better* than something else that does not do this as well?

"Correct!"

Also, vice versa. What is supposed to be *better* than something else must expand the limits of our actuality, the boundaries of our existence, or prevent a greater limitation of the same. For nothing else is meant by advancing perfection and holding off imperfection.

"I must grant this, of course."

Oh, then I have won! Suppose all these analytical comparisons, these analyzed concepts instead of those employed by Lindamour. According to him, we can *prefer* a *state of not being conscious*, annihilation, or that state can be *better* than a conscious one; it can stave off a greater *imperfection*; it can prevent a limitation of our actuality more than the *consciousness* of our imperfection or a lesser degree of our actuality can. For, according to our definition, nothing else was an imperfection. Can a rational person think in so undisciplined a manner that our annihilation is regarded as expanding the boundaries of our existence or preventing a greater limitation more than a lesser degree of our existence might?

> "You have succeeded, Theocles! I am now actually at the point where I must yield. Yet perhaps my weapons are too weak to mount an adequate opposition to you; perhaps Lindamour would have defended himself better."

I really do not know, Euphranor, how the sharpest mind could have mounted a better defense of those who commit suicide. It would always amount ultimately to a certain degree of *being better, being more wished for, preferring* that cannot in any way be combined with our annihilation. The truth remains: *the feeling of a lesser degree of actuality advances our perfection infinitely more than its annihilation does.*[s]

Mendelssohn's *Philosophische Schriften*

Fifteenth letter

Theocles to Euphranor

Naturalists cannot be kept from suicide by the foregoing arguments, Other reasons, also from this system of doctrine, to corroborate the reprehensibility of suicide.

Scarcely had the sun risen today when I saw the British Eudoxus enter my room with a troubled countenance. Why so early, my friend? I called to him. "Theocles," he replied, "a rare discontent has robbed me of my peace today." That could, indeed, be read in your eyes, I responded, but discontent about what?

> "About myself. About the clumsiness with which I defended suicide yesterday."

So today you appear presumably armed with mightier weapons.

> "With weapons so mighty that I believe myself able to repel the most vigorous attack. Not so? You may think that you have done everything to prove that religion must inspire an unsurmountable love of life in an orthodox believer, and that, on the other hand, a disbeliever's own system, the system of annihilation after death, must inspire the same love of life in him."

Was this not enough, then? What was still left to do?

> "Everything, my dearest friend! Everything was still left to do. The things that tempted a person to commit suicide appear to me to have been contained in a third system against which all your reasons are impotent. One could call it an intermediate or mixed breed of believers and nonbelievers."

A mixed breed of believers and nonbelievers? Somehow like the souls of that philosopher are a mixed breed of simple and composite entities?

> "Don't joke, Theocles! I would like to explain myself in more detail. The Theocleses of the world may well have embraced the teachings of this intermediate breed. I mean those philosophers

64

over whom no revealed religion has any noticeable power, in other words, those who do not heed the commandment which commands them to bear their cross with joy, even should they be able to toss it aside. They consider any means of altering their condition permissible, indeed, laudable if it meets with the approval of reason alone. They have followed philosophy wherever it leads them. They have even dared to venture beyond the shores of this life with their arguments and posit the indubitability of the immortality of the souls and a philosophical sort of reward and punishment. These thinkers don't regard death as an annihilation of their existence! They regard it instead as a transition to another kind of enduring state which is merely exchanged for their present life. If they kill themselves, it is not that they seek to exchange an imperfect state for annihilation. They are merely trying to strip away, so to speak, the present cocoon, to leave the vexing husk behind them, and, in a new metamorphosis, to burst forward with transfigured beauty. They are uncertain whether the future state will be better than the one from which they tear themselves away. But they will not shun this metamorphosis. Being in this world a moment longer profits only those who fear that they will be destroyed when they die. For these genuine philosophers, on the other hand, a violent suicide is as right as a worm's metamorphosis, precipitated by heat. What can be reprehensible in this? – Look, Theocles! Do you see the impenetrable fortifications that persons committing suicide surround themselves with? Take your mightiest weapons and see if they can do any damage to this bulwark at all!"

Well, Eudoxus, I replied, I would love to try with what powers I have. Following the practice of someone experienced at war, I will, however, have to find a new type of attack for each new type of defense. I ask you, therefore, as the counsel for these philosophers, whether they do not consider it extremely likely that time and reflection will suppress their presently gnawing worries and pour healing comfort on their wounded soul?

"They might be able to consider it quite likely. But the future life perhaps promises them this comfort with greater likelihood."

Don't back away from the point made here, Eudoxus! The future must promise them this in that life with greater likelihood. For if the hope were the same on both sides, then they would have no reason to leave their present state. But what supports this hopeful expectation?

Before birth the future human being lay wrapped up in an embryo. His state was a constant slumber in which neither distinct representations nor consciousness were to be found. As his limbs developed, the soul also wrenched itself loose from the fetters of that sleep and appeared on the scene, armed with thoughts and consciousness. After death all the limbs decompose once more. The physical mass falls apart, the physical mass for whose organic structure the soul performed such important services. They themselves, the thinking monas, again limit themselves to the region of an embryo. What is more likely than that it will then return to its original old condition and sink again into a deep sleep? Or have your philosophers some sort of revelation which teaches them something better?

"Nothing of revelation! They don't believe in any."

On what basis, then, do they know that the limitation of our power of thinking will suddenly alter at death and no longer depend upon the state of the matter connected with it? Isn't it possible that the embryo, in which my soul lies encased, will constantly travel from plant to plant in the form of lifeless matter or that it will creep into the veins of an animal without ever taking on a more favorable organization and awakening to distinct sentiments? Answer, Eudoxus!

> "What? Our soul is supposed to sink into an eternal sleep? Idle worries! Would a benevolent father let his children, his own creations, become more imperfect and forever remain more imperfect in this way? Would the level, to which he raises them for a time, thus be nothing better than a beguiling stage which puts people from the lowliest rabble on the throne and the next instant casts them back into their nothingness? No, Theocles! We do not need revelation to establish this truth: 'The benevolent creator must elevate from one level to another the entities that he has created and, if they fall down, he must let them fall down only for a short time.'"

I expected you to make this point, Eudoxus! Their hope is thus founded upon God's benevolence and goodness, and they place this hope above the expectation of a better state in this life, the likelihood of which rests not merely upon God's goodness but rather upon the nature of things and the essence of their soul. For, on the basis of the nature of things, it is conceivable that time and reason will probably lessen the misery that they now moan about.

> "Yet, merely add the following: it always remains possible that a greater likelihood of a cure lies in the precipitated metamorphosis than in the expectation of any natural means of help."

But how can I add this, Eudoxus, if I prove that each likelihood stemming from the nature of things must yield a compelling reason for determining our actions that is more important than a likelihood derived from God's goodness? The most orthodox believer cannot doubt his. If we deliberate whether an undertaking is to be carried out, we should not say: we will, of course, probably not succeed in carrying out our project, but God will ordain everything in a wonderful way since God is benevolent. No! the unfathomable wisdom finds no satisfaction in this blind faith. It has endowed us with reason and knowledge; we should consult the nature of things, and at that moment presuppose what is impossible, namely, that the course of things is necessary and not regulated by any wise master. What then seems to us most probable, is what we should expect; we should make decisions in terms of that, and confidence in God's goodness can then impart to us courage and steadfastness to carry out what we have decided. Once this moral maxim is established, people necessarily act contrary to it if they place the probability of becoming happy in this life, which rests upon the nature and the course of things (not to speak of the fact that God's goodness also strengthens us in our hope here) below another probability which is based merely on trust in God's goodness.

You said that we cannot avoid this transformation and, hence, that we lose nothing in the process if we speed it up. This is false, Eudoxus! Whoever, on the basis of the light of reason, assumes a future life must allow for a connection between the future life and the present one. His thinking "I" is supposed to endure, is supposed, even in that life, to remain forever the same "I" that thought, willed, and was conscious of itself in this life. Hence, the changing circumstances, which bind that life with this one, must be grounded in one another.* Whoever departs from this world differently, must enter that world differently. Accordingly, a

---

* See the Seventh letter.

mortal who does not wait for the end of the duration allotted to him in this world, plunges himself into a future state completely different from the state into which he would have been transported by the course of nature. How much the imprudent individual risks, Eudoxus! That single blow influences his entire immortality. Everything will be markedly different from what was determined for him. And does he undertake this audacious change, this great revolution blindly?

Whoever changes the constitution of a political state by violently reversing the order of things, without having as sufficient a reason as possible for supposing that the reversal will be an improvement, is a criminal, an enemy of divine and human laws who takes delight in catastrophes without paying attention to the outcome of his wild ventures. But does not the person contemplating suicide, who believes in an immortality in accordance with reason, find himself in the same situation? In order to avoid present evils, he plunges himself blindly into a horrifying revolution without the slightest hope that he will better his condition by doing so. "Where is the convincing argument," he says, "that this deed is contrary to the divine will?" Where, I ask to the contrary, is the argument for the likelihood of the supposition that it is in accordance with the divine will? Without the likelihood of this supposition no rational man must undertake so important an action, and it is impossible for him to have this likelihood in the case before us. Outside of revelation, we cannot suppose the divine will to be anything other than what proceeds from the forces of nature. What is in harmony with those forces which he has placed in nature must serve us in place of an oracle until an explicit command or the outcome of some matter teaches us something better. As long, therefore, as the forces of nature and of my own body are in accord to maintain this machine which God has given me as a companion here below, it is a crime, a punishable rebellion, if I set myself against these apparent intentions of God, that is to say, if I want something other than God must appear to want for me now. If I want to act rationally, if I want to act in a way that receives God's blessing, then I must try to bring all the forces of my soul into the most perfect harmony with the forces of nature. In other words, I must strive to maintain my body as long as the forces making up my body appear to say to me that God wants to maintain it, and I must leave up to his immeasurable goodness as to how soon it will please him to place me in better circumstances.

Lead your philosophers, Eudoxus, into those festive gatherings where idlers fritter away precious time playing cards. The philosopher can make use of the most dismissed triviality. The more a card is undetected in the same shuffled deck, the more an experienced player bets on it. His hope increases with each loss. If he would toss this hope aside and demand a reshuffling, he would act foolishly. The case before us has a quite similar character. Even when trust in the goodness of God is set aside, the hope that things will get better increases with every stroke of bad luck that befalls us in this world. Those who think otherwise are afflicted by superstitious prejudices like that of those card players who prophesy nothing but bad luck in shuffling a particular deck of cards because some previous shuffles were unlucky. If trust in God's goodness is added, it increases the hope of becoming happy in this life as well as in a future life. Yet, as far as my undeniable maxim is concerned, it is not necessary for this to be considered in the deliberation at all.

> "But, all this considered, indeed, all of it granted, don't you see what a subtle rational inference, what a triviality it comes down to in this most important matter? A mountain range turning on a hair, as that Hebraic poet says."[1]

Oh, Eudoxus, now you are denying the philosophers' character which you presupposed. It is not possible for them to speak this language. They can regard nothing as a triviality that reason commands them. Sacred reason which takes the place of revelation for them! They must bend their knees in reverence before all rational inferences, however subtle or far-fetched they may be. Their happiness depends upon them. All the reasons that you have advanced for suicide I could have applied in general to each case of murder. Your conscientious philosophers would have twisted and turned, and they would have had to reach out quite far to secure the inferences necessary to establish the culpability of this heinous deed.

But I am not faulting this way of proceeding. For reason either everything is beneath contempt or nothing is. Why do we see the objects of our desires always through the lens of the passions and never regard the reasons that keep us from those objects until after we have turned the lens around? The inferences against suicide, one objects, rest

---

[1] "Hagigah" 1:8, *The Mishnah: A New Translation*, by Jacob Neusner (New Haven and London, Yale University Press, 1988), p. 330.

upon truths that have been sought from afar. Indeed! But on what do the compelling reasons that drive us to suicide rest? What worthless trivialities! The loss of our good reputation; the thought of the low esteem into which we have fallen among the worms around us. The regret; an all-too-late, often-useless feeling of a crime that we have made ourselves responsible for. The humiliation; a king who is now shackled to an oar. He commanded and now must obey; he was surrounded with gold and is now surrounded with iron. How trivial and insignificant is all this in the eyes of rigorous reason! And yet does one not assail nature and divinity that they exposed human beings to such calamities?

Nevertheless, the human being himself, the greatness of this imagined king, all his thoughts and actions disappear and become trivialities if one considers them from this side. It is appropriate that a triviality frets over trivialities.

Conclusion

Euphranor could no longer resist the urge to take part personally in Theocles' conversation with Eudoxus. He travelled to them and interrupted this instructive correspondence for a while, in order to receive instruction in the flesh from his English philosopher. Since this, however, took place before Theocles had answered the eighth letter, I believe that I do my readers a pleasant service by adding here in conclusion what was discussed by word-of-mouth between them about this matter. It should be recalled that Euphranor in the cited letter spoke of painfully pleasant sentiments (thus, for the sake of brevity, they labelled the sentiments that, in terms of appearances, are connected with some imperfection) and advanced the thesis that these sentiments contradict Theocles' theory since they appear to attest to anything but knowledge of a perfection. He acknowledged, in front of Theocles, that Du Bos had seduced him into this way of thinking.* This writer heaps up countless examples of amusements of entire nations, in which cruelty appears to have had a far greater part than humanity has. As proof that souls long merely to be moved, even if they have to be moved by unpleasant images, he cites the gladiatorial arenas, jousting tournaments, bullfighting, the cock fights of the English, and finally the tragic stage. Euphranor and the others all agreed on this point, that Du Bos must never have distinguished the soul's pleasure from sensuous gratification and compared the former, in its element, with mere willing. For since the determination of our power of representing is the same in both cases and is only distinguished as a matter of degree,** that pleasure, just like the will, can have no other basis for motivation than a true or apparent good. Indeed, Eudoxos correctly remarked that, according to Du Bos's hypothesis, human beings would have to be just as pleased by disgust, regret, or terror since the soul is moved by them. But experience testifies to the contrary.

Yet they were not able to agree as easily on how the origin of the

---

* *Réflexions critiques sur la peinture & la poesie.*[1]
** See the Sixth letter.

[1] Jean Baptiste Du Bos, *Réflexions critiques sur la poésie et sur la peinture*, 7th edn. (Paris, 1770; reprint Geneva, Slatkine, 1982). Du Bos (1670–1742) argued that art – as exemplified by tragedy – consists solely in stimulating artificial passions for the sake of avoiding boredom. *Réflexions* went through seven Paris editions between 1719 and 1770.

painfully pleasant sentiments mentioned by Du Bos is to be explained; at least until Theocles finally took over the discussion and tried to remove the difficulty in the following manner.

On the basis of the nature of the soul, he said, it has been proven that it cannot want or take pleasure in anything that does not present itself in the form of a perfection. And does experience contradict this? – That we would like to see. The examples that are cited against this are not all of the same nature. In the case of some bloody amusements one must, so to say, suppress all sympathy, all human feeling, if one wants to find them gratifying. The gentle Greeks had to accustom themselves gradually to overcome their sympathetic sentiments before they were able to acquire a taste for the Romans' gladiatorial bouts. And if merely a single maudlin sentiment is awakened in the spectators of jousting tournaments, hunts, or bullfights, there can be no disputing the fact that it disturbs their pleasure.

Other attractive spectacles, on the other hand, must do the opposite: they must make us rage with sympathy, in order to please us. Tragedies are of this sort, stirring portraits for well-educated people and a bloody scaffolding for the insensitive rabble. The pleasure that tragedies afford us is governed by the measure of sympathy that they arouse in us.

Those painful amusements, in which sympathy has no part, are based upon nothing but the skillfulness of the actions of the persons or animals involved. People admire the agility of their limbs and the skillful turns that they know how to make in order to overcome the obstacle or evade it. It is true, the pleasure is not as great as when the players are in danger although, to all external appearances, they must employ just as much skillfulness. A tumbler gratifies us infinitely more if he dares a leap over swords that have been placed crosswise, pointing upwards, than if he playfully fluttered over wooden sticks without touching them. The higher the tightrope artist stretches the rope, the faster I am drawn to his scaffolding. Even here, unnoticed but streaming along with this sentiment are completely different representations which unite in our imagination and play a role in our awe and admiration. We are astonished at the faith that these performers have in their skill; with what circumspection and presence of mind they defy the terrifying danger; how they evade it when it hovers before their eyes and repeatedly stake life and death on their skill. A leap over the sticks, we would ourselves dare, and perhaps have dared successfully. But how certain must the art be which passes over the tips of the swords! How much admiration a Roman fencer deserved who, at the very moment that he gives up the ghost, was still able to gather himself together, to think back to the lessons of his fencing school, and to extend his dying limbs in a respectable fashion! It is true, the horror aroused by the cruelty of the action would be greater than the pleasure aroused by the play of skill, and, at the outset, this bloody spectacle had precisely such an effect on the gentle Greeks. But by custom, by inborn martial sensibilities, by the respect that they had for corporeal exercises, and finally by a disdain for slaves that had gained ground among them, the Romans had inured themselves against this gentle sentiment. They suppressed the tenderer human feelings and delighted in the skillfulness of the fencers and in their corporeal perfections. The imperfect, considered as imperfection, cannot possibly be gratifying. Since, however, nothing can be absolutely imperfect but instead good is always mixed with evil, it is possible to bring custom to a point where people abstract from the evil and direct attention to the little good that is attached to it. This aptitude is called a *spoiled taste*, and there is no abomination in the world for which we cannot find some sort of taste in this manner. Rome, which created such large and expensive institutions to spoil the taste of the nation, in the end produced a masterpiece of spoiled taste, a Nero who set fire to Rome and took pleasure in watching it burn.

However, in the second type of amusements, none of this takes place. Here no detachment, no spoiling of attention is required in order to find pleasure in distressing images, and the danger that is portrayed cannot enhance our appreciation of the artist's skillfulness. There can be no disputing the fact that it takes as much skill to portray a ship in full sail as it does to portray one on the verge of going under, and the painter in both cases is not in danger. For playwrights composing tragedies, things proceed no differently. The danger, the misfortune, that he portrays does not affect him; thus he can calmly and coolly situate it, and we know, notwithstanding, that we owe him thanks for preferring to portray occurrences of ill fortune over the most serendipitous episodes. Why? Because in those ill-fated occurrences nothing but sympathy is the soul of our pleasure.

Sympathy is the only unpleasant sentiment that we find alluring, and the sort of sympathy that is known to us in tragedies under the name of terror is nothing but a sympathy that suddenly surprises us. For the danger never threatens us ourselves but rather our fellow human being whom we pity. What is it, then, about this sentiment over all others that it can be unpleasant and nevertheless please us?

You have shared your views about this, dearest friends! But what is sympathy? Is it not itself a mixture of pleasant and unpleasant sentiments? A quite noticeable, positive feature presents itself here by means of which this emotion distinguishes itself from all others. It is nothing but the love for an object combined with the conception of a misfortune that befalls it; a physical evil for which it is not responsible. The love rests upon perfections and must afford us gratification, and the conception of an undeserved misfortune renders the innocent object of our love all the more precious and elevates the value of its merits.

This is the nature of our sentiments. If a few bitter drops are mixed into the honey-sweet bowl of pleasure, they enhance the taste of the pleasure and double its sweetness. Yet this happens only when the two types of sentiments, of which the mixture consists, are not directly opposed to one another.

If, to the conception of some present fortune, there is added the poignant memory of that misery in which we previously lived, then tears of joy gush forth, tears that are the epitome of all joys. Why? The concept of a past imperfection does not conflict with the concept of the present perfection. Both can exist next to one another, and that bygone imperfection makes us more sensitive to the gratifying feeling.

However, were this present fortune not complete, were there some distressing circumstances that still pain us in the present, they would erase part of the joy and markedly diminish its intensity. For this reason I said that they must not be directly opposed to one another; they must be able to exist side by side.

What rapture, then, springing from sympathy, must inundate us! And how pitiful are those hearts that remain closed off from this heavenly feeling! The most ardent love is not incompatible with the conception of a physical evil afflicting the object of our love. They can both exist. Indeed, we never feel in its full measure the sweetness of friendship until a misfortune befalls our friend and he deserves our sympathy. All his perfections, his slightest merits shine in our eyes with twice the luster, especially if he is himself not responsible for his ill fortune.

Look at the crowd that in thick heaps swarms around someone

condemned to die. They have all understood what things the scoundrel has perpetrated; they abhor his conduct and maybe even the man himself. Now he is dragged, disfigured and powerless, to the gruesome scaffold. People work their way through the throng, they stand on their tiptoes, they climb roofs in order to see the features of death distort his face. His judgment is pronounced; the executioner approaches him; in an instant his fate will be decided. How longingly at that moment do all hearts wish that he were forgiven! This man? The object of their revulsion whom a moment ago they would themselves have condemned to death? By what means now does a ray of human love become alive in them once again? Is it not the approach of the punishment, the sight of the most gruesome physical evil, which somehow reconciles us even with someone wicked and purchases for him our love? Without love we could not possibly be sympathetic toward his fate.

How much more, then, must the theatrical presentation of innumerable episodes of ill fortune, to which someone virtuous succumbs, enhance our love for his perfections and make him worthier in our eye! Such a sight in nature would be unbearable for us since the displeasure over his undeserved ill fortune would far surpass the pleasure that springs from love. Yet, although this is the case in nature, it is nonetheless pleasing on stage. For the recollection that it is nothing but an artistic deception lessens our pain to some extent[*] and leaves only as much of it as is necessary to lend our love the proper fullness.

[*] See the Fifth letter.

Notes of the Editor

(a) Aristotle himself [*Poetics* viii. 4] makes it clear what sort of doctrine flows from these concepts for those who compose dramas. They can never be sensuous enough, and they must guard against requiring the imagination of the audience to initiate too much. Accordingly, it must be possible for the entire play with all its manifold parts to be grasped sensuously all at once. That is to say, the whole must have its specific size and the parts their specific proportion to the whole.

(b) Descartes was the first to think of giving a material definition of pleasure.[1] He found that we would have to regard an object as something perfect of its sort if it is to afford us gratification; that is to say, according to the nominal definition assumed by a famous writer,[*] if we are to prefer having the representation to not having it. This is the most general formula which encompasses all particular cases. The healthy, the tasteful, the beautiful, the useful, all amusements terminate ultimately in the concept of a perfection if what determines them as subspecies is abstracted from them. Insofar, then, as the theory of sentiments has an influence on the doctrine of ethics, the doctrine of Descartes can be assumed as a theorem confirmed by experience. The teacher of ethics has this in common with the person who gives instruction about nature: the former can appeal to the general laws of sentiments just as the latter can appeal to the general laws of motion that are known to him through experience, without worrying about their more distant cause. But the metaphysician is not satisfied with that. He also wants to grasp this: why does the soul want to have the sort of representations which portray something perfect to it?

(c) Theocles appears here to be aiming at the passage in Plato's *Symposium* where he speaks of two Venuses. ἡ μέν γέ που πρεσβυτέρα καὶ ἀμήτωρ Οὐρανοῦ θυγάτηρ, ἣν δὴ καὶ Οὐρανίαν ἐπονομάζομεν· ἡ δὲ νεωτέρα Διὸς καὶ Διώνης, ἣν δὴ Πάνδημον καλοῦμεν.

---

[*] Maupertuis.[2]

[1] René Descartes, *Les Passions de l'âme*; cf. *The Philosophical Writings of Descartes*, tr. John Cottingham, Robert Stoothoff, and Dugald Murdoch (Cambridge, Cambridge University Press, 1985), vol. 1, pp. 361–2.

[2] *Essai de philosophie morale*, by Pierre Louis Moreau Maupertuis (1698–1759), was published in Berlin in 1755.

To each Venus he attributes her special love. πάντες γὰρ ἴσμεν ὅτι οὐκ ἔστιν ἄνευ Ἔρωτος Ἀφροδίτη.[3] This philosophical fable corresponds in an incomparable way to the doctrine of beauty and perfection. In the same dialogue Socrates, in the name of the prophetess Diotima, recounts another fable of love, which can be given an even more philosophical interpretation. On the birthday of Venus, he says, all the gods had a feast and among them was also Plenty, the son of Diligence. Poverty stood before the gate and begged. Plenty was tipsy from nectar (since at that time wine did not yet exist), and, after sauntering into Jupiter's garden, he fell into a deep sleep. Poverty hit upon the idea of taking advantage of this drunkenness and she succeeded. She embraced Plenty and acquired Love. – If, under poverty, we understand the strivings of our power of representing and under plenty, the beautiful or complete manifold, then it can be quite well explained why love came from their embrace.

(d) As an excuse for the writer cited, one could perhaps say that he has conceived both *sameness* [*Einerley*] and *concordance* [*Einhelligkeit*] of the manifold under the term *unity* (*unité*) and, as a result, subsumed beauty and perfection under a general title. Yet, how could he say of concordance that it makes it easier for us to represent of manifold? The concordance is not there, as is sameness, to limit the manifold. No, it must accomplish precisely the opposite, it necessarily increases the number of our concepts! One can imagine all the springs, wheels, and gears of a clock and, as a consequence, grasp all their manifold parts without thinking of the reason why these receptacles are there and why they are connected with one another the way they are rather than differently. The reason why something is part of a thing does not have the slightest in common with the mere representation of this thing. For, since the representation of both the parts and their harmony is grounded in the positive power of our soul, both demand an exertion and engagement of this original power. Indeed, most of the time, it costs more trouble and attentiveness to see the basis of a thing or its concordance than to represent the manifold parts of it to oneself.

---

[3] "Certainly there is the older goddess, who has only the heavens for a mother and whom we accordingly call 'the heavenly Uranian,' while the younger is the daughter of Zeus and Dione, whom we call 'the earthly Pandemon.'" "We all know that without Love there is no Aphrodite" (180d).

(e) As strange as this sentence sounds, it is just as indubitable. Our body, considered as corporeal, can feel neither moral nor physical evils. Only insofar as it is connected with the soul are certain alterations capable of transpiring within it, which the soul represents to itself as imperfections, and thus arise all unpleasant sentiments.

(f) No one will deny that the essence of a simple thing consists in its powers, when one considers that all alterations, which a simple thing can undergo, must consist in an alternation of degree. For no parts can be displaced, nothing added, nothing even taken from it. Thus the power is the basis of everything which can be attributed to a simple thing, and it is consequently its essence.

(g) The distinction between the Stoic and Epicurean systems is founded upon this subtlety. If Euphranor were right, that is to say, if we call objects good or perfect because they afford us pleasure, then the pleasant sentiment would be the *highest good* (*finis bonorum*). Since, however, the most sensuous rapture itself, as one sees in what follows, is nothing other than a sensuous sentiment of perfection or completeness, then the doctrine of the Epicureans is accordingly refuted, and it is shown irrefutably that the perfection or completeness and not the pleasant sentiment is to be called the *"highest good."*

(h) In this respect Descartes was of almost the same opinion as Theocles.

> "La cause," he says (*Les passions de l'âme*, art. 94), "qui fait que pour l'ordinaire la joye suit du chatouillement, est que tout ce qu'on appelle chatouillement ou sentiment agréable, consiste en ce que les objets des sens excitent quelque mouvement dans les nerfs, qui seroit capable de leur nuire, s'ils n'avoient pas assés de force pour lui resister, ou que le corps ne fut pas bien disposé. Ce qui fait une impression dans le cerveau, la quelle étant instituée de nature pour témoigner cette bonne disposition & cette force, la représente à l'âme comme un bien qui lui apparient, entant qu'elle est unie avec le corps, & ainsi excite en elle la joye."[4]

---

[4]   *Passions de l'âme*, §94, p. 56:

The cause that makes joy ordinarily follow titillation is all that one calls "titillation" or "agreeable sentiment." It consists in the fact that the objects of the senses excite some

One readily sees in what respect this view proceeds from Theocles' system. Wolff, on the other hand, has provided a very incomplete proof of this matter.

> "Voluptas & taedium," he says, "ortum trahunt ex perceptione confusa perfectionis & imperfectionis. Oriuntur enim voluptas & taedium extemplo, dum perfectionem aliquam, vel imperfectionem in re percepta intuemur; id quod unusquisque in se ipso experitur. Enim vero cum cognitio intuitiva, qualis cum ad voluptatem (§511) tum ad taedium (§518) requiritur, demum distincta evadit, ubi attentionem nostram successive promovemus ad ea qua ideae rei insunt (§682. Log.) taedium ac voluptas distinctam perfectionis ac imperfectionis ideam minime praesupponunt."*

However, is this expression "least presuppose" (*minime praesupponunt*) sufficient? The postulate reads: "gratification and pain arise from an obscure concept of perfection and imperfection," and this is confirmed, for the most part, by experience. But then one hears the consequence that flows from this proof: "hence, gratification and pain presuppose no distinct concept of perfection and imperfection." Must they then *necessarily* spring from *obscure* concepts since they presuppose no *distinct* concepts? Could they not, as far as this proof is concerned, at the very least arise as much from distinct concepts as from obscure ones?

---

*Psychol. emp. S. 536.[5]

> movement in the nerves which would be capable of injuring them if they did not have sufficient force to resist that movement or if the body was not well disposed. What makes an impression in the brain of the sort that has been instituted by nature to testify to that good disposition and that force, represents it to the soul as a good of the soul inasmuch as the soul is united with the body and thus excites the joy in the soul.

> Cf. *Philosophical Writings of Descartes*, tr. Cottingham, Stoothoff and Murdoch, vol. 1, pp. 361–2.

[5] Christian Wolff, *Psychologia empirica* (Frankfurt and Leipzig, 1738), in *Gesammelte Werke*, Division Two, vol. 5, ed. Jean Ecole (Hildesheim, Olms, 1968), §536, pp. 414–15:

> Gratification and pain begin from the confused perception of perfection and imperfection. For gratification and pain arise immediately when we consider some perfection or imperfection in the thing perceived; something which each individual experiences in himself. For, indeed, since intuitive knowledge of some sort is required both for gratification (§511) and for pain (§518), and since it ultimately passes over distinct things where we increase our attentiveness to the properties contained in the idea of the thing (§682 of the *Logic*), pain and gratification *least presuppose* a distinct idea of perfection and imperfection.

> Having identified the rules of mathematical and philosophical method, Christian Wolff (1679–1754), a major force behind the German Enlightenment, attempted to convert all fields of study into a system of rationally-ordered knowledge.

(i) Pain is an inward feeling of the separation of what is constant in the human body. This constancy must, to be sure, consist in such parts as stand in combination with the soul by means of the brain; otherwise the soul could feel nothing of the separation. Thus, there are many insensitive parts in the animal body and the nerves themselves can be insensitive if, through ligature, their communion with the brain is interrupted. Furthermore, this separation does not necessarily have to be visible. In the course of each severe stretching, constant parts can come loose from one another which we cannot notice with the eye but can feel inside. If someone still does not like this explanation, then the explanation of pain might be articulated in the following way: pain is an inward feeling of the actual or feared separation, and so on. – All this holds merely for the distinct pain which has its seat in the body. Often, however, we feel an indistinct pain in the body and do not ourselves know where. This is nothing other than an inward sentiment of the imperfection of our body in general, for in this case we are not conscious of the separation which takes place somehow in this or that part. – In his *Philebus* Plato gives an explanation of gratification and pain that leaves us amazed by his profound insight into the nature of sentiments:Λέγω τοίνυν τῆς ἁρμονίας μὲν λυομένης ἡμῖν ἐν τοῖς ζῷοις ἅμα λύσιν τῆς φύσεως καί γένεσιν ἀλγηδόνων ἐν τῷ τότε γίγνεσθαι χρόνῳ . . . Πάλιν δὲ ἁρμοττομένης τε καὶ εἰς τὴν αὐτῆς φύσιν ἀπιούσης ἡδονὴν γίγνεσθαι λεκτέον.[6] That is to say, if what is supposed to be harmonious in an animal body loses its harmony, then the nature of the animal runs the risk at the same time and pain results. If, however, this harmony is restored, then gratification or a pleasant sentiment results.

(k) About sensuous pain Descartes says the following

> La cause qui fait que la douleur produit ordinairement la tristesse, est que le sentiment qu'on nomme douleur, vient toujours de quelque action si violente, qu'elle offense les nerfs; en sorte qu'étant instituée de la Nature pour signifier à l'ame le dommage que reçoit le corps par cette action, & sa foiblesse, en ce qu'il ne lui

---

[6] "I say, then, that when the harmony in us living beings is disturbed, our natural condition is disrupted, and at that time pain is generated . . . But if the harmony is restored and returned to its natural condition, then I say that that pleasure results" (31d).

a pu resister, il lui represente l'un et l'autre comme des meaux, qui lui sont toujours desagreables.[7]

(l) Everyone readily understands what is meant by the "simple proportions within the oscillations [of the music]." For it is well-known that two chords yield a single pleasing sound [*Wohllaut*] when they are stretched in a simple relationship to one another. That is to say, if the number of oscillations of the one chord relates to the number of oscillations of the other in the same time, such as 1:2, 2:3, 4:5, 5:6, or the reverse, such as 3:4, 3:5, and 5:8. However, the oscillations in the dissonant sounds [*Uebellaut*] relate 8:9, 8:15, 45:64, and the like. In composition, one looks above all to the pleasure the soul takes in foreseeing certain consequences, expecting certain things, and in being deterred, disappointed, or satisfied in regard to those expectations. Nothing is as pleasing, that philosopher said, as the resolution of doubt. The musician lets us enjoy this pleasure in many sorts of ways, and Theocles reckons it with beauty since the powers of spirit must accordingly be engaged in a simple manner. – But what he understands by the tension of our nerve vessels, a tension in harmony with all chords, may not be so easy to see. Yet people have been convinced for some time that certain nerve vessels of hearing vibrate harmoniously with the sounding strings and that we do not even feel the sound until they have communicated this vibrating movement of the air in the tympanum. Indeed, one meets persons every day who cannot hear certain sounds without quivering in every bone and indicating this sentiment by automatically chattering their teeth.

Hence, it is extremely likely that all the nerves of our body are set in certain tensions that harmonize with chords and that the oscillations of pleasing sounds in general are conducive to the tone of a healthy life. Leibniz was on to this thought in one of his letters and even believed, if I am not mistaken, that this side of medicinal art was quite promising

---

[7] *Passions de l'âme*, §94, pp. 399–400:

> The cause that makes pain ordinarily follow sadness is that the sentiment which one calls "pain" always proceeds from some action so violent that it injures the nerves. Being the sort of sentiment instituted by nature to signify to the soul the damage this action does to the body as well as the body's feeble powers of resisting it, this sentiment represents to the soul both as evils that are always disagreeable to it.

Cf. *Philosophical Writings of Descartes*, tr. Cottingham, Stoothoff, and Murdoch, vol. 1, p. 362. (There is no note "j", probably because "i" and "j" were not distinguished at the time.)

since many sicknesses could be cured through the restoration of the tone. In Plato's *Symposium*, Erixymachus, who knew something about medicines, has a similar thought which appears to have been the source of the idea in Leibniz.

(m) Here Theocles tries to formulate in a few words a distinct concept of *charm*, a word whose significance would otherwise be very unsettled. People seldom speak of a charming flower, a charming building, but they do speak of a charming demeanor, charming gestures, charming expressions, a charming turn of phrase, and so on. In all these cases the line of beauty occurs, not as standing there all at once in space, but rather as a line gradually sketched by movement. The painter expresses charm by a flame-like line which our imagination always combines with the concept of movement. "In the movement, positioning, and stance of the body," a French writer says, "people principally distinguish the charm that is so enchanting. If the limbs have the suitable dimensions for this use, if nothing conflicts with this development, if the joints and the insertions are so perfect that nothing stands in the way of the demand to move, and the movements themselves glide softly and in the most loving order relative to one another, there then arises in us the idea that we express by the word 'charm.'" (*Dictionnaire encyclopédie*, article on "grace" by Mr. Watelet.)[8] This description, like Theocles's definition which agrees with it, properly extends only to charm in painting and sculpture. But in other arts, too, there appears to be something that may be referred back to a similar concept.

(n) Perhaps this invention could also provide occasion to express the imitations of human passions in a melody of colors. Each passion is connected as much with certain sounds as with certain movements of the limbs. The former are expressed in music by similar sounds, but the latter could perhaps be imitated by the movements of colors. A line, suddenly interrupted, could portray fear to a certain extent, and many lines travelling quickly through one another could portray anger, just as the line of a wave proceeding slowly and artlessly could portray a kind of profundity.

---

[8] Henri Watelet, "Grace," in *Encyclopédie, ou Dictionnaire raisonné des sciences, des arts et de métiers*, ed. Diderot and d'Alembert (Paris, 1751–65; reprint, 1st edn., Stuttgart and Bad Cannstatt, Frommann, 1966, vol. 7, pp. 800–6).

Against the invention of a melody of colors in general and especially against Krüger's invention of the unification of the latter with a melody of sounds, one could perhaps still recall the following.* It is indisputable that we are able to discriminate far more colors than sounds in the same time. For experience teaches that each individual color still sustains itself within the eye for a while if, at the same time, we have closed our eyes. Hence, in a melody of colors the impression which the foregoing colors have left behind them must be mixed with the present ones and produce an effect completely different from the one demanded. The nerves of the sense of hearing appear to retain the impression for a shorter time if the sound does not cause a very large vibration in the air. Indeed, although it may be hoped that, by habitualizing the nerves of the eye, one could even bring things to this point (since in the case of hearing itself it is very much a matter of habit), at least at the outset one would still have to let the colors follow upon one another more slowly and after lengthier intervals than do sounds, and only after long practice be mindful of a unification of the melody of the colors with the melody of sounds.

Père Castel first came up with the idea of putting a melody of colors into practice, and Krüger improved this invention considerably. But neither must have thought of this difficulty or any of the others mentioned by Theocles. Otherwise they would have been able to claim with much less confidence that a melody of colors must afford us far more and at least as much pleasure as a melody of sounds. Even Krafft, who wanted to demonstrate the impossibility of this invention in a public address, passed over the most important difficulties and dwelled on trivialities. No other judgment can be passed on this address, at least from what Krüger has reported of it.**

In passing I must make mention of one more item. Père Castel sought to assist his machine to some extent by letting the colors represent certain small pictures. But against this procedure Krüger recalled already that the portrayal of entire objects belongs more to painting than

---

* See *Miscel. Berol.* T. VII, p. 345.[9]   ** Ibid., p. 348, §6.

[9] Mendelssohn is referring to Johann Gottlob Krüger's essay "De novo musices quo oculi delectantur genere," published in *Miscellanea Berolinensia* (Berlin, 1743) and (below) to the criticism of Castel's "clavicymbalum oculi" ("piano for the eye") by Georg Wolfgang Krafft, in his address to the Petersburg Academy on 24 April 1742. Krüger (1715–59), philosopher and physician, is the author of *Doctrine of Nature* (Halle, 1740–9).

to the actual harmony of colors which he undertook to bring about. Theocles's suggestion of applying a line of beauty is quite far from this mistake.

(o) In algebra there are three kinds of signs: signs of quantities such as a, b, y, z, and so forth; signs of operations which are to be performed on these quantities, such as $+$, $-$, $\times$, $\div$ $\sqrt{}$ and so forth; and, finally, signs of relations such as $=$, $<$, $>$, $\approx$, and so forth. In the case of constant quantities the signs $+$ and $-$ are employed to indicate the position and region spoken about, since these regions, in relation to one another, must be regarded as quantities to be set off from one another. From this one sees that the signs $+$ and $-$ alter nothing in the quantity but rather the operations that are supposed to obtain with regard to the quantities. Adding a negative quantity means subtracting a positive quantity equal to it; thus also in reverse, subtracting a negative quantity means adding a positive quantity equal to it. Why does a positive quantity result when I multiply two negative quantities together? This is not difficult to answer. Multiplying means taking a quantity as many times as the units that are comprised by another quantity. Thus if I multiply $-a$ with b, then I must subtract a as many times as there are units in b, that means $= -ab$. However, if I multiply $-a$ with $-b$, then a negative quantity must be subtracted or, what amounts to the same, a positive quantity equal to it must be added as many times as the units that are comprised another quantity. Thus, the product is a positive or additive quantity.

(p) My dear friend, Mr. Abbt,[10] wanted to defend Lindamour's comparison, at least that which concerns the characterization of quantities, against the reasons advanced by Theocles. In 1761 from Frankfurt where Abbt was professor at the time he sent me some remarks which the reader will hopefully enjoy here. I must, however, remind readers in advance that the remarks refer in part to expressions which I employed in the first edition of the *Letters* ["On sentiments"] in which I appeared to make negative quantities merely into quantities to be subtracted. On this point Mr. Abbt wrote me as follows.

"It seems to me that when I want to think of negative and positive separately, I then think of them merely as such quantities which

---

[10] Thomas Abbt (1738–66), critic and philosopher, best known for his *On Death for the Fatherland* (*Vom Tode Fürs Vaterland*, Berlin, 1761), was a particularly close friend of Mendelssohn.

through their combination destroy the previous repetitions without applying them to income and expenditure, ascending and descending, left and right, above and below. The abstract concept of son, indeed, also demands the relation to the father but it does not suppose that, under the concept of son, I now think Cajus Sempronius and so on. Just as I can think of that son and several sons together without having the fathers in mind, so I can also think of negative quantities *in abstracto* and together without positing something positive as long as the relation to a position or something of the sort lies at bottom. The best mathematicians have said a thousand times that negative quantities are actual quantities, that they are as actual as positive quantities. As long as it is not a matter of a reciprocal determination, then I can leave that out of consideration and regard the quantities merely as positive without thinking of the negative. For example, strictly positive logarithms are given for positive and negative sines, tangents, and the like. For in such a case it is merely a matter of determining their quantity, not their position which the algebraist then determines more precisely. Negative quantities sometimes become impossible but this is not due to the fact that they cannot be thought *in abstracto*, but rather due to the fact that, because of other circumstances, they do not allow themselves to be thought as that for which they are put forward.

"Thus, the square root of $-x^2$ cannot be thought because the fourth proportional to $+ - -$ cannot be thought as negative. For, otherwise I can think of $-x$ just as well as $+x$.

"The algebraist can accordingly never say that a negative quantity is less than zero. The algebraist could just as well say that a positive quantity is less than zero. A negative quantity can, indeed, must be infinite just as well as a positive quantity. This way of speaking is upsetting merely because the transition from positive to negative passes through the infinite or through zero. Thus it always appears as though one falls below if one then passes over to the other side. Now, in common life, people have almost always taken as their sole example that of assets and debts, and here it was natural to have begun from the positive and to have passed through zero into the negative. In such a case, the negative would be less than nothing; for one would first have to return to zero, not before one had something, but before one had something positive. But take note! Even here, before you come back from the negative to zero, you must decrease the negative. Yet if it were to conform to the mistaken idea, then the negative would have to become less and less, less than nothing, the more it distances itself from zero; that is to say, in its distance from zero it would have to decrease and not increase.

"In other examples, however, where one proceeds from the negative through zero into the positive, the positive could just as well signify something less than zero, since I must turn back from the positive before I arrive at zero. And how, then, do matters stand with the transition through the infinite which is common to both types? If similarly good examples of this were to be found in common life, then the incorrect idea would probably not have gained ground so easily. Wolff has strengthened this idea considerably by his wondrous proofs of universal subtraction.

"Since I am now in this material, allow me to express my thoughts on this subtraction. I have not read it as far as I know but it is probably well-known to you already.

"For me subtraction is nothing but the method of finding what prevents two quantities from being equal.

"For example, why is $+B$ not equal to $+A$, or how would it have to be if they were to be equal to one another? Now people have, in my view, made the following inference. If, on the one side of the equation, A were to stand and nothing else, then both members of the equation would indeed be equal. However, in order for *nothing else* to be standing there, I cancel what is there by its opposite: thus, $+B-B+A = A$.

"Now I see, indeed, what prevents this equation, namely, $-B+A$. Because this is always the case and rests upon the simplest truths, the general rule has been abstracted: if the sign of the quantity to be subtracted is inverted and the quantity is combined in this manner with the quantity from which it is supposed to be subtracted, then you have the difference.

"And then Lindamour is probably not so wrong to compare pleasure and displeasure with positive and negative quantities and the condition of not having a sentiment with zero. Its abstract concept can be applied, to be sure, to pleasure and displeasure; but, as in the entire *mathesi intensorum*, it cannot be calculated since no one can determine exactly the unity which such an intensive quantity would yield through a uniform repetition.

"In the designation of the quantity, therefore, Lindamour is not wrong. However, I would deny that someone committing suicide could ever compute and suitably compare the entire sum of his positive and negative quantity, that is, of his pleasures and displeasures, whether he were to limit himself to this life or even to extend the duration of his consciousness to some state after death. It remains as impossible in the former case as in the latter, though in the latter there is, in addition, the risk that the sum of his pleasures will increase in another state. This is something that always remains a risk in this case, even without assuming the punishments of hell, since our pleasures depend upon our way of thinking, and we have seen people who, after their fortunes took a turn in the best possible way, were sad and upset merely by the memory of some bygone misfortune. The person committing suicide cannot see in advance whether or not a happier hour might still be able to take hold in his life, a time in which he would later pass from the world by a natural death (since it is impossible to determine that only his negative quantity will always grow). For this reason, then, he is able to plunge into a misfortune that he would have avoided by refraining from suicide. Yet we are treating Lindamour too gently. In addition to the fact that he cannot make his calculations precisely, he also does not make them correctly.

"Who commands him to take only pleasures into account, pleasures which emerge from observing his own perfections? Lindamour's calculations thus will not hold as far as strict morals are concerned. His calculation will be rejected even as far as politics is concerned. The state obliges him to remain a member until either it relieves him of his citizenship or death calls him away. Politics can never allow someone to make the decision for himself about his own uselessness and so forth."

In the second edition of the *Letters* ["On sentiment"] I made use of these recollections of my friend and altered somewhat the passage to which they refer, though only in the manner of expression which, to be sure, was faulty in the first edition. However, the reasons on the side of Theocles appear to me irrefutable, nonetheless. It is true, if one takes into account the use which mathematicians make of negative quantities, the concept of them is not completely exhausted by subtraction. The only contrast which is possible in the case of numbers is that of adding and taking away. In the case of other quantities, however, there are still other contrasts which can be no less expressed by signs. For example, considered from a point within the body, the three dimensions of the body have two sides standing opposite one another, which contrast one can express in a completely appropriate manner through + and —. One can make use of the same signs in the case of intensive quantities which are opposed to one another. Warmth and cold, desire and aversion, beauty and ugliness, fear and hope, and still others are of this sort; hence, they can be characterized by + and —. In all these cases + and — are signs of the operations performed on the quantities, but this operation at times can be represented under the concept of subtraction and addition only in a very inappropriate way.

But all these considerations do not prove useful to Lindamour's comparison. If zero is supposed to express nonbeing, then it is as impossible for an imperfect existence to be expressed as it is for a negative quantity. On this point, I will have to be somewhat long-winded.

In regard to constant quantities, as Mr. Abbt correctly notes, it does not matter which of the two sides standing opposite one another we want to name positive or negative. In regard to intensive quantities, insofar as they are represented by extensive quantities for the sake of calculating, it can also be a matter of indifference how we want to posit the signs. Mr. Abbt is accordingly correct in maintaining that the negative quantity is something actual just as much as the positive quantity is and that it is merely placed in operation on the other side. In the metaphysical understanding of them, by contrast, there are no positive concepts which, as such, would be opposed to one another. Among concepts actually opposed to one another, the one must be actually affirmative and the other actually negative. Hence, one can properly posit nothing opposite the true reality except a true negation. If realities appear to be mutually contradictory, this is so by virtue of the alterations that accrue to them. For one can imagine the same reality under various alterations which cannot obtain together; in which case a contrast actually results but not between reality and reality, but rather between limitation and limitation. If the reality A can be entertained with the alteration b as well as with the alteration not-b, then Ab is opposed to A-not-b, because the modifications are mutually contradictory. Gratification and pain contrast with one another, not insofar as they are sentiments, since in this consideration they are far more in agreement, but rather because the former is a sentiment of the reality, the latter a sentiment of the deficiency. Reality and deficiency, however, are actually opposed to one another. Movement is properly only opposed to the deficiency of movement. However, since the movement is also capable of various directions which mutually cancel one another, in this sense one can also posit one movement opposed to another. From this consideration one sees that no property of the things that is actually affirmed of them could be opposed to some other affirmative property, except insofar as their limitations and modifications reciprocally cancel one another.

Since Ab as well as A-not-b are affirmative concepts, it does not matter which of the two one wants to mark with + and −. Zero signifies the point of transition from the modification b to the modification not-b and leads as much from + to − as from − to +.

As soon, however, as one posits the negation of a reality and characterizes this negation as zero, this zero leads back neither to a negative nor to a positive quantity. For the denial of a reality is directly opposed to the affirmation of the same reality and permits no further advance. An example from mechanics: if the state of rest follows upon forces of motion in opposing directions striving against one another, then the positive velocity can be transformed into a negative one. If, however, we keep in mind that the state of rest cancels all forces of motion, then this zero can lead neither to a positive nor to a negative velocity.

In order to apply these considerations to the state of pleasant sentiments, one can, to be sure, oppose the prevailing gratification to the prevailing pain and mark the one with + and the other with −. In this case zero would be the condition in which the gratification is equal to the pain. But if, as Lindamour intends, zero is supposed to mark a nonbeing, then no opposite quantity can be perceived beyond this zero. Nonbeing is a complete canceling of reality and from this point no further advance takes place; hence, too, no state relative to which annihilation is to be preferred.

(q) Dialogues bring with them a convenience that is very important for careless writers, namely, that of being able to have the opponent (who is supposed to be defeated) give in at the proper time. If this happens, then the reader is authorized to appear on the scene and to take up the part of the defeated opponent. Considered from another angle, however, no material of importance can be elaborated in a conversation where the main persons involved are not provisionally in agreement about certain points. Otherwise the longest conversation would scarcely suffice to establish the requisite definitions of the words employed. In the present case it was all the more justified to have Eudoxus agree, since the proposition that no free choice could take place without sufficient reason had been proven in a thoroughly rigorous manner by our philosophers. In my "On probability" I dare to give a new proof of this proposition, a proof which, if it is correct, has the advantage of not being dependent upon any particular system.

(r) "Perfection" is Leibniz's name for the reality which accrues to a thing if one considers it apart from its limitation. However, he names the reality taken together with the limitation, "degree." In the case of our soul, for example, the power of representing the world to itself or striving to do so would be its perfection. If, however, the limitation is added, the limitation, that is, by virtue of which the soul can represent the world to itself only from the position of its body and sensuous limbs, a degree of perfection results (see Leibniz's *Principia philosophiae more geometrico demonstrata*, definition 140.[11]) If I am not mistaken, Wolff has rightly deviated from this type of definition in regard to composite things since, according to Leibnizian principles, no true reality is to be ascribed to them insofar as they are composite things. For bodies are not actual substances but rather only phenomena ("phenomena substantiata," as Leibniz calls them) which are opposed to reality (see Wolff, *Theologia naturalis, part. posterior*, §5.[12]) Hence, Wolff defines the perfection by the harmony of the manifold; but he calls harmony the striving to maintain something in common. Of course, as Theocles reminds us, this concept may in each case also be applied in regard to simple things and reduced to the Leibnizian definition. For since the purpose of simple things is the representation, then they are all the more perfect, the more precisely their representations agree with each other as well as with the matters represented; that is to say, the greater the degree of their power, the more perfect they are. However,

---

[11] Gottfried Wilhelm Leibniz, *Principia philosophiae, more geometrico demonstrata: cum excerptis ex epistolis philosophi (Principles of Philosophy, Dermonstrated in a Geometrical Manner, with excerpts from the philosopher's letters)*, ed. Michael Gottlieb Hansch (Frankfurt and Leipzig, Petri C. Monath, 1728).

[12] (Frankfurt and Leipzig, 1736), in *Gesammelte Werke*, Division Two, vol. 8, Part 2, ed. Jean Ecole (Hildesheim and New York, Olms, 1981), §5, pp. 3–4.

in regard to simple things the Leibnizian definition is more fruitful, and, given any number of equally valid definitions, the philosopher like the mathematician is free to presuppose the one that leads him to his goal by the shortest route.

One notices, however, that Wolff appears to have deviated from the rigor of the mathematical manner of teaching when he assumes (*Theol. nat. parte posteriori* §6) an arbitrary definition: "Ens perfectissimum dicitur, cui insunt omnes realitates [compossibiles] in gradu absolute summo."[13] For since he would define the perfection not by the reality but rather by the harmony of the manifold, he should not have defined even the most perfect being (*Ens perfectissimum*) by the highest degree of all possible realities as long as he did not prove (as has been done here) that the two manners of definition cited are equally valid.

(s) The ancients have always said, "every nature wants to preserve itself."[14] Every nature strives to maintain itself. One can as little imagine a power that is to retain in itself the basis of its own annihilation as one can think a motion that would contain the sufficient basis for complete rest. Now the soul that could *want* its own annihilation would be nothing other than a power whose inner vocation is oriented towards its self-annihilation; since the will is an inner orientation of our power of representation. And if the opponent would even want to deny the simplicity of the soul and make the capacity of representing things a property of composite things, this recourse would nonetheless not save him. A power of something composite can naturally cease if the composition itself is dissolved by other natural powers. But neither a simple nor a composite power can be oriented towards and, even less, orient itself towards its own annihilation. Hence, if in our power of representing, be it simple or a property of something composite, existence and annihilation vie for the upper hand, then the will must always decide the issue for existence; otherwise the power of representation would determine itself to be destroyed. In this consideration, each thinking entity must prefer being exposed to every possible pain over

[13] Ibid., §6, p. 4: "That being is called most perfect in which all compossible realities exist in the absolutely highest degree." "Compossible" is a technical term from Leibniz, indicating that a specific possibility is able to obtain together *with* (*cum*) another specific possibility. Cf. G. W. Leibniz, *Textes Inédites*, ed. Gaston Grua (Paris, Presses Universitaires, 1948), vol. 1, p. 325: "*Compossibile* quod cum alio non implicat contradictionem."
[14] Cicero, *De finibus bonorum et malorum*, iv. 16: "*omnis nature vult esse conservatrix sui.*"

wishing to be annihilated. If an eternal damnation were possible, then someone malicious would nonetheless have to prefer it to his annihilation. – Is this image revolting and does it appear to contradict our feelings? – Of course! But for no other reason than that our soul cannot conceive of annihilation at all. For we are created for immortality and can never imagine annihilation as genuine annihilation. By it we always think of a kind of sweet sleep uninterrupted by dreams and we prefer this sleep to our consciousness of pain. Maecenas who regarded his soul as mortal might very well see the infinite importance of this life in terms of his system. He expressed a wish which any rational human being must almost regard as mad; yet even by his own erroneous principles nothing was more reasonable:

> *Debilem facito manu*
> *Debilem pede, Coxa:*
> *Tuber adstrue gibberum,*
> *Lubricos quate dentes.*
> Vita dum superest, bene est.
> *Hanc mihi, vel acuta*
> *Si sedeam cruce, sustine.*[15]

"There can be no doubt," Bodmer says, "that he knew nothing better than the fact that his entire being would cease with his death. *He would prefer the most painful life to this complete annihilation.*"[16]

In Mr. Cochius's splendid, prizewinning work "Investigations of Inclinations" ["Untersuchungen über die Neigungen"], he tries to maintain, on the basis of reason, the possibility of wishing to be annihilated. According to his theory, the instinct for perfection or, as he calls it, for expansion is the first, fundamental instinct of human nature which the instinct for preservation can in certain cases contradict and from which preservation would then necessarily have to deviate.

I want to cite his own words: "Since, unless it exists, this instinct (for

---

[15] P. Lunderstedt, *De C. Maecenatis fragmentis* (Leipzig, Teubner, 1911), Fragment 1, p. 35: "Disable my hand/ Cripple my foot and hip/ Erect a swollen hump on my back/ Shatter my shivering teeth./ While life still breathes in me, it is fine./ Save my life, even if/ I am lying on a piercing cross!" Mendelssohn is probably citing this text from Seneca's, *Ad Lucilium Epistulae Morales*, tr. Richard M. Gummere (Cambridge, Mass., Harvard University Press, 1953), Epistle 101, line 11, vol. 3, pp. 164–5.

[16] Opposing criticism that rested solely on rules or on sentiment, Johann Jacob Bodmer (1698–1783) (and his fellow Swiss critic Johann Jacob Breitinger [1701–76]) championed the role of poetic phantasy and, in a celebrated debate with Johann Christian Gottsched, defended the work of Milton.

expansion or extension) could not have an effect, this appears precisely to obtain for the inclination to our preservation and, in contrast, for the aversion to our annihilation. But it obtains only, as it were, in the second degree. For our existence is not essential to us; we can think of a human soul that would be merely possible but would not have an instinct to extend itself. Since our existence is that very condition of our essence in which we produce and undergo changes, have representations, and take in impressions, it conforms to the essential instinct, and, to that extent, the inclination to preserve itself is natural. But if, in the case of the actual extension of itself, it were to find sheer resistance, then it would be canceled in turn. So as not to suppose some impossible case, in one pan of the scales place several, lively representations which are at odds with the instinct and in the other pan a few feeble representations that conform to the instinct; the result follows of itself. Under such conditions, one could give up the inclination to preserve one's existence, although at bottom there would always be an error. For here it is a matter of whether the representations themselves are there, but not whether they are there with some or no basis. To be sure, as far as suicide is concerned, at bottom in most cases there would be a secret inkling of survival, that is to say, lying in profound obscurity there would be a representation of continuing to exist after ending the present life. But it is difficult to maintain that there would never be a case of a suicide committed with the intention of self-annihilation. However, were there such cases, then the inclination to preserve one's existence could have become so feeble that not only an aversion to the contrary, but even a desire would take its place, a desire which would generally go much further. For, from the canceled inclination nothing more would follow than that one would, with a certain composure, forfeit existence. That one would take one's life itself demands more than the lack of an inclination to maintain it."

Permit me to make a few remarks about this passage. One can be satisfied with this philosopher's identification of the instinct to expand or extend oneself as the basic instinct of the soul only if one does not in the process forget that this instinct also strives not to lose what has already been attained. The novel charms us considerably, to be sure, but we are not for that reason completely indifferent to what has been preserved for some time, not as indifferent, for example, as we are to things which can never come within the sphere in which we are able to expand ourselves. If we are more inclined to maintain than to lose what has been attained, then the basic instinct of the soul must be oriented not only towards extending and acquiring new realities, but at the same time towards preserving what has been attained.

Mr. Cochius acknowledges that, unless it exists, the instinct to extend ourselves cannot have an effect. If this is the case, then the termination of existence is as opposed to this instinct as it is to the instinct for preservation. It is, accordingly, utterly impossible for the basic instinct of the soul to be oriented towards self-annihilation since without existence no extension can take place, and since no instinct can be oriented towards its own *ineffectiveness*.

"We can think of a human soul," Mr. Cochius says, "that is merely possible but does not have an instinct to extend itself." If something is to be inferred from this, then it is nothing further than that we must prefer existence to the *instinct itself of extending ourselves*. But we cannot lose this, and I am also not speaking of this. Yet the *fulfillment* of this basic instinct remains far less essential than existence to us. We can indeed think of a soul whose instinct to expand itself is obstructed; indeed, a soul can even exist whose instinct to expand itself finds resistance and obstacles at every turn. Now, since in our case existence does not come into conflict with the instinct itself but rather with its satisfaction, then, indeed, the argument that existence is not essential cannot decide the matter.

According to Mr. Cochius's theory, it must be possible for the wish or desire to annihilate oneself to express the instinct to expand oneself. The concept of *expansion* must, therefore, be able to be determined in such a form that it contains the concept of *annihilation*; that is to say, under certain conditions the annihilation must be an expansion.

I must confess that I cannot make any sense of this. One might consider what the philosopher himself says, that for self-annihilation the canceling of the inclination to preserve oneself is insufficient and that it must be possible for a desire to that effect to emerge. According to Mr. Cochius's theory, this must be able to be brought under the general formula of expansion. For all desires and inclinations must be branches of the basic instinct. As more determinate concepts, they must lie in the general concept of expansion and be able to be traced to it. Now obviously one cannot think of any case in which annihilation and expansion should be able to be affirmed and denied of one another. For without existence no instinct can have an effect. How, then, would it be possible for the soul's power of extending itself ever to pass over into a desire for annihilation? "In one pan of the scales," Mr. Cochius says, "place several, lively representations which are at odds with the instinct and in the other pan a few feeble representations that conform to the instinct; the result follows of itself." – What result? The only genuine result is, in my view, that a strong desire to alter this condition will arise in the soul. For the greater weight of the many lively and, at the same time, contrary representations aim at this. But a desire not to be, this appears all the less to be the result of the greater weight since, taken individually, each contrary representation presses for change. Each need demands satisfaction, this is its natural tendency. And if it does not receive this satisfaction, then the desire becomes more powerful, but a tendency towards satisfaction cannot pass over into a tendency towards annihilation, however great the obstacles that stand in the way of satisfaction.

Hence, the thought that any sort of genuine desire for annihilation should be able to arise in the human soul appears even more absurd according to Mr. Cochius's theory which traces all the soul's inclinations to a general instinct of expanding itself.

Dialogues

First dialogue

Philopon and Neophil

PHILOPON. So, if I correctly understand what you are saying, you do not regard Leibniz as the person who first invented the preestablished harmony?

NEOPHIL. I do not know how you would infer this from what I have said.

PHILOPON. Oh, the inference is obvious. Did you not say that Leibniz assumed this hypothesis and brought it into his system?

NEOPHIL. You are paying much too close attention to the words. Allow that I may have misspoken. We do not want to interrupt the discussion that we've been having.

PHILOPON. No, dearest friend! You are not allowed to sidestep me in this way! It would not be the first time that I would have learned something from your little acts of hastiness. I must stop you now in your tracks if I want to experience a thought that you would have perhaps never intentionally revealed.

NEOPHIL. You're pushing me far too much. I see now that one must be very careful with people of your astuteness. A single word reveals our entire sense to them. Well, then! I confess to you that I do not regard Leibniz as the inventor of the preestablished harmony, although I know that no one has ever contested his reputation for this and that Bayle

96

himself, in the name of the learned world, congratulated him for this great discovery.

PHILOPON. And in the name of all Leibnizians I demand from you the proof.

NEOPHIL. I have it ready although I would not have believed that I would need it today. But take note. I am maintaining merely that another philosopher found the essential part of this view first, and I am happy to acknowledge that Leibniz is the first to give it the name "preestablished harmony."

PHILOPON. Now, indeed! You do not want to make things good again with this qualification, do you? I would have thought that a name is not a very remarkable invention. Indeed, I have always wondered at the fact that Leibniz took the trouble to contradict Bayle when Bayle wanted to ascribe the invention of this name to a P. Lamy.*

NEOPHIL. True, Leibniz could very easily have been generous with such a triviality. It is more than parsimoniousness if people worth millions are not willing to have even a farthing stolen from them. And yet Leibniz is to be excused here. You have to assume that he was so selfishly exact not towards Bayle the philosopher, but towards Bayle the critic. Towards Bayle the critic, I say, who has often made crimes out of smaller historical inaccuracies . . . But I will hurry to the proof which you have demanded of me in the name of all Leibnizians. But before anything else, let us see whether we are in agreement about the meaning of this view. What do you understand by the preestablished harmony?

---

* See Bayle's *Dictionary*, the note to the article "Rorarius."[1]

[1] See Pierre Bayle, "Rorarius," in *Historical and Critical Dictionary: Selections*, ed. and tr. Richard H. Popkin (Indianapolis and Cambridge, Hackett, 1991), pp. 213–54 and Leibniz, "Réponse aux réflexions contenues dans la seconde édition du Dictionnaire critique de M. Bayle, article Rorarius, sur le système de l'harmonie préétablie" ("Response to reflections contained in the second edition of M. Bayle's Critical Dictionary, the article 'Rorarius' on the system of pre-established harmony"), *Journal des Sçavans* (19 August 1702), in *Die philosophischen Schriften*, ed. C. J. Gerhardt (Hildesheim, Olms, 1960), vol. 4, pp. 554–71. Bayle (1647–1706), a French Protestant *émigré* living in Rotterdam, is best known for *Dictionnaire historique et critique* (Rotterdam, 1695–7; 2nd edn., Rotterdam, 1698) and its skepticism about reason's capacity – be it in the form of science, theology, or philosophy – to make the world intelligible.

PHILOPON. What all Leibnizians understand by it. A doctrine according to which everything in our soul that harmonizes with the changes in the body arises in the soul at the instigation, to be sure, of the body, but through the power interior to the soul and not through the influence of a substance distinct from it. In the same way, everything in our body that harmonizes with the alterations of the soul is produced in the body at the soul's instigation by nothing other than mechanical corporeal powers. If, therefore, one were to ask a Leibnizian, "By what means are body and soul united with one another?", he would answer, "God has, from all eternity, ordained such a harmony between them that certain movements in the body follow upon certain representations in the soul, movements that have their sufficient reason or ground in both at once. That is to say, the ground *through which* they arise is located in the mechanical powers of the body, but the reason *why* or *to what end* they arise is to be found in the state of the soul. When, on the other hand, certain representations in our soul ensue from and harmonize with certain movements in our body, the ground *through which* they emerge lies in the original power of our soul and the foregoing state of it, while the reason *why* they arise is to be found in the movements of our body. The Leibnizian simile of two clocks is well-known."

NEOPHIL. You have understood this view perfectly. Indeed, I see that you are way beyond all objections that Bayle has brought against it. Of all the opponents who later challenged it, Bayle is, in my judgment, the one who understood it best and, even by Mr. Leibniz's admission, contested it from the right side.

PHILOPON. Before we go further, however, I must insist on some explanation for the following. Has it not appeared to you as though Leibniz was not consistent in regard to this view? For example, in his *Monadology* he expounds it in a way completely different from the way in which he first made it known to the world in the *Journal des Sçavans*. Indeed, I believe that he would have been able to respond to Bayle's objections with far stronger reasons, had he remained constantly faithful to his own system.

NEOPHIL. Leibniz merely expounded his view under various forms as demanded by his purpose on each occasion. In the *Monadology* he demonstrates it as a consequence of his system of monads.[2] Here is where it radiates in its complete light, where it in fact ceases to be an hypothesis and maintains its rank among proven truths. Hansch[*] has analyzed this quite well, and after him Baumgarten has demonstrated it so convincingly that it would be superfluous to tarry on it. – What kind of challengers could it find from this side? Only those, certainly, who directed their weapons against its basis, I mean against the monads themselves. As soon as one concedes this in the sense in which Leibniz took it, one is compelled to ban all physical influence of substances from nature, and then the defenders of the harmony have won. But our philosopher did not want to allow the fate of the harmony to depend absolutely on the fate of the monads. He knew quite well that if a truth can be arrived at only in one way or if it merely fits into some chain, then it is considered by a general prejudice to be a truth only halfway. What, then, was more natural than to seek to make it valid outside of his system as well? He undertook this in the *Journal des Sçavans*.[3] And here we see quite well that, against Bayle, he could only make use of those weapons which the common philosophy had put in his hands. What he maintains about all substances in the *Monadology*, he had to limit to body and soul alone in the *Journal* and limit in such a way that Bayle began to doubt whether such a machine, such as the body of an animal, did not have to be a preestablished harmony and also whether it was something impossible. Leibniz contented himself with shifting the burden of this proof to his adversary since he could not use his real weapons in this context. That theory of the original forces of simple entities from which, when they are placed together, the appearances of extension and movement emerge, could not help him at all against this opponent; although that theory, in the context of this system, both

---

[*]   In his *Principiis Philosoph. Leibnizianae*, etc.[4]

[2]   "Monadology" refers to an unnamed 1714 manuscript that has been so designated since J. E. Erdmann adopted it in his edition of Leibniz's collected works (*Opera omnia*, Berlin, 1840), in keeping with the designation of the first published version, a German translation, *Leibniz's Theorems on the Monadology* (*Leibniziens Lehr-Sätze über die Monadologie, etc.*; Frankfurt and Leipzig, 1720).

[3]   "Système nouveau de la nature et de la communication des substances, aussi bien que l'union qu'il y a entre l'âme et le corps" ("New System of Nature and of the Communication of Substances as well as the Union that there is between Soul and Bodies"), *Journal des Sçavans* (27 June 1695) in *Die philosophische Schriften*, ed. Gerhardt, vol. 4, 477–87.

[4]   Michael Gottlieb Hansch, an enthusiastic defender of Leibniz's philosophy, held lectures on philosophy at Leipzig from 1703 to 1711; see p. 90, n. 11.

provides the basis from which the preestablished harmony flows as a proper consequence and permits no more doubt about the possibility of the artifice necessary to it.

PHILOPON. I find this remark reasonable, and I also understand now why Wolff assumed the preestablished harmony only as it had been defended by Leibniz against Bayle.* For since he did not trust himself to determine what it is in which the forces of the simple things actually consist, he also could not regard it as established whether all simple things had representations, and whether the extension and powers of movement of composite things can be explained by these representations.

NEOPHIL. You're absolutely right, and from this you can see with how much attentiveness one must read a systematic writer before one can make objections to him or refute his reasons at all.

PHILOPON. Good! And hence we are perfectly in agreement, as far as the meaning of this doctrine is concerned. Will we also be in such agreement with regard to the rest of it? My curiosity is so piqued that I will be quite troubled if I don't soon hear who was a Leibnizian on this point before Leibniz.

NEOPHIL. At the outset I will merely cite the words of this philosopher without mentioning his name. The work from which these words are taken was printed in 1677, in other words, eighteen years before Leibniz made his hypothesis known to the learned world. Listen to a passage that I took such notice of that I should be able to translate it from memory. "The body cannot determine the soul to think, and the soul cannot determine the body either to move or to be at rest or to anything else (if something else is possible)." And in a note the author adds: "Since I do not corroborate this by experience, I scarcely believe it possible to persuade someone to ponder my reasons without prejudice, so convinced are people that the body, at the behest of the soul and by its effect, is set in motion at one time and at rest at another. But no one has yet determined what the body can do; that is to say, no one has yet

---

* See Wolff's Latin cosmology, §206, 213.[5]

[5] Christian Wolff, *Cosmologia Generalis* (Frankfurt and Leipzig, 1737) in *Gesammelte Werke*, ed. Jean Ecole (Hildesheim, Olms, 1964), Division Two, , vol. 4, §§206, 213, pp. 157–8, 163.

learned from experience what the body is disposed to do by virtue of the laws of motion (insofar as they are regarded as corporeal) and what it must be determined by the soul to do. No one is so well acquainted with the inner structure of the body that the person could grasp all its capabilities. Indeed, in the case of animals, one notices things that surpass all human acumen. In sleep the sleepwalkers do much that they would not have understood how to do awake. From this it becomes quite evident that the body, via the laws of motion, is capable of much that subsequently amazes the soul itself."[6]

PHILOPON. If I am not mistaken, I believe that I recognize these words as Spinoza's.

NEOPHIL. You are not mistaken, Philopon! It is the second proposition in the third part of his *Ethics* and the proposition that immediately follows it reads: "The actions of the soul spring from adequate concepts (*ideis adaequatis*) and the passions from inadequate concepts." He proves this proposition by appealing to the fact that the essence of the soul consists in its thoughts. All thoughts, on the other hand, are composed of adequate and inadequate concepts. What, then, follows from the nature of the soul, that is to say, whatever has the soul as its immediate cause on the basis of which it can be explained, must follow either from an adequate or an inadequate concept. Since, however, he has demonstrated elsewhere that nothing but passions follow from inadequate concepts, he infers from this that the actions of the soul must spring from its adequate concepts.

PHILOPON. I still see nothing here that is supposed to betray the essential part of the Leibnizian harmony. If Spinoza maintains at the same time that soul and body do not reciprocally affect one another, then it is at least possible that he adhered to the system of occasional causes.

NEOPHIL. Impossible! Nothing can run more counter to Spinoza's philosophy than the system of occasional causes. The defenders of this view must grant a free will to the entity through whose mediation body

---

[6] Spinoza's *Ethica* was published posthumously in Amsterdam, 1677; cf. *Ethica*, in *Opera*, ed. Carl Gebhardt (Heidelberg, Winters, 1972), Pt. III, proposition 2, vol. 2, p. 141: "The body cannot determine the mind to think, nor can the mind determine the body to motion or rest, or to anything else (if there is anything else)."

and soul are connected with one another, and how could Spinoza consent to this? Spinoza, who considers intellect and will one and the same? You see, too, that he explicitly maintains that all changes that transpire in the body can be explained on merely mechanical grounds or, in his words, on the basis of the laws of corporeal nature. This is a view with which the defenders of the occasional causes could not possibly be satisfied. Indeed, Spinoza even avails himself of all the evasions of the Leibnizians. He appeals, like them, to our ignorance about the inner structure of our body and finally to the fact that no one has yet demonstrated the impossibility of such a machine that could produce, in a mechanical manner, all the actions to which this or that individual body is determined.

PHILOPON. But was Spinoza permitted to have recourse, like Leibniz, to the wisdom of God? You know how much the latter appealed to this divine property which could not have helped Spinoza at all.

NEOPHIL. At the very outset I said to you: "Leibniz brought this hypothesis into his system"; that means, he thereby made use of all the advantages that his system afforded him.

PHILOPON. Suppose I have to concede to you that Spinoza cannot accept the system of occasional causes. Even then he acknowledges only one side of the harmony, namely, what concerns the alteration of the body and the manner of its succession. On the other hand, he observed a perfect silence, I believe, about everything that relates to the soul and the succession of its concepts. He says, to be sure, that the actions and passions of the soul spring from their adequate and inadequate concepts. But what explains those alterations of the soul that are apparently based, not on the foregoing state of the soul, but on the movements of the body instead? If sensuous concepts are things the soul undergoes, where does Spinoza show us the way in which we are to derive these from inadequate concepts (without the help of the body and its limbs)? On the other hand, if he did not think of this difficulty, then this hypothesis is as absurd as several other senseless views that this strange mind wanted to force into a system.

NEOPHIL. The entire world acknowledges that Spinoza's views are quite absurd. Actually, however, they are absurd only insofar as he wanted to apply them to this visible world outside us. When, on the other hand, the world is considered which, to speak with Leibniz, existed in the divine intellect as a possible combination of various things prior to God's decision (*antecedenter ad decretum*), many of Spinoza's views can coexist with true philosophy and with religion. Yet let us leave this for another time. I content myself for the present with showing you that Spinoza must very well have thought of the difficulty that you touched on. The experience that the succession of our thoughts is interrupted by sensuous sentiments is too common for a philosopher to have been able to overlook it. In the seventh proposition of the second part of his *Ethics*, Spinoza says: "The order and connection of concepts is one and the same with the order and connection of things." Remember now what Leibniz brings to his defense against Bayle when the latter objects that, without the effect of another substance upon the soul, it would be inconceivable how the soul is frequently able to pass over immediately from pleasure to displeasure and from sadness to joy. Did he not also assert that changes in the soul can be explained by the same reason or ground through which changes in the visible world can be understood? Did he not assert that everything in the soul succeeds something else just as it does in the context of things? What else does this mean but what Spinoza says in the words cited: "The order and connection of concepts is one and the same with the order and connection of things?"

PHILOPON. You appear in fact to be right. How wonderful is the makeup of the human intellect! Through erroneous and bizarre principles Spinoza almost stumbles precisely into the view to which Leibniz was led by the soundest and most correct concepts of God and the world. But now tell me, what should one think of a view that can be inferred from opposite principles with equal correctness?

NEOPHIL. Spinoza has not come to his important doctrine through what is false and absurd in his system, but rather through that in it which is true. There has never yet been a system that could have consisted of purely false principles, and one can say of the Spinozistic system in particular that the most erroneous propositions of it are not so much false as they are incomplete. He erred because he contented himself, so to speak, with one half of the philosophy that cannot exist, however, without the other half. What wonder, then, that, by means of the correct principles contained in his system, he could discover many other truths and could interweave them into the sequence of his inferences? Whoever examines them more closely, notices that they are, nonetheless, utterly inconsistent with the absurdity that is to be found in his system.

PHILOPON. Do you know that you have now put me in a rather embarrassing situation regarding the uprightness of our Leibniz? How can he allow the learned world to congratulate him for this discovery since he knew that it did not belong to him alone?

NEOPHIL. As inappropriate as this behavior would have been for a philosopher like Leibniz, I nevertheless believe that he is to be excused in this case. We would have to chat far into the night, if I were to explain myself fully on this matter. It is sufficient for us to know that there are people who also pass judgments on truths according to a certain genealogy. To repudiate a doctrine, they need only to know that, in the case of this or that writer, it stood in a pernicious kinship with errors. They cannot imagine that one can tear it free and cleanse it of the poison which had entered it through the infection of errors that, along with it, constituted a whole. If Leibniz had openly confessed that he borrowed the essential part of his harmony from Spinoza, tell me, would these people not have believed from the outset that they found, in the reference to Spinoza's name, the basis for refuting this doctrine? Quite certainly. Indeed, they would not have neglected to call to mind the silliness that one must guard against using even a single piece of household furniture of someone who has died of the plague. That such likenesses make an impression, Leibniz knew; he who was not merely the greatest, but also the most careful philosopher. But it is late, and I should not trouble you further. You know how indispensable it is for our thinking monad from time to time to set itself down a few degrees in order to revert to the condition of a sleeping monad. There is no more metaphysical way for me to tell you good night.

Mendelssohn's *Philosophische Schriften*

Second dialogue

Philopon and Neophil

PHILOPON. But what do we care whether conversations about metaphysics belong among those considered stylish and fashionable? It is enough that they contain for us as many matters of importance as of grace.

NEOPHIL. Only for us? The abstract basic truths must contain this importance and grace for all thinking beings. This is particularly the case for those truths that refer to the doctrine of spirits. They have, to be sure, no immediate influence on human life. Nevertheless, they are the noblest and worthiest knowledge since their themes are the noblest and worthiest.

PHILOPON. People at the present time must have completely forgotten to consider metaphysics from this perspective. God, in what disdain it languishes, this former queen of the sciences! Because it was so much loved, so much exalted by the Germans in the past, I am flabbergasted and cannot find the reasons why it has sunk so low in the present day.

NEOPHIL. Cannot find? And hence they must lie so hidden that one has to search for them? No, my dearest friend, no. You have undoubtedly overlooked a source from which we, unfortunately, must derive several evils. I have in mind our slavish imitation of a people that appears, as it were, made to seduce us. This people, which does not have a single metaphysical mind to show for it since P. Malebranche,[1] saw that rigorous and fundamental matters are not its expertise. Hence, it made the stylishness of manners its sole concern and made a practice of heaping the most biting sarcasm on those who indulged in profound meditations and did not know how to live in the society according to a certain exaggerated tenderness of taste. The few philosophers that there still were among this people began to lose their frown and become

---

[1] Nicolas Malebranche (1638–1715), author of *The Search after Truth* (*De la recherche de la vérité*, Paris, 1674–5), proposed that God alone is the source of causal agency, acting only on the *occasion* of certain material and/or psychic conditions; hence, the label "occasionalism" for the theory.

charming. Ultimately they also thought in a charming way. They wrote works *pour les Dames, à la portée de tout le monde* [for women, at the gate of the entire world], and so forth, and very wittily derided the gloomy heads whose writings continued to contain something more than the beautiful sex wanted to read. Honorable Germans derided right along with them. And how could they do otherwise? Germans who would gladly give away half their intellect if the French would only concede to them that they know how to live.

PHILOPON. Will the Germans, then, never recognize their own worth? Will they forever prefer to exchange their gold for the fool's gold of their neighbors? They could, indeed, be quite content with the fact that they have the greater philosophers, and the French the more charming philosophers.

NEOPHIL. Certainly! Leibniz, Wolff, and their various successors, to what a level of perfection and completeness they have brought philosophy! How proud Germany can be of them! Yet what does it help to claim more for oneself than is right? Let us always acknowledge that even someone other than a German, I add further, someone other than a Christian, namely, Spinoza, has participated immensely in the work of bettering philosophy. Before the transition from the Cartesian to the Leibnizian philosophy could occur, it was necessary for someone to take the plunge into the monstrous abyss lying between them. This unhappy lot fell to Spinoza. How his fate is to be pitied! He was a sacrifice for the human intellect, but one that deserves to be decorated with flowers. Without him, philosophy would never have been able to extend its borders so far.

PHILOPON. The misfortune of this man has always touched me in an extraordinary way. He lived in moderation, alone and irreproachable; he renounced all human idols and devoted his entire life to reflection, and look what happened! In the labyrinth of his meditations, he goes astray and, out of error, maintains much that agrees very little with his innocent way of life and that the most depraved scoundrel might wish for in order to be able to indulge his evil desires with impunity. How unjust is the irreconcilable hatred of scholars towards someone so unfortunate!

NEOPHIL. These people believe that they promote the good cause of religion in a nontrivial way when they heap abuse on its naysayer and deluge him, as it were, with calumnies. But the harm they produce outweighs the advantage that they believe themselves to be procuring. The nonbeliever insists on his preconceived opinions all the more stubbornly since he regards calumny as the strongest weapon that can be used against him, while impartial minds regard him as the insulted party and magnanimously take his side. – Of all Spinoza's adversaries, only Wolff is not subject to this reproach. This great philosopher, before he refutes Spinozism, casts it in its proper light.[2] He shows the strongest side of it, and, precisely by this means, he has discovered its weaknesses better than anyone else. Anyone who has read his refutation attentively, will certainly never again be tempted to agree with Spinoza.

PHILOPON. But why do you pass over Bayle? Has he not also shown sufficiently the weakness of this erroneous system?

NEOPHIL. Here and there he has, to be sure, brought up some correct objections to Spinoza. But he has interwoven them with so many sophisms and invalid inferences that he robs them, as it were, of all force. For example, the concept Spinoza appears to make for himself of extension was contested by Bayle with sound reasons, and he showed adequately that extension could not possibly be regarded as an infinite property of God. But what purpose is served by the array of inferences that he burdens Spinoza with? What use is it to indicate that, in the opinion of Spinoza, if Christians take the field against Turks, God would take the field against God, or that all acts of murder, theft, adultery, and incest would have to be attributed to the supreme being? What use are these detested instances and many more like them? In order to make all these objections valid, would he have not first had to demonstrate to Spinoza that there actually are imperfections in God's providence? It is well-known that Spinoza maintains precisely the opposite. As long as Bayle has not torn down this bulwark behind which his opponent safely hides, all the accusations that he makes against that opponent are only so many blows in the air that miss their mark.

---

[2] See Christian Wolff, *Theologia Naturalis* (Frankfurt and Leipzig, 1736), in *Gesammelte Werke*, Division Two, vol. 8, Part 2, ed. Jean Ecole (Hildesheim and New York, Olms, 1981), §706, pp. 715–17 and "Spinoza," in Pierre Bayle, *Historical and Critical Dictionary: Selections*, ed. and tr. Richard N. Popkin (Indianapolis and Cambridge, Hackett, 1991), pp. 288–338.

PHILOPON. You are right. And just now I remember that Bayle himself confesses to having not gone through Spinoza's works very attentively. Nothing but carelessness can make a philosopher like Bayle an unfair adversary. For certainly the zeal against the disbeliever that often deludes the most acute thinker did not guide Bayle's pen.

NEOPHIL. But it is possible that wit led him astray even more. It is, after all, responsible for as many inadequate adversaries as zeal is. How free, in any case, Wolff is of both these charges. Everything that Bayle fails to do and, even with the utmost diligence on his part, would probably have failed to do is accomplished by Wolff. He proves that Spinoza believed that an infinite perfection could, as it were, be composed of an infinite amount of finite perfections, and, finally, he shows the lack of a foundation for this view and does so with such clarity that I am utterly convinced that Spinoza would himself have given it his approval with pleasure. For one must not infer this philosopher's kind of mind from the intractable hardheadedness of so-called "free spirits." He was led astray out of error and not out of the baseness of his heart.

PHILOPON. Yet you showed me yesterday that Spinoza maintained the preestablished harmony. If he had been serious about convincing himself of the truth, would it not have been quite easy for him to infer that the soul has a power and consequently is a particular substance?

NEOPHIL. I do not believe that this follows immediately from the system of harmony. Yet, since you remind me of yesterday, allow me now to put to your judgment a thought that I divulged in passing. It concerned the form under which Spinoza's system can exist with reason and religion. You know, the Leibnizians attribute to the world a twofold existence, as it were. It existed, to use their language, among possible worlds in the divine intellect prior to the divine decree. Because it is the best, God preferred it over all possible worlds and allowed it actually to exist outside him. Now Spinoza remained at that first stage of existence. He believed that a world never became actual outside God and all visible things were not subsisting for themselves, up to this hour, outside God, but instead were still and always to be found in the divine intellect alone. What, then, the Leibnizians maintained about the plan of the world as that plan existed in the divine mind *antecedenter ad decretum* is what Spinoza believed it possible to maintain about the visible world. The former say that God entertained the possibility of contingent things since he could think of his own perfections next to a certain degree of limitation.* In the same way, Spinoza accordingly maintains: "Every individual thing expresses the divine properties in a certain limited manner."[3] According to the Leibnizians, the character of contingent things in the intellect of God (for even *antecedenter ad decretum* the contingency would have had to have its distinguishing character) is such that they cannot be conceived without an infinite series of causes. In almost the same words Spinoza maintains: "The concept of an individual thing that is actually present has God as its cause and, to be sure, not insofar as he is infinite, but rather insofar as the concept of some other thing is to be encountered in him that is likewise actually present. In the same form God is the cause of the latter insofar as the concept of a third something is to be encountered in him and so forth."** How can a rigorous philosopher take exception to this doctrine, if it is applied to the world as it existed in the divine intellect?

PHILOPON. Good! That, then, would be the side of Spinoza's system that borders on the truth. But with this you have still not faced my objection. How could he have a concept of the preestablished harmony and deny that the soul is a substance?

NEOPHIL. That is what I wanted to show you just now. – The world of Spinoza, we have seen, is an ideal world; it is what, according to Leibniz's system, the archetype for this world was before the decree. Now, consider this. Must not each explanation of the community of

---

* Wolff, *Theologia naturalis*, P. II, §92: "Deus possibilia prima omni possibili modo limitat, & omnes eorundem limitationes quam distinctissime ac simul cognoscit."[4]
** See the ninth proposition of the Second Part of his Ethics.[5]

3 A paraphrase of Spinoza, *Ethica* (see p. 101, n. 6), pars, I, propositio 25, corollarium (cf. *Opera*, vol. 2, p. 68).

4 *Gesammelte Werke*, Division Two, vol. 8, Part 2, §92: "God limits the first possibles in every possible way and knows all limitations of them in the most distinct manner and all at once."

5 Spinoza, *Ethica*, Pars II, propositio 9 in *Opera*, vol. 2, pp. 91–2: "The idea of a singular thing, in the act of existing, has God as its cause, not insofar as he is infinite, but insofar as another idea of a singular thing in the act of existing is considered the effect of which God is also the cause, insofar as some third thing is the effect, and so on to infinity."

soul and body conform as much to this eternal archetype as to the visible replica of it?

PHILOPON. Indisputably.

NEOPHIL. Now, in this archetype the concept that expresses the human soul is no substance and has no particular power that could effect changes. If, therefore, Leibniz were to have explained the community of body and soul by reference to this archetype, he would have had to remain silent about the concept that the soul effects changes by its own power, and his system would still have remained worlds apart from the system of occasional causes. For according to his system, the subsequent representations in the archetype of our soul can be intelligibly explained on the basis of foregoing representations, which does not happen according to the system of occasional causes. Since, however, Spinoza did not countenance the actual emergence of a replica but instead allowed for the archetype alone, he could of course have a concept of harmony without inferring from it that the soul has a power of subsisting for itself. There you see how insufficient harmony alone would have been to disabuse him of his error.

PHILOPON. I understand this all very well and now see how much we owe Spinoza's error. It was only a small step for him to the truth. People generally believe that Spinoza makes no distinction between necessary and contingent things. But is it not enough for him to declare explicitly that it is possible, on the basis of divine properties, to give an intelligent explanation for the necessary insofar as God is infinite, but for the contingent, on the other hand, insofar as there is an infinite series of other contingencies to be encountered in him? His mistake was, therefore, something completely different from what perhaps all his adversaries regard it to be. – Still what must have moved him to deny God freedom?

NEOPHIL. If he has come to any error innocently, then it was most certainly this one. He simply regarded the *indifferentia aequilibrii* [indifference of equilibrium] as genuine freedom, and he shares this error with countless philosophers who are orthodox believers. But he did not lack the sagacity to see that the choice of an intelligent entity is always determined by compelling reasons. Hence, he considered this indifference impossible and denied every intelligent entity freedom.

Leibniz has fortunately dispelled this error and demonstrated irrefutably that genuine freedom consists in a choice of the best, and that compelling reasons can determine the choice and cancel mere chance but never bring about a necessity. One is amazed at the capriciousness of human beings! Leibniz would necessarily have vindicated the development of this concept, even for a Spinozist.

PHILOPON. Enough for today! Let me first become versed with this new outlook that you have shown me today, and you can show me some more of it tomorrow. I see, indeed, that the remark made by Bacon in particular regarding philosophers holds for philosophy in general. In their development both have the same fate: in the beginning superstition [*abergläubisch*], then disbelief [*ungläubig*], and finally orthodox belief [*rechtgläubig*].[6]

NEOPHIL. But do not forget as well that God directs everything in the world to the good. Spinoza's dangerous errors must have contributed to the priority of truth.

---

6   Francis Lo. Virulam, *The Essayes and Counsels, Civill and Morall*, newly enlarged (London, 1625), in *The Works of Francis Bacon*, ed. James Spedding, Robert Leslie Ellis, and Douglas Denon Heath (London, Longman, 1861), Essay 16 ("Of Atheism"), vol. 6, p. 413: "It is true that a little philosophy inclineth man's mind to atheism; but depth in philosophy bringeth man's mind about to religion."

Mendelssohn's *Philosophische Schriften*

Third dialogue
Numesian and Kallisthen

NUMESIAN. Have you read *Candide*, then?[1]

KALLISTHEN. The most biting satire on our German doctrine of the best world, who wouldn't read it?

NUMESIAN. The author seems to me to have exposed the weakness of this hypothesis quite successfully. Tell me the truth, as German and metaphysically minded as you are, did you not have to laugh?

KALLISTHEN. Who can deny a Voltaire laughter? With the exception of passages that are actually unworthy of him, I read the little novel with pleasure.

NUMESIAN. Not even with some shame that you were otherwise enamored of this view? Be honest!

KALLISTHEN. Not in the slightest, truthfully. For I remained nonetheless attached to this doctrine. Don't you believe that things, about which one can laugh, can still be true?

NUMESIAN. At least Lord Shaftesbury, your favorite writer, does not believe this. Along with that Greek sophist, he considers levity the touchstone of the true.

KALLISTHEN. Whoever maintains this, it was certainly not what the Greek sophist, Gorgias of Leontini, had in mind.[2] This much can be inferred from the connection in which Aristotle cites Gorgias' utterance. The sophist wanted merely to teach a rhetorical device which could be useful in public disputation and exchange. He said, "One must destroy the laughable by the serious, and the serious by the laughable."* That is

---

* Aristotle, *De Rhetorica*, Bk. III, ch. 18.

[1] *Candide ou le enthousiasme* (Paris, 1759) is Voltaire's satire on enthusiasm and the Leibnizian doctrine that this world is the best possible one. In the work Pangloss, Candide's foppish old master of philosophy, repeatedly attempts to defend the best possible world doctrine at the most inopportune times.

[2] Gorgias (483–375 BC) is the author of the nihilist tract "On Non-Being and on Nature."

to say, if by some serious observation an opponent has succeeded in commanding attention, then try to dispel the seriousness by means of something that can be laughed at. If, on the other hand, he has charmed the laughers, then take pains to dispel the happy mood by means of something serious. Since the time of Gorgias many a sophist has known how to make successful use of this device, at least the first half of it. – But listen, now, to how Lord Shaftesbury takes this passage. "A wise man from antiquity had already said that a joke is the sole touchstone of seriousness, just as seriousness is the sole touchstone of a joke. For what can bear no raillery is suspicious, and a joke that survives no serious investigation is surely false wit."* There we have a touchstone,** instead of a means of debate, though a touchstone of the serious and mirthful which can still be defended to some extent. In the end the English writer makes even the laughable into a criterion of truth. Oh, if only the Lord had written the thirty-odd volumes of such criteria for which we have Voltaire to thank.

NUMESIAN. This much I know, the Lord protested against misuse and qualified his proposition so much . . .

KALLISTHEN. So much that the qualifications leave practically no room for the proposition, as always happens to friends of the truth who allow themselves to be seduced into maintaining something paradoxical. In the end, out of respect for the truth, they must do so much qualifying and take such precautions that their proposition, which sounded so peculiar at the outset, is gradually reduced to something quite common. "The laughable is a touchstone of the truth": this sounds strange and promises something novel. But after all the concessions and reservations which the truth extorts from the wise Shaftesbury, this proposition does not say anything more than we have long known already, namely, that the truth cannot have in itself something absurd that deserves to be laughed at. For where else does the Lord's distinction lead, the distinction between being made laughable and being laughable!

---

*   *Essay on the freedom of wit and humor.*[3]
** Not for nothing does the Lord cite the somewhat ambiguous words of the translation: *seria risu, risum seriis discutere* [to discuss the serious with laughter, laughter with serious things].[4]

[3]   Earl of Shaftesbury, "Treatise II: *Sensus Communis*; An Essay on the Freedom of Wit and Humor," in *Characteristics of Men, Manners, Opinions, Times* (London, 1711), ed. by John M. Robertson (Indianapolis and New York, Bobbs-Merrill, 1964), vol. 2, pp. 41–99.

[4]   Ibid., p. 52, n. 1.

NUMESIAN. But this distinction is self-evident; for what can someone mischievous not make laughable?

KALLISTHEN. That is to say, someone mischievous can bring the most serious things into a contrast in which they arouse laughter. But with this, matters are not yet settled. Even when a subject appears to be laughable in and for itself, in its natural setting, it can be fundamentally true.

NUMESIAN. Here we come to the distinction between appearing and being. This, too, is presupposed.

KALLISTHEN. But consider the fact that, in general, almost everything in the case of the laughable is a matter of appearance or of the viewpoint from which the object is considered. To be sure, like the pleasant, painful, and offensive, the laughable is a feature of reproach but only insofar as it is suited to making an impression of a certain sort on certain subjects. Of course, in addition, the reproach requires a certain makeup to produce this impression; but also a certain disposition in the subject to receive this impression. From the side of the subject, being is not at all distinct from seeming, for the impression and its effects can in both cases be the same. Thus, too, in regard to the person laughing, everything that moves him to laugh is laughable. We must return to the objective basis of the laughable, to the sensuous absurdity, if we want to distinguish what is laughable from what appears to be laughable. What in fact contains such an absurdity, a conspicuous defectiveness, that is laughable; what, however, is truly free from this can at most have only the appearance of being laughable. In this regard we can say that a subject matter can appear laughable without truly containing the objective basis for being laughable, that is to say, without being absurd. If, therefore, Lord Shaftesbury praises the laughable as a touchstone of truth, then he must in fact have meant the objective element of the laughable, namely, the absurd. His proposition teaches us nothing more than this: considered from the right perspective, the truth can contain nothing absurd and does not deserve to be laughed at. Who has doubted this? Or was this the peculiar view that had made us so attentive at the outset?

Let us now return to *Candide* which was the occasion for this investigation. Let us set aside the fact that the poet has basically distorted providence and compressed into a small span of space and time more evil than has probably ever taken place in such a span. Let us set aside the fact that in this small span itself he does not even talk about the good that, by the laws of nature, must be bound up with the evil dreamt up by him. Let us also not take into account the fact that he betrays the talent – which we certainly do not begrudge him – the talent of imbuing the most innocent subject matter with a tinge of evil and, so to say, finding a hell where God has planted a paradise. Rather, conceding all his premises and accepting the truth of the circumstances, I would like to know what we should infer from this? That a more perfect world is somehow possible? That this immense world of bodies and spirits can be governed according to physical and moral laws that do not permit in any corner of some part of the world such evils as are described in *Candide*? This would be obvious nonsense or, what many would perhaps fear more, utterly ridiculous. Consider how Voltaire behaves when some mediocre journalist wants to criticize one of his tragedies. Should he allow himself more freedom towards the creator than he allows Freron toward himself?[5]

NUMESIAN. It would appear that you would not permit yourself to be dissuaded from your system, even if *Candide* were a true story instead of being a novel.

KALLISTHEN. Certainly not! One must simply not know what is at issue if, as another French writer has done to repudiate the German system, one drafts a portrait of the history of France and analyzes the chain of evils out of which this country's affairs of state are composed. Civil wars, the bloody wedding, persecution by dragoons, Law's system, Ravaillac, Clement, and so forth. What does this matter to our system, what do even a thousand other ridiculous or lamentable things which have so often turned the political world of France on its head matter? With utter composure Pangloss can wrap himself in his mantle and say: "The world is still the best!"

NUMESIAN. You believe then that there is no major objection to this doctrine?

KALLISTHEN. On the basis of experience, none unless it were an

---

[5] Elie-Catherine Freron (1718–76), traditionalist-minded French journalist, engaged in a celebrated literary feud with Voltaire.

experience completely different from what we inhabitants of earth are capable of having. – It follows so naturally and so unforced from the concept of an infinite wisdom that I do not comprehend at all how the proposition can be doubted: "Supreme wisdom will prefer what is best to what is less good."[6] And yet there remain difficulties in this doctrine that I cannot resolve to my satisfaction. Leibniz stirred up one difficulty of this sort in his *Theodicy* itself and if I had this splendid work at hand, I could show you how important the doubt is and how feebly Leibniz appears to remove it.

NUMESIAN. You will still be able at least to recall the thought, or is it absolutely necessary to cite his words?

KALLISTHEN. I remember that I wrote down the entire passage in my handbook. Here it is: "Someone might object," it says, "that it would be impossible to produce the best (the best world) since there is no perfect creature and since a more perfect can always be produced. I answer that one must not apply to the entire world what can be said of a particular substance that can always be surpassed by another. For the world is meant to endure forever, it is something infinite. Moreover," the philosopher continues, "in each of the smallest parts of matter there are infinitely many creatures since what endures is in fact infinitely divided. However, the infinite, that is, the sum total of an infinite number of substances, is, properly speaking, no whole, no more than is the infinite number itself which one cannot say is odd or even. The subject of discussion here is not of a creature, but rather the entire universe, and the opponent would have to maintain that one universe could always be better than another and so on ad infinitum. But he would deceive himself in this respect and not be able to prove his point."[7] What do you think of his answer?

NUMESIAN. That it rightly places the burden of proof on the opponent. As long as it has not been demonstrated that, for every world, the possibility always exists that there is a more perfect one in an infinite progression of worlds, the Leibnizian always has good reason to regard

---

[6] Cf. G. W. F. Leibniz, *Theodicée, Essais sur la bonté de dieu, la liberté de l'homme et l'origine du mal*, in *Opera philosophica*, ed. J. E. Erdmann (Berlin, 1840), enlarged with a preface by Renate Vollbracht (Meisenheim and Glan, Scientia Aalen, 1959), §195, p. 564 (also in *Die philosophische Schriften*, ed. C. J. Gerhardt (Hildesheim, Olms, 1961), vol. 6, p. 232).

[7] Ibid., §§195–6, p. 564.

this world as the best because it has been preferred by the supreme being to all the rest.

KALLISTHEN. The universe, Leibniz says, is no whole because it is destined to endure eternally and because the smallest part of matter contains infinitely many creatures. We must posit one of two cases: either the array of creatures, as they endure eternally, cannot *in any way* be taken together and regarded *as a whole*, even by the infinite intellect itself, because taking things together in this way contradicts the nature of eternal duration; or the infinite series can, to be sure, be canvased in the most distinct way by the infinite intellect, but together it constitutes no unlimited whole but rather something immense, and the opponent has to prove that this immensity can be surpassed by another. The former case is incompatible with the system of this philosopher. However endless and eternal the quantity intended, it must have been possible for this infinite array of creatures to be completely canvased in its eternal future by the infinite intellect and compared with others, since no choice of the best takes place without this comparison. Indeed, the immense future must be constantly present to the infinite intellect and thus be capable of being grasped by him and, indeed, in a single idea, as a whole.

I well know that, in the opinion of some philosophers, it is utterly impossible for the progression into infinity to be completely comprehended, precisely because the essence of such a series consists in ceaselessly progressing. Hence, they say, the mathematically infinite is a magnitude whose boundary one does not determine and which, therefore, can always be extended further and further without ever being completely canceled and leaving a boundless magnitude in its wake. In the same way they maintain that, therefore, time can continue to endure for an eternity but it will never have endured an eternity. Moreover, if one says of matter, it is infinitely divisible, then from this it does not follow that the number of its parts is infinite but rather the very opposite, that it remains forever finite and can be constantly increased by further division. Some philosophers have expressed themselves in this way with regard to the mathematically infinite. – But even if Leibnizians have thought in this manner, Leibniz himself did not. According to the system of this philosopher we find the infinite everywhere in nature. According to that system, each part of matter is not only *infinitely divisible* (which would merely be a progression into infinity), but is *infinitely divided* in actuality. Each organized entity consists of an infinite number of smaller entities which are no less organized. Each present condition of a created thing contains as much forwards (the entire series of effects without end, or the future in its eternal duration) as backwards (the series of causes without end, in which naturally the concept of a contingent being can be analyzed). Every concept of the human being leads to the infinite and contains an impenetrable depth that can only be completely fathomed by the infinite intellect.

I tell you nothing new when I say that this infinite which we encounter in nature is essentially distinct from the infinity of God. It is merely a picture, a copy of that supreme infinity, but one that is implanted within us and which we also find again everywhere outside us that we look. If, however, this universe, in spite of its infinity and eternal duration, must present itself as a whole to the divine intellect, then a definite degree of perfection will also have to be ascribed to it, regarded as a whole. Of course, it will be a limited, not an infinite degree. Contrary to Spinoza, it has been proven very successfully that an infinite number of finite perfections, taken together, constitutes a merely finite perfection of the whole. By heaping up many parts or taking them together, one sustains an *extended magnitude*, but no *unextended magnitude*, no *strength*. Thus, too, when infinitely many limited perfections are taken together, they constitute an infinite perfection in terms of extension, but not of strength.

If, however, the perfection of every universe, however infinite in number and duration it may be, is still limited, then it is difficult to understand why another universe is not possible which, considered as a whole, possesses a higher degree of perfection. Leibniz demands the proof that this is possible. But the proof appears to lie in the propositions that in the infinite intellect the universe, while infinite in the number of creatures and eternal in duration, nevertheless constitutes a whole, that this whole must possess a limited degree of perfection, and that a limited degree can always be surpassed by another.

To be sure, the Leibnizian always wins when he infers from the result. This universe has been produced by God, hence there must be no more perfect system of the world. If the series of possible worlds, each surpassing the other in perfection, were infinite, then God could not have produced any of them. "He cannot act without sufficient reason," Leibniz continues in the cited passage, "and in this case he would even have had to act contrary to the principle of sufficient reason. Thus it is just as if one should imagine that God decided to produce a ball without having the slightest reason for its having a definite size. Such a decision would be without result for it would bring with it what would necessarily impede its execution."[8] These reasons are patent. If something better were possible, then the supreme goodness could only choose what is better. But we would still like to see more distinctly how the perfection of the whole, without being infinite, can nevertheless not be greater than it actually is.

Another difficulty which I cannot fully settle is this. You know that we have important reasons for believing in *creation in time*, at least for considering it rationally as possible as a *creation without beginning*. But can a creation in time be compatible with the system of the best world?

It has been established that the concept of a contingent entity proceeds forwards to an endless series of effects as much as it does backwards to an endless series of causes. It suited God to let this endless series of possible causes and effects actually begin and continue at the point where he found it good. But what reason could the supreme wisdom have found to prefer one member of this chain to the other, since they all remain part of the system of the most perfect universe?

Suppose that *b*, *c*, *d*, *e*, and so forth represent the series of causes and effects that God allowed actually to exist. By virtue of the concept that we have of the contingency of things, there is also a possible condition *a*, from which, if it had been actually present, the condition *b* would have naturally followed and on the basis of which it could be intelligibly explained. This possible condition *a* would have had to have actually existed and the conditions *b*, *c*, *d*, *e*, and so forth, which represent the series of the best world, would have followed upon it according to the laws of nature. Hence, *a* belongs to the series of the best as much as *b* does, and it could have been actual, without harm to the most perfect world. What reason, then, can the supreme wisdom have for letting the series of causes and effects begin with *b* rather than *a*? You see that one can push this question to infinity.

One would have to assume, of course, that even here the law of the

---

[8]   Ibid.

best was decisive and if there had to have been a beginning, that member would have been chosen as the beginning, which would lead to progress towards a higher perfection by the closest, shortest, and most immediate path. But this answer is not completely satisfying, and I wish to see clarified more distinctly how the first condition, which actually came to be, could involve an earlier condition without this earlier condition having belonged to the choice of the best.

NUMESIAN. Now, it no longer amazes me in the slightest that you are not intimidated by a satire of this system. For I see that serious difficulties cannot bring you to the point of abandoning this doctrine. But are you not letting yourself be blinded by respect for its great inventor?

KALLISTHEN. I don't think so. I am conscious, to be sure, of my great esteem for these immortal philosophers. Leibniz and Newton! I cannot pronounce these names without, as that student of Plato in his time did, thanking providence that it let me be born after them. In fact, if I am created to contemplate God's works, then I can now better fulfill the purpose of my existence. For I now look upon God's works with eyes completely different from those I would have looked upon them with before these two great men. – Yet the esteem for the man cannot seduce me into blindly accepting his thoughts and opinions without testing them. But I have already said to you that the doctrine of the best world flows immediately from the properties of God, and Bayle himself had to acknowledge as much, considered from this point of view. Since, therefore, it has its proven certainty, objections and difficulties cannot keep us from agreeing with it. They can capture our attention and provide us with an occasion for reflection. However, the once proven truth stands fast as long as the foundations on which it rests are not shaken. For my own peace of mind, I would not like to do without this doctrine since it is the only one that is able to satisfy me. Through the consideration that the slightest objects around me are parts of the most perfect world, they acquire a sublimity that makes them worth revering.

Mendelssohn's *Philosophische Schriften*

Fourth dialogue
Kallisthen and Numesian

NUMESIAN. What painter, what sculptor ever finished two pieces that were perfectly similar to one another? Indeed, even . . .

KALLISTHEN. Wait, my dear friend! You are wrong. Did you not want to challenge the principle of indiscernibles?

NUMESIAN. And?

KALLISTHEN. Yet you cite an experience to which the defenders of this doctrine can appeal the most.

NUMESIAN. Not at all! This experience teaches us, to be sure, that finishing two similar things surpasses all human skill. But won't we be able to regard the production of them, precisely for this reason, as a prerogative of the divine art?

KALLISTHEN. I can let this stand for the moment, although I would, nonetheless, have much to say against it. But what follows from this that is disadvantageous to the Leibnizians?

NUMESIAN. You should soon hear what. Only do not demand back again what you have now granted me. What, in fact, do you think? Are two things that cannot be distinguished absolutely impossible?

KALLISTHEN. Not if they are supposed to exist in a different combination of time and space.

NUMESIAN. Good! And, therefore, divine omnipotence can actually have produced two such things?

KALLISTHEN. Indisputably, if it were not necessarily the case that manifold things gave divine wisdom more pleasure.

NUMESIAN. You always have your qualifed "if" in readiness so that you do not become ensnared. Yet this time your "if" will not protect you. If completely similar things prove more art than manifold things do, if, I say, they can be regarded as a mark of divine insight, then divine wisdom must have been more pleased by them.

KALLISTHEN. You do well, my friend! not to listen to the doctrines of philosophers like oracles but rather look for doubts and objections to them in the only place they are to be found. One can never be convinced if one has never doubted with reason. I remember having read this objection or something similar in Voltaire's short philosophical writings.[1] However, as is typical for overly animated minds, they are too restless to read through any profound work with the requisite effort. They merely look around with fleeting glances for thoughts that stick out and are akin to strokes of insight. They oppose them with strokes of insight that are more dazzling and believe that they have philosophized. It is completely certain, in particular, that Voltaire at most glanced at the writings of Leibniz for Leibniz was still a German although he wrote his theodicy in French. Here Voltaire may have noticed by chance that Leibniz maintained that it is unsuitable for divine wisdom to have put two indistinguishable things into the world. Voltaire believed that he read that it would require more art, more skill to produce manifold things than to produce things perfectly similar. Without troubling himself any further with the philosopher's system or his reasons, he contents himself with investigating, in his own way, whether it is more difficult to produce manifold or similar things. But listen, now, to how Leibniz took it. You know that he demonstrated by irrefutable proofs that divine wisdom can choose nothing without sufficient reason. If, therefore, two indistinguishable things should be encountered in diverse places or at diverse times, then it must be possible to understand why the one is present here rather than there, or at this time rather than that time. But since no difference is to be found in the things themselves and since space and time cannot in themselves tip the scales in favor of a particular choice, no compelling reason can have determined the divine will, and, hence, it is not possible for a choice to have been made. Do you see, now, why Leibniz says: perfectly similar things would not be suitable for divine wisdom? It is not that manifold things would somehow require more skill, but rather that,

---

[1] See *Elements de la philosophie de Newton* (Amsterdam, 1738), critical edn. by Robert L. Walters and W. H. Barber, in *The Complete Works of Voltaire* (Oxford, The Voltaire Foundation, 1992), vol. 15, pp. 210f.

since wisdom directs everything according to space and time, it cannot set one and the same thing down at diverse places or diverse times.

NUMESIAN. I am ashamed. This time you have snatched victory all too quickly from my hands and the reproach which you make of Voltaire falls back on me with twice as much right.

KALLISTHEN. For some time now one has become accustomed to this splendid writer's lack of profundity, and, aside from the great masses, few people allow themselves to be seduced any more by the shingle of philosophy hung out by him. But even people of profound insight in philosophy venture many a clever pronouncement and believe themselves able, by some lucky and sudden stroke of inspiration, to decide the most difficult disputed questions.

NUMESIAN. You are thinking of the philosopher who recently published an entire treatise against the Leibnizian proposition of the indiscernible . . .

KALLISTHEN. Do not try to guess who it is that I have in mind. There are too many unauthorized judges of the same ilk in the anarchy of philosophy for us both to hit upon the same one at the same time. I am speaking of the author of the *Pensées sur la liberté,*[*] a scholar who certainly did not lack the talent to deserve the name of a true philosopher. But he must have lacked the patience to analyze the notions that occurred to him and to trace them all the way back to the first principles of human knowledge.

NUMESIAN. Good, good; he shares this lack of patience with many. Even I have never been able to bring myself to read attentively and in the proper order the abstract doctrines of ontology which seem at bottom to have nothing more to say than what we have already known for some time. A kind of self-denial is actually required to turn back

---

[*] A work of Mr. Prémontval.[2]

[2] André Pierre Le Guay Prémontval, *Pensées sur la liberté, tirées d'un ouvrage manuscrit qui a pour titre: Protestations et declarations philosophiques sur les principaux objets des connaissances humaines* (Berlin and Potsdam, 1754); in November and December of 1753 and February 1754, Prémontval (or "Le Guay") (1716–64) delivered these *Thoughts on Liberty* to the Royal Academy of Sciences in Berlin. He was a prominent member of the Academy and a leading critic of Wolffian philosophy.

from the steep, untrodden path (on which one believes that the truth is to be reached) in order to practice walking on flat land.

KALLISTHEN. And yet no one who has not first measured his steps on flat land takes a sure step on high ground. – I can cite for you, precisely from the little work of which we are now speaking, some examples of how easily the sharpest minds can fail because of an inadequate knowledge of ontology. You will unquestionably remember what kind of a proof of the principle of indiscernibles the author promises in a footnote. He affirms, namely, that one can regard all individual things at the same time as species and genera: as species in regard to the genera in which they are immediately contained and which are commonly regarded as the lowest level of species; as genera, on the other hand, in consideration of the various alterations to which they are subject and which have their subspecies in turn and so on ad infinitum. Now, he says further that since it is completely absurd to assume two completely similar species or genera in nature, this can be claimed just as little of two individual things. For the series of species and genera proceeds, in his opinion, to infinity.

NUMESIAN. Well? Do you find something in this proof to which you take exception?

KALLISTHEN. If it is true, as this writer assures us, that these reasons led him to the principle of indiscernibles a long time before it was known to him that there is a Leibnizian philosophy, if this is true, then we have, I say, one more example of how impossible it is to infer the truth of the reasons from the correctness of the inference. For, in the first place, it is false that it ought to be possible to regard an individual thing as a genus in regard to its alterations. A thing is an *individual thing* only when everything that is a part of it is completely determined. As long as it is not yet established whether this or that is a part of it or not, the thing still belongs to a species or to a genus and can be encountered nowhere other than in abstraction. For the concept of a species is something universal, the likes of which is found in nature only in the individuals conceived under it. Everyone knows that everything must be completely determined in a thing, including its contingencies and alterations, if it is to be actually present. Now, tell me how our writer could believe that subspecies are still to be found in an individual thing, a thing that is completely determined in every regard? Or did he want to claim that there would never be a thing determined in every regard? But, then, how is it possible for it to be present?

NUMESIAN. But are you not also imposing on our philosopher a definition of species and genera which he would never concede? You assume the Wolffian definition of a species while he perhaps may understand by it nothing other than an assortment of similar things, taken together, without it being necessary to suspend the complete determination of these individual things. They can always remain different in some respect and yet, taken together, constitute a certain species or a certain genus.

KALLISTHEN. Good! He can take the words the way he wants, but the fact of the matter remains the same. I say that, by this very definition, all things which have precisely the same similarity in common with one another must belong to one and the same species. For the particular differences among them do not thereby come into consideration. Do you see now why it is absurd to assume two completely similar species? But how can one extend this to two individual things? Why can two things not have alterations that are completely identical and exist in a different context of space and time? I do not find the slightest connection between these two propositions. Two species cannot possibly be differentiated in terms of space or time because space and time do not come into consideration at all in the determination of species and genera. But why can this not be said of individual things? But perhaps our writer wanted merely to prove that no two perfectly similar things could be encountered at the same time and in precisely the same space. If this is the case, he is perfectly correct. But then his doctrine contains nothing other than what people have seen for centuries prior to Leibniz, and his doctrine is still very far apart from what one calls the principle of indiscernibles.

NUMESIAN. I am really sorry to have to acknowledge that you are right. For since Leibniz gave no proof of his principle, then it would be highly desirable if our writer's reasons were as correct as they were novel.

KALLISTHEN. Do we not have enough reasons to demonstrate the truth of this principle in a convincing manner? It is true, Leibniz appears to have contented himself with induction. But has there been any lack of proofs given by his successors? Nothing can, in my judgment, be more convincing than the proof given of it by Wolff.[3] Indeed, this principle flows so naturally from the universal harmony of all things that it is impossible to challenge this principle without denying that harmony. For if all things are connected with one another in the most precise manner, then it is impossible to encounter two completely similar things without the entire series on both sides being completely similar. But how does this happen if we do not intend to transport these two things into two similar worlds?

NUMESIAN. Well, if there is nothing further, then let us allow two similar worlds to be present. Anyone who accepts the existence of two indistinguishable things will certainly not have any reservations about also considering, along with Democritus, completely similar worlds to be possible.

KALLISTHEN. Oh, but Democritus' view is even less able to withstand the Leibnizians' attack. Nothing will be easier for them than to prove the impossibility of several completely similar worlds. For either they are connected with one another or not. If they are connected with one another, then they do not constitute more than a single world since everything belongs together in a single chain. If they are not connected with one another, then either they must be different in some respect or they are completely similar to one another. As for the first case, it is not possible for something completely similar to be found in both worlds since in each world one thing must be connected with everything in the most precise manner. In the latter case, on the contrary, these two worlds are not at all distinguishable from one another, I mean, they are not distinguishable even in space or time. If, however, they are not to be distinguished, not even in space or time, then they do not constitute several, but rather in fact only one and the same world, and the multiplicity that we thereby imagine is a mere chimera.

NUMESIAN. A mere chimera? And why? Doesn't this require the assumption of the principle of indiscernibles precisely where one is supposed to prove it?

KALLISTHEN. Not at all! You know that two similar things that cannot

---

[3] Christian Wolff, *Cosmologia Generalis* (Frankfurt and Leipzig, 1737), in *Gesammelte Werke*, ed. Jean Ecole (Hildeshim, Olms, 1964), Division Two, vol. 4, §195, p. 152.

even be known and distinguished from one another in space or time counted, centuries before Leibniz, as two things that are not two. One may posit a single concept as many times as one wants, but these positings constitute a multiplicity only because the one is assumed either after or alongside the other. But what does this mean other than that they have been assumed in a different space or at different times? If one cancels this difference, then all these concepts must, as it were, flow together and constitute merely a single thing. If Leibniz concedes the internal possibility of two completely similar things, then he would understand it only in the sense that God could entertain the very same thing in a different combination of time or space and even actually produce it if, in his infinite wisdom, he would find it to be good.

NUMESIAN. Is it, therefore, impossible for God himself to entertain two things that do not have either an internal or at least an external difference?

KALLISTHEN. It is as little possible for him to do this as it is for him to entertain two things that are not two.

NUMESIAN. Now, good night, Hazard! Or have you still not read what trouble this very author took in a more recent work (*du hasard sous l'empire, etc.*) to urge upon the Leibnizians a scenario in which their God is supposed to be forced to act?[4] By now it is quite certain that his rhetorical figures are put to use to no avail. For the two completely similar things which he assumes in the divine intellect prior to creation, one of which God would have to have chosen arbitrarily, can be, as Leibniz would put it, nothing other than a single concept entertained by God in diverse spatial or temporal combinations. Hence, he had merely to choose between two different combinations, in which case there could not possibly have been a shortage of compelling reasons determining his will.

KALLISTHEN. I have not yet read this little work by Prémontval. But this writer's objections to the Leibnizian philosophy are almost all of the same stripe. One need merely consult the ontology a little in order to see perfectly the feebleness of his reasons. The main objection, on

---

[4] Prémontval, *Du hasard sous l'empire de la providence, pour servir de préservatif contre la doctrine du Fatalisme moderne* (*Of the Hazards within the Empire of Providence, to Guard Against the Doctrine of Modern Fatalism*) (Berlin, 1755).

which he relies throughout his *Pensées sur la liberté* and which is supposed to cancel the Leibnizian distinction between necessary and contingent truths, is in my opinion nothing but a caviling, specious inference, the weakness of which can be uncovered with little trouble.

NUMESIAN. And yet I am acquainted with many a zealous Leibnizian whom this objection has perplexed. A contingent truth, it says, presupposes a certain condition under which that truth takes place. But then someone shows them that, in the case of each mathematical proposition, there is a condition which renders the proposition true. How, then, can this circumstance be what distinguishes the so-called contingent truths? You seek, of course, a distinction between the condition that is presupposed in the case of mathematical truths and the condition that belongs to a contingent truth. But you seek in vain.

KALLISTHEN. That may be; for the most zealous Leibnizians are not always those who best know how to make use of his reasons. The spirit of partisanship blinds the eyes of the acutest philosophers. – We will not be able to talk at length today. But a few more words! And, indeed, no more than a few words are necessary to show you that the entire difficulty that people believe they find in this doctrine is based merely upon a misunderstanding. Prémontval, just like those who did not know how to refute his reasons, believed that it would be sufficient for a truth to be conditional if in such an instance one were able to employ the little word "if." As a result, they were readily perplexed by the fact that they saw that they were able to express all mathematical truths with an "if." To Leibniz and Wolff, on the other hand, this would not have appeared strange at all. They knew all too well that one can transform each categorical proposition in mathematics into a conditional proposition if one makes the essential determination of the subject in its subspecies into a condition.[*] But are the truths, therefore, contingent? We will see. I will make use of Prémontval's example. All the corners of a triangle together are equivalent to two right angles, or, in order to express this

---

[*] See Wolff's Latin Logic, §226: "Praepositiones categoricae aequivalent hypotheticis & ad eas reduci possunt."[5]

[5] *Philosophie Rationalis sive Logica* (Frankfurt and Leipzig, 1728), in *Gesammelte Werke*, Division I, vol. I, Part 2, ed. J. Ecole (Hildesheim and New York, Olms, 1983), §226, p. 229: "Categorical propositions are equivalent to hypothetical propositions and can be reduced to them."

proposition conditionally, if a space of three sides is enclosed, then there are, etc. What does this theorem presuppose? That a triangle is actually present at hand? By no means! It merely presupposes that three sides can, without contradiction, enclose a space. This truth is necessary since the concept of a triangle necessarily contains no contradiction. Now draw a triangle on the table and say: this triangle has three angles which are equivalent to, etc. What now does this proposition presuppose? Undoubtedly it presupposes that the figure drawn by you is a triangle. But was it necessary that you drew a triangle here? Certainly not! For the contrary, "this figure is no triangle," contains no contradiction. Therefore, your proposition is contingent and true only in a specific instance. You can apply this very easily to all truths without distinction and draw from this the conclusion that a proposition which presupposes a mere possibility is unconditioned and necessary. For a possible thing is necessarily possible, or what contains no contradiction, necessarily contains no contradiction. A proposition, on the other hand, that presupposes something actual that is not necessary, is only contingently true. These are the borders that separate the practical geometer from the natural philosopher. The former merely presupposes the possibility of certain concepts instead of preoccupying himself, like the latter, with things as they actually are.

NUMESIAN. I understand this all very well. But a single difficulty still lies in my way, a difficulty that I beg you to remove for me. Does it not follow from your explanation that each proposition which presupposes a necessary condition must itself be necessary?

KALLISTHEN. Irrefutably.

NUMESIAN. But, now, the existence of this world presupposes a necessary truth, the existence of God, and yet the Leibnizians acknowledge that it is contingent.

KALLISTHEN. Your objection would be perfectly well-founded if this world presupposed nothing further than the existence of God alone. But for the existence of the world the will of God is required as much as his existence. His will, however, is not necessary.

Part II
Rhapsody or additions to the Letters on sentiments

In the "Letters on sentiments" ["On sentiments"] I assumed with *Monsieur Maupertuis* the following nominal definitions: *The pleasant sentiment is a representation which we prefer to have than not to have; the unpleasant, on the other hand, a representation which we prefer not to have than to have.* In this definition, however, there is a small error that deserves to be noted. For the smallest error in the basic definition of any subject matter can, in subsequent considerations, lead us astray into the most significant misunderstandings. On the basis of the content of the definition, we would have to despise every unpleasant sentiment and wish to see it purged from our soul and destroyed. If we pay attention to ourselves, however, we notice that, in the case of some unpleasant sentiments, our disgust is not always directed at the representation but very often at the object of the representation. We do not always prefer *not to have* the representation, as required by the definition, but in very many instances merely prefer instead for the object *not to be*. We disapprove of the evil that has occurred; we wish that it had not happened or that it stood in our power to make things right again. Once, however, the evil has occurred, and if it has occurred without our being in any way responsible for it and without our being able to prevent it, then we are powerfully attracted to the representation of it and long to acquire that representation. Lisbon's demise in the earthquake attracted countless people to take in the sight of this terrible devastation with their own eyes.[1] After the bloodbath at *** all our

---

[1] Lisbon was destroyed by an earthquake in 1755. Fires throughout the city were followed by a massive tidal wave, taking 10,000–15,000 lives.

citizens hurried over to the field of slaughter, strewn as it was with corpses. After the deed was done, the sage himself,[2] who would have taken pleasure in preventing this evil by offering up his own life, waded through the human blood and felt a frightful fascination at the sight of this terrifying place. If what we love is in danger or misery, we have no intention – at least as far as the initial sentiment is concerned – of accepting this, but instead have every intention of removing the evil. However, if there is no way to remove the evil, we nonetheless want to be apprised of each circumstance and yearn to learn even the most unpleasant news as soon as it happens. In all such cases it is clear that our disapproval, our repugnance is aimed more at the matter at hand than at the representation of it. Each individual representation stands in a twofold relation. It is related, at once, to the matter before it as its object (of which it is a picture or copy) and then to the soul or the thinking subject (of which it constitutes a determination). As a determination of the soul, many a representation can have something pleasant about it although, as a picture of the object, it is accompanied by disapproval and a feeling of repugnance. Thus, we must indeed take care not to mix or confuse these two relations, the objective and the subjective, with one another.

In order to keep these two relations apart from one another and within their proper boundaries, we must return to their origin and look for the trace of them there. By means of each thing's determination, either something is posited or something is nullified in it. That is to say, by means of each distinguishing feature of a thing, something is either affirmed or denied of it. All finite things have affirmative and negative features. The former ascribe some *content* [*Sachliches*] to the thing, the latter withhold some content from it. One should understand me to be speaking here of genuine affirmations and negations, not of such that consist merely in words. A verbal affirmation can be in fact a negation as far as the content is concerned, just as a verbal negation can be a genuine affirmation as far as the content is concerned.

The affirmative features of a matter constitute the elements of its perfection, just as the negative features of the same constitute the elements of its imperfection. For the affirmative features, insofar as they are in fact affirmative, are in accord with one another, as I pointed out

---

² I.e. Frederick the Great.

quite distinctly in the first part of this work. Thus they provide the thing with a multiplicity which harmonizes in something common, i.e., a *perfection*. The negative features, on the other hand, deny the content either a multiplicity of things or their harmony with one another. For the realities themselves, insofar as they are combined in something finite with negations, can contradict one another and thus cancel each other out. But we call the lack of a multiplicity of things or its disharmony an *imperfection*.

The elements of perfection, i.e., all the features that posit some sort of content in a thing, are satisfying and comfortable to us. By contrast, the elements of imperfection or the features denying a thing some sort of content are perceived with dissatisfaction. I am speaking here of perceiving and recognizing some thing or, in other words, of *intuitive knowledge*, not of a mere consciousness of signs and words that suggest these features. For the consciousness of signs and words leaves the soul in an indifferent state, arousing neither satisfaction nor dissatisfaction. On the other hand, when we perceive and know some thing itself, we are not able to discover any features of it that would not arouse either satisfaction or dissatisfaction, once that intuitive knowledge posits or negates something in the thing in which it is perceived.

This satisfaction or dissatisfaction refers, however, to the object; they apply only to the thing that possesses the affirmative or the negative features. We feel gratified or not by the organization and constitution of the thing after we perceive realities or deficiencies in it. In relation to the thinking subject, the soul, on the other hand, perceiving and cognizing the features as well as testifying to enjoying them or not constitutes some *sort of content [Sachliches]* that is posited in the soul, an affirmative determination of the soul. Hence, every representation, at least in relation to the subject, as an affirmative predicate of the thinking entity, must have something about it that we like. For even the picture of a deficiency in the object, just like the expression of discontent with it, are not deficiencies on the part of the thinking entity, but rather affirmative and material determinations of it. We cannot perceive a good action without approving it, without feeling inside a certain enjoyment of it, nor can we perceive an evil action without disapproving of the action itself and being disgusted by it. Yet recognizing an evil action and disapproving of it are affirmative features of the soul, expressions of the mental powers of knowing and desiring, and elements of perfection which, in this connection, must be gratifying and enjoyable. It is the same for all other good and evil properties, merits and deficiencies, virtues and shortcomings of things. They must be considered in two sorts of relations, in relation to the *object* or to the matter which they are part of outside us and in relation to the *mind's projection* or the thinking entity's perception of them. In both relationships what is good is pleasant, i.e., it is not only an element of the perfection in the object, but rather, considered as a representation, it also adds to the affirmative features of the thinking entity, and, in both considerations, it necessarily makes us fond of it. The evil, on the other hand, is unpleasant from the side of the object, considered as the original picture [*Urbild*] outside us, because in this connection it consists in a deficiency, a negation of some sort of content. However, considered as a representation, a picture within us that engages the soul's capacities of knowing and desiring, the representation of what is evil is itself an element of the soul's perfection and brings with it something quite pleasant that we by no means would prefer not to feel than to feel.

According to this remark, the imperfect, evil, and deficient always arouse a mixed feeling that is composed of an element of dissatisfaction with the object and satisfaction with the representation of it. Considered as a whole, such a representation will be pleasant or unpleasant, depending upon whether the relation to the object or the relation to us is weightier, becomes the dominant relation, and obscures or even suppresses the other. If the object gets too close to us, if we regard it as a part of us or even as ourselves, the pleasant character of the representation completely disappears, and the relation to the subject immediately becomes an unpleasant relation to us since here subject and object collapse, as it were, into one another. The representation then has nothing pleasant about it but rather will be simply painful. We can rightly say of this sort of representation that we would prefer not to have it than to have it. For every impulse of the soul sets itself against this representation and seeks to get rid of it.

Sensed pain is of this sort. Insofar as its object is the body from which we are not in a position to separate ourselves, the distinction between the relations, noted above, disappears. For mind's projection and object are united in the most inseparable manner. Thus, for us there is nothing pleasant about this sentiment, as long as it is present and holds sway in the soul. Merely in its absence, if we are freed from it, does it leave behind a memory that we call *being happy* and is in fact a pleasant sentiment, but this is not the place to consider it. – The consciousness of a deficiency in us in body or soul, the consciousness of an evil that adheres to us or is impending, and so forth, is absolutely unpleasant in most cases and we would prefer not to have such a representation at all since in this case we are as much the object as the projection of the evil and, hence, probably cannot distinguish the relation to us that, in the representation, is supposed to be pleasant. Still, traces of subjective satisfaction continue to reveal themselves here. Fear and terror, for example, are not entirely devoid of charm for the soul. Otherwise, how would they be able to be appreciated in what is sublime and majestic? – Indeed, if fear becomes quite palpable and takes complete control of the soul, then we are very often in danger of doing precisely what we are so afraid of. If we look down from a dizzying height, the body moves as it were mechanically and takes up precisely the position which is the most dangerous for it. I have known a melancholy soul who feared saying certain words more than death, and, in the fear of having articulated them against his will, he repeated them countless times. The danger itself has such a charm for human beings that everyone strives to become more closely acquainted with a lesser or greater degree of the same. To their great vexation, the educators of young men have very often made the same remark. If one portrays too vividly the danger that is connected with a certain action, one merely arouses in the noblest minds an all the more powerful drive to withstand the challenge that the danger presents. It is true, if the danger is surmountable, the concept of *courage* comes along and seduces the brave youth to put his powers to the test in the face of the danger, since courage is one of the greatest perfections of the human being. But even where the danger cannot be overcome, the soul always finds something attractive about it. If a phoenix were to appear or the head of Medusa were to be seen, I believe that each of us would shrink from the danger and turn his eyes away but just as certainly have to withstand a powerful attraction and contend, as it were, with himself.

If the evil does not affect us ourselves, but rather our fellow creatures, then it depends upon temperament and education. Crude minds which do not so easily feel sympathy with other beings, can take pleasure in spectacles where their fellow creatures suffer and are miserable.

Bullfights, racks, insane asylums, bloody scaffoldings for executions, and the like appeal to them far more strongly than does the depiction of the most moving story, and, as unethical as it might be, what the crudest minds do must have its basis in the nature of the human being. In the first part, to be sure, I have correctly distinguished the cases where, due to a harmful indulgence, the sympathy must be suppressed if the audience wants to feel pleasure and the cases where the pleasure of the audience is grounded solely and singularly in the sympathy which is aroused by the suffering of fellow creatures. Even the causes of the pleasure which I presented there still appear to me not unfounded. In the first case one diverts attention away from the suffering of living creatures and looks merely at the agent's good properties that give us pleasure; in the second case it is the love combined with the suffering, that is so very alluring. These considerations are based upon the nature of the human soul, but they are not the only causes of the pleasure afforded us by stirring objects. The nominal definition touched on at the beginning of this essay can mislead one into believing that each representation of some objective imperfection is absolutely unpleasant. But how is it that sorrowful spectacles can nonetheless be very pleasant? In order to salvage the assumption that the basic definition is true, one must search for the objective perfections which somehow flow, un-noticed, into the experience and are, as one believes, the sole causes of the pleasure. However, according to the observation I made above, there is, independently of these causes, a source of pleasure that is far more universal. I have shown that the objective imperfection arouses no sheer discontent, but rather a mixed sentiment. On the side of the object and in relation to it, we feel, to be sure, discontent and disfavor in the intuitive knowledge of its deficiencies. But on the side of mind's projection, the soul's powers of knowing and desiring are engaged, that is to say, its reality is enhanced and this must of necessity cause pleasure and satisfaction. As long as an observer is not sensitive enough to sympathize with the suffering being, as long as he does not see himself in his fellow creature but, instead, is sufficiently thick-skinned to put himself at a certain distance from others, then he is quite capable of separating the objective from the subjective and regarding the suffering of his fellow creatures, particularly when he is not responsible for it, with a kind of satisfaction.

Hence, it was not right for me to criticize Du Bos for saying that the soul longs merely to be moved, even it is to be moved by unpleasant representations. This is true in the most precise sense of the word since, in relation to the mind's projection, the movement and stirring which is produced in the soul by unpleasant representations cannot be anything else but pleasant. To be sure, like the will, pleasure is based on nothing else but a genuine or apparent good. But this good may not always be sought in the object outside us, in the original picture. Even the deficiencies and evils of the object can, as representations, as determinations of the thinking projection, be good and pleasant. If it is the case that the soul finds nothing pleasant in certain emotions and wishes to be able to divest itself of them completely, then this happens only if we ourselves are the object of them or if the object comes so close to us that we are accustomed to put ourselves in its place and to empathize in the liveliest way with everything that affects it. The objective side of the representation will then take complete control of the soul and suppress the subjective side.

The gruesome objects of nature that amuse crude people are too violent for more sensitive and better educated minds. Their sympathy with their fellow creatures is too vivid. Placing themselves in the position of the one suffering, they feel his pains as their own and, as a result, enfeeble the pleasant side of the representation too much. If those sorts of representations are to please them, then the objective side of the representations must be weakened, set at some distance, or moderated and obscured by neighboring concepts. The most terrifying events also please them, but events of this sort in tales and, of course, tales of bygone times and faraway places rather than in nature. They read with pleasure and satisfaction the history of major upheavals and troubled periods of which they certainly could not have been spectators. The gentlest souls or, to speak with the poet, the *most tenderhearted* souls of children delight in the telling of tales of terrifying adventures, tales from prehistorical times; they delight and tremble with fear. To ascribe these innocent amusements to an innate maliciousness, a natural joy at others' misfortune, would be to think of the nature of the human soul in a way that is more than misanthropic. Lucretius absolved it of this criticism long ago:

Non quia vexari quemquam'st jucunda voluptas;

He adds:

137

Sed quibus ipse malis careas, quia cernere suave'st.[3]

But a far better account can be given of such phenomena on the basis of our earlier observations. As soon as we are put in the position of separating the relation to ourselves from the relation to the object, the awareness of the evil, the disapproval of it, and the expression of disgust with the scourge are very attractive preoccupations of the soul, which cannot take place without a sense of satisfaction.

Another means of rendering the most terrifying events pleasant to gentle minds is the imitation by art, on the stage, on the canvas, and in marble, since an inner consciousness that we have an imitation and nothing genuine before our eyes moderates the strength of the objective disgust and, as it were, elevates the subjective side of the representation. It is true, the soul's sentient knowledge and capacities to desire are deceived by art and the imagination is so swept away that at times we forget every sign that it is an imitation and fancy that we truly see nature. But this magic lasts only as long as is necessary to give our conception of the object the proper vitality and fire. In order to have the most pleasure, we have accustomed ourselves to diverting attention from everything that could disturb the deception and directing attention only at what sustains it. However, as soon as the relation to the object begins to become unpleasant, a thousand factors remind us that we are looking at a mere imitation. Added to this is the fact that art adorns the representation with many sorts of beauties which strengthen the pleasant sentiment and help attenuate the unpleasant reference to the object.

By this means it is possible to grasp why people who are not accustomed to the illusory representations do not enjoy dramatic tragedies. We have seen that a certain refinement is required to abandon oneself to the illusion and to relinquish consciousness of the present to it as long as it is pleasurable. However, as soon as it begins to become unpleasant, it is necessary to rescind the attentiveness and let the spirit be present. Whoever is not accustomed to this, feels bored as long as he is not caught up in the illusion. As soon as art exercises its power to deceive him and seduce his senses against his will, he feels a conflict, sometimes annoying, sometimes ridiculous, between his reason and his

---

[3] *De rerum natura*, II. 3–4: "Not because another's adversity is scrumptiously satisfying;/ But because it is sweet to see what afflictions you're spared." Cf. Lucretius, *De rerum natura*, tr. W. H. D. Rouse, rev. Martin Ferguson Smith, 2nd edn. (Cambridge, Mass., Harvard University Press, 1982), pp. 94–5.

imagination. The former reminds him at an inappropriate time of the imitation, and the latter wants nonetheless to persuade him that he is beholding nature. Thus one often hears the common man burst out in loud laughter during the most moving passages of a tragedy. This laughter does real credit, as the dramaturge notes somewhere quite correctly, both to the playwright and the actors. It is proof that their artistry has been powerful enough to make a lively impression on the most inexperienced member of the audience, someone who is not used to letting his senses be deceived.

The difference between the material of the imitation and the material of nature, the marble and the canvas are the most obvious sensed features which, without damaging the art, call the attention back from the illusion whenever necessary. Because of this, one also sees why the closer that painted statues come to nature, the more unpleasant they are. I believe that the most beautiful statues, painted by the greatest artists, could not be contemplated without revulsion. Life-size and fully clothed wax figures leave an impression that is quite disgusting. Since no sensed feature conveys to us that we have a mere imitation before us, we are put off by the lack of the sign of life: movement. In miniature or bas-relief, the sight would be even more painful since here, despite the art, imitation of nature can be quite easily discerned.

There is an infantile taste which is offended by the imitation of something unpleasant if the expression is strong and sketches the object in a lively way. To satisfy this sort of taste, the objective side of the representation would have to be weakened too much, that is to say, the illusion itself would have to be frustrated. By this means the play would lose its charm and become tasteless. Art must summon all the powers of genius to make the imitation and the illusion sustained by it complete, and art can certainly leave it to contingent circumstances, to the adornment, to the place, the material, and a thousand other things that do not fall under its sway to provide the soul with the necessary reminder that it has art and not nature before it. This consideration provides a basis for determining the boundaries both for the playwright and for the actors, in other words, to what extent they must strive to be similar to nature.

I have said of gratification of the senses [*Sinnenlust*] that it consists in a feeling of the improved condition of the body that is pleasant to the soul. I have also regarded the body's movements as the object, the soul merely as a spectator that takes pleasure in this representation because it perceives an objective perfection; to be sure, the sort of perfection that comes closer to it since the object of the representation is an entity with which it is bound up in the most precise manner. But there is yet another source of the pleasure we take in sensuous gratifications that must not be disregarded. The soul enjoys the well-being of its body not merely as a spectator, that is to say, not merely in the general sense that it somehow perceives the perfection of an object with ease. Rather, by virtue of sensuous gratification, there accrues to the soul itself a no lesser degree of perfection, and by this means what is pleasant in the sentiment becomes incomparably more lively. Harmonious sentiments in the soul correspond to harmonious movements in the limbs and the senses. In a state of sensuous rapture, the entire neural structure is set in motion, one harmonious motion, and since this is the case, the entire basis of the soul, the entire system of sentiments and obscure feelings, must be moved and put into play as well, one harmonious play. By this means every capacity for sentient knowledge, every power of sensuously desiring is engaged in the way most conducive to it and sustained in the exercise. In other words, the soul itself is transported to a better condition. In this way, in the case of a sensuous gratification, the pleasure of the soul does not spring merely from the feeling of the body's well-being but at the same time from the reality which the harmonious engagement and exercise of the powers of sentiment and desire add to the soul itself.

I scarcely expect here the reproach that, by these considerations, I grant too much to sensuous rapture by elevating it to a perfection of the soul. For some time now people have moved far beyond the dismal moral doctrine which condemns all amusements of the senses and prescribes to human beings duties to which their creator has not ordained them. We are called in this life not only to improve our powers of understanding and willing, but also to educate feeling by means of sentient knowledge and to raise the obscure impulses of the soul to a higher perfection by means of sensuous pleasure. When we neglect the latter, we act as contrary to the intentions of the creator as when we neglect the former. We only make ourselves miserable when we lack a sense of proportion, preferring the trivial to the important, the lesser perfection to the higher one, the passing moment to the lasting future. To be sure, the enjoyment of anything sensuously gratifying furthers, at least for a short time, for a few moments, the well-being of the body as well as the perfection of the sentiments and impulses of our soul. But if the proper measure is exceeded and the ultimate purpose is missing, then the rapture brings both body and soul, but especially the soul, deleterious consequences which infinitely outweigh the good that it affords. If a person, while deliberating, considers the consequences, allows the higher determinations their importance, and only permits sensuous gratification a suitable share in his happiness, he obviously acts in accord with the intentions of his all-bountiful creator and can include the enjoyment of sensuous amusements among good actions.

What has been recalled here about sensuous gratification, holds *mutatis mutandis* also for sensuous pain. The soul perceives disharmony in the strain of fevers, imperfection in the movements of the limbs, and, as cited at the end of the Tenth letter, attains a feeling, composed of a thousand individual sentiments, of its body's imperfection and of the danger threatening it. But in this case, due to the agreement between the soul's sentiments and alterations in the limbs and senses, a subjective imperfection is added to this objective imperfection which the soul perceives as an observer. If some disorder or discord transpires in the movements and alterations of the nerves, as happens in the case of pain, then this is also communicated to the soul and disrupts the system of sentiments and obscure drives. Thus, a lack of harmony arises in the depths of the soul, an impaired reality, and the consciousness or even the obscure feelings of that reality cannot be anything but unpleasant to the soul.

In the *conclusion* to the letters I had my philosopher express some thoughts on mixed sentiments, composed of gratification and its opposite. However, the matter is too vast for someone to be able to be cover it so quickly. From this simple mixture of pleasure and displeasure spring countless sorts of sentiments, all of which are distinct from one another and reveal their identities outwardly by completely diverse features. This is the nature of our soul! When it cannot distinguish two sentiments which it has simultaneously, it combines them into one phenomenon which is distinct from both and has almost no similarity with them. If one, however, alters the slightest circumstance in the simple sentiments, then the phenomenon that springs from them will also be changed and take on a completely different form. Sympathy, for example, is a mixed sentiment composed of love for an object and discontent at its misfortune. The movements through which sympathy reveals itself are distinct from the simple symptoms of love as well as discontent. But how diverse this phenomenon can be! Were one to change merely the time in the pitied misfortune, the suffering would reveal its identity by means of completely different characteristics. Through our sorrowful sentiments we sympathize with Electra, weeping over the urn of her brother, since she regards the misfortune as over and done with and grieves for what she has lost. What we feel about Philoctetes' pains[4] is likewise sympathy but of a somewhat different sort. For the torment that this virtuous man must endure is present and overcomes him before our eyes. But if Oedipus is horrified as the great secret suddenly unfolds, if Monima is terrified as she sees the jealous Mithridates begin to fade,[5] if the virtuous Desdemona fears for herself when she hears her gentle Othello speak so threateningly to her, what do we feel then? Sympathy, every time! But sympathetic horror, sympathetic fear, sympathetic terror. The movements are diverse, but the essence of the movements is one and the same in each case. For since every love is bound up with the willingness to put ourselves in the position of the beloved, we must share all sorts of suffering or pathos with the beloved person, what one very emphatically calls *sympathy*. Why, then, should it not be possible for fear, terror, anger, jealousy, desire for revenge, and, in general, all sorts of unpleasant sentiments, even envy, to arise from sympathy? – One sees from this how very clumsy it was for most critics to divide the tragic passions into terror and sympathy. Terror and sympathy! Is theatrical terror, then, not sympathy? For whom does the audience feel terror when Merope draws the dagger on her own son? Certainly not for themselves but for Aegis whose survival is everyone's wish and for the deceived queen who regards him as the murderer of her son.[6] If we want, however, to call "sympathy" the mere discontent about the evil presently confronting another, then we have to distinguish, not the terror, but all other passions communicated to us by someone else, from

---

[4] Electra, Philoctetes, and Oedipus are protagonists of the correspondingly named Sophoclean tragedies to which Mendelssohn is alluding here.

[5] In Act III, Scene v of Racine's *Mithridates* (Paris, 1673), King Mithridates turns pale as Monima, his fiancée, admits her love for his son, Xiphares.

[6] In Act III, Scene iv of Voltaire's *Mérope* (Paris, 1743), Queen Mérope is on the verge of killing her son whom she sent away as a child for his safety and whom she does not now recognize but takes for her son's killer.

sympathy proper.* – In the conclusion that has been cited, I touched on this consideration a little and, on the basis of it, sought to explain why we find the sad emotions played out on stage so pleasant.

The mixed sentiments have the peculiar property of not being as gentle as pure pleasure, of course, but of penetrating deeper into the mind and appearing to sustain themselves there longer. What is merely pleasant quickly leads to a point of satiation and ultimately tedium. Our desire always extends further than our enjoyment and if it does not find complete fulfillment, the mind longs for change. By contrast, the unpleasant mixed with the pleasant captures our attention and prevents us from being prematurely sated. Everyday experience shows that, when it comes to the sense of taste, sweetness alone quickly becomes boring if it is not mixed with something sour. What has been noted here, however, is universally the case, and it is also confirmed by experience of emotions. Anger and grief are not by any means as pleasant as jokes and cheerfulness, and yet, for someone who believes himself justified in feeling angry or grieved, they have a charm so inexpressible that more than stoic self-control is needed to get rid of them. Nothing is more gratifying to an angry person than his indignation; someone mourning the loss of a friend retreats into solitude in order to indulge his sense of grief without being disturbed. It is readily apparent to everyone that grief is a mixture of pleasant and unpleasant sentiments, and the same can be just as easily established with regard to

---

* In his *Dramaturgy*, with his characteristic philosophical acuteness, Lessing proves that Aristotle posited, not *terror* and *sympathy*, but *fear* and *sympathy*.[7] By "fear" he understands, in his explanation of Aristotle, what we feel for ourselves, by "sympathy" what we feel for our fellow man. What is thereby gained is at least the internal consistency of what the wise Greek says. For these are his thoughts, expressed by him in diverse ways, namely, that we take ourselves into consideration during the dramatic presentation of tragedy. But I deny that we do this. At least it is not necessary if we are supposed to sympathize with others. How often is the object of sympathy in circumstances of the sort that we could never be in? It cannot, of course, be denied that we are more easily moved to be sympathetic if we are in similar circumstances, if we have to endure or fear a similar misfortune. But this does not come, as Aristotle appears to believe, from selfish fear since it is certainly not selfishness that opens our heart up to sympathy. What intensifies our sympathy is rather the livelier *feeling we ourselves have* of a similar evil since that feeling is what enables us to regard the suffering soul as someone all the more deserving of our pity. For an identical reason, each animal of a certain species sympathizes merely with the cry of another animal of the same species since it connects this sound, in the most intense manner imaginable, with the inner suffering which it has itself felt at another time. This thought might deserve to be elaborated further; but this is not the place for that.

7 Aristotle, *Poetics* 1449 b 23; Gotthold Ephraim Lessing, *Hamburgische Dramaturgie*, Sections 74–82 (1768) in *Werke*, ed. Herbert G. Göpfert (Munich: Hanser, 1973), pp. 574–623.

anger. One knows that anger is composed of the discontent over an insult that has been received and the desire to avenge it. These images reverberate together in an enraged mind and produce completely opposite movements as first one, then another image gains the upper hand. Blood soon rushes into the extremities of an angry person, the eyes protrude and become fiery, the face turns red as he stomps his feet, swings his fists in the air, and raves like a madman; these are the telltale signs that the desire for revenge is in control. The blood quickly returns to the heart, the wild fire in his eyes dies out as they sink back into their sockets, the face regains its normal paleness, and his external limbs hang powerlessly at his side; these are the unmistakable signs that his discontent over the insult now prevails. This conflict of sentiments in the mind of someone angry has been sketched splendidly by the poet:

> Now he must either impotently sink down
> Or his benumbed blood must become a fire once more
> And violently lift him up again. It surged and
> Became inflamed and gushed upwards from the swelling
> Heart into his countenance. . .
> And he leapt up and stepped high out of his ranks and became
> incensed.[8]

If the anger does not lack the desire to avenge itself, the enraged mind that in the heat of passion loves revenge as its happiness will revel in this image, and it will be difficult for it to heed reason's reminders to the contrary. Anger accordingly belongs to the mixed sentiments, and hence the powerful attraction which an irate mind finds in it.

An immense object that we can contemplate as a whole but cannot comprehend likewise arouses a mixed sentiment of gratification and its opposite, a sentiment which initially sets off a trembling sensation and, if we continue to contemplate it, a kind of dizziness. This immenseness may consist in an extended or unextended, constant or variable magnitude [*Größe*]; but the sentiment in each case is the same. The unfathomable world of the sea, a far-reaching plain, the innumerable legions of stars, the eternity of time, every height and depth that exhausts us, a great genius, great virtues that we admire but cannot attain; who can look upon these things without trembling? Who can

---

[8]   Friedrich Gottlieb Klopstock, *Der Messias*, 3 vols. (*Songs I–III* [Bremen, 1748]; *Songs IV–V* [Halle, 1752]; *Songs VI–X* [Copenhagen, 1755]); ed. Elisabeth Höpker-Herberg, 2 vols. (Berlin and New York, de Gruyter, 1974), vol. 1, Bk. I, Song 4, ll.271–6, p. 72.

continue to feast his eyes upon them without experiencing a pleasant sort of dizziness? This sentiment is composed of gratification and its opposite. The magnitude of the object affords us gratification, but our inability to comprehend its boundaries adds a certain degree of bitterness to this gratification, making it all the more alluring. Still, the following difference is to be noted. If the large object, in regard to its immensity, presents us with no multiplicity to contemplate (as in the case of a placid lake or a fruitless plain that is not punctuated by any objects), the dizziness ultimately changes into a kind of revulsion at the monotonousness of the object, discontent gains the upper hand, and we must turn the confused look away from the object. This conforms perfectly to the theory of sentiments, and it is quite amply confirmed by everyday experience. By contrast, the immensity of the structure of the world, the magnitude of an amazing genius or of sublime virtues are as differentiated as they are enormous, as perfect as they are differentiated, and the discontent bound up with the contemplation of them is grounded in our feebleness. Thus they afford an inexpressible pleasure of which the soul can never get enough. What soulful sentiments surprise us when we consider the immeasurable perfection of God! Our inability accompanies us on this flight, to be sure, and drags us back into the dust. But the ecstasy over that infinity and the displeasure with our own nothingness blend together into a holy trembling, a more than rapturous sentiment. After a brief pause we try a second and a third time, and the source of pleasure is as inexhaustible as before. No sense of tedium or revulsion, no discontent with this or that side of the object intermingles with our sentiment here, and we would be happy if our entire life could be an uninterrupted attempt to grasp the divine perfection.

Contemplation of the divine perfection itself is, as far as the object is concerned, infinitely exalted beyond every defect. If such contemplation, as far as we are concerned, can nonetheless not be separated from discontent with our own feebleness, then one can with some certainty conclude that, for a finite being, there is absolutely no pure pleasure. Still, it is even less the case that there is a pure displeasure. The object of pure pleasure at least exists and exists necessarily; but the object of unmixed displeasure is not to be found even in the realm of possibility and, hence, is an absurdity. Even the chimerical concept which people make of the most imperfect entity must afford some pleasure; otherwise our poets would not be able to make such profitable use of it. It is true, in order to please our imagination they invest their fictitious entity with all the more power and knowledge, the higher they allow its moral maliciousness to climb. But reason finds the contrast ridiculous and is ashamed of the imagination for being able to be amused by so monstrous an image.

Everything evil that is to be encountered in nature and can simply be conceived is mixed with something good. The most perfect evil would be an entity to which nothing but negative features are ascribable, sheer absurdity! Given the fact, as has been elaborated in the foregoing, that the affirmative features of a thing always arouse gratification if they can be intuitively known, then the representation of no entity, even considered in relation to the object, can be merely unpleasant. The determinations of content, without which no entity is thinkable, never fail to arouse a corresponding degree of comfortableness, by means of which the representation of what is imperfect in nature is still far more composite (than the imperfection itself). The positive determinations produce a twofold satisfaction, in the twofold relation to the object and to the thinking subject, a theme treated at length at the beginning of this essay. The negative determinations, by contrast, arouse dissatisfaction in relation to the object and satisfaction in relation to the mind's projection which intuitively knows and disapproves the object. All these considerations must be compared with one another and weighed against one another before the soul can know whether the pleasant or the unpleasant outweighs the other. The simplest sentiments which the objects of nature afford us are mixed and interwoven in a wondrous fashion with one another. How much more wonderful must they become if, at the same time, one looks to the neighboring concepts which are bound up with each representation in an inexpressibly multiple manner by the inner as well as the external connection of things, by space and time, cause and effect, similarity and contrast!

When I wrote the "Letters on sentiments" ["On sentiments"] I had, to be sure, a flimsy concept of the nature of mixed sentiments. But I only saw a flickering of the astonishing and myriad effects of them until I had the opportunity to read the splendid English work on the sublime and the beautiful for the *Library of Fine Sciences*.[9] The author of the

---

9   Edmund Burke, *A Philosophical Enquiry into the Origin of Our Ideas of the Sublime and the Beautiful* (London, 1757); ed. with an introduction by James T. Boulton (Notre Dame, University of Notre Dame Press, 1968). Moses Mendelssohn, "Philosophische Untersuchung des Ursprungs unserer Ideen vom Erhabenen und Schönen," *Bibliothek der schönen Wissenschaften*, 3, 2 (1758); reprinted in Jubilee edition, vol. 4, pp. 216–36.

work is a keen observer of nature. He heaps observation on top of observation, each of which is as basic as it is discerning. Yet, whenever it comes down to explaining these observations on the basis of the nature of the soul, his shortcomings become apparent. One sees that he was unacquainted with the psychology developed by German philosophers. Mere experience was not sufficient for him to be able see these profound doctrines in connection with one another. The basic principle that intuitive knowledge of perfection is gratifying was regarded by him as a mere hypothesis and the slightest experience which seemed to contradict the hypothesis was reason enough for him to reject it. However, anyone convinced that this basic principle of sentiments is no hypothesis, but rather an established and irrefutable truth is not going to allow experience to lead him astray, however much it may appear to present the opposite. Such a person considers the matter further and finds the most precise kinship between reason and experience, something that frequently is to be found only with difficulty, though it is always at hand.

In no way do I flatter myself with having provided the psychological basis for all the experiences noted by the Englishman. Our sentiments have such depths that poking my eye in their direction is all too fatuous. I wish rather, by my effort here, to have encouraged a philosophical mind to undertake this worthwhile investigation. My friend still owes the world a translation that he promised to give of the English work along with emendations and notes.[10] If only he would fulfill my wish!

Given the astonishing mixture of pleasant and unpleasant sentiments which are interwoven in a way infinitely more refined than that of the most delicate network of fibers in the human body, one must surely wonder at philosophers who have wanted to compute the sums of pleasant and unpleasant sentiments in human life and compare them. The author of the "Essay on Moral Philosophy" imagined this consideration in a very facile manner.[*] He calls the

---

[*] *Essai de philosophie morale.*[11]

[10] Lessing is the friend.

[11] P. L. Moreau de Maupertuis, *Essai de philosophie morale* (London, 1750); reprint of 1758 Berlin edition in *Oeuvres*, introduction by Giorgio Tonelli (Hildesheim and New York, Olms, 1974), vol. 1, pp. 171–252. A pirated edition with a Berlin imprint was available in 1749 (see David Beeson, *Maupertuis: An Intellectual Life* (Oxford, The Voltaire Foundation, 1992), p. 194, n. 36).

product of the strength of a pleasant sentiment as long as it persists "the moment of happiness" and the sum of these moments "human happiness." He subtracts from this sum the sum of the moments of unpleasant sentiments, and so forth. I do not have at hand the little work in which this computation was laid down as the foundation. But if my memory serves me right, then nothing can be more unreflective than this idea. Two presuppositions without which the idea cannot get off the ground are at odds with both reason and experience. One must assume, first, that our sentiments are either sheer gratification or sheer discontent and, second, that each discontent absolutely decreases the sum of happiness. Is it still necessary to refute this chimera?

Some philosophers who think they understand the mass and weight of sentiments have endorsed the notion that there must be more misfortune than good fortune in the world since one hears more crying than laughter. – To maintain this thought seriously one must have laughed more than he has reflected in his life. It is false that crying is always a sign of misfortune in this life and just as false that laughter is always a sign of good fortune. At first glance these two movements appear to be diametrically opposed to one another, and yet they have completely the same origin in nature just as black and white appear to be opposed to one another and in nature are very closely related. For all phenomena this is quite usual, and since the emotions are phenomena, one should not be amazed when the inference from the appearance to the truth can no more be drawn in their cases than it can in the others.

Crying is a sentiment that is a mixture of gratification and discontent, springing from intuitive knowledge of the contrast between a perfection and an imperfection, both of which are quite proximate to us. Thus we cry when we feel sympathy; for the sympathy itself is founded on the contrast between a person's moral perfections and physical imperfections. So, too, we cry when we are happy and vividly remember our previous misfortune – these are tears of joy – or when we are unhappy and remember the previous good fortune – which really are the tears which our philosophers regard as signs of misfortune. But how false! If discontent over a present misfortune is so huge and vivid that it prevails in the soul, suppressing all adjoining concepts, then our eyes are dry, we stand there with petrified looks on our faces, and cannot cry.* Only when adjoining concepts are re-awakened in the soul, when we can compare our present misfortune with past good fortune, do we become melancholy. Only then does the heart become lighter and the blank stare soften into pleasureful tears which, for the one grieving, are more pleasant than the most alluring sensuous gratification. Is anything more needed to prove that crying is a sentiment composed of gratification and its opposite, and that a person is not always unhappy when he can let things come to tears?

Laughter is just as little an unerring sign of good fortune. Rather it is founded, as much as crying is, on a contrast between a perfection and an imperfection. The only difference is that this contrast must be of no importance and not be very proximate to us, if it is to be laughable. The foolishness of humans, which has important consequences, arouses sympathetic tears; however, the foolishness that is not dangerous makes it merely laughable or ridiculous. People call such a contrast an *absurdity* and thus say that everything laughable presupposes some absurdity. Every lack of harmony between means and end, cause and effect, between a person's character and behavior, between thoughts and the way that they are expressed, in general, every contrast of the great, venerable, illustrious, and very significant with the insignificant, despised, and small is laughable as long as the consequences of the contrast are not awkward for us. Think of that philosopher who sought the sublime divinity in the Egyptian temple with all its splendor and, on the altar, saw an ape to whom this proud building had been erected. He must have had to laugh at first. But very quickly he must have considered the tragic consequences of this brutish ignorance, and the object must then have been more repulsive than laughable. The audience laughs equally at Tartuffe's pranks and Orgon's simplemindedness as long as neither appears to have any dangerous consequences.[12] But the moment one sees the deceiver in all his light and the one deceived in

---

* Quin ipsa tanti pervicax clades mali
   Siccavit oculos: quodque in extremis solet,
   Periere lacrimae.[13]

[12] In Molière's *Le Tartuffe ou l'Imposteur* (Paris, 1669) the gullible Orgon almost loses his wife and possessions to the scheming Tartuffe, whom he has taken into his home as his spiritual director.

[13] Seneca, *Oedipus Rex*, ll. 57–9: "No, that persistent agony of so much evil/ Dried up eyes and, as usual in such desperate straits,/ Tears perished." Cf. *Seneca's Tragedies*, tr. Frank Justus Miller (Cambridge, Mass., Harvard University Press, 1938), vol. 1, pp. 432–3.

danger, the mood of laughter is transformed into disgust and sympathy. – The same circumstance can appear laughable to one person and depress someone else, depending upon whether they participate more or less in the fate of the affected person. The foolishness of our friends commonly vexes us, pleases enemies, and amuses persons who are neutral. Hence, laughter is a particular emotion that accompanies a certain sort of mixed sentiment but, in and for itself, is as little necessary to our happiness as the trembling sentiment we have when we behold something immensely large. The philosopher who wept over the foolishness of human beings was perhaps happier than the individual who constantly laughed about it.

Like various other errors in theoretical philosophy, these false conceptions of the measure of happiness are the fruits of the refined Epicureanism that some philosophers have pulled out of the dust once again. They place the highest good – the final purpose of all our wishes and what all inclinations, needs, desires, and passions in the end reduce to – in the pleasant sentiment instead of analyzing it further, as they should, and looking for it either, with the Stoics, in a state of harmony with nature or, with modern philosophers, in the original drive for perfection. To be sure, every good act, every virtuous action is joined with a sentiment of the soul that is sweeter than all sensuous gratification. In practical ethics, one can accordingly countenance the basic principle of pleasant sentiments without danger and, by means of it, even awaken in someone a love for virtue by sharpening his feelings and making them capable of a higher level of rapture, to be found only in doing what is good. But one must not transport this principle into theoretical ethics, where there can be no spurious principles without spurious consequences. Our philosophers prove irrefutably – I have also presented such a proof in the "Letters on sentiments" ["On sentiments"] – that the power of our soul, of each spirit generally, is originally oriented to the good and perfect, and that the choice of a spirit which is free could not possibly have anything but perfection as its sufficient reason. Since perfection is the only thing that accords with the nature of an entity that is free, it is one and the same whether perfection or being in accord with our nature is posited as the highest good, the *primum naturale*, [the naturally first thing] the aim of all our wishes. In order to prevent any misunderstanding, however, one has to make clear to himself what is meant by this "being in accord with nature."

As far as pleasant sentiments are concerned, they are an effect of perfection, a gift of heaven inseparable from knowledge and from the choice of the good. But they can be analyzed and reduced to the original drive for perfection. In the soul, a pleasant sentiment is nothing other than the *clear, but indistinct intuiting of perfection*, and, insofar as it is accompanied by a sensuous gratification, by a certain comfortableness on the part of the body or a harmonious tension of neural fibers, the soul also enjoys a sensuous, but indistinct intuiting of the perfection of its body. I have put this matter beyond doubt in the "Tenth letter on sentiments" ["On sentiments"]. From this it then follows irrefutably that everything, in the final analysis, must amount to the original drive for perfection. For one flatters himself in vain of having arrived at the ultimate ground of things when one has not ascended to its essence. For it is the perfection and not the pleasant sentiment that is immediately grounded in the essence of a spirit. Thus, too, perfection and not pleasant sentiment must be called "the supreme ground [*der höchste Grund*] of all free actions," that is to say, "the *highest good*" [*das höchste Gut*].

Those who are fond of contesting every philosophical principle, may always object that in this manner we have made human beings into selfish creatures by referring everything to the human being and its perfection. A reasonable person simply laughs at this objection. It is the same melancholy whimsy of some fanatics who have scruples about finding pleasure in the love of God since they fear loving the supreme being selfishly. In order to endorse such a notion, one must know neither what love is nor what selfishness is. How can it be endorsed? Do I love my friend selfishly if I regard his well-being as my own, if I look upon everything good that crosses his path as if it had crossed my own path? Do I act selfishly towards my fatherland if I regard its prosperity as a part of my own happiness and seek to promote my own perfection in its perfection? Or does one believe that the principle of perfection allows me to close myself off within my own private enclave and transform everything around me into a miserable wasteland as long as I am promoting my own perfection? What an illusion! As if there could be a world in which a thinking being could *isolate* itself or as if a thinking creature that tears itself away from every bond and closes itself off within itself could also be perfect in itself, happy with itself! As if advancing the well-being of my fellow creatures, imitating God, and making everything around me more perfect (as much as I can and it is in my power to do), as if being proficient at doing what is good, at loving and being loved, as if being charitable, being generous, acting justly, defending freedom and virtue were not the innermost perfection of a thinking creature! As if true love of perfection could be envious, uncharitable, misanthropic and could delight in others' misfortunes like someone full of avarice or jealousy! These traits are selfish for their strength consists in selfishness. They would weaken if they were communicated or shared much like the warmth of an extinguished flame weakens when it flows over to neighboring objects. But true perfection is a living flame, constantly fanning out and becoming stronger and stronger the more it is able to fan out. The inclination to communicate itself and to reproduce the good that one enjoys is implanted in the soul as much as the instinct to preserve oneself. We become more perfect, if everything that surrounds us is perfect; we become happier if we are able to make everything around us happy.

No love, no friendship can exist without the benign reproduction of itself. Love is a readiness to take pleasure in someone else's happiness. That means, if one reduces the concepts of happiness and pleasure to their elements, that love is the readiness to regard another's progress to a higher level of perfection as an increase in our own perfection and, vice versa, the readiness to regard another's decline into some imperfection as a worsening of ourselves. In the case of the general love of humanity, this takes place to a lesser degree; but in the case of friendship this readiness grows into the inclination to put ourselves completely in the position of our friend and to feel everything that affects him as though it affected us ourselves. – In Philostratus' play[14] Ajax asks Achilles:

> "What heroic deeds were the most dangerous for you?"
> "Those that I undertook for my friends," he answered.
> "But which ones," Ajax continued, "came easiest to you?"
> "The very same ones," Achilles replied.
> Ajax asked further: "What wound caused you the most excruciating pain?"
> "The one that Hector inflicted on me," Achilles responded.
> "Hector?" Ajax rejoined, "as far as I know, he never inflicted a wound on you."
> "Oh, yes," Achilles said, "the most deadly wound; for he killed my friend Patroclus."

[14] *Heroicus*, ed. Ludo de Lannoy (Leipzig, Teubner, 1977), p. 63.

Far from canceling the mutual interest of moral entities or even weakening it in the slightest, the basic principle of perfection is instead the source of universal sympathy, of this brotherhood of spirits [*Verbrüderung der Geister*] – if I may be allowed the expression – which engulfs and entwines each person's own interest and the common interest in such a way that they can no longer be separated without destruction on all sides. No lifeless thing can become more perfect without an element of happiness being produced thereby in the realm of spirits, and this element reproduces itself endlessly through participation and ignites itself the more it ignites others. For if the essence of a spirit consists in thinking and willing, then it must itself become all the more perfect, the more perfect its concepts are and the more perfect the objects are which it imagines. Its happiness grows with the abundance and magnitude of the perfection which it has produced or advanced by its free will. Human politics strives for a goal which is attained to the highest possible degree in God's wise and peaceful government, namely, the goal of having each member advance what is best for the community by working on his own well-being. For no rational being can promote his true happiness without becoming a benefactor of the entire creation – so precisely, so inseparably do particular interests and universal interest hang together in the state ordained by God.

And the rebels in this state cannot escape the fate that they forever deserve in the human government. Due to an interest that they have woefully misunderstood, they detach their selfish existence from the whole and dissolve the bonds of universal kinship on their side. As a result, they become destroyers of their own happiness and moral death is the consequence of this moral dissolution. Contemplate the state of a soul in which the following thoughts are able to arise:

> No let not Nature's hand
> Keep the wild flood confin'd! Let order die!
> And let this world no longer be a stage
> To feed contention in a ling'ring act;
> But let one spirit of the first-born Cain
> Reign in all bosoms, that, each heart being set
> On bloody courses, the rude scene may end,
> And darkness be the burier of the dead![15]

---

[15]   Shakespeare, *Henry IV*, 2, Act I, 1.

And yet the wretch, for whom there is nothing but himself, is on the road to this horrifying curse. If he be granted what he is striving for, namely, the capacity to detach himself completely from everything, he will repeat in a cold-blooded manner all the curses of the raving Northumberland and, in the end, add merely the little prayer of that slave:

Unum me surpite morti![16]

But who does not see that this hatred of all creatures can no more exist with the true spirit of perfection than hatred of oneself can? This universal law, this nerve of happiness, runs through all parts of creation, blooms in the rose, stirs in the worm, and thinks, wills, and feels blissfully in the human being. The essence of God consists in perfection; it is the plan of creation, the source of all natural and supernatural events, the goal of all our desires and wishes, the guiding principle of our actions and omissions; it is the supreme principle in ethics, in politics, and in the arts and sciences of pleasure. It is the sun in the system of sciences, and without it everything falls back into night and confusion.

When one still used to search in philosophy for a particular principle for each phenomenon, one believed that one could explain even moral phenomena (which are so often contradictory) only by attributing two souls to each human being, one of which incited him to good, the other to evil. Like the two gods of Zoroaster, these souls must have constantly wrestled with one another for domination, and, as one gained the upper hand for a while and then the other, so they propelled the same individual at one time to virtue, at another time to vice. Various philosophers, the same ones who have seen the impossibility of a perfectly evil God, have nonetheless believed it possible to assume the existence of a perfectly evil soul in order to explain the origin of moral evil. I do not know whether one ought to number Xenophon among these philosophers or whether he is not serious when he has the remorseful Araspes (who has permitted himself, as it were, against his

---

[16] Horace, *Satires*, II. III. 283: "Snatch me alone from death!" Cf. Horace, *Satires, Epistles and Ars Poetica*, tr. H. Rushton Fairclough (Cambridge, Mass., Harvard University Press, 1966), pp. 176–7.

will to be overcome by an unpardonable love) say the following to Cyrus:[17]

> My King! Now I am utterly convinced that I have two completely different souls in me. The cunning sophist, love, has taught me this philosophical doctrine. One cannot possibly believe that one and the same soul is good and evil, virtuous and vice ridden at the same time, and thus self-contradictory. No! There must be two of them. If the good soul dominates, then we act appropriately; but if the evil soul dominates, then we act basely. I have experienced this. When, at odds with my duty, I sucked in the poison of forbidden love and was prepared to perform atrocities, the evil soul mastered me entirely. Because you stood by me, my King, the good soul has now risen up again. I am no longer the man I was. I have a completely different sense, a different reason, a different will. I am free and gladly distance myself from the object that previously I could no more leave behind than my own life.

This cunning sophist taught Araspes a very important truth. For, in contrast to Cyrus, this hero had maintained a while earlier that the will is perfectly free in matters of love and hate and that anyone who firmly resolves not to love does not run the slightest risk when he goes around with a beauty and shows her friendly courtesies. Because this ingenious story sheds light quite nicely on the doctrine of mediate and immediate freedom, allow me to cite a part of Araspes' conversation with Cyrus. Cyrus did not want to see the beautiful prisoner whose charms Araspes had so much extolled, and the more eloquent the young hero was in trying to arouse the prince's curiosity, the less he was able to move him to contemplate so extraordinary a beauty.

> "How is it possible," Araspes exclaimed in wonderment, "not to see her! For her beauty surpasses anything that you have ever seen!"
>
> "Precisely for this reason," the prince responded, "I want to avoid her. If I should allow myself to be so bewitched by the mere report of her beauty, her countenance would most likely bewitch me even more. I would then have to visit her more and more often, and, in the end, no time would be left for my most pressing

---

[17] Xenophon, *Cyropaedia*, VI. 1. 41; cf. Xenophon, *Cyropaedia*, tr. by Walter Miller (London, Heinemann, 1914), vol. 2, pp. 140–3. For the exchange between Araspas and Cyrus below, see ibid., pp. 2–13.

matters. The surest means of protecting oneself from fire is distance."

"You're joking, my Prince!" Araspes replied. "A beautiful face does not have so much power that it would be able to dominate the will itself and force people to set their duties aside. By no means does love have the nature of fire; for fire burns all combustible things without discrimination while love ignites only those who want to be ignited. We see that we have complete power over our inclinations in specific instances, and if we have it in specific instances then we must be able to have it in every instance. We do not want to fall in love with our kinsmen and relatives, and we do not do so. The laws forbid it. Would these laws not be as unfair as they are fruitless if they dictated something to us that was not in our power, in regard to which our will is not free?"

"That does not follow," Cyrus answered. "To be sure, it is up to us whether we want to begin to love; but whether we want to stop is not in our power. We have an immediate freedom to want what seems good to us and, duped as we are, we also believe ourselves completely free to deem whatever we want good. No, Araspes! In this respect our power is limited. We must flee the first impression, or our freedom is done for. Have you not witnessed examples of people who, before they loved, put great stock in their freedom and, afterwards, were forced into groveling slavery? Chains of iron or diamonds could not have tied them up any more firmly than do the shackles of love."

"Oh, indeed!" Araspes responded. "I have often heard such wretched souls whining, people who, if one were to believe their complaints, are in fact wretched and lost without help. You can hear them complaining just as miserably about life itself. However, so many doors stand open to them to take leave of this life, and yet they do not go but instead remain where they are. They have just as many ways to escape the bondage that exists merely in their imaginations, and they would rather complain. These slaves of love often become so shameless that, under the pretension of some irresistible compulsion, they lust for another's bed. But what do the laws do? Are these people somehow punished less than other thieves because of the pretext of their bondage and the obedience they owed their tyrants? Or you yourself, Cyrus! Would you ever pardon such a crime for this reason? No, my prince! Beauty is not responsible for in no way does it have the power to compel us to any sort of wickedness. Libertines compel themselves on the basis of their own instincts and shift the blame to love. An upright and virtuous man can love and admire everything that is beautiful without overstepping the bounds of well-being and righteousness in the slightest. What does a man of your virtue have to worry about, Cyrus? What temptation do you have to fear? – You see, my Prince! I am still perfectly in control of myself although I have seen the countess. I have even spoken with her, I have admired her intellect and her noble bearing as much as her beauty. But, for all that, I remain who I was, and you should find me as faithful to my duties as I ever was."

"Good," the king said. "Only make sure that you remain this way. I hereby commission you with the responsibility for the care of this distinguished prisoner. Take her under your protection, and let her feel her difficult situation as little as possible. Because of her attributes, she deserves to be treated in a considerate way, and her person can perhaps be of enormous importance to us in this war."

Araspes took over the office with pleasure. He visited the incomparable Panthea daily and took care of every possible matter in regard to serving her. The outcome of this story is well-known. The splendid qualities of these two persons and their daily dealings with one another made them friends. After a while, Araspes' friendship turned into the most passionate love, and one day, as the virtuous lady humbly refused his proposal with friendly admonitions, he went into such a rage of love that she had to send one of her slaves to the king. The king ordered Araspes to come before him and went alone with him into an adjoining tent. One can easily imagine how ashamed Araspes must have been when he came face to face with Cyrus, how he looked to the ground in embarrassment to avert the eyes of the king. The king sympathized with him and consoled him. The king made himself responsible for commissioning a young hero to so dangerous a post since he should have probably seen the danger. Araspes thanked the king for his generous sympathy that would otherwise be denied a guilty person, and his observations on the nature of the soul, cited earlier, followed.

One sees that Araspes did not understand the lesson that love had given him. The sophist simply taught him that our reason is not always our master, that the practical will, the resolve that breaks out into deeds, does not depend unqualifiably on judgments of the intellect, and that there must instead be something in the soul which in specific instances

157

could be mightier than reason and capable of bending the stiff neck of the wise man himself under its yoke. Araspes should have looked for this "something" in the soul itself, but he should not have made it into a particular entity, into a second soul. And how did he light upon the idea that an evil soul could be the origin of it? One could with just as much right ask: is there something to be so named? A more fortunate experience could have taught him that licit love, virtuous love itself, acts according to the same laws and could not, therefore, be on the basis of some other principle such as that of two suns, the one burning and the other warming.

Plato sought another way out of this labyrinth.[18] Since he saw quite well that we are able to want the evil, never as evil, but rather under the illusion of the good, he concluded that the basis of moral evil must always be a lack of insight. The passions, he states, can never overwhelm us since they are not compelling but persuasive. They must get it into our heads that the place to which they want to seduce us is good; they must deceive our powers of knowing before they can direct our will. Plato even cancels the distinction between the good and the pleasant, the evil and the unpleasant. If the good, indeed, appears unpleasant for a while and the evil pleasant, then in his opinion one is looking only at the present. As soon, however, as one takes the future into consideration, the unpleasant good must subsequently become all the more pleasant and the pleasant evil all the more unpleasant. One has, Plato says, to distinguish four different sorts of things: (1) the absolutely pleasant, (2) the absolutely unpleasant, (3) the pleasant that subsequently becomes unpleasant, and (4) the unpleasant that subsequently becomes pleasant. In regard to the first two, no seduction by the passions takes place. For the most rational passion cannot render the absolutely unpleasant pleasant. Only in regard to the last two can we deceive ourselves if we falsely weigh the present gratification against the future discontent or the present discontent against the future gratification, and on an incorrect scale believe ourselves to have found what is weightier. The basis of all moral evil lies, accordingly, in this erroneous weighing or reckoning, and each mistake for which we are responsible presupposes a mistake in knowing. From this Plato concludes that virtue is a science and, like other sciences, can be learned.

---

[18] *Protagoras* 352–7.

On the basis of this theory the moderns have constructed their doctrines of proficiencies or perfected habits and of the difference between speculative and pragmatic knowledge. Each insight that passes over into the capacity to desire and produces a desire or aversion is called an instance of *effective* or pragmatic knowledge. By contrast, the insight that has no marked influence on the capacity to desire is called an instance of *ineffective* or speculative knowledge. Each instance of effective knowledge is an active impulse of the soul, an impulse which, if it finds no resistance, unfailingly brings about its specific effect. If opposite impulses contend with one another and each maintains a weight equal to the other, they both lose their efficacy, and the soul passes into a state of indifference. If, however, the impulses are mightier on one side, the soul inclines to the side of the superior force and carries out or omits an action, depending upon whether the drives for or against it have had a more powerful effect on the soul. In analogy with the designations given in mechanics, the force of knowledge that actually comes to be exercised is called a *vital force*, while the force whose activity is checked by resistance is called a *dead force*. All of this can transpire in the mind by virtue of the nature of our souls, without the soul necessarily having to be conscious of this weighing of impulses against one another. It may feel a drive to do something or not to do it; it may also feel the resistance of contrary desires and aversions and decide to do what it feels the mightiest attraction to do. However, if the effective knowledge is distinct, then its effects on the capacity to desire are called "compelling reasons." In practice these compelling reasons often have to contend as much with obscure inclinations (which we have called "impulses of the soul") as with compelling reasons to do the opposite. The capacity of the soul to compare compelling reasons for and against an action and, in the wake of this comparison, to decide is called *freedom*.

These distinctions provide some light but they do not remove all difficulties. There is effective knowledge and there is also ineffective knowledge? Fine! But why is it that reason's distinct insight into things often is not as effective as the senses' indistinct knowledge of things? Why are impulses so often mightier than compelling reasons? – Further, what do proficiencies add to this matter? How can an instance of speculative knowledge through constant practice become pragmatic: in other words, how can a dead force by means of a proficiency, a perfected habit become a vital force?

To remove these difficulties, I will risk taking a step that is not without danger. I will attempt to determine the power of impulses mathematically by means of an hypothesis, and, on the basis of this more precise determination, I will attempt to explain an assortment of psychological phenomena which have been a stumbling block for many philosophers. If my hypothesis is false, then it can at least pave the way to the truth.

A representation or bit of knowledge is effective insofar as it presents us with a perfection or an imperfection. There is no longer any doubt about this; but I will go further. The degree of this effectiveness is proportional to (1) the degree of perfection. The greater a perfection is, the more pleasant is the intuitive knowledge of it and the mightier, too, is the drive to possess it. The degree of this effectiveness must be proportional, moreover, to (2) the degree of our knowledge. The more distinct, the more certain, the truer, and so on, our knowledge of one and the same perfection is, the more effective is the desire for it. And I will dare to add even a third proportion: the degree of effectiveness is proportional to (3) the speed involved. The less time is demanded to consider the perfection presented to us by a certain concept, the more pleasant is the intuitive knowledge of it and the more passionate the desire to enjoy it. According to this hypothesis, one could thus say that the effective force of impulses is (1) proportional to the magnitude of the good that they strive for, (2) proportional to the magnitude of our insight, and (3) inversely proportional to the time required to consider this good.*

If this presupposition is allowed to stand, then it follows quite naturally that a representation could often be less distinct, less certain,

---

* In many instances several other considerations could be added and make the proportion more complex, e.g., the difficulty or ease of possessing the good. Up to a certain degree the difficulty increases the desire for some matter. But if it oversteps this degree, then it defeats the desire. Much depends here on the confidence that we have in our powers, something that varies, depending upon the subject, time, circumstances, opportunity, and so on. In addition, there is novelty. To the extent that we cling to the usual, the novel also increases our desire, as long, that is, as it is not altogether alien. But it is not my purpose here to count all the variables of the proportion that can be calculated. I wanted merely to adduce the most essential aspects which have led me to the consideration that follows. Besides, all the conceivable variables of the proportion fall into three classes. They refer either (1) to the object or (2) to the soul or (3) to the relation of the object to the soul. They are, accordingly, objective, subjective, or relative. The variables of the proportion cited by me agree considerably with this division. The objective pertain to the magnitude of the true or apparent good, the subjective to the magnitude of our insight, and the relative to the enjoyment which the soul promises itself in regard to this object.

less true and yet have a greater power of working on the capacity to desire; namely, if it has in its object a greater magnitude of perfection or if it is possible to ponder this perfection more quickly. This should be easily conceivable on the basis of the rules of the complex proportion.

Thus emotions and sensuous sentiments are so often mightier than reason. Araspes could have said with as much right as Medea: *Aliud cupido, mens aliud suadet; video meliora proboque, deteriora sequor.*[19] By a correct, rational inference the soul can be convinced that A is good and yet decide on B if it perceives in B a greater number of good things and can consider them in a shorter time, even though it does not perceive those things in B as distinctly or as surely as it perceives what is good in A. If this happens, then the magnitude of impulses for B is mightier than the magnitude of motivating reasons for A, and B gains the advantage. Now the emotions are nothing but indistinct representations, arising simultaneously in the mind, of some considerable good or evil. Thus, the emotions are capable of defeating reason in two sorts of ways, through the quantity of good or bad involved and through the speed with which it can be pondered. Sensuous knowledge can likewise become mightier than reason by virtue of (1) the quantity of features that we perceive, (2) their constant presence,[*] and (3) the pace at which we entertain all the good things that are contained in a given instance of sensuous knowledge. Reason's distinct concepts cannot have the liveliness or array of features that a sensuous concept has. They are also not present to our soul as constantly, and they require some time and leisure to be pondered. Thus, for all their certainty, they have a slighter effect on the capacity to desire.

Many a person scurries to a height out of fear if a rampart is burned, even though no one would be shooting at him if he remained where he was and even though he recognized in advance that no harm could come to him. Other people are completely certain that the powder in a

---

[*] This, too, can provide a variable of the proportion. The representations of reason are not always present to the soul. In accordance with their nature, they alternate with related representations which take their place and divert attention further and further away from the matter at hand. The soul must exert itself to come back from this distraction to the rational foundations that are important to it here. What is sensed is, by contrast, always present without the slightest effort and is constantly appealing. Thus, it becomes easy for the senses to surprise the soul and become master of it in an unguarded moment if reason is, as it were, absent.

[19] Ovid, *Metamorphoses*, VII. 19–20: "Desires persuade me of one thing, my mind of another; I see and attest to what is better but pursue what is worse." Cf. Ovid, *Metamorphoses*, tr. Frank Justus Miller (Cambridge, Mass., Harvard University Press, 1966), vol. I, pp. 342–3.

vacuum-sealed shell cannot be ignited and yet refuse to be present at munitions tests. Why? An accounting of this can be given on the basis of my hypothesis. The conviction that no danger is at hand is based upon a rational inference, but the fear is based upon an almost intuitive knowledge. The rational inference is more convincing, but the intuitive knowledge is more vibrant and quicker. It thus exerts a stronger force on the capacity to desire, producing arbitrary movements in the body.

And for the same reason people are no longer upset if they have frequently seen a gun being fired. For habit can bring it about that the judgment "the bullet will not hit me" ensues as quickly as the idea of danger, awakened by the frightful blast, with the result that the fear disappears. Habit and practice transform every capacity of the soul into a proficiency; because of them, it is possible for an action to be performed speedily which, in the beginning, had required some time to carry out. This principle is well-known from everyday experience; however, it can also be proven on the basis of psychological principles.

A *proficiency* or *perfected habit* consists in a capacity to perform an action so speedily that we no longer are conscious of everything that we are doing in the process. Now for each performance it is necessary that there be a succession of concepts which harmonize with a series of arbitrary movements in the body at times. Those concepts follow all the more quickly upon one another in the soul, the more precisely and firmly they are combined with one another, that is to say, the more similarities and relationships our soul perceives among them. For our power of imagination is constantly engaged in passing from one concept to the other by virtue of associations. The more similarities and relationships we thus perceive among concepts, the easier and quicker it must be for the imagination to be able to run from one concept to the other and, finally, to run through the entire series.

Habit is a more frequent repetition of one and the same action. *Practice* is as well, only with the difference that the same action is diligently and deliberately repeated. Whenever we repeat some performance, we must ponder the series of concepts that are part of this performance, and these concepts are combined with one another more precisely each time. For the more often we entertain a series of concepts, the more relationships and proportions we perceive between them. Thus we can ponder more rapidly a succession of images that we have often had, until finally the concepts follow upon one another in so short a time that our soul is no longer distinctly conscious of them. If this occurs, our capability has been transformed into a proficiency. Thus it is explicable in a quite distinct way how, through habit and practice, each capacity of the soul can become a proficiency. This explanation, it is true, still does not explain what transpires in the human body as a proficiency emerges, how it happens that even our bodily capabilities can become proficiencies through constant practice. But I must leave this to those engaged in researching nature's secrets, who in general have not yet investigated suitably what habit is capable of doing to our bodies. It is sufficient for me, meanwhile, if I have given an account of what transpires in our soul in this regard.

If we have achieved a proficiency in the performance of a certain action, then the lack of consciousness does not prevent obscure impulses from having an influence on the capacity to desire and producing the arbitrary movements attributed to them. For what causes consciousness to stop? The quickness with which concepts succeed one another. Thus, although the degree of our knowledge is lessened by the lack of consciousness, the quantity of effective impulses remains the same in this case. For what is lost in the degree of knowledge is gained in the shortness of the time or in the quickness. This point is based once again on the rules of the complex proportion. According to our hypothesis, the force of the effective impulses is proportional to the degree of the good that we desire, to the degree of our knowledge, and to the speed with which we ponder matters. Given this hypothesis, the magnitude of the effect must remain the same if the speed increases to the same extent that the degree of our knowledge decreases.

This explains how, without thinking about it, we can perform a number of habitual actions which in the beginning required deliberations and reflection. What array of automatic movements are part of speaking and writing? How slowly and deliberately they proceed in the beginning and how quickly they follow upon one another, often unconscious to ourselves, once we have achieved a proficiency in this regard. At the outset the pianist must look at each key before he strikes it; through constant practice he brings things to the point where he can play the most splendid music almost without thinking about it. The same thing is true for a typesetter. At the outset he must look at each box before he can find a letter. However, after continuous practice we can scarcely follow the speed of his hands with our eyes and, before we even notice it, he finds what he is looking for. I believe that all these phenomena can be explained with complete clarity on the basis of what has been advanced above. We have seen how a proficiency arises through practice, how consciousness then ceases, and yet the effect on the capacity to desire is not any less because the concepts become obscure. If this effect on the capacity to desire finds no resistance, it produces in parts of the body the motions attributed to it [the effect]. Is anything more required to give an account of the phenomena cited as well as countless other wondrous phenomena?

Let us apply these remarks to ethics generally where they actually belong and where they in fact appear to have fruitful consequences. The ancients have already investigated whether virtue is a science and could be learned, that is to say, whether the basic principles of ethics suffice to form a virtuous man, whether the influence of the basic principles on actions is so reliable that one would be able to infer this with certainty from that and vice versa. On this score experience does not appear to support any universal assertion. Many people have great command of their inclinations and know how to direct them according to their principles. One sees them direct the course of their lives differently, as often as they alter their principles. Over others, on the other hand, the inclinations have far more power though they know how, through various kinds of sophistry, to change principles according to the inclinations dominating them. Still others oscillate between inclinations and principles and live, as it were, in contradiction with themselves. They have principles and live as if they had none; they are clever in theory and fools in practice.

On the basis of the observations made above, it is evident how these experiences that appear to contradict one another can be unified and explained. It is also evident how the basic principles must be constituted if they are to influence inclinations successfully. I merely submit the following additional remarks in order to make the application easier.

The philosopher can treat ethics as an object of curiosity, and then he is content, like the master of measurement, with dry demonstrations. A single proof is more convincing than countless probabilities. Yet while the demonstration convinces, it rarely arouses. What it teaches acquaints us with the ethically good and thus enhances one of the variables of the complex proportion, the degree of our knowledge. However, the other two variables must not be neglected. Every possible impulse to virtue must be set in motion, and impulses that are merely persuasive are no exception. Moreover, we must learn to ponder a number of compelling reasons quickly. The degree of perfection is increased by the number of impulses, and the time is decreased by the proficiency at pondering them; by this means the effectiveness of the ethically good must increase in a threefold proportion.

Enhancement of the compelling reasons depends not only on the number, but also on the importance of them. One must become acquainted with the true dignity of the human being and consider the sublimity of the human being's ethical nature in the proper light. As an ancient philosopher put it, if someone has the appropriate respect for himself, then he will be all the more inclined to obey the voice of virtue. The shortest path to ethical depravity is to have a low estimation of human nature. Initially this estimation presents itself in the form of self-knowledge, humility; but it is false as soon as it is applied more to the human race than to the individual and more to what we are as human beings than to what is peculiar to each of us on our own. Then it produces misanthropy rather than self-knowledge, pusillanimity rather than humility, demoralizing the powers of the mind far too much and making us almost indifferent towards good and evil. With true humility in his heart, a person may be proud of the human being's dignity and of the rank which humanity occupies in creation. We must be something important in our own eyes, and what we do and refrain from doing must be of some significance, if we are to espouse the cause of the good with zeal and energy. One should learn to consider every human action in connection with the ever-present lawgiver of nature and in relation to eternity. One should get used to having these considerations before one's eyes in every act that one performs. If one does this, a wholesome enthusiasm for virtue will be awakened in us, and each reason motivating us to be virtuous will attain an ethical majesty through which its influence and its effectiveness on the will is strengthened.

If one wants to learn to ponder more quickly the reasons motivating us to virtue (which was our second requirement), it is important to see that this can happen in two sorts of ways, through *constant practice* and through the aid of *intuitive knowledge*. We saw previously how practice can transform each capacity into a proficiency and the slowest rational inference into, as it were, a quick sentiment. Assume that a person ponders these inferences of practical philosophy frequently, considers them in their connection with one another, and has applied the principles drawn from them in cases that come before him. In important cases, such an individual will show wondrously how much power the demonstrated ethical doctrine is capable of having over inclinations and passions. However, if that individual has not had the appropriate practice, then reason comes for the most part too late. The concepts required for the moral inference do not succeed one another as quickly as the situation demands; as a result, their effect on the will is much weaker than the inclination that is resisting them. Virtue is, to be sure, a science and can be learned; but if it is be carried out, then it demands not merely scientific conviction, but also artful practice and proficiency. Indeed, anyone who grapples with the highest stage of ethical perfection and strives for the blessed condition of bringing the subordinate powers of the soul into a perfect harmony with the superior powers of the soul, must do this with the laws of nature just as the artist must do so with the rules of his art. He must continue practicing until, in the course of the exercise, he is no longer conscious of his rules,* in other words, until his principles have turned into inclinations and his virtue appears to be more natural instinct than reason. Then he has attained the heroic greatness which is far beyond the battle of common passions, and he exercises the most admirable virtue without vanity. If an individual's principles are on his lips in every good action performed by him, then virtue has not yet become second nature to him, and he has still failed to take an important step towards ethical perfection.

The second means of increasing the quickness is *intuitive knowledge.* We achieve this if we trace the abstracted concepts back to individual, determinate, and actual instances and carefully observe the application of the concepts. It is easy to grasp how the life of knowledge is enhanced by this artifice. In the application of the general inferences to particular cases we survey at a glance, as it were, all the general concepts' combinations and consequences that, in abstraction, we could only ponder little by little. Thus we reduce the time required to think over the moral inference and this reduction of the time must enhance the effectiveness, the vitality of the knowledge.

Here the inestimable utility of the fine sciences in ethics presents itself, not only for common intellects that are too shallow for the depths

---

* See the First part, p. 246f [end of Third letter].

of demonstration, but even for the philosopher himself if he does not want to ignore any means of awakening the dead knowledge of reason to genuine ethical life. Divine *rhetorical eloquence* not only knows how to bring to light a larger assortment of compelling reasons; in addition, if I may be allowed to express myself poetically, it transforms all impulses into penetrating arrows and dips them into the enchanting nectar which the goddess Suada[20] received from Venus, her mother. *History* transforms the general principles into examples and shows us the application of the abstracted concepts to genuine instances in nature. One does not always have the opportunity of utilizing one's principles oneself and by this means transforming symbolic knowledge into a case of intuitive knowledge. Because of this, the examples of others help us to recognize the consequences, the utility, and the use of general laws of nature in individual cases and to attain a proficiency which we can otherwise manage to have only through practice linked with danger. Finally, if an artist does not misuse the arts of *poetry*, *painting*, and *sculpture* for some ignoble purpose, these arts show us ethical rules in examples that are fictional and have been beautified by the art, examples which again animate knowledge; each dry truth is transformed into an ardent and sensuous intuition. Indeed, in certain instances fictional examples are preferable to genuine examples from history, as Lessing has shown quite clearly in his "Essays on the Fable."[21]

However, someone who desires to be virtuous can no more arrive at his goal by the path of intuitive knowledge alone than he can be satisfied with symbolic knowledge. In the first place, because it only persuades but does not convince, it cannot yield the certainty which makes a virtuous person *tenacem propositi*[22] and not allow himself to be swayed from his resolve by any reversal of fortune.

Moreover, intuitive knowledge is also deceptive because our power of judgment can be easily seduced if it becomes satisfied with examples without proofs. Finally, examples are not recalled with as much ease as is necessary to be able to have an effect on the will. If our soul wants to move from one particular thing to something similarly particular, then it

---

[20] The poetic divinization of the Greek Πειθώ indicating the persuasive power of speech over the heart of the listener.

[21] Lessing, "Fabeln – Abhandlungen" ["Fables – Essays"] in *Werke*, ed. Göpfert, vol. 5, pp. 352–419.

[22] "Stick to his principles", Horace, *Carmina*, III. iii. 1; cf. Horace *The Odes and Epodes*, tr. C. E. Bennett (Cambridge, Mass., Harvard University Press, 1952), pp. 178–9.

finds its path by means of the universal. For since the two particular instances agree solely in regard to something universal, our imagination finds only one way of passing over from one to the other, namely, by moving from the particular to the universal and then from the universal to some other, similar instance which is supposed to be an example of it. If a person has not acquired the proficiency of tracing each present instance back to a general principle, he will remain dangerously on one shore and find no way of crossing over to the examples that should save him. But if a person combines both types of knowledge, then he gives his practical judgment a firm character through the force of the demonstration involved. In each case that comes before us, the general principles come to mind again. The imagination ranges over all the particular cases in which we have ourselves applied these general principles or seen them applied by others. The greater the speed with which this happens, the livelier our knowledge becomes. The effectiveness of the impulses increases and produces the fervent and constant resolve capable of keeping the most furious passions in check. At that point a virtuous person attains the mountaintop high above the clouds where no storm is any longer to be feared. "Nihil est tam difficile et arduum, quod non humana *mens* vincat, et in familiaritatem perducat assidua meditatio; nullique sunt tam feri et sui juris affectus, ut non disciplina perdomentur."[23]

---

[23] Seneca, *De ira*, Liber II. c. 12: "Nothing is so difficult and arduous that the human mind does not conquer it and assiduous meditation does not become familiar with it, and there are no passions so wild and independent that they are not subdued by discipline." Cf. Seneca, *Moral Essays*, tr. John W. Basore (Cambridge, Mass., Harvard University Press, 1970), vol. 1, pp. 192–3.

On the main principles of the fine arts and sciences

For the virtuoso fine arts and sciences are a preoccupation, for the amateur a source of pleasure, and for the philosopher a school of instruction. The profoundest secrets of our soul lie hidden in the rules of beauty, which the artist's genius feels and the critic reduces to rational inferences. Each rule of beauty is at the same time a psychological discovery. For, since it contains a prescription of the conditions under which a beautiful object can have the best effect on our mind, it must be possible for the rule to be derived from the nature of the human spirit and explained on the basis of its properties. Thus, if the philosopher pursues the traces of sentiments on their obscure paths, new perspectives in psychology must open themselves to him, ones which he would otherwise never have uncovered by rational inferences and by experience. The human soul is as inexhaustible as nature; mere reflection cannot possibly establish everything about it, and everyday experience is rarely decisive. The happy moments in which we, as it were, catch nature in the act never escape us as easily as when we want to observe ourselves. At such moments the soul is much too preoccupied with other concerns to be able to perceive what transpires in it. Hence, one will have to analyze carefully the phenomena in which the impulses of our soul are most moved and compare them with the theory in order to shed a new light on this theory and extend its borders through new discoveries. Yet are there any phenomena that move every impulse of the human soul more than the effects of the fine arts do?

Beauty is the self-empowered mistress of all our sentiments, the basis of all our natural drives, and the animating spirit which transforms speculative knowledge of the truth into sentiments and incites us to active decision. It enchants us in nature where we encounter it originally but diffusely, and the human spirit has learned to imitate and multiply it in works of art. Through different senses, poetry, rhetoric, beauties in shapes and sounds pervade our soul and dominate all its inclinations. They can make us happy, then sad at will. They can arouse our passions and tame them in turn,[*] and we willingly submit to the power of the artist who has us hope, fear, become irate, be soothed, laugh, and then pour out our tears. All these various effects must flow from a single source. Two different sources of the movement would make our soul a composite being, and we are convinced that it is simple.

Our sentiments are always accompanied by a definite degree of satisfaction or dissatisfaction. It is as little possible to conceive of a spirit without the capacity to love and to abhor things as it is to conceive one without the power to represent things. It must be possible for all the different degrees and modifications of this satisfaction and dissatisfaction, all our inclinations and passions, to be explained on the basis of this fundamental capacity to love and to abhor things. Hence, if the power of controlling our passions cannot be denied the fine arts and sciences, then they all must work on this fundamental capacity of our soul in different ways and be able to move the most hidden impulses of our soul. But what do the various objects of poetry, painting, rhetoric, and dance, of music, sculpture, and architecture, what do all these works of human invention have in common that enables them to harmonize for the sake of a single final purpose?

Batteux, who is as insightful a student and critic of the fine sciences as he is a fine writer, maintains like many others before him that the imitation of nature is the general means by which the fine arts please us, and he believes it possible to derive all particular rules of the fine sciences and arts from this single principle.[1] In his hands, everything becomes an imitation of nature, and it will not have been difficult for a captivating writer like Batteux to bring the most beautiful thoughts and the most instructive principles to bear on the most barren principle.

---

[*] One cannot entirely deny architecture itself the capacity to arouse passions. It can stir us at least by means of an adjoining conception which the soul always combines with the main conception. Thus, buildings of majesty and splendor arouse reverence and trembling. Castles in the air summon a sense of mirth, country houses a sense of peace and innocence, hermitages a sense of seriousness and profundity, and a tomb can arouse grief and sadness.

[1] Charles Batteux, *Les beaux arts réduits à un même principe* (Paris, 1746); see also *Einschränkung der schönen Künste auf einen einzigen Grundsatz* (Leipzig, 1751).

We will not now insist upon the insufficiency of this principle. It will become clear of itself in what follows. Let this much, then, be granted, that the imitation of nature is the only reason why the fine arts are pleasing to us. Will this answer also satisfy the philosopher who only posed the question in order to develop a more precise acquaintance with the nature of the soul? The imitation of nature is the sole means of pleasing. That can be! But does anything become more understandable through this assertion? Is not nature pleasing as well, without imitating? What means did the supreme artist employ so that the original image [*Urbild*] would please us? We must search out these more original laws of nature which are binding on the most perfect inventor as well as on the imitator as soon as either of them has the intention *to please*. And we must, in any case, have recourse to these laws to do this without having recourse to the creator when we want to make a selection in nature and distinguish the objects that deserve to be imitated. Hence, we repeat our question in, to be sure, a somewhat more general way: *what do the beauties of nature and of art have in common, what relation do they have to the human soul, such that they are so pleasing to it?*

Let no one refer us to the immediate will of God. Let no one create, along with that English philosopher,[2] a new sense for beauty, which the supreme being, on the basis of wise intentions, was supposed to have placed in our soul, as though by decree. This is the shortest way to cut off the train of rational investigations suddenly and transform nature, the most perfect whole, into a patchwork. The system of divine intentions must be distinguished from the system of efficient causes. The most perfect craftsman knows how to fulfill the wisest intentions through the wisest means. His wisdom has chosen the best final purpose but, through the wisest arrangement of the efficient causes, he has also made it a reality. Hence, if the benevolent creator has found it to be in keeping with his intentions that human beings should take satisfaction in beauty, then he will have also let their souls be of such a constitution that this satisfaction flows naturally from it and can be intelligently explained on the basis of it.

Perhaps what is known of the soul from theory can lead us closer to our final goal. In the foregoing essays light has also been thrown on

---

[2]   As Otto Best notes (*Asthetische Schriften in Auswahl* [Darmstadt, Wissenschaftliche Buchgesellschaft, 1974], p. 175, n. 133), Hutcheson is probably meant; cf. Francis Hutcheson, *An Inquiry into the Original of our Ideas of Beauty and Virtue* (London, 1738).

various materials that are germane here so that nothing remains but the application of them to the fine arts in order to uncover the source of the pleasure that they afford us. Each concept of perfection, harmony, and flawlessness is preferred by our soul to the deficient, the imperfect, and the discordant. This is the first level of satisfaction and dissatisfaction which alternately accompany all our representations. The truth of this principle has been proven on the basis of the mere definitions of a spirit, and experience is in full agreement with this principle.

If the knowledge of this perfection is sensuous, then it is called "beauty." An instance of knowledge is called "sensuous," however, not simply if it is felt by the external senses, but in general whenever we perceive a large array of an object's features all at once without being able to separate them distinctly from each other. It has already been shown on another occasion why neither distinct nor obscure representations are compatible with the sentiment of beauty and also how as well as why the clear concepts of beauty influence the capacity to desire with an allure that is so powerful. The intellectual perfection illuminates the soul and satisfies its original drives for cogent representations. If, however, it is to set in motion the impulses of the capacity to desire, then it must transform itself into a beauty. The individual concepts of the manifold must lose their tiresome distinctness so that the whole can shine forth in an all-the-more transfigured light. The further elaboration of this is to be found in the "Letters on sentiments" ["On sentiments"].

From this it follows that everything capable of being represented to the senses as a perfection could also present an object of beauty. Belonging here are all the perfections of external forms, that is, the lines, surfaces, and bodies and their movements and changes; the harmony of the multiple sounds and colors; the order in the parts of a whole, their similarity, variety, and harmony; their transposition and transformation into other forms; all the capabilities of our soul, all the skills of our body. Even the perfections of our external state (under which honor, comfort, and riches are to be understood) cannot be excepted from this if they are fit to be represented in a way that is apparent to the senses.

We have now found the universal means of pleasing our soul, namely, the *sensuously perfect representation*. And since the final purpose of the fine arts is to please, we can presuppose the following principle as indubitable: the essence of the fine arts and sciences consists in an artful, sensuously perfect representation or in a sensuous perfection represented by art.

This representation by art can be sensuously perfect even if, in nature, the object of the representation is neither good nor beautiful. We have seen in the previous essay that what is evil and imperfect in the object itself arouses a mixed sentiment, one which also conveys something pleasant along with it. We also saw, however, that this slight degree of gratification is suppressed by discontent and is scarcely able to be noticed when sensitive minds sympathize too easily. It was shown there, furthermore, that the unpleasantness of the object is lessened by the artful representation, and the pleasantness is, as it were, elevated. The pleasantries of art increase the satisfaction even if they produce a deception, that is to say, even if they stir the senses so intensely that we believe we are seeing the real thing. Yet, in every case, many attendant circumstances remain which do not belong to the domain of art and remind us at the right time that we are not viewing nature itself. Hence, whenever the works of art have a paradigm in nature that they imitate, this paradigm can just as well be unpleasant as pleasant in and for itself, and, in both cases, the imitation of it can be satisfying. Nevertheless, the following distinction is to be noted in this regard: in and for itself, the pleasing paradigm in nature will be gratifying in relation to the object as much as it is in relation to the sketch of it. This pleasure is enhanced by the beauties of the artistic imitation and transformed by the deception of the senses, as long as it continues, into a sweet enchantment. On the other hand, the recollection, following quickly upon this, that we are viewing art and not nature conveys something unpleasant since we would rather see the pleasing paradigms themselves than see replicas of them. – However, the imitation of paradigms that in nature are unpleasant produces a far more mixed sentiment. The representation of them is, in and for itself, unpleasant in relation to the object, but is mixed with some gratification in relation to the sketch of them. This pleasure is enhanced by the beauties of art, and the sensuous deception will also be pleasant here because it assures us of the perfection of the imitation. However, the moment this deception brings the objective reality too much into relief and begins to become unpleasant, we have the benevolent recollection that we do not have the original image itself before our eyes, and, by this means, the pleasant character of the experience becomes dominant and completely masters the soul.

Let us look more precisely at this composite sentiment which is aroused by works of art and derive from it the rule for both the expression and the makeup of the art-worthy object. If the artworks have a paradigm in nature, then the expression must, in the first place, be faithful, that is to say, it must depict all the parts of the paradigm just as we would have perceived them in it itself by means of the senses. The depiction of an object that agrees precisely with all the parts of it is called an "imitation." Hence, in this case imitation is a necessary property of the fine arts and sciences.

All the parts of a correct imitation harmonize with the common final purpose of faithfully representing a specific original image. Thus, in and for itself, each imitation already conveys with it the concept of a perfection, and if our senses can perceive the faithfulness or similarity of the imitation, then it is capable of arousing a pleasant sentiment. Pictures of objects in tranquil water or in a dark room and the figures of bodies cast in plaster please us merely on account of their similarity. Since the similarity with the original image is, however, only a simple perfection, it also arouses in us only a very slight degree of gratification which is often scarcely noticeable and only touches, so to speak, the surface of our soul.

Added to this in the imitations of art is the artist's perfection that we perceive in them. For all works of art are visible imprints of the artist's abilities which, so to speak, put his entire soul on display and make it known to us. This perfection of spirit arouses an uncommonly greater pleasure than mere similarity, because it is more excellent and far more complex than similarity. It is more excellent to the degree that the perfection of a rational being is more sublime than the perfection of inanimate things, and it is also more complex because many of the soul's abilities and, frequently, diverse skills of the external limbs as well, are required for a beautiful imitation. We find more to admire in a rose painted by Huysum[3] than in a river's reflected image of this queen of the flowers, and the most enchanting landscape in a camera obscura does not charm us as much as it can through the brush of a great landscape painter.

The pleasure we take in the beauties of nature itself is inflamed to the point of ecstasy by the reference to the infinite perfection of the master

---

[3] The Dutch painter, Jan van Huysum (1682–1748), is celebrated for his paintings of flowers and fruits.

who produced them. How cold, by contrast, must be the pleasure of an atheist who must content himself merely with the beauties of the objects themselves. Given the cited properties of the beautiful expression, one also sees why genius in works of art pleases us more than does the utmost diligence and hard work. Genius demands a perfection of all the powers of the soul as well as their harmonization for a single, final purpose. For that reason the signs of that purpose, which the hand of a master strews over the work, must be far more pleasing to us than the signs of patience and practice that hard work demands.

The properties of the paradigm in nature have been treated in the foregoing discussion. The paradigm must be, to a noticeable degree, either pleasant or unpleasant in and for itself. The indifferent is rightly excluded since, in and for itself, it arouses no sentiments at all and thus is capable of arousing merely a lukewarm satisfaction with the imitation. By contrast, art's replica must unite all the requirements of a beautiful object. Hence, in the first place, it will have to have multiple parts. The monotonous, the meager, and the sterile are unbearable to good taste.

Furthermore, the parts must harmonize in a sensuous manner to constitute a whole. That is to say, the order and regularity which they observe in their succession must be apparent to the senses. Parts that are dissonant, confused, and in disarray are even more so when a sufficient reason for this condition is lacking. If their order is not apparent to the senses, if it is hidden and must first be extracted by reflection, then our soul falls, as it were, into a state of confusion. It wanders all around without a clue and nowhere finds a resting point where it can revive itself and leisurely think over the whole. As far as our senses are concerned, a hidden order is indistinguishable from a complete lack of order.

The whole must not overstep the determinate boundaries of the magnitude. Our senses must not lose themselves in either the enormous or the minute. Where the objects are too small, the mind misses the multiplicity, and where they are too big, it misses the unity in the multiplicity.

The object of the fine arts must, furthermore, be decent, novel, extraordinary, fruitful, and so forth, all of which can be demonstrated with little trouble from the definition.

From this one sees in what case it is appropriate for art to take leave of nature and not imitate objects completely as they are found in the original image. Nature has an immeasurable plan. The multiplicity incorporated in that plan extends from the infinitely small to the infinitely large, and its unity is far beyond all astonishment. The beauty of external forms in general is only a very small portion of its purposes, and at times it has had to put greater purposes ahead of beauty. Is it, then, very possible that the limited space of nature which we are able to contemplate, that this space insofar as it strikes our senses should exhaust all the properties of ideal beauty?

The human artist, on the other hand, chooses a dimension that is suited to his powers. His purposes are as limited as his capabilities. His entire ultimate purpose is to represent, in a limited arena, the beauties that strike the human senses. Hence, he will be able to come closer to the ideal beauties than this or that part of nature has come, since no higher purposes force him to deviate from this. He gathers together in a single viewpoint what nature has diffusely strewn among various objects, forming for himself a whole from this and taking the trouble to represent it just as nature would have represented it if the beauty of this limited object had been its sole purpose. Nothing else is meant by the usual expressions of the artist: "to beautify nature," "to imitate beautiful nature," and so on. They want to depict a certain object just as God would have created it if sensuous beauty had been his supreme, final purpose and no more important final purposes were able to cause him to deviate. This is the most perfect, ideal beauty, and it is to be encountered nowhere in nature other than in the whole and is perhaps never fully to be attained in the works of art.

The artist must accordingly elevate himself above common nature, and, since beauty is his sole, final purpose, he is free to concentrate this beauty everywhere in his works so that it might move us all the more intensely.

All those who are versed in the art of sculpture rank the figures of nature below those of the ancients. The contours of nature are somewhat spare, and their heads not as noble, not as expressive as the heads of the ancients.

For those, then, who do not possess sufficent genius to abstract the ideal beauty from the works of nature, assiduous observation of the ancients can be more useful than contemplation of nature.

The local colors of nature are not as fresh, not as lively, as the local colors of a skilled colorist. The former paints an infinite space for infinite time and alters its immense painting at every moment. What an astonishing multiplicity of colors it will have to use! Yet, the smaller the number of colors, the purer and livelier they can be. Indeed, the colors of the colorist himself appear rather dull and brownish in comparison with those of someone who dyes colors. For the latter's ultimate purpose is limited to a single color. But will one, for this reason, be able to ascribe more knowledge to a common dyer than to a Rubens or a Titian?

Nature has perhaps never had to produce a human character such as Charles Grandison,[4] but the poet takes the trouble to portray him as, in keeping with the prevailing will of God, the human being he would have had to become. He set up an ideal beauty as a standard and looked for features in nature that, taken together, portray such a complete character. He beautified nature.

This truth is far more distinctly evident in the case of music.

The sounds of nature are, to be sure, full of expression but seldom melodic, and the artist must beautify them if he wants to please. The dancer does the same thing if he, for example, imitates the unaffected movements of a shepherd but combines them with propriety and art.

The boundaries that I have prescribed for myself in this essay do not permit a more expansive investigation of the general properties of the fine arts. I have neither the intent nor the capability to erect an entire system, and I am satisfied if I have sketched the initial, basic contours of a system somewhat correctly. I turn now to the division of the fine arts in their particular classes.

The signs by means of which an object is expressed can be either natural or arbitrary. They are natural if the combination of the sign with the subject matter signified is grounded in the very properties of what is designated. The passions are, by virtue of their nature, connected with certain movements in our limbs as well as with certain sounds and gestures. Hence, anyone who expresses an emotion by means of the sounds, gestures, and movements appropriate to it, makes use of natural signs. Those signs, on the other hand, that by their very nature have nothing in common with the designated subject matter, but have nonetheless been arbitrarily assumed as signs for it, are called "arbitrary." The articulated sounds of all languages, the letters, the

[4] Samuel Richardson, *Sir Charles Grandison* (London, 1753), ed. with an introduction by Jocelyn Harris (Oxford and New York, Oxford University Press, 1986).

hieroglyphic signs of the ancients, and some allegorical images, which can rightly be counted among the latter, are of this type.

The first major division of the sensible expression into fine arts and sciences (*beaux arts & belles lettres*) flows from this observation. The fine sciences, by which poetry and rhetoric are understood, express objects by means of arbitrary signs, perceptible sounds, and letters. Since a combination of many words, based upon reason, is called "a statement," we arrive quite naturally at the well-known definition by Baumgarten: a poem is a *sensuously perfect statement*.[5] This definition has at the same time provided the occasion to locate the essence of the fine arts generally in an artistic, sensuously-perfect representation. Poetry distinguishes itself from rhetoric by means of the ultimate purpose. The main, ultimate purpose of poetry is to please by means of a sensuously perfect statement, while that of rhetoric is to persuade by means of a sensuously perfect statement.

The means of rendering a statement sensuous consist in the choice of the sort of expressions that bring an array of features to mind all at once so that what is designated is felt by us in a more lively way than the sign. By this means, our knowledge becomes intuitive, visible. The objects are represented to our senses as though they were right in front of us, and the subordinate powers of our mind are deceived since they frequently forget the signs and believe themselves to be catching sight of the subject matter itself. The worth of poetic images, similes, and descriptions and even that of individual poetic terms must be judged on the basis of this general maxim.

All things, possible and actual, can be expressed by arbitrary signs as soon as we have a clear concept of them. Hence, the domain of the fine sciences extends to every purely imaginable object.

The poet can express everything of which our soul can have a clear concept. All the beauties of nature, its colors, figures, and sounds, the entire gloriousness of creation, the cohesiveness of the immense system of the world, the commandments of God and his infinite properties, all the inclinations and passions of our soul, our subtlest thoughts, sentiments, and decisions – all of this can serve as material for poetic inspiration.

The object of the fine arts is more limited. These arts make use of

---

[5] Alexander Baumgarten, *Meditationes de nonnullis ad poema pertinantibus* (Halle, 1735), §9, p.7.

natural signs above all. Expression in painting, sculpture, architecture, music, and dance does not presuppose anything arbitrary in order to be understood. Very rarely does it appeal to the consent of human beings in order to designate this or that object in one way rather than another. Hence, each art must content itself with that portion of natural signs that it can express by means of the senses. Music, the expression of which takes place by means of inarticulate sounds, cannot possibly indicate the concept of a rose, a poplar tree, and so on, just as it is impossible for painting to represent a musical chord to us. The various types of natural signs will provide us with the occasion for dividing the fine arts into groups.

The natural signs of which one avails oneself in the fine arts have an effect on either the sense of hearing or the sense of sight. No fine arts are yet known to us for the other senses. Music accomplishes the first of those two effects, all the other arts accomplish the second of them.

The beauties which can be felt in inarticulate sounds are the sensuous arrangement, the harmony of the individual sounds with the whole, the mutual relation of the parts to one another, the imitation, and finally, all inclinations and passions of the human soul which tend to make themselves known by means of sounds. Music is able, furthermore, to represent the multiple parts of beauty either successively or alongside one another. The former is called "melody," the latter "harmony."

In the same way, the natural signs that effect the sense of sight can be represented either successively or alongside one another; that is to say, they can express beauty either through movement or through forms. Dance accomplishes this by means of movement. There is a coherence to the succession of the various positions of the body, the movement of its extremities, and gestures, and, taken together, they constitute a beautiful whole.

Next to the arrangement and agreement of the parts, the beauties that are expressed in the common or lower art of dance are the skillfulness of the limbs of the body, the imitations, the positions and movements in beautiful lines, and finally the lines of beauty which are drawn on the ground by the feet of the dancers. The higher or theatrical art of dance has, in addition, the expression of inclinations and emotions and the imitation of all human actions that can be expressed by movements.

The visible natural signs that appear alongside one another must be represented by lines and figures. This can occur either by means of surfaces or by means of bodies. In painting this occurs by means of surfaces, in sculpture and architecture by means of bodies. Architecture differs from painting as well as from sculpture in regard to the perfections that it has to express. In addition to the order, symmetry, and beauty of lines and figures in pillars, doors, and windows, architecture gives sensuous expression mainly to the comfortableness and solidity of the building as well as to the excellence and prominence of the proprietor's public position. Splendid buildings show the wealth, the dignity, and the comfort of their proprietors. Everything must have the look of splendor, comfort, and solidity since this actually is the ultimate purpose of a building.* By contrast, neither painting nor sculpture has to deal with the excellence and prominence of some external position or with durability. They can, to be sure, often erect a monument of honor and dignity, but this determination is not essential to them. The lines of beauty in painting must have a much freer sweep to them than those in architecture. The regularity and rigidity in the outward lines of the pillars and openings in architecture give them an apparent solidity that the painter as well as the sculptor must often avoid. The beauties that can be expressed by these artists are the genius and thoughts in invention and composition, the harmony in the organization, the imitation of beautiful nature in sketching, a rich variety of beautiful lines and figures, the liveliness of local colors, the harmony of their shading and the truth and unity in the apportionment of light and shadow, the expression of human inclinations and passions, the most skillful positionings of the human body, and finally the imitation of natural and artificial things in general that can be recalled by means of visible images.

Since the painter and sculptor express beauties that are alongside one another, they must choose the instant that is most favorable to their purpose. They must assemble the entire action into a single perspective and divide it up with a great deal of understanding. In this instant

---

* Imitation appears to have no role at all or at least a very small role in the beauties of architecture. It is, of course, maintained that the order in architecture should have a certain similarity with the figure of a well-developed human being. But the builder's purpose is by no means to imitate the human shape. The first inventors merely abstracted from the structure of the human body the rules according to which the concept of solidity can be combined with the beauties of external form. The origin of the order, moreover, could perhaps have been derived more naturally from other reasons as some modern thinkers have actually done.

everything must be rich in thoughts and so full of meaning that every accompanying concept makes its own contribution to the required meaning. When we view such a painting with due attentiveness, our senses are all at once animated, all the capabilities of our soul suddenly become lively, and the imagination can fathom the past from the present while reliably anticipating the future.

We have, of course, placed the domain of natural signs within the borders of the fine arts and the domain of arbitary signs within the borders of the fine sciences. But one must acknowledge that these borders often blur into one another, indeed, that they often must do so, given the rule of composite beauty.

A poet frequently makes use of words and syllables whose natural sound has a similarity with the designated subject matter, and an artist seeks to incorporate into his artworks allegorical images, the meaning of which is often merely arbitrary. But the virtuoso must know how to handle this deviation from one domain into the other and treat it with a great deal of circumspection. The poet who overdoes the imitation of sounds is in danger of giving his poem a trivial appearance that can only please children. And those who dabble in music have often made themselves ridiculous when they wanted to express concepts the likes of which stand in no natural connection to the sounds. I now want to investigate the extent to which the painter and the sculptor are free to use arbitary signs.

It has been established that painting does not occupy itself merely with the sort of objects that are visible in and for themselves. Even the subtlest thoughts, the most abstract concepts, can be expressed on canvas and recollected by means of visible signs. Herein consists the great secret of portraying the soul, as Aristides did,[6] and painting it for the intellect. The artist can execute this in a variety of ways. One way he can do this is, like the composer of fables, by imposing a certain general maxim, an abstract concept on a particular example and thereby representing the subtle thought in a lively and visible manner. Thus, it is possible for Homer to portray the hero who defies the power of love in the person of Diomedes as he wounds Venus, the tenderness of marital love in Hector's departure from Andromacha, and a child's love in the person of Aeneas who carries his father away from Troy on his

---

[6]   The Greek painter Aristides (fourth century BC) was renowned for his soulful paintings.

shoulders with flames and swords all around them.[7] A painter can express temperance in the use of wine or the mixing of wine with water through Thetis' embrace of Bacchus. A philosopher sitting deep in contemplation while enemy soldiers lay waste to the entire city and one of them runs violently towards him with sword exposed would be able to represent a picture of profound meditation.

Another way of painting thoughts can be executed by means of allegory. A person assembles the properties and features of an abstract concept and from this forms a sensuous whole that can be expressed on canvas by means of natural signs. Portrayals of this sort include the portrayal of *opportunity* as a person with a bare neck and lock of hair over the forehead and the portrayal of *silence* through a boy who lays his finger on his mouth.

An image of prayer, says Winckelmann, a great defender of allegorical painting,[*] can be gathered from Homer. Phoenix, Achilles' house steward, was seeking to comfort the hero entrusted to him, and he does this in an allegory.

> "Achilles, you must know," he says, "that prayers are Jupiter's daughters. They have become twisted by so much kneeling; their faces are full of cares and wrinkles, and their eyes are constantly directed to heaven. They are a retinue of the goddess Ate[8] and follow behind her. This goddess goes her way with a bold and proud expression and, light-footed as she is, she runs through the entire world, scaring and tormenting human progeny. She seeks to elude the prayers that follow her ceaselessly in order to heal the very person that she wounds. Whoever reveres these daughters of Jupiter when they draw near enjoys much goodness from them; if, however, a person rebukes them, they ask their father to give the goddess Ate the command to punish that person on account of the hardness of his heart."

---

[*] See the *Thoughts on the Imitation of Greek Works in Painting and Sculpture*, second edition, p. 154.[9]

[7] In *Iliad* v, 334–54 the Greek hero Diomedes wounds Aphrodite (Venus), the Trojan goddess of love and beauty; in *Iliad* vi, 399–493, not yielding to Andromache's pleading; Hector affectionately leaves her and their infant son to fight the Greeks; in the *Aeneid* ii, 707–29, Aeneas carries his father away from the burning city of Troy.

[8] Ate is the daughter of Zeus and the embodiment of tragic delusion; cf. *Iliad* IX, 501–12; XIX, 91–131.

[9] Johann Joachim Winckelmann, *Gedanken über die Nachahmung der griechischen Werke in der Malerey und Bildhauerkunst*, 2nd, enlarged edn. (Dresden and Leipzig, 1756).

In a similar way it is possible, in the manner of Milton, to portray death and sin and, in the manner of Voltaire, discord.[10]

Meanwhile, the artist must take care that his allegories do not become too subtle. They must be both natural and intuitive. That is, the constitution of the sign must be grounded in the nature of what is signified, and we must be able to see this agreement with so little trouble that we think about the signified subject matter more than about the sign. The artist must, therefore, consider that he is supposed to speak, to be sure, with our soul, but only with our lower and sensuous powers. As soon as rumination, reflection, and concentration of wit are required to fathom the significance of the signs, they cease to be sensuous.

Should a butterfly signify the soul, should a golden heart hanging on a person's breast signify a benevolent heart, should a certain tree signify wisdom, should a deer signify at one time a nagging conscience, at another time I know not what; these are merely symbolic signs and far less intuitive than the most arbitrary words. It is not only that such an expression departs from the essence of painting, but rather that it denies the character of fine arts in general and belongs to the subtleties that obscure the beauties of a piece. For one then satisfies wit instead of enrapturing the senses.

If, as Winckelmann proposes, one is supposed to paint the prayers in the manner of Homer, who knows whether one would not likewise be making this mistake?

Satire in painting is far more compatible with the symbolic sign and seems to require such signs much more, just as in poetry and rhetoric it demands more wit than sentiment. Hogarth's prints, some descriptions of which one finds in the appendix to the second edition of his *Analysis of Beauty*, are full of such examples.[11] In the earlier mentioned work, Winckelmann cites a very beautiful example from the fables of Gabrias[12] where a donkey, carrying the picture of Isis, interpreted the reverence paid by people to the picture as reverence towards him. If the donkey's mistaken notion can be suitably expressed with the artist's

---

[10] Though Voltaire criticized the allegorical figures "Death" and "Sin" in Milton's *Paradise Lost* (London, 1667), Discord appears as a character in Voltaire's epic poem *La Henriade* (London, 1728).

[11] William Hogarth, *The Analysis of Beauty* (London, 1753); see p. 51 n. 3.

[12] "Gabrias" is the medieval writer whose name Mendelssohn, like Winckelmann, confuses with "Babrius," the Greek writer of fables in the manner of Aesop around 200 AD.

brush (which is perhaps dubious), Winckelman is right to ask: "Can the pride of the ignorant masses, among the great things in the world, be given a more sensuous expression?"

The attempt has been made to incorporate a type of allegory into architecture as well, but the result would appear not to have been very successful. A dream of the Emperor Constantine provided the occasion for the attempt to give churches a similarity with the crucifix. The altar would have to take the position of the head, the large entrance in front would be in place of the feet, and the two adjacent parts would be in place of both arms.

The ancients adorned the temple of virtue with a single solitary entrance in order to suggest, by this means, that one is unable to arrive at virtue by any detour.

Plutarch relates that Marcellus had two temples built, one for virtue and the other for honor, and had them built next to one another in such a way that one would have to proceed through the temple of virtue in order to come to the temple of honor.[13] The meaning is obvious, but the undertaking itself seems to be far too removed from the genius of architecture. This description of such a building makes the sense of the allegory far more visible than the building itself. An infallible sign that the idea belongs to poetry more than to architecture.

Up until now we have spoken merely of the nature of individual arts and treated their particular and shared objects. But often two or more arts have also been combined in order to make the expression even more sensuous and to storm our minds, as it were, from all sides. These combinations have their particular rules which are to be explained on the basis of the nature of the composite perfections.

In a composite perfection, that is to say, an assembled whole, a single main objective must dominate, and the particular objectives must be in harmony as means to that main objective. Where many final purposes have an equal share in the organization of a thing, interest is divided, the multiplicity is not in harmony, and one finds no reason why these diverse final purposes have been gathered together. This remark pertains equally to beauties and to perfections. In neither may the harmony among the final purposes be left out. Moreover, since we have already seen that each art has a particular final purpose, the artist who

---

[13] See *Plutarch's Lives*, tr. Bernadotte Perrin (London, Heinemann, 1968), vol. 5, "Marcellus," ch. 28, pp. 512–13.

intends to combine arts must choose the final purpose of a single art as the main objective and subordinate the remaining arts to the latter in such a way that they can be regarded as means to the main purpose. For brevity's sake, let us call the former "the main art" and the latter "the auxiliary arts."

Particular rules flow from the particular final purposes by means of which each art is determined in its group, and these particular rules belong to each art respectively as its own, prior to all others. These particular rules can conflict with one another in the composition of the arts, and then exceptions are unavoidable.

If such a conflict of particular rules is not to be avoided, then the smallest exception possible must be made, of course, on the side of the auxiliary arts. In the composition these should serve merely to elevate the main art and lend it certain beauties that it does not possess. Hence, they must always yield to it and relax some of the strictness of their particular rules. The very rules that flow from the general determination of fine arts can never be contradicted in the composition of many particular arts. However, if the particular rules of the main art conflict with the general rules of the auxiliary arts such that the intended combination of arts would be absolutely impossible and the particular rules of the main art are supposed to be discharged completely, then the exception ought, of course, to occur on the side of the main art. It must provide the accompanying arts with the opportunity to give their help and to beautify it with their contribution. Let us apply these general maxims to particular cases.

Music stands in a natural connection with the live performance of the fine sciences. The voice especially must be sometimes raised, sometimes lowered in the expression of sentiments, inclinations, and passions. The reader must know how to express the strong, the heroic, the terrifying, the melancholy, the fearful, and the tender by appropriate sounds, by suitable inflections in the voice, by rising and falling, shortening, pausing and beginning more quickly. All this is part of music. However, as long as music is only used to give a greater emphasis to the arbitrary signs of poesy, all necessary exceptions must take place from the side of music. The poet surrenders to his inspiration without restraint and satisfies the rules of his art perfectly without worrying whether this or that expression will conflict with the rules of music. The auxiliary art must relax the strictness of its particular rules and sacrifice everything to the beauties of the main art. The poet, meanwhile, must use caution. If his poem is to be recited, that is to say, if it is determined to become combined with music, then he must avoid the sort of beauties that cannot be recited and, as a result, make the required combination impossible. In the tragedies of some English writers such as Thomson, Young,[14] and others, one finds some passages which are superb for reading and yet do not distinguish themselves very well on stage. There are beauties of poesy, however, that cannot possibly be combined with music. Poets almost always shift the blame to the actors, but often unfairly. There are passages which can bring the most competent actors to despair, and these are indisputably mistakes committed by the poets out of a lack of sufficient acquaintance with recitation. It is pitiful to listen to how the most excellent actors torment themselves if they have to recite our usual untheatrical translations. The arrangement of words is often so clumsy and the phrasing so atrocious that the great talents of an Eckhof, a Stark,[15] and so on are squandered in vain. I have seen Stark, this ornament of the German stage, perform some miserable translations. In the process the only thing that gave me pleasure was the observation: what would such actors accomplish if they had poets who work on behalf of the actors and were as great in dramatic composition as the actors are in the art of acting.

The recitation of the ancients, although it was set to notes, was indisputably devoid of all genuine musical adornment. It was merely supposed to give the actual delivery of the arbitrary signs on stage a greater impact, and the most unaffected music was the sort most suited for this purpose.

Their choruses and hymns, on the other hand, already had a more precise kinship with music. The more intense the inspiration of the person reciting, the more his voice had to vary in modulation, and the more noticeable the inflections and alterations in it had to be. Here, from the outset, the poet must comply somewhat more with the musician. His thoughts could have been bold, sublime, profound, and full of poetic ornamentation, but the expression, in accordance with music's need, had to be harmonious, divided into short singable

---

[14] See James Thomson, *The Tragedy of Sophonisba* (London, 1729); *Agamemnon* (London, 1738); and *Tancred and Sigismunda* (London, 1744); and Edward Young, *Busivis, King of Egypt* (London, 1718); *The Revenge* (London, 1721); and *The Brothers* (London, 1752).

[15] Konrad Eckhoff (1720–1778) was a leading actor in the Hamburg National Theater; Johanna Christiana Starke (1731–1803) was a popular actress who appeared principally in Leipzig.

sentences and measured stanzas, and frequently supplied with repetitions (refrains). All the while, expression in arbitrary signs remained the highest final purpose, and most exceptions fell to the side of music.

It is not, however, impossible to combine these two arts with each other so that the expression in natural signs is the main final purpose. The expression of sentiment in music is intense, lively, and moving, but indeterminate. One is pervaded by a certain sentiment but it is obscure, general, and not limited to any individual object. This lack can be remedied by the addition of distinct and arbitary signs. They can establish the object from all sides and make the sentiment into an individual sentiment which breaks out more easily. If this more intimate determination of the sentiment in music takes place by means of poetry and painting or stage design, the result is the modern opera.

In this sort of combination of arts, music or the sensuous expression by the natural signs of sounds is the main final purpose, and, hence, all exceptions must take place on the side of poetry. It can legitimately depart from its particular rules such as the unity of place, time, and action as well as occasionally from plausibility in the ordering if it happens to be what is best as far as the music is concerned. The poet must be guided, in all his expressions, by the needs of the musician. He may not give his genius free rein but must instead always look back to the main art at whose final purpose everything should aim. His words, his meter, and the cadence of his verse must be musical, and his figures and similes must owe more to the objects of hearing than to the objects of sight. Indeed, he is not permitted to adorn even these with the beauties of his art to such an extent that they should seem able to dispense fully with the music. He must sketch the sentiments, images, and all musical beauties only, as it were, in outline and provide music with the opportunity of elaborating them and giving the sentiments their true fire, the images life, and the comparisons their similarity. If, on the other hand, the poet has already formed his sentiments in a way appropriate to his art, nothing remains for the musician to do but to sketch the recitation with notes, something which has, to be sure, considerable value but does not agree with the project of letting music be the main art. – The musician has only to look to this, that he does not cancel the possibility of the combination of his art with poesy. In theatrical works he must avoid the general confusion of sentiments which can be appropriate at the right place in a symphony.

Furthermore, he must work in accordance with the poet's plan since it is far easier to consider a distinct plan in arbitrary signs. As for the rest, his art maintains its primacy in this kind of combination of arts, and if a conflict of rules arises, it must be hampered by the fewest exceptions.

Dance has the same connection to poetry that music has. At times it merely accompanies the recitation as it adds the movement of the head and the extremities of the body which enliven the expression of certain sentiments; it is then called natural or prosaic dance. The movements of the limbs accompanying the choruses and hymns were somewhat more artful and approached the high art of dance, as has already been remarked in the case of music. By contrast, the poetic art of dance, the low art as well as the high art, is related more precisely to music than to poetry. Music is the probable cause of the violent movements of the dancer; by means of the cadences, music indicates the order in the sequence of those movements and supports the expression of the dance because it helps transport the spectator into the passion that the dancer wants to arouse. Since, in this case, music is regarded as the cause of dance, but the effect is always the final purpose for which the cause is used as a means, one must look upon music as an auxiliary art which in all its pieces must accommodate the needs of the art of dance.

Dance can also be combined quite well with poetry and music at the same time, although the combination is, of course, more difficult when three arts are supposed to have an effect at the same time. Among the ancients as well as among the moderns (in the case of the French) the combination of these three arts is very common.

> Among others, a certain chorus from Rameau's opera, *Les Indes galantes*, from which the dance melody is rather well known under the title, *Les Sauvages*, is a very nice example of this. On the opera stage in Berlin, one saw an example of this in the last chorus of the opera, *Montezuma*, which was portrayed very well.[16] After Cortes gave the command to plunder and destroy the city of Mexico, the Spaniards enter by force, and the chorus, composed of Mexicans, flees from all sides while the cry rings out: *Fuggiamo, o giorno orribile*, and so on. The dancers represent Spanish soldiers who seek to overtake the Mexican women who are fleeing before them.

[16] Jean Philippe Rameau's operatic ballet *Les Indes galantes*, text by L. Fuzelier, premiered in 1735; a fourth entrée, entitled *Les Sauvages* was added in 1736. *Montezuma* is a opera first staged in Berlin in 1755; music by Karl Heinrich Gaun, French text by Frederick the Great, Italian text by G. P. Tagliazucchi. At l. 8 the translation is "Oh day of horror! Flee!"

As soon as they had overtaken them, they stood still, and two Spaniards who sought to overtake a Mexican woman danced a *pas de trois.*

Only with great care can painting be combined with poetry and rhetoric as such. The expression of inclinations and passions in painting is, to be sure, not as lively and moving as in music, yet it is nevertheless more distinct and definite. Hence, it needs the help of arbitrary signs far less than the sentiment in music does. Here the action is more distinctly evident to the senses, and the countenances, positions, and gestures of the persons acting give the passions with which they are represented an individuality that they lack in music. Thus, only the most miserable bunglers have recourse in painting to a note with words coming, as they would have it, from the mouths of the persons they depict. The true condition, the performance, and the action of each person must be represented in a manner that is, in an absolute sense, purely a matter of the painting.

Yet it is often difficult to abstract from the actions of all the participating persons the event to which they refer. We know what each person wants in particular and their matching emotional state. But we do not see the reason why the persons are there and what sort of final purpose binds them together. The plan of the artist depends upon an event or a fabrication that is not very obvious to the senses. In this case, a short inscription can animate the entire action and briefly indicate the ultimate purpose underlying the harmony of all the parts. An example of this type is Poussin's painting that represents a shepherd-boy and a shepherd-girl as they stand with a contemplative and tender countenance at the grave of a shepherd-girl on which the inscription is to be read: *ET IN ARCADIA EGO.*[17] These few words explain the entire painting and instruct us about the pretext of the painter which we perhaps otherwise would not have fathomed without arduous reflection.

The inscriptions also serve as a means of combining poesy with architecture. They explain the ultimate purpose and the function of a building which one could otherwise not recognize from the outer arrangement of it. The veterans' home in Berlin bears the beautiful and impressive inscription: *LAESO ET INVICTO MILITI.*[18] These words

[17] "And I am in Arcadia," which is also called *The Arcadian Shepherds.*
[18] The veterans' home was established by Frederick the Great in 1748. The inscription reads "For the invincible and injured soldier."

explain the function of the building, and, at the same time, they are a panegyric to the sensibility of its exalted founder who wants to let the wounded and unconquered combatant pass the rest of his days in peace and comfort.*

Architecture in general, insofar as it belongs among the fine arts, is to be regarded only as an accompanying art. The need to protect themselves from the violence of weather and seasons has driven people to erect buildings while all other arts owe their origin merely to pleasure. Hence, all beauties in architecture, as has already been recalled, must be subordinated to their first function, comfort and durability. In the case of painters, by contrast, whose works are not permitted to have the look of rigidity, it has already been recalled above that they must give a freer sweep to their lines, and it has been noted that the greatest artists, if they introduce buildings into their paintings, represent them mostly from the side in order to procure the eye a greater variety. Or if this is not possible, then they interrupt the stiff lines of architecture with a cloud or a tree by means of which they cover a part of the building.

The most difficult and almost impossible combination of arts takes place when the arts that represent beauties alongside one another are supposed to be combined with arts that represent beauties successively. Nature has almost kept this secret to itself alone. In its immense plan it combines the beauties of sounds, colors, movements, and figures in the most perfect harmony by means of infinite times and unbounded spaces. By contrast, human art can unite painting, sculpture, and architecture with music and dance only in an inauthentic way, that is, by means of adornments. In an opera, for example, about some well-known fable, one can have an entire city or a beautiful building arise by the magic power of the harmony, or place the dancers as immovable pillars, which, gradually animated by the music, express their first sentiments in joyous movements. But who does not see that these cannot be called connections except in some inauthentic sense?

We must, meanwhile, make an exception to these general maxims. Music actually combines harmony with melody, since the former represents the beauties alongside one another but the latter represents

---

* Voltaire rebukes his mother tongue for being especially inept at short inscriptions and cites this inscription among others as an example which cannot be given in French without lengthy circumlocutions. Our mother tongue has to reproach itself for this inflexibility far less.

them successively. But the reason for this exception is easy to find. The sounds in harmony are not arranged alongside one another in a space, and, hence, they collapse into one another and we feel nothing more than a single, composite sound. This can vary subsequently according to a beautiful arrangement. Where, however, the beauties have to be arranged alongside one another in one space as is the case in painting, sculpture, and architecture, they can hardly be altered subsequently without confusion. The figure of the space itself which the parts occupy alongside one another, would have to be varied subsequently according to a beautiful arrangement, and a person will scarcely find a means of subsequently combining diverse figures successively according the laws of beauty.*

The topic is still tremendously fruitful but I am not sufficiently initiated in the secrets of the arts to dare to venture more deeply without risk into its sanctuary. Hence, I break off and await with my readers the instruction of a philosopher who is familiar enough with the arts to consider their secrets with philosophical eyes and make them known to the world, as he has promised for some time.[19]

---

* One might look at the letters *On sentiments*, p. 87 [p. 50] where, for precisely the same reason, the possibility of combining melody and harmony in colors is doubted.

[19] Lessing.

On the sublime and naive in the fine sciences

If one reads through Longinus' treatment of the sublime, one can only regret that Caecilius' writings on the subject have been lost.[1] To be sure, Longinus said of him that "he merely took the trouble, through countless examples of the sublime, of making a concept of it for us as though no one were acquainted with it; on the other hand, he completely omitted the most essential feature, namely, the means by which we are able to accustom our spirit to genuine majesty."[2] However, Longinus concerned himself only with the latter, presupposing the former as something that either ought to be familiar to everyone in his view or at least was known to Terentian[3] from Caecilius' writings. As a result, a very necessary part of our acquaintance with the sublime is missing, namely, the distinct definition of it. Some translators and interpreters of Longinus have tried to make up for this lack, but they do not appear to have succeeded very well in doing so.

Given the principles that have been established in the previous essays, principles of the nature of sentiments and the sources of fine sciences generally, perhaps a somewhat more perspicuous analysis can be given of the concept of the sublime which, as Longinus says, constitutes the height of perfection in writings.

We have seen that what is genuinely beautiful has definite boundaries which it may not overstep. If the full dimensions of the object cannot be

---

[1] Caecilius was a Sicilian rhetorician working in Rome during the first century AD. His work on the sublime, mentioned by Longinus, has been lost entirely.

[2] Longinus, *On the Sublime*, tr. W. Rhys Roberts (New York and London, Garland, 1987), p. 41.

[3] Longinus' work is dedicated to Terentian. See *On the Sublime*, pp. 41–3 and Introduction, pp. 18–20.

taken in by the senses all at once, then it ceases to be *sensuously beautiful* and becomes *gigantic* or *enormous in extension*. The sentiment that is then aroused is, to be sure, of a mixed nature. For well-educated minds, those used to order and symmetry, there is something repugnant about this, since the senses ultimately can perceive the boundaries, but cannot comprehend them and combine them into *one* idea without considerable difficulty. – If the boundaries of this extension are deferred further and further, then they ultimately disappear completely from the senses and, as a result, something *sensuously immense* emerges. The senses, which perceive things insofar as they are homogeneous, begin to ramble in an effort to comprehend the boundaries and end up losing themselves in what is immense. The result, as was shown in the first essay,[4] is initially a *trembling* or shudder that comes over us and then something similar to dizziness that often forces us to divert our eyes from the object. The unfathomable world of the sea, a far-reaching plain, the innumerable legions of stars, every height and depth that is beyond the reach of the eye, eternity, and other such objects of nature which appear immeasurable to the senses, arouse the sort of sentiment which in several instances, as was elaborated in that passage, is quite alluring, but in many cases is upsetting.

Because of the pleasantness of these sentiments art also makes use of them, seeking to produce them through imitation. The imitation of the sensuously immense in art is named straightforwardly "the grand or the enormous" [*das Große*]. By this is meant not an unlimited magnitude [*Größe*], but one that appears boundless and is able to awaken a pleasant shudder. In art there is a particular means of arousing this sentiment where what is genuinely immense cannot be presented. At equal spatial or temporal intervals, a single impression is repeated without alteration, uniformly, and frequently. The senses then do not perceive any symmetrical movement or any rule of order in terms of which they could somehow suppose the end of this repetition, and, by this means, they fall into a kind of unrest that is similar to shuddering at something immeasurable. An example in architecture is a straight corridor of pillars where they are similar to one another and stand at equal distances from one another. There is something *grand* about such a corridor of

---

[4] Mendelssohn is referring to "Rhadpsody," pp. 144–5.

pillars that disappears as soon as the uniformity of the repetition is interrupted and something sticks out at certain places. The monotone repetition of a single sound, at equal intervals, has the same effect in music and is employed for the purpose of expressing reverence, fright, horror. In the fine sciences there are oratorical embellishments with a similar effect. An accumulation of conjunctives sometimes accomplishes this:

> *And* the screaming *and* the deadly rage *and* the thundering heavens.

thus, too:

> . . . *and* still is *and* still thinks *and* curses . . .[5]

Sometimes, too, this is accomplished by accumulating nouns while omitting conjunctives. Longinus cites an example from Xenophon: "They slung their shields together, closed ranks, fought, killed, perished" and another from Demosthenes: "For when someone is on the offensive he can employ many things that the offended party cannot even recount; gestures, glances, and things he says, in part as a daredevil, in part as an enemy, in part with the fist, in part in the face."[6] Here the nouns accumulate, sometimes with conjunctives, sometimes without. The climax, increasing step-by-step by the same degrees, has a similar effect (although it also is pleasing for other reasons which this is not the place to elaborate).

Just as there is an immensity of extended magnitude, the effect of which we have just described, so there is an *immensity of strength* or unextended magnitude that has effects similar to the former. Power, genius, virtue have their unextended immensity that likewise arouses a spine-tingling sentiment but has the advantage of not ending, through tedious uniformity, in satiation and even disgust, as generally happens in the case of the extended immensity. The instances of the immensity of strength are as diverse as they are enormous, and, as has already been called to mind in the cited passage, the sentiment that they arouse is unmixed from the side of the object. This is why the soul indulges in them with such fervor. The term commonly applied to what is

---

[5] Klopstock, *Der Messias*, Bk. I, Song 4, ll. 7, 10, p. 65: "*Und* das Geschrey, *und* der tödtenden Wut, *und* der donnernde Himmel"; see p. 144 n. 8 and p. 211 n. 42.

[6] Longinus, *On the Sublime*, XIX, XX, pp. 98–9, 100–1.

intensively enormous is "strength," and strength in perfection is designated "the sublime." In general, one could also say: each thing that is or appears immense as far as the degree of its perfection is concerned is called *sublime*. God is called "the most sublime being." A truth is said to be "sublime" if it concerns a quite perfect or complete entity such as God, the universe, the human soul and if it is of immense use to the human race or its discovery would require a great genius.

In the fine arts and sciences the sensuously perfect representation of something immense will be *enormous, strong,* or *sublime* depending upon whether the magnitude concerns an extension and number, a degree of power, or, in particular, a degree of perfection.

The sentiment produced by the sublime is a composite one. The *magnitude* captures our attention, and since it is the magnitude of a perfection, the soul enjoys latching on to this object so that all adjoining concepts in the soul are obscured. The *immensity* arouses a sweet shudder that rushes through every fiber of our being, and the *multiplicity* prevents all satiation, giving wings to the imagination to press further and further without stopping. All these sentiments blend together in the soul, flowing into one another, and become a single phenomenon which we call *awe*. Accordingly, if one wanted to describe the sublime in terms of its effect, then one could say: "It is something sensuously perfect in art, capable of inspiring awe."

Each perfection that goes beyond our customary conceptions because of its magnitude, surpassing the expectation that we have of a certain object or even transcending what we can think of as perfect, is an object of *awe*. Regulus' resolve to return to Carthage, while aware of the torture that awaited the likes of him, is sublime and awe inspiring because we would not have believed that duty, the duty to keep a promise even to an enemy, could have had so much power over a human heart.[7] The startling reconciliation of Augustus with Cinna in Corneille's famous tragedy produces the same effect because we would have outfitted the prince's character with a completely different way of proceeding. In *Cannut* the grace which Ulfo experiences does not

---

[7]   The Roman general, Marcus Atilius Regulus (c. 250 BC) was captured by the Carthaginians and then released for the purpose of conveying the Carthaginians' conditions for peace to Rome. After he argued for pursuing war further, he returned to prison in Carthage where he was tortured and killed.

produce so sudden a sentiment since it was not unexpected from a character as kind as Cannut's.* [8]

Finally, the properties of the Supreme Being which we recognize in his works inspire the most ecstatic awe and admiration because they surpass everything that we can conceive as enormous, perfect, or sublime.

Since the enormous and the sublime have such a related nature, it is apparent why artists so often support the sublime by means of the enormous and prepare us, as it were, for the spiritual representation of the sublime through the sensuous impression of something enormous. They enlarge the measure or the proportions of things that they want to represent as sublime. Artists make use of a bright glow which blinds because of its *strength* or else of a *darkness* that allows the boundaries of the objects to recede; but they never use a moderate light. No picture of the sublime is clearly distinguished; some features are enlarged hyperbolically, and the rest are left indefinite so that the imagination may lose itself in their magnitude:

> . . . I stretch my head up into the clouds
> My arm out into eternity . . .

The sublime in literary composition is accompanied by the enormous in music, by the artificially immense in the repetition, and so forth. Not that everything enormous is also sublime, as one would commonly believe, but rather because similar sentiments mutually reinforce one another and because the enormous is for the outer sense precisely what the sublime is for the inner sense. The impression on the inner sense must, therefore, be strengthened if the outer senses are harmoniously attuned to it by a similar impression.

In the works of fine arts and sciences, the awe, like the perfection which it presupposes, belongs to two different genera. Either the object to be represented possesses awesome properties in and for itself, in which case the awe at the object becomes the dominating idea in the

---

* Thus, if Cannut could be put in circumstances in which his grace would be unexpected and would not flow so immediately from his general kind character, the effect would be indisputably far stronger. See *Bibliothek der schönen Wissenschaften*, Erster Band, Erster Theil, p. 56.[9]

8 Corneille, *Cinna* (Paris, 1640) and Johann Elias Schlegel, *Cannut* (Copenhagen, 1746).

9 Friedrich Nicolai, "Abhandlung vom Trauerspiel," *Bibliothek der schönen Wissenschaften und der freyen Künste* (Berlin, 1757) vol. 1, Part 1, p. 56. (Nicolai's entire essay is to be found on pp. 17–68).

soul; or the object in itself is not so extraordinary, but the artist possesses the skill of elevating its properties and showing them in an uncommon light. In this case the awe is directed more at the imitation than at the original, more at the merits of the art than at the merits of the object. Because of this and insofar as each work is also a copy of the perfection of its creator, the awe in this case is directed, above all, at the artist and his splendid qualities. One admires his great wit, his genius, his imagination, and his soul's capacities that harmonize for so worthy a final purpose, the hidden essence of which he knew how to reveal in his work. What especially pleases us in the case of art, considered as art, is the reference to the spiritual gifts of the artist which make themselves visibly known. If they bear the characteristics of an uncommon genius or some otherwise extraordinary talent, then they inspire awe on our part.

This division will provide us with the opportunity of deciding the extent to which the sublime is compatible with an embellished expression and in what case it refuses to assume such a form. We will begin with the type of sublimity where the awe and admiration spring from the object itself.

The value of perfections of the external condition are all too slight to be able to be held in awe by someone intelligent. Thus, riches, splendor, stature, and undeserved power are easily excluded from the sublime.

Longinus puts it quite ingeniously, "When things are of the sort that despising them is regarded as something great, they can never themselves contain anything actually lofty in itself."[10] In fact we do not admire those who possess great riches or superior positions of rank as much as those who can have them and reject them out of noble magnanimity. Thus, too, the representation of these things in architecture and the ornamental arts, where enhancements of the external condition come into play, can become illustrious, proud, and magnificent, to be sure. But the representation can reach the level of the sublime only by means of a *noble simplicity*, that is, through avoidance of anything that would appear to place great value on those enhancements. Not the disappearance of wealth and splendor but rather a wise indifference to them elevates our soul and teaches it its own dignity. They only remain important to the garish individual who wants to stake his pride on them.

---

[10] Longinus, *On the Sublime*, ch. 7, pp. 54–7.

Uncommon physical strength without courage, a beautiful shape in an insignificant place on the body, a beautifully formed face that betrays neither spirit nor sentiment, an uncommon agility without charm and bearing, and so forth are all bodily perfections that can, to be sure, inspire a slight degree of awe and admiration.* But we will never be so enthralled by them as when we admire the perfections of spirit. An enormous intellect, enormous and uncommon sensibilities, a fortunate imagination joined with penetrating sagacity, noble and passionate emotions that elevate themselves above the conceptions of commoner souls (be their goal a true or apparent good), and generally all great qualities of a spirit that take us by surprise sweep our soul up with them, elevating it, as it were, above itself. The immensely enormous character of those qualities (qualities that, given the absence of any expectation, must also appear *novel*) anchors the attentiveness of the spirit and so weakens all other adjoining conceptions that the soul can find no way of moving to another object. Instead, the soul is momentarily stopped in its tracks and gazes, *astounded*, at this immensity, if I am permitted to use this word in the sense in which it has already been used by good writers. If this inability to leave the object persists for some time, such a condition of the mind is called *astonishment*.

Meanwhile, the awe is almost comparable to a lightning bolt which blinds us in one moment and disappears in the next, provided that its flame is not sustained and nourished by the fire of a gentler sentiment. If we love the object of which we are in awe or if it deserves our sympathy because of an undeserved agony, the awe alternates with the more familiar sentiment in our mind. We wish, hope, and fear for the object of our love or our sympathy and admire his or her great soul that

---

* The Dutch translator must not have understood me correctly here since, in an added note, he cites against me the examples of Helen, Zeuxis, Venus, and Antinous[11] as well as Apollo and Laocoön, each of which arouses not a slight degree, but the highest degree of admiration. As if the masterpieces of ancient art did not please more through the fullness of soul that they express than through mere bodily beauties? Does Venus or Antinous de' Medici have merely a beautiful and rule-governed form that reveals neither spirit nor sentiment? If, moreover, the translator wanted to see the awe extended to the visible knowledge of each important and particular novelty, then he did not consider that in German we distinguish "amazement" and "awe." Amazement is the condition of a soul looking at the novel and unexpected; but awe is its condition when it looks at the unexpectedly good.

11 Zeuxis was a Greek painter (fl. 400 BC) celebrated for his portrayal of human figures in superhuman proportions. Antinous (110–AD130), a favorite of the Emperor Hadrian, was depicted in sculptures and on coins as a model of youthful beauty. See Introduction, p. xxxix on the translation of 'awe'.

is beyond hope and fear. If an artist by his power of enchantment can put us into such a frame of mind, then he has reached the pinnacle of his art and satisfied the worthiest calling of the fine arts. It is a pleasant spectacle for the gods, an ancient philosopher says, to see a virtuous soul wrestle with fate, to see him surrender everything to it but his virtue. "Ecce spectaculum dignum, ad quod respiciat intentus operi suo Deus: ecce par Deo dignum, *vir fortis cum mala fortuna compositus!*"*

These, then, are the most distinguished sorts of awe which can spring from the object itself without its being necessary to draw the perfections of the artist into consideration as well. We want to see the extent to which an external embellishment in the expression is compatible with it.

As has been recalled in the foregoing discussion, the genuinely sublime occupies the powers of the soul in such a manner that all adjoining conceptions which are somehow attached to it have to disappear. It is like the sun that by itself illuminates and by its radiance obscures all weaker lights. Also, in the moment when we perceive the sublime, neither wit nor imagination administer their office in order to direct us somehow to other conceptions. For the sublime or the object of awe was never linked, by laws of the imagination, to some other conception in our soul upon which it could naturally follow. If someone doubts this, he need only reflect on the fact that the unexpected, the novel is an essential determination of the sublime, according to our explanation. This is precisely the source of the strong impression that awe makes on our mind, which is not infrequently followed by an astonishment or even a type of stupor, an absence of consciousness.

It becomes clear from this that excessive embellishment in the expression of things is not compatible with something sublime of the first type. Expansion by means of adjoining conceptions is unnatural since the latter must all, as it were, recede into the darkest of shadows. Because of the length of time it takes, the analysis of the central concept would weaken the awe since it would let us feel the sublime only little by little. Similes, just like other decorations of speech, can take place even less since the sources of them (wit and imagination) cease to act in the course of the perception of the sublime and instead allow the soul

---

* Seneca, *De Providentia*, C. II. 9.[12]

[12] "Behold a spectacle worthy of God's attention as he contemplates his work; behold what is worthy and fitting for God, *a brave man confronted with misfortune!*"; Cf. Seneca, *Moral Essays*, tr. John W. Basore (Cambridge, Mass., Harvard University Press, 1970), vol. 1, pp. 10–11.

the appropriate leisure to give itself up to the concept of the sublime in order to consider it all its magnitude. The central concept of the sublime is actually this:

Judicis argutum quod non formidat acumen.[13]

One can say of it, "it prefers to be seen under the light" [*volet haec sub luce videri*], in contrast to what is the case for the adjoining conception, "that loves the dark" [*haec amat obscurum*].[14] Thus, in representing something sublime of this type, the artist must devote himself to a naive, unaffected expression which allows the reader or spectator to think more than is said to him. The artist's expression, meanwhile, must always remain intuitive and, where possible, be traced back to individual instances so that the mind of the reader is awakened and inspired to reflect.

We will clarify these ruminations with some examples. In this sentence, "What God willed, came to be" there resides the same elevated concept that we admire in the well-known sentence, "God said, 'Let there be light,' and there was light."[15] But the former expression is abstract and is not sufficiently inspiring. The sensuous action of speaking and this individual object "light" make the concept intuitive and animate it.

Reges in ipsos imperium est jovis
Cuncta supercilio moventis.[16]

This is an uncommonly sublime thought. However, if one had said "mind" (*mente*) or "will" (*voluntate*) instead of "wink" (*supercilio*), or "governing" (*regnantis*) instead of "moving" (*moventis*), then a portion of its majesty disappears because the concrete concepts have been changed to abstract ones. The almighty wink, *supercilio*, and the sensuous effect, *moventis*, arouse in our imagination the sublime image of a Jupiter of Phidias. We see the almighty, if I may be permitted so to speak, face to face,

---

[13] Horace, *Ars poetica*, l. 364: ". . . that it does not fear a judge's critical insight." Cf. Horace, *Satires, Epistles and Ars Poetica*, tr. H. Rushton Fairclough (Cambridge, Mass., Harvard University Press, 1966), pp. 480–1.

[14] Ibid., ll. 361–5.

[15] Genesis 1:3.

[16] Horace, *Odes*, III. 1.7: "Over kings themselves is the rule of Jupiter/ Moving everything with a wink"; cf. Horace, *The Odes and Epodes*, tr. C. E. Bennett (Cambridge, Mass., Harvard University Press, 1952), pp. 168–9.

> *Qui totum nutu tremefecit olympum.*[17]

In the following passage from Horace,

> *Si fractus illabatur orbis,*
> *Impavidum ferient ruinae*[18]

the danger in which the sage finds himself is perfectly drawn. By contrast, the state of his soul, which is actually supposed to inspire awe on our part, is suggested merely by a single word: "undaunted" (*impavidum*). Let us suppose the following addition:

> *Si fractus illabatur orbis,*
> *Justum et tenacem propositi virum,*
> *Impavidum ferient ruinae.*[19]

Where is the admired sublimity now? The poorly suited paraphrase of the subject has allowed the fire of expectation to burn out, having detained the mind of the reader all too long, anxious and eager as it was at the beginning.

One will notice the same phenomenon in the case of the author of the holy psalms and, to be sure, in the passage where he elaborates a similar thought, perhaps in even more dignified fashion than Horace.

> Hence we are not afraid when the earth is transformed,
> And mountains sink into the sea.
>
> – Psalm 46. 3

Here the danger is described just as completely as it is by Horace, but in a way far more commensurate with the truth. Yet what can be expressed in simpler and more unadorned fashion than the effect of trust in God: "We are not afraid" (for which the Hebrews did not need more than three syllables).[20]

One might take note, in passing, of the careful choice of expressions made by these two great poets, if one be permitted to compare them in different ways. Horace describes the state of mind of a Stoic sage who has been hardened against all adverse contingencies by the consideration

---

[17] Virgil, *Aeneid*, IX. 106 and X. 115: "who with a nod made all Olympus tremble"; cf. Virgil, *Works*, tr. H. Rushton Fairclough (Cambridge, Mass., Harvard University Press, 1935), vol. 2, pp. 118–19 and 178–9.

[18] *Odes*, III. iii. 7–8 (see next note); cf. Horace, *The Odes and Epodes*, pp. 178–9.

[19] Ibid.: "If a shattered world were to cave in,/ On a man just and tenacious in his resolve,/ Its ruins would strike someone undaunted by them."

[20] In German: "Fürchten wir uns nicht."

that fate is necessary and unalterable. He can, of course, fear all evils; the ruins of a shattered world really are his undoing: "its ruins would strike" *(feriunt ruinae)*; but he is not terrified by this. No misfortune befalls him unexpectedly. He has composed himself for every blow of fate. By contrast, the holy poet speaks of the state of mind of a pious individual who is fully at peace with God and puts his trust in him. This person can be terrified by the sudden threat of a danger. Yet he thinks back to God:

> Therefore he is not afraid.

As far as their nature is concerned, some things are so perfect, so sublime that they cannot be reached by any finite thought, cannot be adequately intimated by means of any sign, and cannot be represented as they are by any images. Among such things are God, the world, eternity, and so on. Here the artist must exert all the powers of his spirit to find the most worthy signs by means of which these infinitely sublime concepts can be aroused in us intuitively. He can accomplish this all the more surely since the signified matter always remains far greater than the sign that he makes use of, and, consequently, his expression, however full it may be, always remains naive in comparison to the matter. The holy poet sings: "Lord! Your grace extends beyond the heavens and your truth above the clouds. Your justice, like the mountain of God and your law, an unfathomable depth!"[21] Herr von Haller sings of eternity:

> Swiftly soaring, faster
> Than time and sound and wind
> And even light's wings, thoughts grow
> Weary of you and hope for no barriers.[22]

Does he not appear, with these sublime images, to have found the most worthy measure for the immeasurable itself?

In sublime passages where much is left to the reader to ponder, poets have the great device of getting the reader's attention through unfinished verse, interrupted inferences, or monosyllabic words. These sorts

---

[21] Psalm 36. 6–7.
[22] Albrecht von Haller, "Unvollkommenes Gedicht über die Ewigkeit" (Bern, 1736), in *Die Alpen und andere Gedichte*, ed. Ludwig Hirzel (Stuttgart, Reclam, 1968), p. 77 ll. 63–6: "Die schnellen Schwingen der Gedanken,/ Wogegen Zeit, und Schall, und Wind/ Und selbst des Lichtes Flügel langsam sind,/ Ermüden über dir und hoffen keine Schranken."

of unresolved cadences do not completely comfort the reader. He longs for the conclusion and finds enough material in the present thought to think it through to the end himself. The following passages may serve as examples of this.

> *Ne dubita, nam vera vides . . .*
>
> — *Aenead*, III. 316

> *Constitit Anchisa satus, et vestigia pressit*
> *Multa putans . . .*
>
> — *Aenead*, VI. 330

> *. . . Manet imperteritus ille,*
> *Hostem magnanimum opperiens, et mole sua stat.*
>
> — *Aenead*, X. 771[23]

> . . . silence the tremolo of chords there
> Then you extol the Lord with more dignity
>
> — *Springtime*[24]

> *Supremamque auram, ponens caput, expiravit.*
>
> — Vida[25]

> And he bowed his head and died.
>
> — Klopstock[26]

We find a masterpiece of this sort in the fifth song of the *Messias* where the poet, at one of the most sublime thoughts, breaks off the verse in the middle in order to allow the reader time to grasp the great thought appropriately.

> . . . God thought to himself of the world of spirits that remained
> faithful to him;
> And of the sinners, the human race. At that point he became
> furious and stood then

---

[23] Virgil, "Doubt not, for what you see is real . . ."; "Anchises' son halted his steps and stood still,/ Pondering much . . ."; ". . . Undaunted he remains,/ Steadfast in his bulk, awaiting his noble foe"; *Works*, vol. 1, pp. 368–9; vol. 1, pp. 528–9; vol. 2, pp. 222–3.

[24] Ewald Christian von Kleist, "Der Frühling" (Berlin, 1749; revised 1756), in *Werke*, Pt. 1, ed. August Sauer (Bern, Lang, 1968), p. 227: ". . .Verstummet dann bebende Saiten,/ So preißt ihr würdiger den Herrn."

[25] Marco Girolamo Vida, *Christiados* (Cremona, 1535), Bk. V, 995: "Bowing his head, he exhaled his last breath." *Christiados libri sex* was first published in 1535. Cf. Marco Girolamo Vida, *The Christiad, A Latin-English Edition*, ed. and tr. Gertrude C. Drake and Clarence A. Forbes (Carbondale and Edwardsville, Ill., Southern Illinois University Press, 1978), pp. 238–9.

[26] Klopstock, *Der Messias*, Song X, l. 1052, vol. 1, p. 227. "Und er neigte sein Haupt, und starb."

> High on Mt. Tabor, holding the quivering globe so
> That it would not perish [*vergieng*] in front of him.[27]

How well thought out this is by the poet who says *vergieng* instead of *vergehe* in order to interrupt the cadence even more through the masculine closing syllable, although grammatically *vergehe* would have been more correct.[28]

Sublime sensibilities or the heroic which, as we noted above, constitute a subgroup of the sublime of the first type, consists in the sort of perfections of the powers of desire that inspire awe. If the hero is introduced speaking for himself and voicing such sensibilities, he must express himself as briefly and in as unadorned a fashion as possible. A great soul expresses its sensibilities uprightly and emphatically, but not bombastically. It is a greater perfection if noble sensibilities have become, as it were, our second nature, if we think and act in a superior way without knowing it and without making ourselves out to be particularly deserving because of this. Hence, the emphatic brevity in the answer of old Horace, "Qu'il mourut," of Voltaire's Brutus, "Brutus l'eut immolé," and the unaffected proposal of friendship in Corneille's *Cinna*: "Soyons amis, Cinna!"[29]

Here is also the place for that Spartan's response, when a Persian boasted that the number of arrows and javelins of the Persian army would screen out the sun. "Then we will fight in the shadows," he replied. Even Simonides' epitaph to the Lacedaemonians who remained behind at the battle of Thermopylae is of this sort:

> Die hospes Spartae, nos te hic vidisse jacentes;
> Dum sanctis patriae legibus obsequimur.
>   – Cicero, *Tusculan Disputations*, Bk. I, l. 101[30]

---

[27] Ibid., Song V, ll. 322–5, vol. I, p. 109. ". . . Gott dachte sich selbst, die Geisterwelt, die ihm getreu blieb;/ Und den Sünder, das Menschengeschlecht. Da ergrimmt er, und stand itzt/ Hoch auf Tabor, und hielt den tieferzitternden Erdkreis,/ Daβ er nicht vor ihm vergieng."

[28] Mendelssohn is contrasting "vergieng" (see n. 27) the variant of the subjunctive mood (*Konjunktiv II*) of "vergehen" that expresses a contrafactual or impossible condition, with "vergehe," the variant (*Konjunktiv I*) that expresses an uncertain or possible condition. He is calling attention to the fact that the last syllable in "vergieng" is accented, while the penultimate syllable is accented in "vergehe": a cadence is masculine when the final meter is monosyllabic and accented.

[29] Corneille, *Horace* (Paris, 1640), III. 6: "Let him die"; Voltaire, *Brutus* (Paris, 1730): "Brutus slaughtered him"; Corneille, *Cinna*, V. 3: "Let's be friends, Cinna!"

[30] "Stranger, tell Sparta that you saw us lying here,/ Keeping the laws of our holy fatherland." Cf. Cicero, *Tusculan Disputations*, tr. J. E. King (Cambridge, Mass., Harvard University Press, 1966), pp. 120–1.

These patriotic men regard their death as amply compensated if only Sparta learns that they fell in battle because they obeyed the holy laws of the fatherland.

Yet to the same degree that a hero's sensibilities are unalterable and that his soul briefly yet emphatically makes these sensibilities known once a decision is made, a hero's soul must reveal his thoughts to be rich and inexhaustible when he reflects on his actions and is still uncertain which path virtue commands him to take. He must act in neither an obstinate nor an arbitrary manner, and if the case is dubious, he must discern with great care the reasons for and against what he envisages doing, before being swayed in one direction or another. Then, the expression of the sublimity of these sensibilities will be embellished in the richest possible way; every spark of oratorical eloquence is applied to show the compelling reasons on both sides and to show them in their strongest light. The undecided soul sways from one side to the other, as if driven by waves, and sweeps the listener along with him until he finally recognizes the voice of virtue which tears him free of that uncertainty. All at once, every doubt is defeated, every obstacle is overcome, the decision is made, and, from that point on, nothing can make him waver again.

Sublimity of the latter sort is the source of the monologues in tragedies which have come into vogue so much in modern times with the doing away of the chorus. Masterpieces of this sort are the monologues by Augustus in *Cinna* (Act IV, Scene III), Rodogune in the tragedy of the same name (Act III, Scene III), Agamemnon in *Iphigenia* (Act IV, Scene III), Cato in Addison's *Cato* (Act V, Scene I), and Aeneas in Metastasio's opera *Dido* (Act I, Scene XIX).[31] Yet they are all surpassed by the famous monologue of Shakespeare's *Hamlet* in the third act (Scene II). Allow me to translate the latter for the sake of those readers who are not familiar with the English language. Hamlet has a well-founded suspicion that his mother and her present spouse conspired to assassinate his father, the legitimate king. This thought gnaws at his soul and causes him so much anguish that he falls into a deep melancholy. He has resolved to avenge the death of his father, but he is not yet fully convinced. The uncertainty plunges him into despair and

---

[31] Joseph Addison, *Cato* (London, 1713) and Pietro Antonio Metastasio, *Didone abbandonata* (Naples, 1724).

brings him almost to the point of committing suicide. Deep in these despondent thoughts, he steps forward and reflects:

> To be, or not to be; that is the question:
> Whether 'tis nobler in the mind to suffer
> The slings and arrows of outrageous fortune,
> Or to take arms against a sea of troubles,
> And, by opposing, end them. To die, to sleep –
> No more, and by a sleep to say we end
> The heartache and the thousand natural shocks
> That flesh is heir to – 'tis a consummation
> Devoutly to be wished. To die, to sleep.
> To sleep, perchance to dream. Ay, there's the rub,
> For in that sleep of death what dreams may come
> When we have shuffled off this mortal coil
> Must give us pause. There's the respect
> That makes calamity of so long life,
> For who would bear the whips and scorns of time,
> Th'oppressor's wrong, the proud man's contumely,
> The pangs of disprized love, the law's delay,
> The insolence of office, and the spurns
> That patient merit of th'unworthy takes,
> When he himself might his quietus make
> With a bare bodkin? Who would fardels bear,
> To grunt and sweat under a weary life,
> But that the dread of something after death,
> The undiscovered country from whose bourn
> No traveller returns, puzzles the will,
> And makes us rather bear those ills we have
> Than fly to others that we know not of?
> Thus conscience does make cowards of us all,
> And thus the native hue of resolution
> Is sicklied o'er with the pale cast of thought,
> And enterprises of great pith and moment
> With this regard their currents turn awry,
> And lose the name of action . . .[32]

Of all the types of sublimity, the passionate sublimity of a soul suddenly bewildered by terror, regret, fury, and despair demands the most

---

[32] *The Complete Works*, ed. Stanley Wells and Gary Taylor (Oxford, Clarendon Press, 1986), III.i. 58–90.

unaffected expression. A mind in anger is preoccupied with its emotion alone, and any conception that would put distance between it and the emotion is torture. At the moment of a violent emotion the soul is working under a torrent of images. They all press to the point of exploding, and since they cannot all be expressed at the same time, the voice stammers and can scarcely utter the words that first occur to it.

What, for example, could Oedipus say at that horrifying moment when the entire mystery became clear to him from what the old palace servant said, and he sensed that he would have to endure the terrible curse that he issued against Laius' murderer? "Oh! Oh! Now everything is clear!" Sophocles has him exclaim.[33] On this subject Oedipus was acquainted with so many oracles, testimonies, and circumstances which appeared, in part, to contradict one another and, in part, to contradict his own consciousness. Now he recognized to his horror that they were all completely consistent and coherent with one another and that he was the most miserable creature of all mortals. "Oh! Oh!" is the expression of nature in the first moments of bewilderment, the sigh released by an unfortunate soul when no words come to him. The first idea that could have arisen in Oedipus' soul had to refer to the way the circumstances agreed with one another: "Now everything is clear!"

All this appears much too calm to Seneca who, by contrast, has his Oedipus rage in a completely different manner in the same situation.

> Dehisce tellus, tuque tenebrarum potens
> In Tartara ima, rector umbrarum rape.[34]

One sees that the more the words bellow, the colder they leave the heart. For we feel that we hear the poet posturing and not the unfortunate Oedipus.

In Shakespeare's *Macbeth* MacDuff hears that Macbeth has taken his castle and killed his wife and children. MacDuff falls into a deep melancholy. His friend wants to console him but he does not listen, thinking instead of ways of avenging himself until, finally, he breaks out in the terrifying words: "He has no children!"[35]

---

[33] *Oedipus Rex*, 1182.
[34] Seneca, *Oedipus Rex*, ll. 868–9: "Open up, earth! and take me down, you power of darkness/ And ruler of the shadow world, down into the deepest pits of Tartarus". Cf. *Seneca's Tragedies*, tr. Frank Justus Miller (Cambridge, Mass., Harvard University Press, 1938), vol. 1, pp. 508–9.
[35] IV. iii. 216.

These few words exude more vengefulness than could have been expressed in an entire speech.

When Joseph in his melancholy could no longer restrain himself and dismissed all those present in order to make himself known to his brothers, what words was he to find to express the state of his soul? How was he to make it clear to his brothers all at once that he is the brother mistreated by them, but still their brother? "I am Joseph," he says, "is my father still alive?"[36] And his brothers could not answer him for they were terrified of him.

Longinus has already noted that the truly sublime can more often be sustained by sheer silence. "The sublime," he says in the ninth section of his essay, "is nothing but an echo of a great spirit. And for this reason we sometimes admire a human being's mere thinking even if he does not utter a single word, like the silence of Ajax in hell,* which in itself contains more sublimity than anything that he could have said."[37] Such eloquent silence has been imitated by Virgil,** where he says of Dido who is addressed by Aeneas in the Elysian fields:

> Illa solo fixos oculos aversa tenebat,
> Nec magis incepto vultum sermone movetur,
> Quam si dura silex, aut stet Marpesia cautes.
> Tandem proripuit se se, atque inmica refugit
> In nemus umbriferum.[38]

Among the moderns Klopstock has likewise sought to put this sublime silence to work precisely when Abdiel is addressed by the penitent Abbadona who was his friend before the revolt.[39] I do not trust myself to determine how successful Klopstock's effort was.

If this mute eloquence, if one can so call it, is joined with sublime passions at the right place, then it can have the most propitious effect on the mind of an attentive audience.

In Sophocles' *Oedipus* (Act IV, Scene III) the Corinthian shepherd says to Oedipus, in the presence of Jocasta, that he could return to

---

* Homer, *Odyssey*, Bk. XI. v. 563.   ** Virgil, *Aenead*, Bk. VI. v. 469.

[36] Genesis 45. 1–3.   [37] *On the Sublime*, pp. 60–1.

[38] *Aeneid*, VI. 469–73: "Turning away, she held her eyes fixed in one direction/ And as he begins to speak, her face is no more moved/ Than if she were set in hard flint or Marpesian rock./ Suddenly she flung herself away and, as his enemy,/ Fled back into the shady grove." Cf. Virgil, *Works*, vol. 1, pp. 538–9.

[39] *Der Messias*, Song II, ll. 757–61, vol. 1, pp. 40–1.

Corinth without worrying, that Merope was not his mother and Polybius was not his father. The shepherd says that he found Oedipus on the mountain Citeron and brought him from there to Corinth. This news must have struck the mind of Jocasta like a thunderbolt. Now she is fully informed of her horrible fate. She allowed her son to be exposed on this very mountain out of fear that he would at some time, in keeping with the oracle, kill his father, Laius. Oedipus was found on this mountain and is now her spouse. Tiresius' obscure utterances and the entire terrible secret now suddenly become clear in her soul. But she remains silent. The pain has so stupefied her that she stands there like a pillar. Her spouse and son continues to probe the shepherd. What despair there must have been in her eyes during this discussion! Oedipus, tortured by the most terrifying doubts, allows himself to be driven by his inquisitiveness to put a question to her. At that moment she awakens as it were from the slumber of the dead.

> *Jocasta.* "How can this be!" she replied, "What did he say? – For heaven's sake, if you have any love for yourself, stop probing any further! I am miserable enough."
>
> *Oedipus.* "Just calm down! If I were the progeny of three generations of slaves, it could not be a disgrace to you."
>
> *Jocasta.* "Obey me anyway! I beg you! Oh, don't do it!"
>
> *Oedipus.* "No! I must bring the truth to light."
>
> *Jocasta.* "Oh, if you knew what important reasons I have for keeping this from you."
>
> *Oedipus.* "But it is precisely these secret reasons that increase my uneasiness."
>
> *Jocasta* (to the side). "All the more lamentable! – May you never know who you are!"
>
> *Oedipus.* "Have someone quickly bring the other shepherd here. Let the queen be forever ashamed of my class and fancy herself great with her own."
>
> *Jocasta.* "Alas! alas! The most hapless of all mortals. This is all that I still have to say to you – I am no longer able." (departs)[40]

This is the way that truly sublime passions speak. The silence of Jocasta as long as the exchange was not directed at her; the wild, despairing looks, the anguish, and the convulsive trembling in all her

---

[40] *Oedipus Rex*, ll. 1060–72; in *Sophocles*, tr. F. Storr (London, Heinemann, 1977), vol. 1, pp. 98–101.

limbs (which a good actress couples with this frightful silence) cast the entire scene into the most extreme terror, a scene in a state of constant expectation, sustained by Oedipus' impatience and by the gradual unfolding of the great secret. He is, to be sure, not yet fully informed of Jocasta's fate. But the intimations brought about by her behavior, the oracle, and Tiresias' utterances are all the more terrifying. Finally she speaks, but what words! What confusion! "How can this be! What did he say? – For heaven's sake" and so on. In departing, she lets us know quite clearly what designs she nourishes in her bosom and rushes to carry out without witnesses. "This is all that I still have to say to you – I am no longer able." Who does not tremble in fear for her life at this moment? Who does not accompany her with their eyes, wishing that she not be left to her despair? But Oedipus is all too preoccupied with himself and does not suspect any danger from her side. She departs and at the outset of the fifth act we learn that our concern was all too well-founded.

Enough has been said about the first type of the sublime in which the basis for awe is to be found in the very matter to be represented. Perhaps I have dwelled far too long on this type. But sublime sensibilities demanded a far more extensive elaboration since there is hardly a single one that is to be placed in this class among all the examples of the sublime cited by Longinus. I consider Ajax's silence an exception which actually belongs to this type, as does the famous plea of this hero (cited by Longinus in the ninth section): "Oh, father Zeus! Save the Greeks from the darkness, let it become light that our eyes might see again. If you have decided to do so, at least kill us on a bright day!"[41]

The second type of sublimity is that in which the awe and admiration redound more on the art of the representation than on what is represented and, thus, as was previously shown, mostly on the genius and the extraordinary capabilities of the artist. In itself the object often can contain nothing elevated in stature, nothing extraordinary. But we admire the enormous talents of the poet, his effective imagination, his capacity to compose, his profound insight into the nature of things, into characters and passions, and the noble manner in which he was able to express his splendid thoughts. A human being who dies wandering

[41] *Iliad*, XVII. 645.

around the battlefield is in itself not an object deserving our awe or admiration. But there is no one who is not in awe of Klopstock's genius when he sketches this object. The first fortunate insight by means of which he opens up a field to great thoughts was his portrayal, not of an ordinary person, but of an atheist in this condition.

> . . . The approaching victor
> And the prancing horse, the din of the clanging armor,
> And the screaming and the deadly rage and the thundering
>   heavens
> Storm around him. He lies and sinks with his head split in two
> Mute and without a thought among the dead, believing that he is
>   perishing.
> Then he lifts himself up one more time and still is and still thinks
>   and curses
> The fact that he still is, and with pallid, dying hands he spews
> Blood towards heaven. God he curses and still wants to deny.[42]

What painters call a "fracas," the wild tumult on a battlefield which is sketched here with such splendid strokes, sets the mind of the reader in motion, the most extreme motion. In the midst of this powerful din, the furious despair of the atheist who now feels that a God exists draws all our attention to it, filling us with disgust and dismay. The dreadfulness, the horror storms our soul from all sides; everywhere we find the *sensuous immensity* that arouses shudder after shudder and, as was shown above, undergirds the sentiment of the sublime. – What a thought! ". . . God he curses and still wants to deny."

How sublime the following depiction of someone about to die is:

> . . . the eyes of the one dying grow dim and stare,
> Seeing no more. The countenance of the earth and sky vanish
>   from him
> Deep into the night. He no longer hears a human voice
> Nor the tender laments of friends. He himself cannot talk,
> And with quivering tongue scarcely stammers out the anguished
>   departure.

---

[42] *Der Messias*, Song IV, ll. 5–12, vol. 1, p. 65: ". . . Der kommende Sieger/ Und das bäumende Roß, der rauschenden Panzer Getöse,/ Und das Geschrey, und der tödtenden Wuth, und der donnernde Himmel/ Stürmt über ihm. Er liegt, und sinkt mit gespaltenem Haupte/ Dumm und gedankenlos unter den Todten, und glaubt zu vergehen./ Darauf erhebt er sich wieder, und ist noch, und denkt noch, und fluchtet,/ Daß er noch ist, und spritzt mit bleichen sterbenden Händen/ Blut gen Himmel. Gott fluchtet er, und wolt' ihn gerne noch läugnen."

He exhales deeply; a cold, anxious sweat runs
Over his forehead, the heart beats slowly, then stands still, and he
is dead.[43]

This description has, as far as its intrinsic value is concerned, a great similarity with the description of Sappho's jealous love, which Longinus has preserved for us.[44] This fragment of a poem, the English *Spectator* says, is for poets what the well-known ancient torso was for Michelangelo.[45] – Now all these sort of objects such as death, a battlefield, despair are not, in and for themselves, admirable, and they become so merely in the imitation of them by the genius of the artist. But by their very nature they are frightening and dreadful, and support the sentiment of the sublime because of the sensuous immensity inherent in them. For this reason artists also prefer to select them.

However, there are also objects of a completely indifferent nature that do not provide the artist with the slightest support. It is left completely up to the artist's powers as to how sublime these objects appear to us, that is to say, to what extent they would deserve our awe and admiration. An example of this type is the passage in Demosthenes praised by Longinus.[46]

> Tell me the truth, do you want to keep running around, asking one another: "Is there any news?" What more do you need to hear than the news that a man from Macedonia is waging war on all of Greece? "Has Philip died?" No, by God he has not; he is merely indisposed. But, oh, you Athenians, what does this matter to you? If we suppose that something human did befall him, you would surely create some other Philip.[47]

Where does the greatness lie here? What else arouses the idea of the

---

[43] Ibid., Song V, ll. 217–23, vol. 1, p. 106: ". . . Dem Sterbenden brechen die Augen, und starren,/ Sehen nicht mehr. Ihm schwindet das Antlitz der Erde und des Himmels/ Tief in die Nacht. Er höret nicht mehr die Stimme des Menschen,/ Noch der Freundschaft zärtliche Klagen. Er selbst kann nicht reden,/ Und mit bebender Zunge den bangen Abschied kaum stammeln./ Athmet tiefer herauf; Ein kalter ängstlicher Schweiß läuft/ Ueber sein Antlitz, das Herz schlägt langsam, dann stehts, dann stirbt er."

[44] *On the Sublime*, ch. 10, pp. 68–71.

[45] Joseph Addison and Sir Richard Steele, *The Spectator*, No. 229 (Thursday, Nov. 22, 1711); in *The Spectator*, ed. Gregory Smith (London, Dent, 1958), p. 180.

[46] *On the Sublime*, ch. 18, pp. 96–7.

[47] Demosthenes, *Phillipica* I. 9–12. Cf. Demosthenes, *Works*, tr. J. H. Vince (London, Heinemann, 1930), p. 75.

immense here but the admirable spirit of the speaker who knows how to make use of the most trivial circumstances so successfully in order to impart life, emphasis, and spirit to his address?

No one is more successful than Shakespeare in knowing how to draw some advantage from the most ordinary circumstances and to make them sublime by some effective twist. The effect of this sort of sublimity must be all the more intense, the more unsuspectingly it surprises and the less people expect such important and tragic consequences from so insignificant a cause. I will cite a few examples of this from *Hamlet*. The King arranges some amusements to dispel the Prince's melancholy. Plays are performed. Hamlet sees the tragedy *Hecuba* performed. He appears to be in a good mood. The social gathering disperses, leaving him alone, and – now one is astonished at the tragic consequences that Shakespeare is able to draw from these common circumstances – the Prince speaks with himself:

> O, what a rogue and peasant slave am I!
> Is it not monstrous that this player here,
> But in a fiction, in a dream of passion,
> Could force his soul so to his whole conceit
> That from her working all his visage wanned,
> Tears in his eyes, distraction in 's aspect,
> A broken voice, and his whole function suiting
> With forms to his conceit? and all for nothing!
> For Hecuba!
> What's Hecuba to him, or he to Hecuba,
> That he should weep for her? What would he do
> Had he the motive and the cue for passion
> That I have? . . .
>
> – Hamlet, Act II, Scene II

What a masterstroke! Experience teaches that dejected souls find a way at every opportunity, often in the midst of our attempts to cheer them up and when we least expect it, of making the transition to the prevailing image of their melancholy. The more someone believes that he has drawn them away from that melancholy, the more suddenly they plunge back into it. This experience guided the genius of Shakespeare whenever he had to portray melancholy. His *Hamlet* and his *Lear* are full of the same unexpected transitions that cannot help but shock the audience.

In the third act, at the behest of the King, Guildenstern, an earlier intimate of Hamlet, attempts to sound him out and find the secret cause of his melancholy. The Prince notices this and becomes indignant.

> *Guildenstern.* O my lord, if my duty be too bold, . . .
> *Hamlet.* I do not well understand that. Will you play upon this pipe?
> *Guildenstern.* My lord, I cannot.
> *Hamlet.* I pray you.
> *Guildenstern.* Believe me, I cannot.
> *Hamlet.* I do beseech you.
> *Guildenstern.* I know no touch of it, my lord.
> *Hamlet.* 'Tis as easy as lying. Govern these ventages with your finger and thumb, give it breath with your mouth, and it will discourse most eloquent music. Look you, these are the stops.
> *Guildenstern.* But these cannot I command to any utterance of harmony; I have not the skill.
> *Hamlet.* Why, look you now, how unworthy a thing you make of me! You would play upon me, you would seem to know my stops, you would pluck out the heart of my mystery, you would sound me from my lowest note to the top of my compass; and there is much music, excellent voice in this little organ, yet cannot you make it speak. 'Sblood, do you think I am easier to be played on than a pipe? Call me what instrument you will, though you can fret me, you cannot play upon me.[48]

No one but Shakespeare may dare to bring such circumstances onto the stage for no one but he possesses the art of putting them to good use. Must not the audience be as taken aback as Guildenstern who senses the Prince's superior sagacity and leaves the scene full of shame?

If in his work the artist wants to convince us in visible and sensuous fashion of the perfection that he possesses to a high degree, then he must direct his attention to the finest and greatest beauties capable of animating his imagination. Minute brushstrokes testify, to be sure, to the artist's finishing touch, the toil and the care he took to please us. But the sublimity that warrants our awe and admiration is certainly not to be sought in them. Awe is a debt that we owe the extraordinary gifts of

---

[48] III.ii. 336–60.

spirit. These gifts are called, in the narrowest sense of the word, "genius." Accordingly, where sensuous marks of genius are to be found in a work of art, we are ready to give the artist the admiration he deserves. Yet the insignificant attendant circumstances including the final execution of a picture (which, of course, is part of the painting but not essential to it) show only all too clearly the toil and trouble that the work cost the artist, and we are accustomed to subtract from the genius as much as we attribute to the toil.

Thus, one sees that in this type of sublimity the artist is free to apply all the wealth of his art in order to place in their true light the beauties that his manner of thinking has been fortunate enough to produce. This type of sublimity is thus distinguished from the first since preference is necessarily given a naive and unaffected presentation. At the same time, however, one sees that there are small beauties here as well that could perhaps preoccupy a lesser spirit at length but that the artist should not consider worthy of his attention and toil and that he may indulge only if they present themselves, as it were, of themselves. It will suffice to cite a single example of this. The holy poet of the psalms says of the sun (Psalm 19.6):

> The sun rises like a groom from his bedroom
> And delights, like a hero, in running the race.

Both similes are uncommonly sublime, and Hogarth finds a thought similar to the latter in particular in the image of Apollo, so famous in antiquity, whom the artist characterized quite splendidly as the god of the day because of the speed with which he seems to appear and shoot his arrows (where the arrows signify sunbeams). But where it has not completely vanished, the sublimity of these splendid beauties has, even in the hands of as great a master as Rousseau, at least been considerably diminished by a belabored development.

He writes:

> Cet astre ouvre sa carrière
> Comme un Epoux glorieux,
> Qui dés l'Aube matinale
> De sa couche nuptiale
> Sort brillant et radieux.
> L'univers à sa presence

215

Semble sortir du néant.
Il prend sa course, il s'avance,
Comme un superbe géant.[49]

Here the eight words from the basic text have been extended to nine verses but how much they have suffered by this extension! Kramer left the first simile its brevity but the second has lost, in his translation, almost even more than it did in the French.[50]

Our definition makes clear that this second type of the sublime can consist as much in thoughts as in the expression of them. This type of sublimity, in other words, can consist (1) in the understanding as well as in the imagination, in the invention, the similes, sentences, sensibilities, sketches of characters, passions, and mores of human beings, and of objects in nature, and (2) in the use of embellishments, in the selection of the sort of adjectives that designate the most sensuous properties, in the order and combination of the words, and, finally, in the melody and in the harmony of the phrase. For the artist can make his extraordinary talents known by means of all these beauties.

It will not be necessary to recall that one very often meets with both types of the sublime in the works of art. With regard to the notion of imitation, the essay "On the main principles of the fine arts and sciences" has already indicated that our pleasure in the similarity of an artistic imitation is far greater than our pleasure in that of a copy produced by nature itself. For in the former case, regard for the artist is part of the mix and elevates the pleasure. Now this obtains not only for imitation but for all beautiful things in general, as was also recalled in the essay mentioned. They are far more pleasing when they are regarded at the same time as imprints of the perfections of the artist who produced them. However little he may himself seek to appear and to shine, footsteps of his genius will always be left behind which from time to time betray him and allow us to know the giant who is responsible for them. Hence, subjective sublimity can in many cases be combined with

---

[49] Jean Baptiste Rousseau, *Ode II, tirée du pseaume XVIII*, : "That star rises/ Like a glorious groom/ As the light dawns/ Coming, bright and radiant,/ From his nuptial bed./ In its presence the universe/ Seems to emerge from nothing./ The sun takes its course, it advances/ Like a proud giant." Cf. Rousseau, *Odes* (Paris, Librairie Sacrée, 1822), pp. 8–9.

[50] Johann Andreas Kramer (1723–83) published his "Poetic Translation of the Psalms with Essays on Them" ("Poetische Übersetzung der Psalmen mit Abhandlungen über dieselben") in *New Contributions to Pleasure of the Intellect and Wit* (*Neue Beiträge zum Vergnügen des Verstandes und Witzes*) (Bremen, 1755).

objective sublimity. Depending, however, upon whether the awe and admiration redound more to the object itself or to the skill of the artist, the expression can be more or less embellished, something that must be judged in each case on the basis of the makeup of the subject treated or of the aim of the artist.

Longinus appears to concern himself solely with the second type of sublimity, and, since his essays are in everybody's hands, it would be superfluous to clarify all these observations by examples as well. My intention was merely to make clearer the concept of the sublime which is treated so diversely in the works of the fine arts and sciences, and I am satisfied if I have not completely failed at this. I am content to add some additional remarks.

Longinus says (in the seventh major part of his work), "generally you can be sure that something is genuinely beautiful and sublime if it is pleasing to everybody everywhere."[51]

Dissatisfied with this proposition of Longinus, Perrault says the following in his reply to Boileau's eleventh remark[52] about Longinus: "If this precept is assumed, the sublime would be found very rarely, since people of different ages, education, and life-styles imagine the very same thing in very different ways."[53] It seems to me that Perrault is not wrong if what is being discussed is the second type of sublimity. A profound insight into the secrets of art are frequently required to be able to admire the artist's talents, and how few noble souls there are who possess this profound insight! But the sublimeness of an object and especially the sublimeness of certain sensibilities must certainly touch people of every sort as soon as they understand the words through which that sublimity has been expressed. Indeed, as long as their feelings have not been completely spoiled, even people with a common way of thinking must find some sublime sensibilities all the more awesome, the more it elevates them above their common way of thinking and the less they would have trusted the human soul with such perfections.

Someone might raise the following objection: Have not the most sophisticated art critics debated about passages as to whether they are to

---

[51] *On the Sublime*, ch. 7, pp. 56–7.
[52] Boileau, *Réflexions critiques sur quelques passages de Longin* (Paris, 1693); the editors of the Jubilee edition note, however, that the tenth and eleventh reflections stem from 1710, at which point Perrault was already dead; see Boileau *Œuvres* (Amsterdam, 1717), p. 276 n.
[53] Charles Perrault, *Parallèle des anciens et modernes* (Paris, 1688).

be counted among the sublime? The passage, for example, from Holy Scripture, "God said, Let there be light, and so forth" belongs indisputably to the first type of sublimity, and yet its sublimity has been doubted by clever minds. Where, then, is there the agreement that we would look upon as a sign of the first type of sublimity?

Consider, however, the fact that Longinus' opponents have never doubted that the event, "God said, Let there be light, and there was light" is in itself sublime. They have merely not wanted to concede that it was the aim of the Lawgiver to say something sublime by this. In other words, they acknowledged that this passage is an instance of the first type of sublimity, and only the sublimity of the second type was doubted by them. When one looks at the polemical treatises that have been exchanged regarding this passage, it is amazing how little the art critics have been interested in finding agreement with one another. One party appeals to the sublimity of the action and the simplicity of the expression; another passes over this in silence and speaks only of the intention of the Lawgiver who, to put it in human terms, certainly had no intention of assiduously applying the powers of his soul to produce something sublime. If they had explained themselves, the debate would have been resolved.

Hence, Longinus is not only right about the fact that what everyone everywhere finds pleasing must actually be beautiful and sublime, but one can also invert the proposition if one is speaking of the first type of sublimity, and say that the sublime must be pleasing to everyone everywhere. The words of the Greek art critic that immediately follow also make it apparent that he is really speaking of the first type of the sublime when he says that it is pleasing to everyone everywhere, even though he does not explicitly present this essential distinction. He says: "If people with many different leanings, with dissimilar lifestyles, who are different in their sciences and in years, are nevertheless at the same time moved by something, then the union, as it were, of so many disunities provides all the greater certainty that the very things that one thus admires must unmistakably contain something majestic."[54]

Moreover, since the sublime only occurs in great and extraordinary capabilities of the soul, ordinary wit (the capacity to detect something common to diverse things, which has no particularly significant con-

---

[54] Longinus, *On the Sublime*, ch. 7, pp. 56–7.

sequences[*]) must be excluded from sublimity of the first as well as the second type. Exaggerated contrasts, epigrammatic insights, twisted and affected wit can amuse us for a while and be charmingly entertaining, but they can never be awe-inspiring. Indeed, they can even obstruct such awe since they are characteristics of a small spirit for whom even an insignificant proportion, once detected, becomes something important. When it comes to expressing passion, such characteristics are completely unbearable. In a state of emotion, the smallest soul has more important things to do than to take note of and dwell on insignificant connections and proportions. Only an indifferent mind has enough idle time to amuse itself frequently with trivialities.

This obtains, meanwhile, only in the case of the ordinary, caviling wit. There is, however, a noble and great sort of wit based, not on empty similarities and vacuous connections and proportions, but on fruitful truths and sentiments that are often dignified. This higher form of wit is a fruitful source of what is sublime and admirable in the fine sciences. Even the most violent passion does not preclude an antithesis that is supported by an important truth or sentiment. The fine writers of antiquity were acquainted with this authentic form of wit which is pleasant, stirring, and instructive all at once. In its place, however, some of their successors have introduced an empty glitter that is more blinding than illuminating. Here are some examples of sublime thoughts draped in wit:

---

[*] The Dutch translator says that this definition appears to be too narrow and to apply only to antitheses. But the antithesis is a figure of speech in which opposite concepts are placed next to one another so that they reciprocally cancel each other, for example,

"*Victrix* causa Diis placuit, *victa* Catoni."[55]

Not good enough to be a god, too good to be an accident.

Proficiency in making antitheses is a type of wit since features that appear to contradict one another must be shown from a single viewpoint in which they are compatible. Wit is, by contrast, more universal. Every similarity, every likeness, every relation, every connection that is perceived among diverse things is an effect of wit. A thought is witty if it notices this agreement even if the things are not explicitly placed in opposition as occurs in the antitheses. In order to distinguish ordinary wit from the higher level wit, I have added, in the definition of the former, that the noticed agreement or commonality must have no important consequences. Thus one also distinguishes an empty sagacity from a fruitful one. It is the ability to discover distinguishing features in things that agree, and it depends upon whether these features have important or unimportant consequences. Properly speaking, in most cases the antithesis presupposes the use of sagacity as well as that of wit.

[55] Lucanus, *Pharsalia*, I. 128: "The victor pleased the gods with reason, but the vanquished pleased Cato." Cf. Lucan, *The Civil War*, Books I–X, tr. J. D. Duff (London, Heinemann, 1927), pp. 12–13.

Alexander's answer to Parmenio when Parmenio said to him: "I would accept Darius' offer if I were Alexander." "So would I," the Prince replied, "if I were Parmenio."

"If someone wants to fear nothing," an ancient philosopher says, "then he must learn to fear God." Racine's sublime verse supposedly sprang from this.

Je crains Dieu, cher Abner! et n'ai point d'autre crainte.

– Athalie, Act I, Scene 1[56]

> Omnia terrarum subacta,
> Praeter atrocem animum Catonis.

– Horace[57]

Neque Cato post libertatem vixit, neque libertas post Catonem.

– Seneca[58]

Tout étoit Dieu, excepté Dieu même; et le monde que Dieu avoit fait pour manifester sa puissance, sembloit être devenu un Temple d'idoles.

– Bossuet[59]

> Deep within it the human race has
> Two civil orders, one in heaven and one in nothing.
> From the sturdiest material God selected it.
> Half for eternity, but half to decompose.
> Ambiguous cross between angel and cattle,
> It survives itself, it dies and would never die.

– Haller[60]

---

[56] Racine, *Athalie* (Paris, 1691): "I fear God, dear Abner, and have no other fear."

[57] *Odes*, II. 1. 23: "All the earth subdued/ Except for the unbending soul of Cato". Cf. Horace, *The Odes and Epodes*, pp. 108–9.

[58] *De constantia sapientis*, II. 2: "Cato did not survive liberty nor liberty Cato". Cf. Seneca, *Moral Essays*, vol. pp. 52–3.

[59] Jacques Benigne Bossuet, *Discours sur l'histoire universelle a Monseigneur de Dauphin: pour expliquer la suite de la Religion & les changemens des Empires* (Paris, 1681), p. 192: "Everything was from God, except God himself; and the world that God had made to manifest his power seems to have degenerated into a temple of idols."

[60] "Über den Ursprung des Übels" (Bern, 1734), in *Die Alpen und andere Gedichte*, p. 62, ll. 103–8: "Fern unter ihnen hat das menschliche Geschlect/ Im Himmel und im Nichts, ein doppelt Bürgerrecht./ Aus ungleich festem Stoff hat Gott es auserlesen,/ Halb zu der Ewigkeit, halb aber zum Verwesen./ Zweydeutig Mittelding von Engeln und von Vieh,/ Es überlebt sich selbst, es stirbt und stirbet nie."

> . . . A human being, where does it come from?
> Not good enough to be a god, too good to be an accident.
>
> – Lessing

> How miserable, how troubled were my first years;
> Not yet mature as a human being, yet mature enough to have its
> needs.
>
> – Ibid.[61]

> Fashion and folly command the world;
> One the body, the other the soul.
>
> – Dusch[62]

Examples of pathetic or passion-arousing antitheses:

> How lonesome sits the city once teeming with people
> The greatest city of peoples, the princess of countries has become
> a vassal.
>
> – Klagel[63]

> Anibalem pater filio meo potui placere. Filium Anibali non
> possum. . .Vultum ipsius Anibalis, quem armati exercitus sustinere
> nequent, quem horret populus romanus. . .tu sustinebis?. . .De-
> terreri hic sine te potius, quam illic vinci. Valeant apud te mea
> preces, sicut pro te hodie valuerunt.
>
> – Titius Livius[64]

> Lève toi, triste Objet d'horreur et de tendresse;
> Lève toi, cher appui, qu'esperait ma vieillesse:
> Viens embrasser ton Pere! Il t'a du condamner;
> Mais, s'il n'était Brutus, il t'allait pardoner.

61 Gotthold Ephraim Lessing, "Die Religion" (Berlin, 1753), in *Werke*, ed. Göpfert, vol. 1, p. 171:
". . . Der Mensch, wo ist er her?/ Zu schlecht für einen Gott, zu gut fürs Ohngefähr"; p. 174,
ll 101–2: "Wie elend, kümmerlich, wuchs ich die ersten Jahre;/ Zum Menschen noch nicht
reif, doch immer reif zur Baare."

62 Johann Jakob Dusch, *Drey Gedichte von dem Verfasser der vermischten Werke in verschiedenen
Arten der Dichtkunst* (Altona and Leipzig 1756), p. 39 (cited by Menselssohn in the Jubilee
edition, vol. 4, p. 66): "Die Mode und der Wahn ertheilt der Welt Befehle;/ Die eine für den
Leib, der andre für die Seele." Cf. *Verhandeling*, p. 56 n. 1 (see p. 5 n. 6 above).

63 Klagel, *Jerusalem*, v. 1: "Wie sitzt die Stadt so einsam, die sonst voll Volks war./ Die größte der
Völker, die Fürstin der Länder ist zinsbar worden."

64 Livy, *Ab urbe condita*, Bk. XXIII, ch. 9: "I was able to reconcile Hannibal to my son. I could not
reconcile my son to Hannibal . . . Will you oppose the face of Hannibal himself, the face that
armed forces refuse to oppose, the face dreaded by the Roman people? . . . But let yourself be
deterred from this here rather than be defeated there. Let my prayers have an effect upon you
as they have had for you today." Cf. *Works*, tr. Frank Gardner Moore (Cambridge, Mass.,
Harvard University Press, 1951), vol. 6 (Bks XXIII–XXV), pp. 26–7.

> Va, ne t'attendris point; sois plus Romain que moi;
> Et que Rome t'admire en se vengeant de toi!
>
> – Voltaire[65]

As has already been mentioned above, sublimity in general and especially the first type of sublimity stands in such a precise connection with naive expression that it is useful to investigate here what it is that the naive consists of and to what extent it is possible to make use of it in works of the fine sciences. There is no German word to designate this property of the expression. "Natural" and "unaffected" say too little since a person frequently expresses himself in a natural and unaffected manner in ordinary life without thereby being naive. "Noble simplicity," on the other hand, says too much and designates only a certain species of the naive; for people also often say of certain comic expressions, that they were naive although they are anything but noble.[*] Hence, our only recourse is to use this foreign word; our aim, however, is to search for the concept that we would combine with this word.

Simplicity is, without dispute, a necessary property of naivete. As soon as an expression is profound, lively, full of emphasis, or furnished with an array of embellishments, it can in no way be said to be naive, and, to this extent, sublimity in the expression is opposed to naivete. But mere simplicity is not enough. Hidden beneath this simple exterior must lie a beautiful thought, an important truth, a noble sentiment, or an emotion that expresses itself in an unaffected manner. Confronted by an expres-

---

[*] The *niais* of the French, of which the Dutch translator speaks at this point, appears to be essentially different from the naive. *Niais* signifies a thoughtless and listless simplicity or an ignorance of the ordinary ways of the world that is the source of stupidity. "Si la simplicité se remarque dans l'exterieur et qu'elle soit accompagnée de nonchalance, elle fait le *niais*. La simplicité, n'est pas incompatible avec la vivacité; jamais niais ne fut actif" (*Dict. Encycl.*).[66] It can provide the occasion for the naive if something with important consequences happens or is said on the basis of this listless simplicity. Moreover, a remark by the translator seems important to me, namely, where he said that *niais* can be better expressed in painting and sculpture than can what is genuinely naive, leaving aside the sublimely naive or noble simplicity. For, in the hands of the plastic artist, what is genuinely naive is transformed for the most part into innocence or imprudence.

[65] *Brutus*, Act V, Scene VII: "Lift yourself up, you sad object of horror and tenderness;/ Lift yourself up, dear support and hope of my old age/ Come embrace your father! He had to condemn you/ But, if he were not Brutus, he would have pardoned you./ Go, do not tarry for an instant; be more Roman than I;/ And let Rome admire you as it avenges itself on you."

[66] "If simplicity calls attention to itself on the outside and is accompanied by nonchalance, it would be *silly*. Simplicity is not incompatible with vivacity, but silliness would never be active." *Encyclopedie ou Dictionnaire Raisonné des Sciences, des Arts et des Métiers* (new facsimile impression of the 1st ed. Paris, 1751–1780); reprinted (Stuttgart-Bad Cannstatt, Frommann-Holzboog, 1966) vol. 11, p. 130.

sion that is merely simple, we remain devoid of sentiment. But if a beautiful thought dwells, like a noble soul, in this unadorned body, our heart is moved by a tender sentiment and we joyfully exclaim: this is naive! The mores which today prevail in the countryside are often the most simple. But are they as naive as the mores of the Arcadian shepherds[67] and other citizens of the golden age that perhaps never existed anywhere but in the imagination of poets? And what else is the cause of this difference but the noble sentiments imputed to those shepherds along with their outward simplicity? One could perhaps also propose the following explanation: if an object is nobly conceived, beautifully conceived, or conceived along with its important consequences and signified by a simple sign, then the designation is deemed naive.

This definition would, of course, be perfectly suited to all those examples where the person who utters something naive actually has beautiful, noble, or important thoughts and only employs simple signs. In his *Eclogue*, for example, Virgil says:

> Malo me Galatea petit, lasciva puella,
> Et fugit ad salices, et se cupit ante videri.[68]

This is uncommonly naive. Galatea's hiding appears to be nothing but innocent playing. Underlying it, however, there is a tender love; "luscious girl" [*lasciva puella*]. By this charming playfulness she lures the shepherd into following her behind the willows. There was no better way for her to make her secret longing known to him.* With the

---

* Here the Dutch translator cites a very cute little poem from the *Anthol. française* (T. III, p. 93) that I would like to share with my readers:

Revenés, charmante verdure:
Faites regner l'ombrage et l'amour dans nos bois!
A quois s'amuse la Nature?
Tout est encore glacé dans le plus beau des mois!
Si je viens vous presser de couvrir ce bocage,
Ce n'est que pour cacher aux regards des jaloux
Les pleurs que je repand pour un berger volage;
A! je n'aurai jamais d'autre besoin de vous. (bis)[69]

[67] "Arcadia," the name of a landlocked, shepherding region of Greece, is also the title of a romance by Jacopo Sannazzaro (Naples, 1504), depicting a dream world of pastoral simplicity.

[68] *Eclogues*, III. 64–5: "Galatea, luscious girl, hits me with an apple and runs/ Off to the willows, hoping that first she is seen". Cf. Virgil, *Works*, vol. 1, pp. 22–3.

[69] *Anthologie française ou chansons choisis, depuis le 13e siècle jusqu'à présent.*, ed. Jean Monnet (Paris, 1765): "Come back, greenery with all your charms/ Make shade and love reign in our woods!/ Why does nature amuse herself?/ Everything is still frozen in the most beautiful of months!/ If I come to urge you to cover that wooden grove,/ It is only to hide from the sight of the jealous/ The tears that I shed for a fickle shepherd;/ Ah! I would never have another need of you."

simplest expressions, Johann, Hagedorn's cheerful soap-boiler, makes known the contentment of his soul, his lack of want, his industriousness, and his trust in providence.[70] He expresses the sensibilities of a philosopher without the latter's boastful verboseness. He puts his rich neighbor to shame without profound postulates, without witty proverbs. His entire behavior is naive.

The inscription on the bronze statue of Myron's cow reads:

> Shepherd, why do you hurry
> So far back to me
> And jab at me with the goad
> And yell: move!
> I am the cow of the artist Myron
> And I am not going anywhere with you.[71]

This inscription is naive precisely because it appears at first glance to be a simple narration, but in fact contains very flattering praise of the artist.* La Fontaine loses his benefactress, Madame de Lasabliere, and meets his friend, Mr. d'Hervart. This honest friend says to him, "My dear La Fontaine, I have heard of the misfortune that has befallen you. You lived with Madame de Lasabliere, and she is no longer alive. I

---

* Occasionally someone who is mocking some thing or person also assumes the countenance of an innocent narrator in order to hide his purpose and thereby make the mockery all the more biting. Praise and blame are each all the more effective, the less they betray design and the more they appear to be, as it were, accidental. For example, from Götz:

> Oh, what wonderful harmony!
> What he wants, she wants.
> He likes to carouse, so does she.
> He likes to play cards, so does she.
> He likes to have lots of money
> And play the lord
> And that's her way as well.
> Oh, what wonderful harmony!
> What he wants, she wants.[72]

[70] Friedrich von Hagedorn, *Werke* (Vienna, Schraembl, 1740), vol. 2, p. 66.
[71] Johann Nikolaus Götz, *Vermischte Gedichte*, ed. Karl Wilhelm Ramler (Mannheim, 1785), p. 12: "Du Hirte, warum eilest du/ So weit zurück nach mir!/ Stichst mit dem Stachel auf mich zu,/ Und rufest: Fort von hier!/ Ich bin des Künstlers Myrons Kuh,/ Und gehe nicht mit dir." Myron was an Athenian sculptor (c. 450 BC) known for the simplicity and natural likeness of his figures.
[72] Ibid.: "O wundervolle Harmonie!/ Was er will, will auch sie./ Er bechert gern, sie auch./ Er lombert gern, sie auch./ Er hat den Beutel gern;/ Und spielet gern den Herrn;/ Auch das ist ihr Gebrauch./ O wundervolle Harmonie!/ Was er will, will auch sie."

would like to propose to you that you move to my house." "I will go there immediately," La Fontaine responded.

The former sergeant-major, Paul Werner (in Lessing's *Minna von Barnhelm*) wants to speak with his departing major to get money from him. "Indeed, I only do it because of the interest," he says, "by the life of my poor soul, only because of the interest! – If at times I thought to myself, 'what will become of you in old age, if you hit rock bottom, if you have nothing, if you have to go begging?' then I thought: 'No, you will not go begging, you will go to Major Tellheim. He'll share his last penny with you and feed you until your death; at his place you will be able to die an honest man.'" The major grabs his hand and asks: "And, comrade, do you still think that?" "No," says the honest Werner, "I don't think that any more. If someone doesn't want to take anything from me when he needs it and I have it, then he also won't give me anything when he has it and I need it."[73]

In general, the naivete of moral character consists in simplicity of

from Boileau:

> On dit que l'Abbé Roquette
> Preche les sermons d'autrui:
> Moi qui sçai qui'il les achete,
> Je soutiens qu'ils sont à lui.[74]

from Rousseau:

> Husiers, qu'on fasse silence!
> Dit, en tennant audience,
> Un President de Baugé;
> C'est un bruit a tête fendre,
> Nous avons déjà jugé
> Dix causes sans les entendre.[75]

Praise occasionally takes on the guise of a scolding and is all the more flattering:

> Hélas, qu'est devenu ce temps, cet heureux tems,
> Où les Rois s'honoroient du nom de fainéeans?[76]

And, in reverse, scolding takes on the appearance of praise and is all the more painful because of this irony.

[73] *Minna von Barnhelm* (Hamburg, 1767), Act II, Scene VII.
[74] Nicolas Boileau, *Œuvres poétiques* (Brossette: Amsterdam, 1718): "People say that Abbé Roquette/ Preaches others' sermons'/ Knowing that he buys them/ I insist that they are his." Cf. *Verhandeling*, p. 63.
[75] "'Soldiers, be quiet!' says/ A President de Baugé, holding/ Audience, "the noise you make/ Gives me a splitting headache./ We have already judged/ Ten cases without hearing them." Cf. *Verhandeling*, p. 63.
[76] "Helas, what has become of that time, that happy time,/ When kings honored themselves with the title of 'Do-nothings'?" Cf. *Verhandeling*, p. 63.

outer appearance, which betrays inner dignity without intending to do so. It consists in being ignorant about the way of the world, in being unconcerned about being falsely interpreted, and in having the confidence that is based, not on stupidity and a lack of ideas, but on nobility, innocence, goodness of heart, and the benevolent persuasion that others will be no more badly disposed to us than we are to them. Hence, when we consider people's outer actions and omissions as signs of their inner morality and dignity, simplicity in the signs along with the dignity and importance of what is signified will be demanded for it to be naive.

Naivete in the shape of a face, which has served painters and sculptors so well, has a similar constitution. It is always something not sought, something unsophisticated in the outer appearance that unintentionally betrays an inner splendidness. Facial features, looks, and gestures of people are signs of their inclinations and sentiments, while each facial feature signifies an inclination and each expression a corresponding movement of the heart. Because of this, a naive character will be supposed to lie behind every feature and gesture if they, as it were, unintentionally, unassumingly, and unselfconsciously betray a propitious and harmonious system of inclinations and sentiments. This is the source of the naivete in the character of the child when, among the otherwise one-dimensional features of a childlike face, tender buds of gentleness, love, innocence, and graciousness sprout forth. – Grace or the sublime beauty in movement is likewise bound up with the naive since the movements of someone with those charms glide naturally, nimbly, and gently into one another. These spontaneous movements unintentionally and unconsciously reveal that their sources, the impulses of the soul and the stirrings of the heart, act in a manner as unforced as the movements themselves, harmonizing in a way just as gentle and unfolding in a way just as uncontrived. Thus, too, the idea of innocence and moral simplicity is forever bound up with sublime grace.* – The more this beautiful movement is combined with consciousness and appears to be a work according to plan, the more it departs from the naive and attains the character of *something sought* as well as *something affected*, if the inner stirrings are not in tune with it. – Nothing is so tasteless as affected naiveté or outer simplicity that we

---

* See Part One, p. 316.[77]

[77] The reference is to footnote m (p. 82).

recognize is intentional and pretentious. – On the other hand, if the simplicity in the movements betrays thoughtlessness and lack of sensitivity, then it is called "stupidity" and if it is accompanied by listlessness, then we have the *niais* which was discussed in a footnote earlier. – On the basis of these considerations, then, it follows that uncontrived simplicity on the outside and dignity or importance on the inside are required in order for something to be naive.

We find examples, meanwhile, of someone saying something naive but not actually thinking anything more than the words that he uses convey. Different circumstances, however, have placed those listening in the position of thinking considerably more or drawing important consequences from the same words that appear neutral. In Molière's, Lubin tells Dandin himself, without knowing who he is, about the illicit affairs of his wife and forbids him to let this reach Dandin's ears. As he leaves, he shouts to him: "But keep your lips sealed!"[78] The situation is naive. Lubin has no evil intention beyond merely gabbing a little, and, by this means, he awakens Dandin's jealousy.

There is the well-known passage from Gellert (*Fables and Stories*, Second Book, page 115):

> What did you say, Papa? You have misspoken; I'm supposed to be just fourteen years old?
> No, fourteen years old and seven weeks.[79]

This passage is uncommonly naive since Fieckchen betrays the most secret wishes of her heart without noticing that she is doing so. She wants rightly to show her father that he miscalculated some seven weeks and thereby shows how precisely she herself had to calculate. Thus, she betrays more than she wanted to say, and her answer is nevertheless called naive.

Thus, in our haste a naive word occasionally escapes our lips that betrays our most important secret. In a group of women amusing themselves with fairy tales, whose tastes ran along the lines of *Gageure des trois comméres*, one of them, when her turn came, told the story of

[78] *George Dandin ou Le Mari Confondu* (Versailles, 1668), Act I, Scene II: "Bouche cousuë au moins!"
[79] Christian Fürchtegott Gellert, "Das junge Mädchen," in *Fabeln und Erzählungen* (Leipzig,, 1748), Pt. II, pp. 114–16: "Was sagten Sie, Papa? Sie haben sich versprochen,/ Ich sollt erst vierzehn Jahre seyn?/ Nein vierzehn Jahr und sieben Wochen." See also his *Fabeln und Erzählungen*, critical edn. by Siegfried Scheibe (Tübingen, Niemeyer, 1966), pp. 234–5.

someone who was supposed to have gone on a journey and she concluded her story by saying: "suddenly the door opened and who was it but her husband himself." – "Her husband," the others said, shocked, "her husband!" "Yes," she replied quickly, "I, too, was scared to death."[80]

If this happens in the heat of an emotion, a naive divulging of our most secret thoughts can have tragic consequences. In Weiss's *Romeo and Juliet* one finds a feature of this sort.[81] The Countess Capulet is far from thinking that her Juliet is in love with Romeo and has reason to believe, instead, that she hates this Montechi just as her entire family hates and persecutes him since he killed their cousin Thebaldo. (Juliet pretends to be distraught over his death since she is really distraught by Romeo's absence.) The countess comes to cheer up her daughter and bring her the news that the Count von Lodrona has sought her hand.

> *Madame Capulet.* . . . I bring you some joyful news, Juliet! Joyful news for us all, especially joyful for you.
>
> *Juliet* (hastily). Has Romeo received a pardon? . . . (in shock) Oh, how weak my head is . . . . Has Romeo been punished?

A French writer (*Dict. Encycl. Art. Naïveté*) distinguishes "*a* naivete" and "*the* naivete," apparently following his use of the language.

> "A naivete," he says, "is what people call a thought, a feature of the imagination, or a sentiment that we unwillingly let slip and that sometimes can be damaging to us. It is an expression of animation, indiscretion, or inexperience in the ways of the world. An example of this naivete is a wife's reply to her dying husband when he described for her the person she should marry after he dies. 'Take him,' he said, 'you will do quite well!' 'Oh,' she replied, 'I have already thought of that.'
>
> "*The naivete*, however, is the language of beautiful genius and insightful simplicity. It is the most elegant painting of a fine and discerning idea, the masterpiece of art in the eyes of the person for whom the idea does not come naturally."[82]

---

[80] Cf. La Fontaine, "Contes," Bk. II, 7 ("La Gageure des trois commères où sont deux nouvelles tirées de Boccace" – "The Wager of Three Gossips"), in *Œuvres completes* (Paris, 1826), pp. 141–4.

[81] Christian Felix Weiss, *Romeo und Juliet: ein bürgerliches Trauerspiel in fünf Aufzügen* (Berlin and Leipzig, 1768).

[82] *Encyclopedie, ou Dictionnaire Raisonné*, p. 10.

Since both types of naivete have certain features in common, it will be necessary to extend the definition of the sublime somewhat further in order not to exclude either of them. If some designated matter, itself important or having important consequences, is understood by virtue of a simple sign, the purpose of the speaker may have been to convey more than he says, or he may have accidentally divulged more, that is to say, unintentionally and, at times, contrary to his intentions. In both cases the designation is called "naive."

Since it is apparent that, in the case of the naive, the designated matter makes an impression on the senses that is greater and more important than the sign, it will necessarily be felt in a more lively manner. That is to say, we will know intuitively the matter designated, since we have intuitive knowledge of something designated if we present or represent it to ourselves in a more lively way than we do the sign. The naive expression affords an instance of *intuitive knowledge* which is, therefore, *perfect* and if it allows an assortment of characteristics to be perceived at the same time, it is an instance of intuitive knowledge that is also *sensuously perfect*. Hence, the naive is in keeping with the ultimate purpose of fine arts. For the essence of fine arts consists in a sensuously perfect representation.

This makes clear, too, the reason why we have called the unaffected expression of the first type of the sublime "naive." For the signs are simple, unadorned, and the matter designated is sublime and of great importance.

It is, meanwhile, also certain that the artist should only make use of a naive expression or of such signs as are beneath the status of the matter designated, when the circumstances, states of mind, and characters of the persons introduced provide some reason for not choosing the sort of signs that are completely suited to what is designated. This occurs in the following instances:

> (1) In the first type of sublimity and especially in the case of sublime sensibilities and passions, as has already been shown above. (2) In pastoral poetry or other artworks about the countryside where the persons introduced are credited with sentiments and thoughts but no studied expressions, attitudes, and gestures. (3) In utterances that are placed in the mouths of innocent children like little Joas in Racine's *Athalie* where this little prince makes the most scathing criticisms of tyranny with the simplest expressions

and like Arabella in Lessing's *Miss Sara Sampson* where this child speaks of sheer good-heartedness and innocence at the very instant that the minds of Mellefont and the inhuman Marwood are torn apart by the most violent passions. Belonging to this group is the masterful passage in Homer where Hector tenderly takes leave of Andromache, perhaps never to see her again, and the little Astyanax becomes frightened of the feathers waving on the hero's helmet and, crying, hides in the wet-nurse's arms. (4) In eulogies and satires in order to conceal the poet's intention and thereby sustain it all the more securely. Finally, (5) in comedies and comic writings generally, where the contrast between the sign and the matter designated can be amusing as in the passage cited from *George Dandin* or in *Ecole des Femmes* by the same writer where Agnese in her simplicity relates to the suspicious Arnolph all the liberties which she has permitted Horace, liberties which, in themselves, were completely innocent from her side at least, but make Arnolph extremely jealous.[83]

The effects of the naive are a pleasant astonishment, a slight degree of amazement at the unexpected importance that lay hidden beneath the simple outer appearance. We gladly fix our attention on an object that permits us to discover more and more, the longer the time we spend with it, an object that, as it were, holds more for us than it seemed to promise. If this inner importance is a high degree of perfection, there then follows the shivering feeling of the sublime that is combined, however, with a joyful sentiment that comes very close to laughter. For the simplicity of the sign contrasts with the importance of the matter designated by it or the consequences which flow from it; the sort of contrast that moves one to laugh and, if not suppressed by stronger sentiments, makes itself known by actual laughing. Overwhelmed by the sublime, it is no longer laughter that the contrast produces, but rather the trace of a gracious smile that spreads across the lips and disappears into a lofty state of awe and admiration. This is always the sentiment that we have if we are surprised by naivete in moral character. An insensitive person who judges merely by appearances will not perceive the morally naive without laughing. For such a person does not see anything beyond the contrast with the way of the world that is better known to him and the lunacy of confidently relying on the goodness of

---

[83] Molière, *L'Ecole des Femmes* (Paris, 1662), Act II, Scene v.

others produces peals of laughter in him. By contrast, a man with a sensitive heart sees through this to the inner dignity at hand, recognizes the high-mindedness from which that ignorance and apparent lunacy spring, and, even while his lips are stirred to laugh, a shudder pours itself out through his heart, reducing this laughter to a reflection, filled with amazement. A naive quality in the features of a face has a similar effect with the difference that here the laughter will present itself by means of much weaker traces since the contrast is not so marked. An insensitive person looks upon it with indifferent eyes since the countenances and features of the face appear to him insignificant. For someone who is acute the effect of the contrast presents itself merely in a gentle opening of the lips and an almost undetectable lengthening of the mouth that is more satisfaction than laughter.

If the inner quality of the naive is an evil that is not dangerous, a weakness, a mistake, a foolishness that does not result in any noticeable misfortune, then the naive is merely *ridiculous*. In this case, what matters is whether the person who says something intends to present more for us to understand than he says or whether we divine more than he intends. In the first case he makes us laugh, in the second he becomes ridiculous himself. Examples of this have been cited quite sufficiently in the foregoing, and the application is so easy a matter that it is fair for us to leave it to the reader.

If, however, the inner quality of the naive is an actual danger, a misfortune that befalls a person in whose fate we participate, then the naive is *tragic*. Of course, if the danger is to be feared as a consequence of naivete, then the effect is terrifying and vanquishes every sentiment that we have towards something ridiculous. An example of this is the passage, cited above, from the tragedy *Romeo and Juliet*. No less an example can be found in Monime's all too candid confession in Racine's *Mithridiat* where, through the machinations of the sly Mithridiat, this princess allows herself to be completely honest and confesses her love affair but during the telling perceives to her horror that Mithridiat grows pale and begins to turn white from anger.[84]

If, however, the evil to be feared is not a result of naivete but rather is combined with it in some other way as a sign with the designated, then the smile that springs from the detected contrast can persist along with

---

[84] *Mithridates* (Paris, 1673).

the most tragic sentiments. Andromacha smiles about the simple fear of the little Astyanax even as hot tears roll down her cheeks. The entire audience laughs at the innocence of the little Arabella without the tragic sentiment being diminished by this. Indeed, our sympathy with these children becomes all the more lively, the more they make it apparent, by their naive actions, that they do not sense the misfortune which affects them the most. From this one sees how unfounded the opinion of some critics is who want to ban from the tragic stage all sentiments which have a tinge of the ridiculous in them. This matter deserves a further elaboration, but it does not belong here to the final purpose that I have set for myself.

On probability[*]

Among the kinds of knowledge that we have to attain, probability can perhaps be regarded as the most necessary since it is suited to our limited sphere and, in most cases, must take the place of certainty. Its influence on what people do and leave undone and, by means of this, on their happiness has always been so evident to philosophers that they dared to make the foundations of truth totter sooner than the foundations of probability. There are doubters who do not want to allow any complete conviction anywhere and even believe that they find uncertainty in the principle of contradiction. Such doubters nevertheless act in common life just like the great majority of human beings do who regard themselves as fully convinced of a considerable number of eternal truths. Bayle, who embraced the cause of universal doubters in the most zealous fashion, pleaded in their defense that they let themselves be guided by probability in their actions. Thus one

---

[*] Preliminary remark: The essay "On Probability" was originally composed as an address for the Society of Literary Friends [*Gesellschaft literarischer Freunde*] which had formed at Berlin in 1755. Nicolai reports on this organization as follows: "A coffee house for savants, organized by Professor Müchler, came into being, a closed society of some hundred persons, mostly scholars or at least friends of erudition. Euler, Aepinus, Jacobi, Gumperz, Wilke, Martini, Bamberger, Resewitz, and many others along with Moses Mendelssohn and myself were members of this society. Every week someone read aloud an essay with a mathematical, physical, or philosophical content. Mendelssohn's essay 'On probability' was written for this society."

As far as the content is concerned, the article follows the work on evidence. In it the mathematical investigations of that time on probability are gathered together. Reference is made, in particular, to Euler, Bernoulli, Pascal, Huygens, Halley, and Fermat among others. At the same time, David Hume's critique of the concept of causality is, to be sure, briefly examined, but in a polemical sense. The application of the foregoing to ideas in metaphysics and the philosophy of religion, such as the prescience and the will of God and so forth, form the latter part of the article.

sees that they are compelled to give probability the approval that they refused to give truth itself.

It has long been recognized that the universal teachings of philosophy and mathematics are all too far apart from the events that occur in nature. If their abstract inferences are to be applied to individual instances, then they must frequently take a step where the rules of the common art of reason abandon us. We must assume principles the correctness of which we are not sufficiently convinced; we must combine causes and effects with one another where their connection just does not seem necessary; we must suppose events on the basis of other events, which are not fully grounded in one another. In short, we must base our thinking on probabilities which, if they do not appear to presuppose another type of inferring,* seem at least to presuppose other basic maxims, a type of premise.

Mathematicians, who expanded the borders of their science more rapidly than philosophers did, have also made great discoveries in the field of probability within the last century. In all types of games of luck, wagers, forms of insurance, lotteries, in some lawsuits, indeed, even in regard to historical believability, they have calculated the probable cases against one another and determined the magnitude of expectation or the degree of probability in terms of this calculation. One need only be familiar with the names of Pascal, Fermat, Huygens, Halley, Craig, Petty, Montmort, Moivre, Bernoulli, and Euler in order to appreciate their discoveries fully.

A philosopher who, in order to fulfill Leibniz's wish, wanted to invent an art of reasoning probabilities would have had to possess the skill of abstracting the universal from the particular rules that these great mathematicians have given us and then to uncover a greater number of particular rules, as it were, a priori.

I do not trust myself as having either the mathematical insight or power of invention necessary to undertake this difficult work. But in the course of investigating the grounds upon which these great minds base their calculations, I have come to some conclusions which can at least provide occasion for further reflection. My principal intention thereby

---

* See Wolff, *Logica*, §588.[1]

[1] Wolff, *Logica* (see p. 128 n. 5), §§573–4, 578, 588, pp. 434–5; *Gesammelte Werke*, vol. 1.2, pp. 434–7, 440–1.

is also to submit an example of the uncommon fruitfulness of the Wolffian definitions to those who doubt the advantages of a systematic mind. One will see in what follows that I have made use of his explanation of the probable and, by means of this explanation, have arrived at consequences to which neither Bernoulli's nor 's-Gravesand's definition of probability would have led me as naturally.[2]

Every truth consists in a proposition in which something is affirmed or denied of some determinate subject. In both cases it must be possible, on the basis of the determination of the subject, to render intelligible why what is said of it belongs to it or not. The determinations of the subject, from which the predicate follows, are called "the reasons for the proposition's truth,"[*] since they contain the reason why a proposition is true.

If all these reasons for a propostion's truth are familiar to us and we grasp the way the predicate necessarily proceeds from them, we are then convinced of the truth,[**] and our conviction achieves the name of a mathematical certainty. All propositions in pure mathematics and in logic itself, as well as some propositions in metaphysics and in theoretical ethics, are of this sort.

If, however, only some of these reasons for a proposition's truth are given to us and we infer from them a conclusion which is not completely determined by them, then the proposition belongs among the instances of probable knowledge,[†] and we cannot be completely convinced of its correctness.

The degree of probability is determined by the relation of the given reasons for its truth to those which are completely certain, and only a slight degree of probability is attributed to a proposition if the fewest

---

[*] Wolff, *Logica*, §573.[3]   [**] Ibid. §574.   [†] Wolff, *Logica*, §578.

[2] Mendelssohn is probably referring to one of the following: Jacob Bernoulli, *Ars conjectandi* (Art of Conjecturing) (Basil, 1713) or Nicholas Bernoulli, "Specimina artis conjectandi ad quaestiones juris adplicatae," (Specimens of the Art of Conjecturing Applied to Questions of Law) *Acta Eruditorum* (Leipzig, 1709) vol. 5, Part IV, Supplement. Wilhelm Jacob's-Gravestand, *Introductio ad Philosophiam, Logicam et Metaphysician* (Leyden, 1736); Mendelssohn cites the German translation *Einleitung in die Weltweisheit* (Introduction to Philosophy) (Halle, 1755).

[3] *Wahrheitsgründe* ("the reason for the proposition's truth") might also be suitably translated "truth factors" or "grounds of truth"; since the ensuing discussion turns on the quantifiability of necessary but insufficient *Wahrheitsgründe*, the term "condition" appears a likely English equivalent but this translation is probably inadvisable inasmuch as "truth condition" has become a standard translation of Ludwig Wittgenstein's *Wahrheitsbedingung* (cf. *Tractatus Logico-philosophicus*, tr. D. F. Pears and B. F. McGuiness [London, Routledte & Kegan Paul, 1961], 4.431).

reasons for its truth are known. If half of them are given, then the proposition is dubious. If, however, more reasons are given than are lacking for certainty, we then would say straightaway: the proposition is probable.[*]

We want to elucidate this proposition with an example. Titius travels with three other persons through an unsafe forest, and it is learned that one of them has lost his life. If we are to maintain with certainty that Titius is dead, then the following three reasons for its truth must be given to us:

1. Caius was not murdered;
2. Sempronius was not murdered;
3. Maevius was not murdered.

Thereupon it follows, without contradiction, that Titius was murdered. As long, however, as these three reasons for the truth of the proposition are lacking and we do not have before us more than the one reason (namely, that one of the travellers was murdered), the degree of the probability that Titius is dead is proportional to certainty as $1:1 + 3$ or $= 1:4$, that is, the quantity of probability $= \frac{1}{4}$ and thus the case is less than dubious.

If, however, two of the party lose their lives, then we would lack only two reasons for certainty. Consequently, the degree of probability in relation to certainty $= 2:4$ and, therefore, $= \frac{1}{2}$; hence, the proposition is dubious.

If three died, then the ratio of the probability that Titius is dead to certainty $= 3:4$. In this case, then, people say that it is probable that Titius is dead.

The familiar principle of mathematicians which they lay as the basis for all calculations of probability rests upon these quite easy inferences. That principle is:

> The relation of the number of cases in which a certain outcome is obtained to the number of all possible cases is equivalent to the relation of the probability of this outcome to certainty.

If one then asks how great the hope of a player is who will win bet *a* if

[*] One can compare the truth, in mathematicians' terminology, with a *maximum* and probability with a variable magnitude. One may not, however, take this *maximum* as, indeed, an *infinitum* since otherwise the degree of probability must be $= 0$. This will become more distinctly evident from examples.

he throws a dice with more than four spots, the answer is $= \frac{a}{3}$. For six different throws are possible with a dice and he wins in two, namely, if the dice comes up with five or six spots; hence, the proportion of hope to certainty $= 2a{:}6$ or $= \frac{a}{3}$. The hope of those he is playing against is, for the same reason, $= \frac{2a}{3}$. Hence, the bet is also to be made according to this proportion.

In *Acta Eruditorum*, 1709, p. 465 someone believes that he detects a logical incorrectness in this inference.[4] "Mathematicians," it is said, "presuppose that all six throws should be equally possible which, however, never is the case in nature since there a single outcome is always determined with certainty and all others are at least hypothetically impossible." Wolff himself, in his Latin logic (§578, Not.), appears to want to validate this objection to the mathematicians' presupposition, or at least he appears not to have sufficiently removed the difficulty. I do not understand how this hypothetical determination in nature is supposed to conflict with the mathematicians' cited principle. Indeed, I venture to maintain that precisely this hypothetical impossibility of all other throws is the ground on which the calculation of the probable case rests.

The question was: "How great is the hope of a player who will win bet *a* if he throws a dice with more than four spots?" That is to say, given a number of reasons for the truth of the proposition that Titius will presently throw a dice that comes up with five or six spots, what is the relation of that number of reasons to certainty?

If we are to be able to maintain this proposition with certainty, then we must be convinced that it is hypothetically impossible that Titius will now throw a dice that comes up with one, two, three, or four spots. We lack four reasons for the truth of this, and they are the hope of the opponent, Sempronius. But Sempronius also lacks the certainty that he will win, the conviction that it is hypothetically impossible that Titius will throw a dice that comes up with five or six spots. He lacks these two reasons, and they are Titius' hope. Consequently, the ratio of Titius' hope to Sempronius' hope $= 2{:}4$ or $1{:}2$. Hence, Titius' hope $= \frac{1}{3}$ and Sempronius' hope $= \frac{2}{3}$.

In all the examples that we have cited up to now, a simple probability

---

[4]   Pierre Remond de Montmort, "Essai d'Analysis sur les jeux de hazard" ("Essay on the analysis of Games of Chance").

was to be calculated. Our judgment was based upon the following universal rational inference:

> The probability of a given outcome stands in the same relation to its certainty as the relation of the number of given reasons for its truth to all reasons for its truth taken together.
>
> Now in the case at hand, the number of all the reasons for its truth = a, the number of given reasons for its truth = b.
>
> Thus, the probability = $b{:}a$.

In our cited examples, the minor premise was mathematically certain. For a as well as b are determined with certainty and no longer subject to doubt. The major premise does not determine the certainty, but merely the probability of the given outcome. Thus, too, the inference in the conclusion must contain a simple probability.

If, however, the minor premise itself, or the relation of the cases in which one wins, to all possible cases is unknown and is first to be found by a probable calculation, then the conclusion attains a composite probability. In his introduction to philosophy, 's-Gravesand gives an example of this:

> "We will suppose," he says, "that someone picks from a bowl of black and white marbles, and we are to say how probable it is that the first one he removes will be black or that it will be white.
>
> "The probability is relative to certainty as the number of black marbles is to the number of all of them; but these numbers are unknown to us.
>
> "However, without worrying about the numbers themselves, we can discover the relation of the one to the others which we seek, if previously one or several of these marbles have been removed. For the number of all marbles which have been thus removed from the bowl is in proportion to the number of black marbles among them as certainty is to the probability that is being sought. This manner of calculating probability," 's-Gravesand adds, "is in fact subject to some small mistakes. But if the number of the marbles which have been taken from the bowl is quite large, then the mistakes in the application should not be considered."

The correctness of this procedure can be shown through the following reasons.

Just as it is probable that so-and-so will happen when the fewest reasons for it are lacking, so it is probable that so-and-so has happened when the most reasons for it are given. If, therefore, one has removed a certain number of marbles, then it is to be supposed that everything ensues according to the proportion of probability and that for which one had the most reasons takes place. It is, therefore, probable that the number of black marbles among those coming out is relative to the number of white ones as the probability that only black ones will come out is to the probability that only white ones will (just as, namely, one had supposed before taking them out) or, as is to be seen from the attached calculation,* as the number of all black marbles which are in the bowl is to the number of all white ones in it. The greater the number of marbles removed, the more probable it is that the alleged proportion is correct. For the more marbles that are removed, the more frequently the outcome would have to have been contrary to the probability, if the deviation from the proportion is supposed to constitute a noticeable difference. We can, therefore, make the following rational inference:

> As the number of black marbles in a bowl is to the number of all marbles in it,** so the probability that a black one will presently come out is to certainty.
>
> The number of black marbles in the bowl is relative to all of them taken together, in the same proportion as the number of black marbles that have been removed is to the number of all the marbles which have come out;†
>
> Hence, the probability that a black marble will presently come out is in relation to its certainty, in the same proportion as the number of black marbles that have come out is to the number of all marbles that have been removed.

By this means, then, 's-Gravesand's proposition is confirmed.

Since, however, in this inference neither premise states a complete certainty but each instead rests solely upon probabilities, it is clear that

---

* Removed black marbles = a
      white marbles = b
Removed black marbles in the bowl = y
      white marbles in the bowl = x
The probability that a + b will be only white marbles = ax + bx. That a + b will be only black marbles = ay + by. Thus, ab = ay + by : ax + bx and a:b = y:x.

** = x + y : y.

† x + y = a + b : a.

in the conclusion there must be a twofold probability. 'S-Gravesand, who treats composite probabilities in particular, could have suitably calculated this sort of probability along with the others. Since, however, the probability of the minor premise is very difficult to calculate, he preferred to avoid looking at the mistakes in the application which would be very small if the number of marbles removed from the bowl is quite large.

Since we must first look for the proportion between the cases by means of a probable inference, Rüdiger calls this type of probability "the medical probability."[*] For in the art of medicine, one infers from the proportion between those who died from a given illness or were cured by a certain medication and the number of those in which this was not the outcome, to the probability in current individual cases (although here one must depend upon the probable connection between cause and effect, of which I will soon have more to say).

From certain observations which had been undertaken at London and Paris for several centuries, people established the number of how many children out of a hundred would die in the first six years, from six to sixteen, from sixteen to twenty-six, and so on. If now, in a present case, it is to be calculated how probable it is that Maevius, who is of a given age and has been absent for a certain time, is still alive at present, the learned Bernoulli teaches how this is to be calculated by an easy application of the universal rules, noted above.[**]

Frequently, probability is also the path by which we arrive at indubitable certainty. If we cannot survey every reason for the truth of a subject all at once, then we first assume some of these reasons in order to see what would result from them if they in fact alone exhausted the essence of the subject. The outcome which is brought about in this form is called "a hypothesis." Then we investigate whether all other reasons for its truth are in agreement with this assumed hypothesis. If this is the case, then the proposition, which initially had only a probability, attains a complete certainty. Outside of algebra, examples

---

[*] Rüdiger, *De sensu veri et falsi*.[5]

[**] Bernoulli, "Specim. artis consectandi ad quaestiones juris adplicatae," *Acta Eruditorum*, V, T. IV, Supplementum, p. 159.

[5] Andreas Rüdiger, *De sensu veri et falsi* (Halle, 1709, 1722). According to the editors of the *Jubiläumsausgabe* 9vol. 1, p. 638), Rüdiger, a physician, defined several types of probability (historical, medical, hermeneutical, physical, political, anthropological, and practical).

will seldom be found where the truth has been uncovered other than by means of hypotheses. The exception to this, I submit, is the *principium reductionis* through which, without making any probable presupposition, we can at the same time find certain truths, as it were, by demonstration.

All our judgments that depend upon experience, upon analogy, and upon induction have been contested by the astute skeptic, David Hume, in his *Philosophical Inquiries*.[6] The German translation of this work is in everyone's hands and we would like to cite from the fourth inquiry (which he entitles "Skeptical Doubts Concerning the Effect of the Understanding") the principal objections which most have the appearance as though they could cancel physical certainty.

> "We always presume, when we see like sensible qualities," Hume says, "that they have like secret powers, and reckon on a similar effect. If a body of like color and consistence with that bread, which we have formerly eaten, be presented to us, we make no scruple of repeating the experiment, and foresee with certainty, like nourishment and support. Now this is a process of the mind or thought, of which I would willingly know the foundation. It is allowed on all hands, that there is no known connection between the sensible qualities and the secret powers; and consequently, our reason cannot have made an inference a priori. As to experience, I do not even grasp how it can be extended to future times, and to other objects, of which we still have no experience."[7]

(One readily sees that the target here is the well-known logical proposition that we never are able to perceive something universal since all our experiences are of individual things which are determined

---

[6] David Hume, *Philosophical Essays Concerning Human Understanding* (London, 1748) renamed *An Essay concerning Human Understanding* in 1758; cf. *Enquiries Concerning Human Understanding and Concerning the Principles of Morals* ed. L. A. Selby-Bigge, 3rd edn. rev. P. H. Nidditch (Oxford, Clarendon Press, 1975). Translated as *Philosophische Versuche über die menschliche Erkenntnis* (Hamburg and Leipzig, 1755), with notes by Johann Georg Sulzer.

[7] This and the following quotation of Hume have been translated from the German, though I have tried to use Hume's formulations whenever possible. Where the German translation cited by Mendelssohn departs from Hume's text, the original is given in these notes. Cf *Enquiries Concerning Human Understanding*, ed. Selby-Bigge, Section IV, Pt. II, p. 33:

> ... and consequently, that the mind is not led to form such a conclusion concerning their constant and regular conjunction, by anything which it knows of their nature. As to past *Experience*, it can be allowed to give *direct* and *certain* information of those precise objects only, and that precise period of time, which fell under its cognizance: But why this experience should be extended to future times, and to other objects, which for aught we know, may be only in appearance similar; this is the main question on which I would insist.

according to time and space and accompanying circumstances.) Hume continues:

> From causes, which appear *similar*, we expect similar effects. This is the sum of all our experimental conclusions. If this inference be made by reason, why is it not just as perfect right at the beginning and for a single example as it is after so long an experience? . . . Now where is that process of reasoning, which, from one instance, draws a conclusion, so different from that which it infers from a hundred instances, that are nowise different from that single one?[8]

In the splendid notes attached by a philosopher to the German translation, these blinding objections are, to be sure, confronted thoroughly enough, but we want to take the trouble, on the basis of the established grounds of probability, to make the inferences from analogy, experience, and so on somewhat more distinct. In his introduction to philosophy, 's-Gravesand proves, on the basis of the will of God, the reliability of these inferences since the all-perfect being must act according to universal laws. But I have some doubts about placing the basis of our experimental inferences in the will of God. One leaves atheists far too many ways out if one, as it were, impresses upon them that they can deny all inferences resting on analogy. Should one have to renounce all proofs for the existence of God, in which merely a single premise is derived from analogy? We would like to see whether we cannot untie the knots in a more advantageous manner.

If we experience a single instance in which two events, A and B, happen at the same time or follow immediately after one another, then either the event B must be grounded in the event A or A and B are subordinated to a third, near or distant cause C or, finally, A and B are effects of completely different causes, whose existence does not at all depend upon one another.

In the first two cases, a reason can be given why A and B occur at the same time or immediately after one another. In the third case, by contrast, there is, in the properties of A and B, no reason that they should be joined, and it should be regarded as a mere contingency that the two causes which produce events A and B meet at one and the same time.

---

[8] Ibid., p. 36: "Now it seems evident, that, if this conclusion were formed by reason, it would be as perfect at first, and upon one instance, as after ever so long a course of experience."

On the other hand, the more often one sees these very same events recur at the same time, the more improbable the assumed third case becomes, namely, where these two events are not supposed to be grounded in one another at all. For the probability that A and B should be joined by a mere lucky accident is related to its certainty as 1 is to the number of the observed instances $+ 1$.* However, the more times one has repeated the observations, the more probable it becomes that it was not an accident but rather that these two events either are grounded in one another or subordinate to a third, common cause. In both cases one can thus infer with probability that A will never occur without B, and, in turn, B will never occur without A.

I would like to provide an example. Let it be supposed that someone feels dizzy whenever he drinks coffee. He will then suppose with probability that this drink is the cause of the dizziness that he felt. Yet the first time that this happens to him, he will not even be able to make this probable inference. There could just as well have been some completely different cause from which this dizziness arose and which by mere chance manifested its effect precisely when he drank coffee. However, the more often he puts this to the test, the more probable becomes the supposition that it was no mere accident and the degree of its probability is to its certainty $= n : n + 1$ (if n signifies the number of observations made). With this degree of probability he is afraid of never being able to drink coffee without becoming dizzy. We would like to apply this to the most well-known experimental inferences. Whenever we have seen light ignited, the objects around us have become visible. If it had only happened by chance that the bodies became visible without this phenomenon having been linked in some mediated or unmediated fashion with the igniting of the light, then the meeting of these two phenomena would have to be reckoned a mere accident whose probability is in relation to certainty as 1 is to the number of observed cases $+ 1$. Consequently, the probability of the opposite is in relation to certainty as the number of observed cases is to certainty $= n : n + 1$.

---

* In the first observation the probability was $= \frac{1}{2}$

in the second $= \frac{1}{3}$

in the third $= \frac{1}{4}$

in the fourth $= \frac{1}{1}$

$\overline{n + 1}$

243

It has been observed that, as long as a body has not met with resistance, it has sunk, and it has been inferred with a probability that is relative to certainty as $n : n + 2$, that heaviness is common to all bodies. However, whether this heaviness is immediately grounded in the essence of the body, or whether there is some material which makes the body heavy, cannot be determined by experience – and the opinions of philosophers, too, are still divided about this.

A similar situation is involved in the example cited by David Hume. The sensuous properties of bread are either immediately connected to its powers of nourishing or they are both grounded in the inner essence of the bread as a common cause of them or, lastly, it is a mere contingency that these external qualities have coincided with its nutritive powers. The probability of the latter case is relative to certainty as $1 : n + 1$; thus the ratio of the probability of the opposite being the case to certainty is $= n : n + 1$. The more often we have the experience, the closer our expectation approaches to certainty, and if n were infinite then we would be completely convinced.

I say, we will only be convinced when n is infinite. This still requires some clarification. For since we have seen that probability always has a definite proportion to certainty, then it would seem that one ought to believe that the probability would have to be able to grow towards certainty through a finite number of throws. But this would be the case if each additional throw were to contribute the same amount to certainty, something which, however, does not happen. Instead, the contribution to certainty constantly decreases according to a definite proportion, and thus an infinite series of such contributions can be required before the finite quantity of certainty is acquired by this means. An example will make this clear. Given the assumption that Titius is supposed to win a bet if he manages to come up with four, five, or six on his throw, then his hope is as great as that of his opponent and both $= \frac{1}{2}$. If he is permitted two throws, then the second throw takes away half of his opponent's hope. For since the second throw only occurs if the first misses, it can bring Titius no more than half of the hope he lacks, in our case $= \frac{1}{4}$. Thus his hope is $= \frac{3}{4}$ and that of his opponent $= \frac{1}{4}$. From this one sees that the second throw's contribution to certainty is not as great as the contribution of the first. For the same reason, the third throw would bring Titius only $\frac{1}{8}$, the fourth $\frac{1}{16}$, and so on. This must be infinite if it is supposed to become $= 1$. Hence, an infinite number of throws is required before Titius' hope can become equal to certainty. If one allows Titius to play with more than one dice at the same time, another calculation takes place since a decreasing series of equations likewise emerges which must be infinite before it takes all hope away from the opposite.

In general, since we saw that the probability $= \dfrac{n}{n+1}$, but

that this formula cannot be $= 1$ unless n is infinitely large, then the probability also cannot become certainty through the amount of throws unless the number of them is infinite. But this does not prevent probability from having a definite proportion to certainty in each particular case.

Our experimental inferences thus have a secure foundation on which they rest. Through frequently repeated experiences and through the credible witness of others who have had these same experiences, we come closer and closer to mathematical evidence although it is certain that we can never arrive at this evidence itself by means of experience.

It has been seen that infinitely repeated experiences can only prove that two events will not have come together at the same time contingently. On the other hand, it still remains dubious, (1) whether these two events are grounded in one another, (2) whether they are subordinated to a third, proximate cause or (3) to a third, distant cause. Hence, it can never be settled by experience which of the three systems, by means of which the effect of one substance on another can be explained, is in keeping with the truth. In other words,

first, whether the alteration in substance B is sufficiently and immediately grounded in the alteration of some other finite substance A, as maintained by the proponents of universal influxes between substances (*Systema influxus physici universalis* [system of universal physical influx]);

second, whether the alteration of substance B as well as the alteration in substance A is immediately subordinate to the supreme being. The Cartesians, along with the universal occasionalists, make this assumption (*Systema causarum occasionalium universalium* [system of universal occasional causes]. Or, finally,

third, whether the two events are subordinated to the Supreme Being by means of the mediation of two harmonizing series of events which Baumgarten calls "the system of universal harmony"

(*Systema harmoniae praestabilitae universalis* [system of universal preestablished harmony]).[9]

Another truth follows from these principles.

> If several phenomena a, b, c, and so on can be explained by a single cause d as well as by several particular causes e, f, g, and so on, then the ratio of the probability that they all have not more than a single cause to the certainty of that cause is the same as the number of phenomena is to the number of phenomena + 1, that is, $= n : n + 1$.

For since these phenomena a, b, c, and so on agree in this respect, that they can all be explained by means of a single cause, then this agreement should not be regarded as a mere accident if each phenomenon is actually supposed to have its particular causes. The probability of such an accident is

$$= \frac{1}{n + 1}; \text{thus the probability of the opposite case} = \frac{n}{n + 1}.$$

Examples of this occur so frequently in ordinary life that, for the sake of brevity, I will be satisfied with some very familiar ones.

In a certain collection of medical observations, it is told that once an entire family was overcome by a night of sleeplessness, exhaustion, blurred vision, and a kind of delirium. The doctor conjectured that there must have been some harmful green in the salad of which all of them had eaten the previous evening. He found that he was not deceived. It was not impossible here that, for each person of this family, a particular event was the cause of the sickness. However, since these several phenomena can also be explained by a single cause, the physician correctly conjectured the latter, and the probability of his conjecture is related to certainty as the number of the sick persons is to that same number + 1, in other words, as $n : n + 1$.

The Copernican system of the world is now generally recognized as more probable than the ancient Ptolemaic system, although the ancients had no lack of eccentricities and epicycles to explain all the phenomena that were subsequently observed. However, in accordance with the modern system of the world, one can explain everything through simple presuppositions and, consequently, by fewer causes since the ancients

---

[9] Alexander Baumgarten, *Metaphysica*, 7th edn. (Halle and Magdeburg, 1779), §450; see also §§448 and 452.

had to conceive each particular phenomenon on some new hypothesis. Thus, to a certain extent, one can determine the greater degree of probability that the modern system of the world has than the ancient.

If the fact that we are able to ascribe a single or even several particular intentions to the various actions that a human being takes up does not contradict his moral character, then the single intention is always the most probable, and the degree of probability is in proportion to certainty as the number of actions which can be determined by an intention is to the same number + 1. This is the basis according to which we judge the intentions of our neighbor in ordinary life.

Since all moral and physical certainties can be discussed in this way independently of the properties of God, they cannot be rejected by the atheist, and he must accept the reasons which are inferred from them for proving the existence of God.

Up until now we have spoken of a probable knowledge which takes place only in regard to our limited intellect. Along with Bernoulli, 'S-Gravesand, Wolff, and others, we have presupposed a determinate truth about the matter itself. Hence, an infinite intellect, from whom no reasons for its truth could be hidden, will have the most certain knowledge of all possible things, and, as far as this intellect is concerned, there is no probability.

It is not, however, to be denied that, in the views of some philosophers, there must also be cases in which nothing but probable knowledge could be ascribed to the All-perfect Being himself without taking some of his perfections away from him. If, namely, there were a kind of truth, the nature and essential determinations of which do not permit complete certainty, indeed, such that perfect certainty in regard to it would contain a contradiction, then one would, without detracting from the Supreme Being's omniscience, be able to deny that he possesses this utterly impossible knowledge just as, without detracting from his omnipotence, one denies that he has the power to make impossible things possible. The very philosophers who believe that genuine freedom is to be found nowhere else but in a completely undetermined choice, an *indifferentia aequilibrii* [indifference of equilibrium] as it is called in the schools, these philosophers, I say, are the ones who claim that free actions cannot be predetermined without canceling the nature of freedom. Hence, they also must have no misgivings about denying that the highest being possesses infallible prescience in regard to our free actions and everything that depends upon them.

Meanwhile, these philosophers do not deny that compelling reasons have an influence on our will. For they would have had to deny their own experience if they doubted this. They merely insist on this, that no complete determination of our free actions should be ascribed to the compelling reasons, since otherwise they would cancel our freedom. Hence, in keeping with the view of the philosophers, one can say that the compelling reasons contain, to be sure, some reason but not a sufficient one why our will determines itself in such a way rather than otherwise.

Now is not the occasion to test all the reasons that people have produced over the ages for and against this view. At the present time I will be satisfied with a single remark to which I have been led by the above thoughts on probability.

If philosophers regard the certain prescience of such things that depend on freedom as utterly impossible, then I maintain that the highest being cannot have even probable knowledge in regard to our future actions.

For if God had a probable prescience of our future free actions, then the degree of this probability must have been determined since a quantity cannot be present anywhere without a definite degree if it, as in our case, is supposed to be finite.

If the degree of divine probability is to be definite, then the proportion between the conditions known to him and certainty must be given since, as we have seen above, the degree of probability is to be determined on the basis of this proportion.

But from what source does God take these reasons for its truth? God takes them, of necessity, from the circumstances in which the entity who acts voluntarily finds himself and from the compelling reasons and impulses which determine his choice. Since the future itself is determined by the free actions, the reason for its truth must be encountered either in the present or in the past. Nothing of the present and past, however, but the circumstances in which beings with free wills find themselves and the compelling reasons and impulses that arise from these circumstances, are connected with the choices made by them.

Now the circumstances in which the free entity finds itself and all the compelling reasons and impulses derived from them do not suffice, in the opinion of the philosophers, to establish with certainty which choice the free entity will make. Thus, the degree of probability cannot be determined from the proportion of the positive compelling reasons to the positive and negative ones together. On the other hand, these compelling reasons still contain some reason why the free entity will determine itself in one way rather than another. Thus, the more positive or the more negative compelling reasons influence our will, the greater is the probability that we will do something or leave something undone. If, accordingly, it were possible that infinitely many compelling reasons could influence our will to the best course of action, then they would constitute an infinitely large degree of probability or a certainty since, in the opinion of these philosophers, the maximum in regard to our free actions is to be sought nowhere else but in infinity. Since only a finite number of compelling reasons influences us in each particular case, the probability of divine prescience in each particular case is in proportion to its certainty, as the finite power of the compelling reasons which occasion our choice is to an infinite number of them; in other words, the degree of divine prescience = 0.

This case should not be confused with the one previously mentioned because the number of throws would have to be likewise infinite before it could constitute certainty. In that case, the ratio of probability to certainty was the proportion of a finite magnitude to a finite magnitude. There the probability for and against a matter, taken together, was always equal to certainty and this was a finite magnitude. The hopes of two players, taken together, are equal to the bet,

just as $\dfrac{n}{n+1} + \dfrac{1}{n+1} = 1$. That an infinite number of

cases was required to constitute a certainty was only necessary if all cases do not contribute the same amount to certainty but decrease in a constant proportion. In our case, however, and in accordance with the presupposition of these philosophers, the certainty is not to be compared with a finite magnitude at all. For even if the positive and negative compelling reasons are taken together, they still do not constitute certainty. Hence, in contrast with probability, certainty is unquestionably an infinite magnitude opposite which the finite magnitude of probability disappears.

If, then, one does not want to deny the Supreme Being even a capacity to foresee with probability all our free decisions, then one must allow the free actions a predetermined certainty, on the basis of which they can be identified and known in advance.

Yet why do I elevate myself to the level of divine properties? Common, daily experience places in our hands reasons on the basis of which this proposition can be presented irrefutably. If it is true that one can make a probable inference on the basis of a person's character and what is known about his way of thinking to what he does and does not do, then all voluntary decisions have a predetermined certainty. For what objectively has no definite certainty, can in no way be known. Could Cassius, for example, not be morally certain that his co-conspirator Brutus would not betray him? Unquestionably, since who would fear a vile action coming from a Brutus? We would suppose that Cassius would have been in a position to lay out separately and distinctly all the circumstances which provide Brutus with the motivation to keep the conspiracy a secret as well as those circumstances which could seduce him to betray it. Let us call the former circumstances *a*, the latter *b*. According to the theory of probability outlined above, the proportion of Cassius' moral certainty to mathematical evidence = a : a + b. For if someone would bet with him that Brutus would betray him, then Cassius' hope = a, his opponent's = b, and, thus, the proportion of Cassius' probability to his certainty = a : a + b, but that of his opponent = b : a + b. One sees from this that the positive and negative reasons or conditions, taken together, must always constitute certainty. Otherwise the proportion of the given reasons for its truth to all of them taken together, that is to say, the quantity of probability, cannot be determined at all.

I believe, therefore, that I have shown, on the basis of divine properties as well as on the basis of ordinary experience, that each willful decision must have its definite certainty in advance. From this it follows that the soul cannot choose otherwise than according to compelling reasons and impulses since the predetermined certainty of future decisions depends upon them. The kind of harmful consequences in regard to freedom and responsibility that trouble people because of this doctrine are mere chimera, the essence of which is due simply and solely to indistinct concepts of freedom.

On evidence in metaphysical sciences

On evidence in metaphysical sciences

Introduction

The criticism is commonly advanced against philosophy that, in its doctrines, no particular conviction is ever to be hoped for since in every century new systems rise up and glimmer for a while only to pass away in turn. In our days the poems, the speeches, the historical and critical writings, the statues, and other artworks of the ancients are still admired as masterpieces, and, to a degree, more is to be gained from the study of them than from the study of nature itself. In philosophy, however, the words of the past have become almost useless in the present day. To be sure, the most famous systems still contain some useful materials, but, as is commonly believed, they are not worth the trouble of searching through the ruins and digging up the rubble that covers them. It is inferred from this that taste or the sentiment of beauty and order is far more durable and reliable than reason or convictions about philosophical truths. For taste has preserved itself in much the same way since Homer while reason changes its shape with every age of humanity, and, hence, the former must be more certain and less subject to doubt than the latter.

Yet the inconstancy of philosophical systems seems to stem from a cause that, in a certain respect, turns out to be to philosophy's advantage. We find such feeble reasons, so little that is compelling and coherent in the systems of the ancients because reason has made such marked progress since that time, because we have come closer to the truth thanks to the efforts of philosophers, because we have learned to see the first principles of nature better and analyze them more distinctly.

In the present day the ancients' teaching about nature is far less useful than their metaphysics because knowledge about nature has, since the time of the ancients, made far more remarkable progress than metaphysics has. In general, the higher an art or science is pursued, the more one distances oneself from those first feeble attempts which, at the time they were made, perhaps demanded more genius than the masterpieces which came later. In the course of time one becomes more and more familiar with the object, the concepts become clearer, a profounder insight is reached with less trouble; one sees with completely different eyes.

In the fine arts and sciences, on the other hand, we are still where we were at the time of the ancient Greeks and have perhaps even taken a few steps backwards since then. A successful imitation of the ancients is the highest perfection that our virtuosos strive for, and the most succesful imitation consists, as always, in pursuing the paragon. In the judgment of those who know, no epic poet has yet attained the level of Homer, no orator that of Demosthenes, and no sculptor that of Phidias.[1] Hence, since we have no better orginal works, is it a wonder that we still look upon the works of the ancients with the same eyes with which they were regarded by their contemporaries? In the dark ages Aristotle meant far more to philosophers than Homer did to poets. For a long time his proclamations were considered certain, that is, until Descartes and Leibniz came along and surpassed him in rigorousness and distinctness. When the moderns produce epic poets who eclipse the *Iliad* as much in beauty as the metaphysics of Descartes or Leibniz eclipse the Aristotelian in rigorousness and distinctness, then the *Iliad* will perhaps seem as useless as the philosophy of Aristotle.

Matters are completely different, however, when it comes to the nature of mathematics. Although greater progress has been made in mathematics than in any other science, the works of the ancients have not, on that account, completely lost their usefulness. Mathematics has its certainty to thank for this prerogative. Its evidence is so great that one could rarely wander far from the truth. One knew less but what one knew were undeniable truths. The discoveries of the moderns have infinitely expanded the boundaries of science, but they have left unaltered the small region that they found already present. Its intrinsic

---

[1] Phidias, Athenian sculptor of the fifth century BC, renowned for the serene grandeur of his works.

constitution was so sound that it was unnecessary to undertake the slightest reform.

In our century the attempt has been made to place the first principles of metaphysics, by means of unerring proofs, on a footing as unalterable as the first principles of mathematics. Everyone knows how great the hope was that one drew from this endeavor in the beginning. But the results have shown how difficult this is to accomplish. Even those who regard metaphysical conceptions as convincing and irrefutable must ultimately concede that they have still not been provided with the evidence of mathematical sciences; otherwise it would not have been possible for them to meet with so much contradiction. The first principles of mathematics convince every rational person who pays a little attention to them. But it is well-known that many a discerning mind of proven ability rejects the first principles of metaphysics and believes that no science other than mathematics can be utterly convincing. Such thoughts appear to have prompted an illustrious Academy to pose the question: whether it is possible at all for metaphysical truths to have the same sort of evidence as mathematical truths, etc.

Part of the evidence of a truth is, in addition to certainty, perspicuity. To say that a truth is perspicuous is to say that anyone who has ever grasped the proof must immediately be fully convinced of the truth and so set at ease that he does not feel within himself the slightest resistance to assuming it. The first principles of differential calculus are just as undeniable as geometrical truths but they are not as evident or as perspicuous. Hence, the evidence of geometric truths cannot be attributed to them. From this one sees that the question raised by the Academy, even in the case where it is affirmed, has two separate divisions. Namely, it must be shown: *first*, whether metaphysical truths can be presented as incontestably as geometric truths, and, if this is affirmed, *second*, whether the proofs of this are capable of the same sort of perspicuity as geometric truths. If the first question, however, is answered in the negative, then it remains to be determined: *first*, what the makeup of the certainty of these truths actually is, and, *second*, what degree of certainty they can be brought to, and, *third*, whether this degree is sufficient for them to be completely convincing.

I venture to claim that metaphysical truths are capable, to be sure, of the same certainty but not of the same perspicuity as geometric truths. That is to say, it is possible, through interlocking inferences, to trace the most eminent truths of metaphysics back to such principles which, as far as their nature is concerned, are as undeniable as the first principles and postulates of geometry, but it is not possible to render this chain of inferences as evident or as perspicuous as it is for geometric truths. In order to prove this claim, I will investigate the nature of mathematical and metaphysical truths separately and then compare them.

Mendelssohn's *Philosophische Schriften*

First section

On the evidence in the first principles of mathematics

The certainty of mathematics is based upon the general axiom that nothing can be and not be at the same time. In this science each proposition such as, for example, "A is B," is proven in one of two ways. Either one unpacks the concepts of A and shows "A is B", or one unpacks the concepts of B and infers from this that not-B must also be not-A. Both types of proof are thus based upon the principle of contradiction, and since the object of mathematics in general is *magnitude* and that of geometry in particular *extension*, one can say that in mathematics in general our concepts of magnitude are unpacked and analyzed, while in geometry in particular our concepts of extension are unpacked and analyzed. In fact, since geometry lays nothing else as its basis than the abstract concept of extension and derives all its conclusions from this single source – deriving them, to be sure, in such a way that one recognizes distinctly that everything maintained in it is necessarily connected by the principle of contradiction with the abstracted concept of extension, there is no doubt that all geometric truths that geometry teaches us to *unpack* or *untangle* from the concept of extension must be encountered all *tangled up* in it. For what else can the profoundest inferences do but analyze a concept and make distinct what was obscure? Such inferences cannot bring in what is not to be found in the concept, and it is easy to see that it is also not possible, by means of the principle of contradiction, to derive from the concept what is not to be found in it. In the concept of extension, for example, there lies the inner possibility that a space is limited by three straight lines in such a way that two of them include a right angle. For it follows from the essence of extension that it is capable of many sorts of limitations and that the assumed sort of limitation of one of its level planes contains no contradiction. If one subsequently shows that the concept of this assumed limitation or of a right-angled triangle necessarily entails that the square of the hypotenuse is such-and-such, then it must have also been possible to find this truth originally and implicitly in the initial concept of extension. Otherwise it could never have been derived from it by means of the principle of contradiction. The idea of extension is inseparable from the idea of the possibility of such a limitation, as was previously assumed, and the limitation is in turn necessarily connected to the concept of the equality of the aforesaid square. Thus, this truth also lay tangled up, as one might say, in the original concept of extension, but it escaped our attention and could not be distinctly known and distinguished until, through analysis, we unpacked all the parts of this concept and separated them from one another. The analysis of concepts is for the understanding nothing more than what the magnifying glass is for sight. It does not produce anything that was not to be found in the object. But it spreads out the parts of the object and makes it possible for our senses to distinguish much that they would otherwise not have noticed. The analysis of concepts does nothing different from this; it makes the parts and members of these concepts, which were previously obscure and unnoticed, distinct and recognizable, but it does not introduce anything into the concepts that was not already to be found in them.

Plato relates in the *Meno* [82–5] how Socrates elicited a profound geometrical principle from an ignorant boy through skillful questioning. If one reads this dialogue, one must confess that the attempt would be easy to repeat if only the individual to be instructed, before answering yes or no, is patient enough to follow us and to pay sufficient attention to the many different questions that we must pose. For in the course of the entire lesson the boy in the *Meno* did not have much more to do than to say yes or no on the basis of the makeup of the matter, and yet Socrates let him find everything out for himself. He does not presuppose in the boy anything more than the concept of extension. He does not disclose to him any nominal definition, axiom, or postulate. Instead, by merely questioning, he directs the boy's attention first to this, then to that member of the underlying concept and lets him gradually find out the geometrical principle together with the demonstration. There is no doubt that, through repeated attempts, he could have done the same with the whole of mathematics and from this one sees that our concepts come down, so to speak, to the last threads if a Socrates takes the trouble to untangle them. Plato relates the story of this episode in order to conclude from it that our learning is nothing but a remembering. For Socrates, indeed, imparted nothing new to the boy and taught him profound truths merely by arousing his attention or, as

Plato calls it, his "power of remembering." This means, in the language of modern philosophers, that no new concepts enter into the soul through learning that were not supposed to have been in it already. For inferences and, in particular, mathematical inferences are nothing but analyses of sensuous impressions or of concepts abstracted from them. Hence, they can make the obscure distinct and disentangle what is tangled up, but can impart absolutely nothing new to the soul. In the sensuous impression of extension, for example, lies the entire sum total of geometrical truths which inferences simply illuminate more. Now it is, however, contrary to reason to ascribe so great a treasure of profound truths to the sensuous impression as a bodily movement perceived by the soul. Moreover, even if one would want to grant this objectively, it is still inconceivable how this infinite amount of concepts can be drummed into the soul all at once by a momentary intuiting. To eliminate this difficulty, Plato hits upon a strange idea: our soul has previously, in some other state, learned and come to know everything that it experiences in this life, and the sensuous impressions are only the occasions or the opportunities for the soul to recall what was forgotten. This is in keeping with a certain mystical doctrine of oriental wise men who likewise maintain that the soul grasped the entire world prior to this life but then forgot everything when it entered this world.

As strange as this doctrine sounds to our ears, there is nevertheless some truth to it. Moderns have, in fact, retained it and even introduced it into their system; they have merely removed the mystical aspect that lends it so absurd an appearance. They say that, since the power of representation constitutes the essence and the inner possibility of the soul, a soul that is present and has absolutely no representations is an obvious contradiction. For it is as little possible for a power to exist without having an effect as it is for a triangle to have four sides.

The soul, then, when it enters into this life, is by no means to be compared with a blank tablet on which the letters first have to be entered, as the Aristotelians would have it. Instead the soul must have representations as soon as it is present, since nothing else is meant by saying that a soul is present. These representations, however, can have the makeup of the tangled concepts which, as we saw above, can always be found in the soul without being noticed by it. We saw that the human soul cannot perceive extension without implicitly representing to itself all geometrical truths. Hence, it is quite possible for there to be a state of the soul in which all its representations are of this makeup, namely, that they are not recognized by it, as, for example, in sleep. An infinite intellect that represents to itself the soul of someone sleeping must perceive representations in that sleeping soul; otherwise the soul would not be present. Yet the soul itself would not then be conscious of those representations and has no representations that are distinct or disentangled from one another. The soul may have had a similar makeup before its entry into this life. If the soul was otherwise present, then an infinite intellect would have had to perceive representations in that soul, though the soul itself was perhaps not able to be conscious of them until the concepts gradually became untangled through prompting by sensuous impressions. Here one sees the transition to the sublime doctrines of modern philosophers: [1] that the soul never ceases implicitly to represent to itself the entire world while explicitly representing to itself only the world relative to the position of its body in it, [2] that sensuous impressions are merely the occasions and opportunities for the representations of the soul to unfold themselves and be perceived, and [3] that this unfolding of concepts in the soul perfectly harmonizes with the unfolding of concepts outside it. But this observation, while near at hand, has already led me too far astray from my theme. Allow me to return.

The entire force of geometrical certainty rests, therefore, on the necessary connection of concepts. That is to say, one analyzes the original concept of extension and shows that there is an indissolvable bond between it and certain consequences derived from it and that, without these consequences, it contains an obvious contradiction. In a word, one shows that the original concept that we have of extension is, objectively considered, one and the same with the concepts and implications derived from it. For although we can perceive an extension without thinking of the geometrical truths that are connected with it, one still knows by means of a correct analysis of the concepts that they are all implicitly contained in the original concept of extension and, hence, objectively considered, cannot be separated from it without contradiction.

What has been shown here for geometry holds for mathematics in general. For extension is nothing other than a static quantity, the parts of which can be found next to one another. If the quantity is not static or is not regarded as static, then the science of it is called "arithmetic."

If the parts of the quantity are not next to one another, but rather follow upon one another, then the measurement of time arises even though people are accustomed to expressing time always by means of either numbers or extended magnitudes, if it is to be measured. The cause of this will become apparent in what follows.

If we consider mathematics from this side, what an extraordinary light it sheds on psychology, a discipline that appears so far removed from it! What profundity! Every ordinary sensuous impression bears within its lap an immense sea of eternal truths. Each concept disappears into an infinity before our eyes. What great minds have worked for unimaginable ages on unpacking the sensuous concept of quantity. Their eyes were always opened by new vistas and unseen distances that are only completely comprehended by an all-seeing eye. And yet until now they have limited the greater part of their efforts to extended quantity alone. Until now there have appeared only isolated, meager attempts to deal with unextended magnitude or the quantity whose parts neither are next to one another nor follow upon one another, but rather collapse into one another such as, for example, degrees and their measurements. What one reads of the measurement of forces of motion, of velocity, of warmth, light, and so on in the works of the moderns can scarcely be counted as a part of this science. For, in the course of measuring these particular types of unextended magnitudes, one still has to make use of artifices to grasp them by lines and figures in order to transform them into extended magnitudes. This would, however, be unnecessary if the first principles of unextended quantity were posited distinctly and separately from one another. These general principles would necessarily be applicable, not only to the cited types of intensive magnitude, but also to the value of things, to their possibility, actuality, perfection, and beauty, to the degree of truth, certainty, distinctness, and inner efficacy of our knowledge, to the goods of moral actions, and so forth. For all these degrees are true quantities and thus capable of measurement and respective comparison. It is scarcely necessary to recall how little of this important theory has as yet been discovered.

Yet, it is not to be denied, meanwhile, that there must be such a theory. For, in the first place, daily experience shows that people of natural, sound reason pass judgments on the degrees of things, make comparisons, and perceive proportions, the correctness of which is confirmed by experience. There is, accordingly, a natural mathematics of unextended magnitudes, and, thus, there must also be an artful one. For if the foundations of this natural science are distinctly analyzed and traced back to general concepts, then the result will be the required, conventional doctrine of magnitudes. Furthermore, the unextended magnitudes are in agreement with the extended ones in regard to the central concept of quantity. But analysis can draw an entire series of implications from the particular concept of extended magnitudes, a series of implications which constitute a binding system. This must, therefore, be possible for unextended magnitudes as well. Why is it, then, that nothing prominent has been established in this respect? I believe that it is easy to show the difficulties which have been found here.

The most necessary and fruitful means of finding something with which to measure a magnitude is the distinct knowledge of its limits. A magnitude without limits is immense. Hence, the way in which a magnitude is to be measured must be conceived on the basis of the makeup of its limits. It is known that all discoveries in mathematics depend upon acquaintance with figures or the limits of extension. Now, the parts of an extended magnitude fall alongside one another and can probably be distinguished with the senses from one another (namely, insofar as they are part of a quantity and here, too, nothing more is necessary). Thus, the various parts of the limits, that is, surfaces, lines, and points (which make up the boundaries of a static extension) can be distinguished with the senses, and, because we observe them individually and afterwards take them together in their appropriate combination, we arrive at a distinct concept of figure. We analyze this distinct concept and arrive at axioms and postulates or theorems and problems, depending upon whether the consequences are immediately or mediately connected with the fundamental idea.

By contrast, the parts of an unextended magnitude collapse into one another and can in no way be distinguished by the senses. Thus, too, their limits cannot be thought in a distinct way by a mere reflection. Missing here, therefore, is the most fruitful means of discovery, that performs such an important service in the doctrine of extended magnitudes, namely, the consideration of figures or the limits of extension, without which one is not in a position to take a single step in mathematics. If one wants ultimately to become acquainted with the limits of an unextended magnitude, then it is necessary to go back to the material of the magnitude or to the quality (since this lies at the bottom of every quantity and constitutes the material of the latter) and learn to distinguish its intrinsic characteristics from one another. But, how difficult it is to attain this abstract insight! An example will illuminate this observation. Let us assume that we wanted to become acquainted with the degree of moral perfection of a character distinctly. To attain this final purpose and grasp the difficulty of this undertaking more distinctly, let us direct our attention constantly at universal mathematics in order to see, with the help of reduction, which means of discovery can contribute something to our project. The material of the ordinary doctrine of magnitudes is a static extension; its various characteristics are length, breadth, and thickness. Two of these (the plane) are the limits of the body; a single one of them (the line) constitutes the limits of the plane; and finally the sign of the absence of all of them (the point) constitutes the limits of the line. All these characteristics can be distinguished by a simple effect of the soul, by mere reflection, and hence it is not difficult to construct for oneself a distinct concept of the limits of an extended magnitude. In the case of the unextended magnitude, cited above, the material is the moral goodness of a character. The characteristics and limits of this material do not occur to the senses and must be produced by the intellect. I must, therefore, return to the definition of moral goodness. This consists in a proficiency at fulfilling one's duties perfectly, despite the obstacles and without a sensuous enticement. These, then, are the characteristics of this quantity, and the limits also may be determined to some extent. For (a) in the first place, the greater the proficiency, second, the more duties, and, third, the more important the duties, fourth, the more the obstacles, and fifth, the stronger the obstacles, and finally (b) the fewer and, sixth, the weaker the sensuous enticements, the greater is the degree of moral goodness. None of these particular characteristics is an original concept. They must be analyzed further and only then can the immediate consequences or the axioms and postulates be produced and posited beyond doubt. Prior to all things, the unextended magnitude of proficiency, the extended and unextended magnitude (namely, the amount and importance) of duties, obstacles, and sensuous allurements must be weighed before one can find a firm footing and lay the foundation of a correct theory. Is anyone still surprised that it is not possible for this to happen very easily?

I have taken a particular case here as an example. However, there are even greater difficulties with the general consideration of the unextended magnitude. For the characteristics of a quality in general are even more abstract and lie even more deeply hidden in the nature of things than the characteristics of moral quality in particular, which I have cited as an example. Indeed, there are particular sorts of unextended magnitudes where the threads being unpacked break off suddenly and it is impossible to proceed further at all without some artificial device of research. One notices this in the case of all *qualitatibus sensibilibus* [*sensible qualities*] other than extension such as, for example, light, warmth, color, hardness, and so forth. The characteristics of these sensuous sentiments can be analyzed neither by the senses nor by the understanding, and thus their limits also cannot be distinctly known in this way. Hence, use is made of some artificial device of research. Since the causes are always appropriate to the effects, one takes up the former where the latter cannot be unpacked. Instead of colors, for example, one takes the constitution of a ray of light, instead of warmth the amount and velocity of fiery particles, and so forth and reduces the concepts of them, where possible, to their first, basic ideas in order to measure the effects by means of their causes. Is there anyone who does not see how far removed all this is from the easy and straight path on which the mathematics of an extended magnitude proceeds?

This very difficulty of constructing appropriate concepts of an unextended magnitude and its limits places one more important obstacle in the path of the mathematical knowledge of qualities, an obstacle that deserves to be considered here. This obstacle consists in the type of notation. The mathematician does not need arbitrary signs since he can put real and essential signs in their place which agree in their nature and connection with the nature and the connection of the thoughts. Geometry, arithmetic, and algebra have this advantage in common though there are differences among them. In its notation geometry has nothing arbitrary at all since its simple as well as its composite signs agree with the thoughts. Lines are essential signs of the concepts which we have of them, and these lines are placed together in figures in the same manner as the concepts are placed together in our soul. In arithmetic and algebra, however, the simple signs, namely, the numbers, letters, and combinative signs are purely arbitrary. Yet in the composite signs as in the formulas and equations, everything agrees exactly with the thoughts.

Hence, in arithmetic a person has to learn only a few arbitrary signs and some rules for combining them in order to understand fully the language of the practicioners of arithmetic and algebra. For, outside these few simple signs and rules for combining them, nothing has been left to convention; everything is determined in the formulas and equations just as it is in our thoughts. In geometry, to be sure, one has no arbitrary signs to retain at all, and, precisely for this reason, geometry comes to beginners more easily than arithmetic does. Yet, considered from another side, the latter science has the advantage of simple signs that are not essential, but arbitrary. That is to say, in geometry nothing can be designated *in abstracto*; rather the signs always represent things *in concreto*. Since even the simple signs in this science are essential, nothing can remain indefinite in a geometrical designation, and, hence, it is always this triangle, this circle, never a triangle in general or a figure in general. In algebra, however, what is supposed to be indefinite in the general concept of it can remain indefinite in the designation. Thus, it is easier to arrive at general concepts in this science than it is in geometry.

On the other hand, everything is arbitrary in the designation of an unextended magnitude since the individual characteristics of it are difficult to distinguish and the manners of combining them are much more difficult to determine and reduce to universal rules. Hence, for the present, research has available to it no means of measuring an unextended magnitude more convenient than designating it by extended magnitudes, as typically happens in dynamics and other related sciences. For by this means one enjoys the advantage of providing an essential and nonarbitrary designation for discovering and grasping the truth.

It is apparent that the certainty of geometrical truths depends merely upon the constant identity of some tangled concept with the derived, untangled concepts. This is the highest degree of certainty but it is only to be found in pure, theoretical mathematics. As soon as we make use of a geometrical truth in practice, that is to say, as soon as we wish to pass from mere possibilities to actualities, an empirical proposition must be placed at the foundation, a proposition which asserts that this or that figure, number, and so forth are actually present. In the entire field of mathematics there is not to be found a single example where one is supposed to be able to infer from merely possible concepts to the actuality of their object. The object of mathematics, the nature of quantity, contradicts such a conclusion. Our concepts of quantity are necessarily connected with other concepts, but not with any actualities. Since, however, one can trust the testimony of the senses and assume it to be undeniable that this or that basic concept has an object actually at hand, the implications that have been drawn from this basic concept must be at hand as well. For contradictory concepts have no object that is actually at hand. I regard, for example, a figure that is present and notice that I can regard each of its sides from an angle at which it appears to vanish completely or to be similar to a mere point. From this I infer that it is a rectilinear figure and thus the figure at hand possesses all the properties which are inseparable from the concept of a rectilinear figure. I count its sides and ascertain that there are three of them; this figure is thus a triangle, and I can assert everything of it that is connected with the concept of a triangle. I come to the angles and notice that one of them is equal to its adjoining angle, and so forth. In all these cases there is an inference, by means of the necessary connection among the concepts, from actualities to actualities, from a subject at hand to the actuality of the predicates inseparable from it. For the fact, however, that such a subject is present at hand, we have no other certainty than the testimony of the senses.

Nevertheless, nothing of mathematics' evidence escapes it because of this consideration. It would be utterly absurd to demand from a doctrine of this sort that it should prove the existence of a quantity through the analysis of a merely possible concept. For no quantity can be absolutely necessary. Each individual thing, however, the existence of which can be inferred from a mere possibility, is necessarily present at hand. Only metaphysics has to identify an example where an inference can be made from a mere possibility to an actuality and it has only a single such example to identify. In every other science, however, and thus also in mathematics, the fact that something is present at hand can be proven in absolutely no other way than by the senses.

But does not this claim expose practical mathematics, if not theoretical mathematics, to the attacks of doubters and idealists who do not trust the senses and regard everything that we perceive by means of them as mere appearances? By no means! They may do this, but then they still must concede that, within the universal delusion, there are constant and variable appearances, and, furthermore, that certain constant appearances are always connected with one another in such a way that one can never perceive one of them without being sure that, from the proper perspective, one must also perceive the other appearances connected with it. If a figure presents me with all the constant appearances of a triangle and one of its angles has the constant appearance of a right angle, then I am convinced that the two other angles together must likewise constantly appear to equal a right angle. The mathematician never troubles himself with the true existence of things. He proves either the coherence of ideas or the coherence of appearances. The metaphysician may, in addition, make out whether these appearances have some external, actual object or not. For the mathematician it makes no difference; his doctrine can neither win nor lose by the resolution of this unimportant subtlety.

I have spoken here of constant and variable appearances. Allow me a brief digression in order to put these concepts into a clearer light. It will be of no small use in the remainder of this essay.

Whenever we perceive an object other than the way it actually is, we say that it only seems so to us and name our representation an "appearance" (*Phaenomenon, apparentia*). I regard a circle from the side, for example, and I see it as an ellipse. A die presents itself to me from a distance as a ball, a pyramid as a cone; the sun appears as a plane surface, the moon as a fiery body. I may let all the colors of the rainbow at one place succeed each other so quickly that I cannot distinguish them and recognize nothing but the mixture of them or the white color. I may let two, three, or more of them quickly succeed one another and perceive a composite color which seems to have nothing in common with the simple colors of which it consists. All objects seem yellow to someone with jaundice, and everything tastes bitter to those afflicted with certain illnesses. All these representations are called "phenomena" or "appearances," since one perceives them as other than they actually exist externally. Doubters say: "Perhaps all our sensuous concepts are merely such appearances, such a sense deception. For we cannot be assured that these objects outside us are so constituted as we perceive them by means of the senses." I have said that mathematicians can *perhaps* allow this to stand without yielding the slightest bit of the certainty of their science, and I want to prove this claim. I believe that no rational person will deny that there are at least two different types of appearances, namely, constant and inconstant appearances. The former have their basis in the intrinsic constitution of the human senses in general but the latter in certain extrinsic contingencies. In the previously cited examples, the basis for the appearance lies, not in the intrinsic, essential constitution of our senses, but rather in the incorrect position from which we regard the objects, in the quickness with which the objects change, or in the debilitated condition of the limbs and juices. These are mere contingencies and thus the appearances caused by them are called "contingent or inconstant appearances." If, however, as the doubters fear, all *qualitates sensibiles* without exception should be a deception of the senses, then the basis of this would have to be found in the intrinsic determinations of human senses. That is to say, we would have to represent sensuous things to ourselves in this way and not another since our senses are constituted in this way and not another. The effects of the sense deception would then deserve to be called "constant appearances." Mathematicians can prove that these constant appearances stand in a necessary connection with one another in such a way that I can infer from one of them to the presence of the other. If I have the constant appearance of a triangle before me, then I can infer indubitably the constant appearance of all the properties of a triangle. Thus, even in the system of a doubter or an idealist, the value of not only pure, theoretical mathematics but even the practical and applied mathematics remains, and it retains its undeniable certainty.

Mendelssohn's *Philosophische Schriften*

Second section

On the evidence in the first principles of metaphysics

Mathematics is a science of magnitudes (*quantitatum*), and philosophy is in general a science of the constitutions (*qualitatum*) of things. If one does not want to acknowledge that philosophy fulfills the requirements of a science, then one may posit that philosophy is *a knowledge of constitutions, based on reason.* I will prove in what follows that this knowledge based on reason deserves to be called a science. Here I first consider merely the basic difference between mathematics and philosophy, a difference that deserves to be elucidated more.

Our soul recognizes in each thing various characteristics and distinguishing marks, the sum total of which fully determines the thing from every side and contains a complete and adequate knowledge of it. Though it is well-known that intrinsic as well as extrinsic characteristics are part of the sum total of these distinguishing marks, I speak here only of the intrinsic ones. These can be regarded in two ways: either insofar as they simply are part of this thing or not part of that thing and in this regard one names them "qualities"; or one weighs whether they are *more or less* part of a thing and names them "quantities." In this definition, everything is distinct, though the words "more" and "less" are in need of some clarification. These are limits of qualities, by means of which they are distinguished from others of the same sort. Thus, for example, I can distinguish one motion from another through velocity and mass; these then constitute the quantity of motion. Similar figures are distinguished by magnitude, light is distinguished from light by virtue of strength and brightness, and inclinations and passions are known and distinguished from other inclinations and passions by their degree of intensity. All these distinguishing marks make known whether the quality is more or less part of the subject matter and they are called "quantities." On the basis of this one recognizes that the quantity or the more-or-less is, to be sure, intrinsically part of the subject matter, but cannot be conceived without comparison with some other thing. For I can never know the *how much* of an object without having compared it either as a part with a whole or as a whole with its part and held them

269

up to one another. But neither comparing things nor holding them up to one another is required to determine whether a distinguishing mark is simply part of a thing or not, for this can be perceived and grasped in the subject matter itself. Hence, either I can simply observe, for example, to what extent extension, contiguity, connection, acting and undergoing, the capacity to know, desire, and detest, contingency, necessity, possibility, and so on are part of a thing or not; or I may consider these features insofar as they are more a part of this and less a part of that. Either I say that the body has an extension while the point has none, or I compare body with body and consider which size is larger or smaller. If I do the former, then I consider extension as the body's constitution; if I do the latter, then I consider it as the body's magnitude. The same alternatives obtain in the case of the other features.

In this regard, the following should not be ignored. If we distinguish qualities from quantities both in ordinary life and in school, this takes place merely in our heads by means of abstraction. The subject matter itself, however, can have no contingent constitution without magnitude any more than it is possible for a magnitude to be actually present without some constitution. This follows quite naturally from the previous observation. Each characteristic – the *how much* or quantity of which I consider – is, in and for itself, a quality. For just as it is more or less part of a thing and, so considered, is to be called a quantity, so it can either be a part of or not be a part of a thing, and, so considered, it constitutes part of the constitution of the thing. Thus, extension or plurality cannot only be larger or smaller (and in this consideration regarded as static and nonstatic magnitudes) but can also be part of the body and of number generally, though not part of a single, simple essence. Consequently, it constitutes a quality of things. In the same fashion figures or the limits of extension have not only their magnitudes, but also their constitutions which are indispensable for knowing quantities distinctly, as is made clear by the first principles of geometry. It is proven, therefore, that no quantity can be present without quality.

However, there is also no contingent or finite constitution without magnitude. For a finite constitution has limits and, to be sure, limits that, it is easy to show, could be otherwise than they actually are. Thus, these limits can set sometimes narrower, sometimes broader boundaries to the constitution; that is to say, in the language of logic, they can more or less cancel the reality of the constitution, through which its quantity or degree is determined. As a result, each individual quality also has its quantity.

Through this consideration, the precise kinship and reciprocal bond between philosophy and mathematics become apparent. Since the former is the science of qualities while the latter is the science of quantities, it is impossible to be a stranger in one of these sciences and have detailed concepts in the other because qualities and quantities are inseparably connected with one another. But this is especially understandable for the mathematics of unextended magnitudes which cannot be discovered without profound insights into the constitutions of things as well as their place and which, if it ever comes to light, must infinitely advance and expand philosophical knowledge. Ordinary mathematics is, by contrast, concerned merely with extension and plurality, and the concepts of these two quantities, insofar as they contribute to the measurement of qualities, can be analyzed and distinguished from one another without particular difficulty. Thus, the link between progress in philosophy and progress in ordinary mathematics is not so immediate that they might hold out the promise of reciprocally furthering and bringing advantages to one another. It is understandable that the occasional influence is not, for this reason, to be denied; nor can the influence of mathematics on the progress of philosophy be denied since it encourages the understanding and, through constant practice, accustoms it to analyzing composite concepts according to certain rules.

Just as there is a purely theoretical mathematics which is not based upon any experiential proposition or actual existence and merely shows the coherence of concepts of quantity with one another, so there is a part of philosophy which, all actuality having been set aside, merely unpacks our concepts of the qualities of things and teaches us how to see their intrinsic coherence. All our concepts are like the seeds of grain of dying plants which, as bad as they look, are nonetheless full of inner virtue and conceal forests of beauty in their husks. If we call a concept fruitless, this is only to be understood comparatively since, in and for itself, each concept is linked to endless truths and can be reduced by analysis to other concepts and truths. Who, then, would want to deny that the concepts of the qualities of things are linked with one another and with other sorts of knowledge and that the latter can be unpacked and derived from the former through undeniable inferences? Who would dispute, for example, that the following two propositions can be demonstrated with as much certainty as any proposition in geometry, namely, that the necessary substance possesses justice to the highest degree while a contingent substance possesses it only to a limited degree? For, since justice is a wise benevolence, the highest degree of it must be possessed by the wisest and most benevolent being. Now, the necessary being possesses these properties, and so forth. The major premise is an immediate consequence of the definition of justice while the minor premise follows from the concept of a necessary being. In this manner it is proven that the highest degree of justice cannot be possessed by any contingent substance, and in precisely the same way an endless array of truths can be demonstrated as irrefutably as the first principles of geometry. For the concepts of qualities can be analyzed and unpacked just as much as the concepts of quantity can. There is, therefore, a purely speculative part of philosophy in which, as was demonstrated above for pure mathematics, attention is directed solely at the combination of concepts and their coherence. In this discipline the same certainty reigns as in geometry.

Yet the principles of this science cannot be explained as perspicuously. The cause of this is not, as one would commonly believe, that in geometry one comes to the aid of the imagination by preparing paradigmatic figures. After all, this would not take place in the case of arithmetic. Instead, there are various causes, and I have paved the way to indicating them by the observation made above. For, in the first place, up until now philosophy has lacked the aid of essential signs. Everything in the language of philosophers remains arbitrary. The words and the connections among them contain nothing that would essentially agree with the nature of thoughts and the connections among them. Hence, definitions are endlessly heaped on top of one another, and a demonstratively executed philosophy acquires, at first glance, the look of vain verbosity. For the soul finds nothing in the designation by means of which it could be guided to the nature of the designated subject matter without an arbitrary association of concepts. Hence, the soul must constantly fix its attention on the arbitrary combination of signs and what is designated, a combination established at some point in the past. For this reason, the slightest inattentiveness makes it possible for thought to lose sight of the subject matter, leaving behind merely the empty signs; in which case, of course, the most cogent philosopher must appear to be merely playing with words. In mathematics, however, this suspicion does not occur since the essential signs lead us, as often as we want, without any particular exertion on our part, back to the subject matters designated by them, and the order and connections among them agree with the order and connections among thoughts.

If we consider the nature of qualities further, even greater difficulties present themselves. These intrinsic characteristics of things are bound up with one another so exactly that one cannot define any of them clearly without an adequate insight into the others. Anyone who is a complete stranger to philosophy, cannot grasp the very first definition distinctly. For if I want to make an intrinsic characteristic *A* distinct for him and he has not made clear his concepts of the other features *B*, *C*, and so forth which are connected to *A*, then some obscurity will always remain in his soul. Because of this, one recognizes the necessity of always returning to the first principles with every step forward that one takes in philosophy. One never makes this journey back to the beginning without enormous benefit, since philosophical concepts cast rays of light that reciprocally lend distinctness to one another and must be pursued. This accounts for the fact that the further philosophers themselves advance, the more they find to improve on the first basic definitions, and, hence, they are always refuting one another or at least seem to be refuting one another. For often it was merely a careless expression by the first philosopher that it was necessary for his successor, in the end, to perceive by constantly going over the first concepts. If one were to say to a beginner, for example, "justice is a wisely administered benevolence," he will neither grasp this definition nor see the necessity of making it so complicated. At the beginning he will be satisfied with the facile definition: "justice is a steadfast will to let each individual have what is his." If he took a few steps further, then he would notice that, by the words "what is his," property cannot be understood but instead everything to which a person has a right. He then posits: "justice is a steadfast will to let each person have that to which he has a right." But he still does not see what capacities of the soul this virtue is based upon. He thus continues: "A right is an entitlement or ethical capacity to make use of certain things as means to one's happiness." Hence, a person who practices justice lets each individual make use of the permitted means to his happiness. Thus, he wants others beside him to be happy but only through permissible means and in proper proportion so that the ultimate aim, the perfection of the whole, is sustained. A person who enjoys seeing others beside him happy is benevolent; a person who seeks to obtain the best final purpose by the best means is wise. Now the concepts have been cleared up, and one sees quite distinctly that justice, reduced to its elements, is nothing else but a benevolence administered with wisdom. From this, however, it also follows that justice is a reality and that the Supreme Being must possess it to the highest degree, which cannot be proven from the previous definition. But what an array of definitions and arbitrary combinations of words with concepts are contained in this inference! What kind of effort is required for all these concepts of the soul to remain constantly present and never disappear into the shadows of words! These proofs contain definitions of wisdom, benevolence, reality, highest degree, and Supreme Being; in addition, the definition of wisdom contains concepts of perfection, means, and final purpose; the definition of benevolence concepts of happiness and of the capacity to desire; the definition of reality concepts of such and such, and so on. Yet what use is it to continue this analysis any further? It is sufficient that one sees to what extent the qualities of things are interwoven, what an array of definitions is required for the simplest philosophical inference, and how often people must transpose these definitions if they are to be applied usefully.

Moreover, if the philosopher has survived all these difficulties, then he has still discovered nothing but certain kinships among concepts. At that point, however, the important step into the realm of actuality must take place. He must show that the object of his basic concepts, from which he infers his truths, is actually to be encountered, so that he can infer from those truths the actual existence of the consequences. The mathematician, as we have seen, can take this step quite easily. He places the testimony of the senses at the foundation of his practical system and does not worry whether the senses assert truths or mere appearances. In both cases he has achieved his final purpose. It is incumbent upon the philosopher, however, to demand that inner and outer senses testify before his tribunal and to distinguish the true from the false, the certain from the uncertain. If he wants to build on the testimony of any sort of sense, then he must first place its nondeceptive-ness beyond doubt. Let us suppose that he has proven that matter cannot think, in other words, that he has demonstrated that our concept of thinking directly contradicts the concept of matter. If he then wants to draw the conclusion that a simple being dwells in us that is different from our body and thinks, then he must show that the concept of matter presupposed by him applies to our visible body and that there is something present in us to which the concept of thinking in the intellect applies, something presently preoccupying him. If he has shown irrefutably that a necessary being cannot exist without being the creator and preserver of all things outside him, then it is still incumbent upon him to prove that such a necessary being exists. In short, it is not enough for the philosopher if, like the mathematician, he has shown the necessary connection between a subject and its predicate. In addition, he must establish beyond doubt either the existence of the subject or the nonexistence of the predicate so that he can conclude, in the first instance, to the existence of the predicate and, in the second, to the nonexistence of the subject. For we do not owe the philosopher thanks for the mere possibility of something if he does not know how to render it actual. Hence, far more is demanded of the philosopher than of the mathematician. The latter proves merely the possibility of a figure and unpacks the properties and accidents of the figure from this possibility. The philosopher, by contrast, is supposed to demonstrate the actual existence of the subjects in order to be able to conclude to the consequences. It is easy to understand that by this means conviction is made more difficult and the evidence diminished, since nothing can be more difficult for the understanding than the transition from concepts to actualities.

In philosophy one has two different paths of arriving at actualities. By the first path, as in practical mathematics, one lays an experiential proposition as the foundation, though it is the sort of experiential proposition of which we are certain that it is not mere appearance. I have in mind the inner conviction "I think" which, as we will see in what follows, is indubitable and from which it can be inferred with certainty: "therefore, I am." It must be possible for the entire philosophical system to be erected on this fundamental principle without relying on any testimony of the external senses. For what the senses perceive of external things is dubious. Only this single, inner sentiment "I think" has the prerogative that one can say of it, with complete certainty, that it is no mere appearance, but rather a genuine reality, as I will show in what follows.

The second path is extraordinary and nonpareil. One moves with sure-footed steps directly from the domain of possibility to the realm of actuality and, of course, that of the supreme and most perfect actuality thinkable. In geometry, for example, these two propositions "an equilateral triangle has equally large sides" and "an equilateral triangle has equally large angles" are inseparably joined. The following propositions are just as rigidly and indissolubly bound up with one another: "the necessary being is possible" and "the necessary being is actual." If, therefore, I can prove that the necessary being is possible, then I have also demonstrated its actuality, and it is well-known that the former can be proven. We have Descartes to thank for these two transitions from the possible to the actual.[2] Before his time one was accustomed in philosophy to laying experiential propositions as the foundation, which left one vulnerable to the skeptics. In fact, the dogmatist was totally defeated as soon as the skeptic cast doubt on the testimony of the senses and thereby dispatched his otherwise so compelling system to the land of chimerae. What was strangest of all, one wanted at that time to make inferences a priori in physics and a posteriori in philosophy. Bacon showed that the testimony of the senses was the most valid in physics and that the testimony of the intellect was the most valid in philosophy.[3] Descartes dared to build his systematic theology on the basis of the doubters themselves. One recognized quite easily, however, that all these types of proof have their difficulties and cannot possibly be carried out as evidentially as was to be wished. In my opinion, these are the factors which make philosophical conviction so difficult and stand in the way of evidence. Still, these are merely the difficulties which lie objectively in the matter itself. However, in regard to the subject or persons who need to be convinced by philosophical truths, there are some important difficulties that are not to be passed over.

Mathematics always finds impartial minds who wait for the outcome of an investigation with the utmost composure. They stand to lose and gain nothing from the fact that the tangent of a circle may make a right angle or some other angle with the diameter. Their whole way of life can remain what it was before if the surface of any circle is proportional to the square of its diameter. Hence, they are interested merely in the

---

[2] Descartes, *Meditations on First Philosophy* in *Philosophical Writings*, vol. 2, pp. 16–23 and 44–9 (see p. 76 n. 1).

[3] Francis Bacon, "Novum Organum," Part II, Aphorism XIX in *The Works of Francis Bacon*, vol. I, p. 245 (see p. 111 n. 6).

truth, and mathematics has no enemy other than ignorance to conquer. Philosophy, on the other hand, also has to do battle with prejudices. The doctrines of the latter have such an immediate influence on our way of life, happiness, and opinions that each individual takes a side from the outset and on the basis of preconceived opinions builds his own system that is quite compatible with his weaknesses. The human mind finally accustoms itself to these prejudices so long that they constitute a part of his happiness. Philosophy would then come along and drive the madness out of this mighty entrenchment. It finds not only ignorant listeners, but ones bigoted against their own best interest who do not want to be convinced. It does not matter how compelling or how evident the reasons underlying philosophy's proofs are; magic has no power if minds are not disposed to it and, instead, defend themselves against it by every possible means. Little is gained if one's willingness to listen to the truth is often fickle. Stubborn patience, commitment, and self-denial are required to lead all his prejudices and cherished thoughts through the fire of this divinity and to wait with dry, manly eyes to see whether they will go up in smoke or reemerge in transfigured beauty. Most of humanity embark on the journey of life with delusion and superstition and with the firm resolve to complete that journey with them. They never listen to the voice of reason without letting themselves be tied up by their prejudices, as Ulysses was by his fellow travelers, and giving them the order in advance: "Pull the rope tighter, the more I squirm and beg to be set free, until we will have lost sight of the Sirens."[4]

Because each individual takes sides in philosophical matters, each individual also believes that he has the right to be in control and pass judgments. Who is the ignorant soul who does not consider himself a legitimate judge in philosophical issues and does not know how to support his magisterial authority by autocratic decrees? The main concepts which are proposed in philosophy are heard so often in common life that each individual believes himself to be sufficiently familiar with them. In mathematics someone who does not know holds back his judgment and awaits the finding of someone who does know. Indeed, why do I say "in mathematics"? In every common art, in every craft no one outside of those with the relevant know-how dares to take

---

[4] Homer, *Odyssey*, Bk. XII, 49–54.

control of an undertaking and contradict someone experienced. Yet in philosophy, in ethics, and in politics each human being's perceptiveness is brazen enough to take over the office of judge. Every fool cricitizes systems, judges ethical actions, and censures forms of government. What confusion must spring from this general anarchy!

Meanwhile, it is not to be denied that this anarchy cannot be steered without seeing despotism with all its dangerous consequences break in from the other side. In each republic the spirit of contradiction is not only a necessary consequence but often also a wholesome underpinning of freedom and general well-being. Not every republican has the capacity to feel the rudder in his hands or to advise the helmsman. But it is in the interest of freedom that everyone speak his opinion, however absurd it may be, so that no one gets it into his head to put forward his own willful prerogatives as wise counsel and impose them on his fellow citizens. Such is the constitution of philosophical freedom. Since not everyone has the capacity to examine philosophers' theses, it is better for such an individual to judge in accordance with his meager insights than to recognize and blindly follow some philosophical pope wherever the latter wants to lead him. Anyone who gripes about this freedom cultivates despotic intentions and is a dangerous citizen in the republic of philosophy. From this, however, one can nevertheless gather what kinds of obstacles stand in the way of philosophical evidence and why it happens that the certainty that reigns in the first principles of philosophy has still not elicited anything like universal conviction.

Mendelssohn's *Philosophische Schriften*

Third section

On the evidence in the first principles of natural theology

My intention here is not to convince atheists of the lack of any basis for their opinion but rather, in the presence of a society of genuine philosophers, to appraise the certainty with which we know the existence of God and his properties rationally. Hence, I can with good reason presuppose a familiarity with all the types of proof which we have in this science and content myself with making general observations about them. In the foregoing section it was seen that all our concepts are infinitely fruitful since each contains an array of implications which can be derived and unpacked from those concepts by means of undeniable principles. Still, the concepts of God and his properties have a wondrous power. They are so intimately connected with one another that one has only to presuppose a single property of God in order to deduce from it everything that we are in a position to know about the Supreme Being. A single chain of inferences combines all perfections of this fecund being. His independence, infinity, immensity, his supremely perfect will, unbounded intellect, and unlimited power, his wisdom, providence, justice, holiness, and so forth are reciprocally grounded in one another in such a way that, without the others, each of these properties would be contradictory. It is possible to derive from certain properties more easily and perspicuously the remaining properties that we know. Moreover, since this perspicuity depends upon insights which are presupposed in people if they are to be convinced, there are also different methods of demonstrating these truths, which have different effects on different minds. In the subject matter itself, however, there is no difference, and whatever property one might want to presuppose, one can ascertain the others. Let the following definition, for example, be presupposed: "God is a being with a supremely perfect will." The supremely perfect will presupposes the most perfect intellect and demands the most perfect might. That will consists, furthermore, in the inclination to every possible good and aversion from every possible evil, according to the standards of their goodness or evil. From this follow justice, benevolence, and wisdom. Since God possesses all these perfections without limits, he is infinite and, consequently, singular. Since no finite thing can be the reason for his existence and no infinite thing exists outside him, he has the reason for his existence in himself; therefore, he is independent and necessary. Furthermore, if finite things should exist, then they must have in him the reason for their existence since outside him there is no necessary being that could contain the reason for them and something contingent cannot be the sufficient reason for them. In addition, he will . . . Yet what is the point of this detailed elaboration which can be found in every compendium? I will be content to make the following remark.

These first principles of natural theology have all the certainty and almost all the evidence of geometrical truths as long as one remains here, as in geometry, with the connection among concepts and merely shows their reciprocal kinship, without inferring from the concepts to actualities. One observes the coherence of these concepts and perceives that one cannot think of any of them without all the others. As soon as one is subsequently convinced by revelation or rational inference of the actuality of one of the properties, then all the truths derived from this likewise take up their position in the domain of actuality, just as in practical geometry I infer from the sensuous perception of a triangle to the existence of all the properties that belong to a triangle.

The atheist, insofar as he is convinced of the existence of none of these properties, behaves towards this theory as an idealist does towards geometry. The latter denies the object of geometry but nonetheless acknowledges the connection among concepts which is shown in geometry and which he cannot deny without contradicting himself. In the same way someone can observe and grant the validity of this system of God and His properties but deny their object as long as he is not perfectly convinced of it.

Up until now, theology has proceeded in tandem with the first principles of geometry. At this point, however, they depart from one another. Theology accomplishes far more than can ever be demanded of mathematics, namely, the fundamental conviction that the object of its science actually exists. Mathematics is satisfied, as we have seen, with the idealists' acknowledgment that at least there are constant appearances bound to certain rules, and it shows these rules a priori. The philosopher, however, must lay the foundation of his system much deeper if it is to stand unshaken, since he must prove a genuine existence of things, not merely a connection of concepts, and this is, indeed, the most difficult knot that he has to untie. In the previous section we spoke of two paths by which one generally proceeds in philosophy from possibilities to actualities, and the same holds for natural theology. One infers either from the possibility of a necessary being to its actuality or from the undeniable intuitive proposition "I think" to my actuality and from this to the actuality of a necessary being, by means of the principle of sufficient reason. The latter method is indisputably the easiest. In our case here where we are speaking of the possibility of the Supreme Being, the former inference from possibility to actuality is completely legitimate, to be sure; but since it is the only instance of its kind and is found in no other setting, many cannot understand it. Yet perhaps the difficulty lies more in the presentation than in the subject matter itself. I want to try to give an easier rendition of the proof.

Since in general the existence of a subject matter is so difficult to explain, let us begin from nonexistence. What is not must be either impossible or merely possible. In the first case the determinations intrinsic to it must be contradictory; that is to say, they must affirm and deny the same predicate of the same subject at the same time. In the second case, they will, of course, contain no contradiction, but on the basis of them it cannot be conceived why the thing should exist rather than not exist. One property as well as another will be able to exist with the essential parts of the same thing, and, on the basis of this, the thing is called "possible." The existence of such a thing is not a possibility intrinsic to it, nor part of its essence nor even one of its properties, and, for this reason, it is a mere contingency (*modus*), the actuality of which can only be grasped on the basis of another actuality. For a contingency is a determination which can be neither conceived nor inferred from the mere possibility, the actuality of which can be only explained by another actuality. Such an existence is, accordingly, not independent but dependent. This needs no further proof. – Now, such an existence cannot be part of the most perfect being since it would contradict its essence. For everyone sees that an independent existence is a greater perfection than a dependent existence is. Thus, the proposition "the most perfect being has a contingent existence" contains an obvious contradiction. For, as was proven above, it cannot be merely possible, and hence nothing further remains for it but actuality or impossibility.

Should the concept of the Supreme Being contain a contradiction, then among its determinations something must be affirmed and denied at the same time. Each determination is either a reality or a deficiency. The former affirms, the latter denies. Hence, no contradiction occurs unless deficiencies and limitations as well as reality are ascribed to a subject matter and, of course, insofar as I ascribe to it a reality and deficiencies opposed to it. Now, all realities are affirmed of the most perfect being, all deficiencies are denied it. Hence, no contradiction can lie in the concept of it. Whoever says "the most perfect being contains a contradiction" contradicts himself, since the subject denies all deficiencies while the predicate intends to affirm some. But if there is nothing contradictory in the concept of the most perfect being, then the latter must actually exist, as is clear from the preceding.

One can convince oneself of the same truth in another way as well. One might simply recall, from the first principles of metaphysics, that a subject matter actually exists as soon as everything determinable in it is in fact determined, that is to say, as soon as it is established for each concept that A can just as well be part of the thing as not, whether the concept is part of the thing or not. Herein lies the characteristic difference between general possible concepts and individual real concepts. In the former neither the affirmation nor the negation of several determinacies is established, but instead left undecided, and they can be determined in one manner as well as another. In the case of individual real things, by contrast, the affirmation or negation of everything that can be affirmed or denied must be established and decided and, conversely, that of which everything down to the most remote relations is established and decided, actually exists. What is not actual must, therefore, be either indeterminable or indeterminate. In the first case, it contains a contradiction and is impossible. In the latter case, there is no reason by which it can be understood how and why it is supposed to be determined in one way rather than another. That is to say, there is a lack of efficient causes which are supposed to produce the possible thing. For "an efficient cause" means nothing else but that through which a possible thing receives all the determinations of it which were lacking for actual existence. Now the most perfect being cannot receive from something external any determination through which it is supposed to become actual. Thus, either it is sufficiently determined by the power of its inner being, or it is indeterminable. That means, either it exists necessarily, or it is absolutely impossible. We have seen from the foregoing that it cannot be impossible, and, hence, it exists necessarily.

Since the discussion of the determinate and indeterminate is so extraordinarily useful in philosophy, I will dwell on this somewhat longer. Each individual proposition is either true or false or indeterminate. It is true if, on the basis of a consideration of the subject, it can be intelligibly explained either absolutely or under certain assumed conditions that the predicate is part of the subject. If, however, it can be demonstrated on the basis of a consideration of the subject either absolutely or under certain assumed conditions that the ascribed predicate is not part of the subject, then the proposition is false. If neither of the two can be demonstrated, then the proposition is indeterminate. Hence, an indeterminate proposition merely says that a predicate can just as well be a part of a certain subject as not be a part of it. That is to say that neither the affirmation nor the negation of the predicate contradicts the subject. If such an indeterminate proposition is to be transformed into a determinate one, then there must be added to the subject the sort of conditions or the subject must be considered under the sort of circumstances that cancel either the affirmation or the negation and thereby render one of the two propositions true, the other false. For example, the following propositions: "a body is extended" and "a body on our earth is heavy" are true. For the predicate of the first proposition may be irrefutably demonstrated on the basis of a consideration of the subject, while the predicate of the second proposition may be demonstrated on the basis of a consideration of the subject under the added condition that the body is to be found on our earth. The opposite of these propositions is false. The following proposition, by contrast, is indeterminate: "a solid body in a fluid material rises to the top." It can be true under certain conditions, false under others. These conditions are that the solid body is either heavier or lighter than the mass of the fluid material which occupies its space. As soon as this condition is added, then the indeterminate proposition is transformed into a determinate one, and, instead of being able to be, as the proposition was, either true or false, it is now established either that the proposition is true or that it is false.

Whenever something determinable is determined and thus an indeterminate proposition is transformed into a determinate one, it must be possible to indicate the reason for this determination. That is to say, I must be able to cite the condition of the subject, on the basis of which it can be understood how the proposition's truth or falsity is not unsettled but instead is settled and determinate. It must be possible for this condition and the determinacy of the proposition that follows from it to be represented and understood in and for themselves, even if it be supposed that human powers do not suffice to see them. For what is being addressed here is not what this or that individual can comprehend, but rather what can be comprehended in and for itself. Yet each individual will grant that everything that cannot be comprehended in and for itself, must also be impossible. Adequate knowledge of this condition and the determinacy of this proposition, following from it, is called "the sufficient reason." Each determination has, therefore, its sufficient reason; that is to say, each determination presupposes a condition of the determinable subject, on the basis of which it can be comprehended why it is determined in one way rather than another. As we have seen above, nothing can be unsettled in the case of a thing actually existing, but rather it must be determined and settled for everything that can be part of it, either that such is part of it or not. Thus, for each actual thing I can form an infinite number of propositions, each of which has its determinate truth. But all propositions that are the opposite of these are definitively false. A sufficient reason for the determinate truth of each of these propositions can be cited; in other words, it can be comprehended how, by virtue of a certain condition of the subject, it is settled whether the predicate is part of the subject or not. Adequate knowledge of all these conditions, from the core of which the *omnimoda determinatio individui* [every mode of determination of the individual] flows, is called "the sufficient reason of the existence of a subject matter," *ratio sufficiens existentiae, actualitatis, entis.*

One might consider the following propositions: "the necessary thing exists" and "contingent things exist." The conditions from which all determinations required for the existence of a necessary being can be inferred lie in its being. The predicate of the first proposition is, therefore, absolutely grounded in the subject. Hence, the necessary being has the foundation of its existence in itself. Contingent things, on the other hand, by virtue of their being, are indeterminate in many respects, and certain conditions must still be added from the outside to the subject before the thoroughgoing determination, required for its existence, can be comprehended. These conditions are free creation and conservation by an independent being, without which the thorough-going determination of a contingent thing is impossible to comprehend and to explain intelligently. Thus, contingent things have the foundation of their existence in the will of a necessary being.

This principle of sufficient reason is founded, as has been seen, on the principle of contradiction. It is absolutely impossible that a determination should be true and incomprehensible. It must be possible to discuss a true proposition on the basis of either the essence or the conditions of the subject. If neither can happen, then the proposition is indeterminate. It is, therefore, absolutely impossible and contradictory that something should be able to be determined without sufficient reason. From this, however, it in no way follows that everything that is determined by a sufficient reason is also absolutely necessary. The existence of contingent things is not absolutely necessary, but rather necessary only under the condition that God might want to create and preserve them. The true sign of absolute and conditioned necessity is this: if the conditions of the subject, on the basis of which the predicate is inferred, presuppose the existence of another subject, then the proposition is hypothetically necessary; if, however, the existence of no other subject is required in order to infer the predicate from the conditions of the existing subject, then the proposition is absolutely necessary. Thus, the existence of God is absolutely necessary because the proposition "God exists" presupposes the existence of no other subject among the conditions of the subject in order, by this means, to determine the predicate. By contrast, the proposition "contingent things exist" pre-supposes the existence and even the will of God among the conditions of the subject that render the proposition true. Thus, the existence of contingent things is not absolutely necessary.

But there is a problem. Is this principle of sufficient reason universal, and does it suffer no exception in regard to the freely willed decisions of rational beings? – I want to contrast this question with another one: in the case of the freely willed decisions of rational beings, is it possible for something to be true and yet absolutely incomprehensible? – But if this is impossible, then all the powers of the mind cannot verify something that is incomprehensible; they cannot determine something where not even an infinite intellect would be able to indicate why it is determined in one way rather than another. If, therefore, a rational being should make a decision for something and, of course, make the decision voluntarily, then it must be possible, since a decision is made, for an infinite intellect, by understanding the inner state of the person making the choice, to indicate why that person decided in one way rather than another. – But do our freely willed decisions themselves then have a certain future? – Of course, and this is not to be denied. For if they did not *objectively* have their certainty established, then all probability in regard to them would vanish. If there did not lie in the soul of a virtuous person the established certainty that he will not maliciously betray his fatherland, then there would also not be a basis for inferring the like with any probability from his character. What is *subjectively* probable, must have its established certainty *objectively*. Since a variety of things may reasonably be supposed about the character of a human being, our freely willed decisions must have their predetermined certainty. Consider these three propositions: first, "a stone that is not supported falls to the ground"; second, "I feel what makes an impression on my sense organs"; third, "I will not betray my friend as long as I remain in command of my senses." These three propositions, I say, are full of indisputable certainty since the predicate may be deduced and confidently inferred from the subject under certain conditions. But this confidence itself has a varied nature. For what makes the predicate necessary is either a part of the conditions of the subject, including a living knowledge of good and evil, or it is not. The former is called "moral necessity," the latter "physical necessity." "A stone in the open air falls to the ground" and "a sensation follows an external impression on the sense organs" are propositions that can be proven without presupposing in the subject one kind of knowledge of good and evil or another. Hence, these propositions are physically certain. The proposition, however, "I would not betray my friend" presupposes among the conditions of the subject especially this, that in accord with my pragmatic knowledge of good and evil, I must find it good not to betray my friend, and, hence, this proposition contains a moral certainty or necessity. A self-determination that can be explained by the knowledge of good and evil is *voluntary*, and, if this knowledge is distinct, it is a *freely willed decision*.

I have the freedom to open my eyes or not. But if I open them, it is no longer up to me whether I want to see objects or not. I explain these propositions in the following way. That I open or close my eyes cannot be intelligently explained other than by the presupposed condition that I find this or that to be good. Hence, this action presupposes certain practical concepts of good and evil and is *voluntary*, frequently even freely willed. But the proposition "With my eyes open I see visible objects" does not presuppose among the conditions of the subject that he find or not find this good, that is to say, no knowledge of good and evil is presupposed. Thus, seeing objects is, as everyone concedes, not immediately voluntary, much less something freely willed.

Here I see before me the path to endless digressions. A further investigation of freedom and responsibility, praise and blame, reward and punishment, insult and atonement could provide me the opportunity to make many a useful remark. Since, however, it would entangle me in a labyrinth from which there is no exit as long as all its turns have not been traversed, I would depart far too much from my goal. Hence, I will break off this discussion here and return to the principle of sufficient reason.

This splendid basic principle is the bond that ties all imaginable truths together. In the divine intellect every science exists, and all possible truths cohere like the propositions of a geometrical demonstration. In our intellect there is always a terrifying gap between possibility and actuality because we can never explain intelligently every possible determination of a thing, and, as a result, experience alone conveys to us the existence of contingent things. An infinite intellect, however, can – if I may speak humanly of the infinite – explain all possible determinations of actual things in the most distinct manner and thus prove their existence a priori. By virtue of the principle of sufficient reason, possibilities and actualities cohere with one another in the divine mind in the most precise manner, and all truths constitute a single whole, a single science, an infinite demonstration, which the Supreme Being surveys at a single glance. If it be supposed that something could exist without any reason, then its existence would be a truth that is connected with no other truth, a solitary island in the realm of truths, to which there is no possible access. Hence, it cannot be an object of the infinite intellect. For just as the divine properties are in the most perfect accord with one another, so, too, all his insights harmonize and constitute a systematic whole in which a single one of them can be rationally explained by all of them, and all of them can be rationally explained by a single one of them. No abstracted fragments, no gaps find a place in this infinite system; they do not belong to the object of divine knowledge and are absolutely impossible.

In order to grasp this sublime harmony of truths more distinctly, one might weigh the following consideration. There are three reasons or foundations for each individual natural event. Such an event can be understood, first, on the basis of the divine power which produces it out of nothing and without which it is absolutely impossible. But it also has a foundation in the system of divine aims, and this, too, is necessarily required for its existence since God would not have wanted to produce it if he would not have found it to be good. Last, its existence can also be made intelligible on the basis of efficient causes in nature. This foundation is always dispensable since God can, in keeping with his aims, miraculously produce something the existence of which cannot be intelligently explained by any *causis secundariis* [secondary causes]. Divine aims harmonize with the effects of his power in the most perfect manner because he produces nothing that is not in keeping with his aims, and there is nothing in keeping with his ultimate aims that he does not produce. But even the system of efficient causes harmonizes in the most perfect manner with his aims as long as God does not interrupt the course of nature by some miracle. Those causes produce no reality that is not in keeping with his aims and he has organized them in such a way that they realize his finite aims in the most exact manner. This in no way conflicts with allowing the presence of evil, as has already been shown extensively by others.

On the basis of this, little is required to decide in which case the principle of sufficient reason leads us to necessary truths and in which case it leads us to hypothetical truths. Many philosophers have been confused about this, and, not knowing how to take care of themselves in this confusion, they have been led to believe that they found unspeakable difficulties in applying this principle. But, on the basis of the considerations described above, nothing is easier than to decide these cases. That everything must have a reason for its determination is an absolutely necessary truth. This truth does not suffer the slightest exception and extends to divine counsel in which it is likewise impossible for something to be decided without some compelling reason. What has a compelling reason can be necessary and also contingent, depending upon whether this compelling reason is to be found in a mere possibility or in an actuality. For what can be explained on the basis of a mere possibility, is absolutely necessary. The existence of something that can only be understood on the basis of the assumption of an actuality, is dependent and, as a consequence, contingent. The necessary being requires only a single reason for its existence, and that reason lies in its intrinsic possibility. Contingent and dependent things demand a threefold reason or foundation: first, an immediately effective, subordinate cause which is not only in itself contingent but also dispensable in every case; second, a mediately effective cause that can produce and conserve out of nothing. This is indispensable and is also necessarily required though it, nevertheless, does not render the existence of contingent things necessary. The third reason or foundation is a final cause without which the Supreme Being can have no compelling reason for producing them. This, too, is required with absolute necessity though it cannot make anything absolutely necessary.

We have, therefore, two different principles on each of which a system of natural theology can be erected. The first is: "What does not exist, must either contain a contradiction or have no reason for its determination, that is to say, by our definitions, it is either indeterminable or indeterminate." The Supreme Being can be neither indeterminable nor indeterminate, since it contains no contradiction and its properties are necessarily determined by its intrinsic possibility. Hence, the Supreme Being necessarily exists.

The second principle is this. "Contingent beings must have the reason for their existence indirectly in a necessary being; I am a contingent being; therefore, etc." The minor premise is composed of two assertions: "I exist" and "I am a contingent being." No skeptic, Descartes says, can doubt the truth of these two assertions;[5] for anyone who doubts exists and anyone who does not know everything with certainty is a contingent thing.

The skeptic can, indeed, generally be in doubt whether the things outside us are as we imagine them to be or whether they only appear so to us. There is no doubt, however, that we imagine them and that they appear to us to be in one way and not another. This is, therefore, the most undeniable experience on which reason can rely, and it must doubtlessly win if it forges all its weapons from this single basic experience without further assistance from the senses.

---

[5] *Meditations on First Philosophy*, in *Philosophical Writings*, vol. 2, p. 17.

From this basic experience reason can draw one more important consequence that is uncommonly useful in the doctrine of God and his properties. Of the properties of things outside us, we never know with convincing certainty whether they are realities or mere appearances and, at bottom, depend upon negations; indeed, in the case of some of them, we have reason to believe that they are mere appearances. Thus, we can ascribe none of these properties to the Supreme Being and must absolutely deny him some of them. Belonging to the latter group are all *qualitates sensibiles* that we have reason to believe are not to be found outside us as they seem to us thanks to our sensuous, limited knowledge and that, therefore, are not realities. This inference can also be inverted. What does not belong to the Supreme Being cannot be a reality since all possible realities are his to the highest degree. From this it follows naturally that extension, movement, and color are mere appearances and not realities. For, were they realities, then they would have to be ascribed to the Supreme Being. The history of philosophy also shows that various philosophers have made the mistake of attaching the most perfect extension to the Supreme Being and some have even sought out the most perfect figure that can be ascribed to him. This absurdity is, in fact, unavoidable the moment one intends to regard figure and extension as something actual, as realities. The final recourse was to an infinite extension which, it was believed, could be appropriately ascribed to the highest being. But the absurdities and contradictions that follow from this hypothesis force us to exclude extension in general from realities and look upon it as a mere phenomenon. There are realities in nature, to be sure, on which this appearance is based. But these realities are not extended at all, but rather simple and what is actual in them is, in fact, the highest being's in *summo grado* [to the highest degree]. But the appearances which we perceive in those same realities must be absolutely denied the Supreme Being, since they depend upon the ineptitude of our knowledge and are not part of things in the way that we perceive them.

But what then are the properties of things, of which we are able to say with certainty that they are actual realities? None other than our soul's capabilities. Our cognitive faculty, for example, cannot possibly be an appearance. For an appearance is nothing other than a concept, the constitution of which must in part be explained by the ineptitude of our knowledge. They are composite representations which we cannot analyze, and hence we perceive them other than they actually are. At the end of the First section we saw that all phenomena are based upon the innate or debilitated constitution of our senses, the angle from which the objects are observed, a false judgment by the sensuous faculty of judgment; in a word, the limitations of our power of representing them. But the foundation of this power and all the different capabilities derivative of it cannot be the limitations of it, and hence the power of representing things and all the capabilities derived from it are true realities. Thus we can rightly ascribe to the Supreme Being all our cognitive capabilities, if we abstract from the deficiencies and imperfections that cling to them, and we can revere in him unfathomable reason, wisdom, justice, benevolence, and mercy.

On the other hand, we know that the way corporeal things appear to us must be based upon certain realities which we incorrectly represent. For no concept can be formed of mere negations. These realities cannot be extensions since extension itself is a phenomenon. Therefore, these realities are simple. But what sort of properties do they have? Leibniz says that they have the properties which are the only ones familiar to us as realities, the *capacities of representing*.[6] He believes he can explain how the appearances that we have of bodies spring from the confusion of these realities. This is not the place to give my explanation of this view. I wanted only to sketch in outline the parts that border on my material. A more detailed description would not be appropriate to my undertaking here.

I have spoken hitherto of two types of proofs of God's existence and shown that they are fully and demonstratively convincing. In no way, however, is it my intention to disclaim all the remaining types of proof that have been elaborated successfully by different philosophers. For theology is supposed to be not only convincing, but edifying, moving the mind and spurring change in conformity with it. Thus, merely demonstrative grounds of proof are insufficient; instead, the life of knowledge must be inspired by an array of cogent reasons. In this respect practical conviction departs from merely theoretical conviction. The latter is content with the driest demonstration, with merely distinct knowledge, but the former does not explicitly demand distinctness and

---

[6] See, for example, Leibniz, "Principes de la Nature et de la Grace, fondés en raison" [Principles of nature and grace, founded in reason], in *Die philosophischen Schriften*, ed. C. J. Gerhardt (Hildesheim Olms, 1961), vol. 6, pp. 598–9.

certainty. It demands instead a living efficacious knowledge, an intense and lively impression on the mind by means of which we are spurred to manage our actions and omissions in keeping with this knowledge. Every probability, every eloquently presented basis of proof contributes something to this life of knowledge, helps increase its energy, as I will elaborate more extensively in the final section. Thus, no one who reveres God must take exception to the slightest basis of proof which brings only a modicum of convincing power with it. – One can divide the reasons on which these types of proof from other quarters depend into the following main classes. First, there are proofs based upon the beauty and order in the visible parts of creation, in all the systems of the world and their coherence, as well as in individual particular regions on earth. Second, there are proofs based upon the beauty and order in the laws of motion. Third and last, there are proofs based upon the undeniable purposes in nature, in general, and, in particular, in ordinary and extraordinary natural events, among which the fates of certain states and even the events of individual persons are to be counted. For even these events, if they are considered as a whole, often make evident the wisest of purposes, purposes that have been sustained by wondrous means.

It is not to be denied that these types of proof still lack a great deal for demonstrative certainty. What concerns beauty and order (not to mention the fact that it first has to be demonstrated that they are not necessary but contingent), even if this is accomplished, one can nevertheless infer from this only that there is a wise and benevolent cause of this order and beauty, not that this all-wise and all-benevolent cause has produced, created everything outside itself from nothing. Perhaps God found himself confronted with a chaos, as some of the ancients dreamed, into which he put order and beauty. Perhaps he merely prescribed orderly and harmonious laws to the disorderly movement to be found in this chaos. These objections can be answered, I admit, but not with the triumphant force with which one can defend a genuine demonstration.

As far as the purposes of things are concerned, nothing but extremely probable conclusions can be drawn from them. For as long as we are not convinced of the existence of a rational being who aims for this or that effect, we can only suppose from the circumstances that the effect must, indeed, have been a purpose of a rational being, that is, if many particular causes come together repeatedly in the same way to produce an effect which is fitting and in harmony with the whole. The more causes, the more often they come together, and the more appropriate and suited to the perfection of the whole the effect is, the more probable is the supposition that this effect was the purpose of a rational being. In our case the probability increases to a very high degree and approaches necessity, but it can never reach this as long as we are not able to observe, in a perfectly distinct way, all the causes whenever they come together or the right proportion of fittingness of a single event to the whole. Last, even from purposes it is only possible to demonstrate a wise arrangement and order, but not a creation from nothing.

These kinds of proof, meanwhile, possess far greater eloquence than the demonstration itself. By their liveliness they make a much greater impression on the mind, awakening the soul to dynamic decisions and producing the practical conviction that should be our foremost purpose in contemplating divine properties. The demonstrative kinds of proof are the fortresses that protect a country against enemy attacks. For peaceful inhabitants, however, they are not the most comfortable and pleasant places in which to live. If someone does not have to contend with an adversary and overcome some subtle doubt, he finds in the method of knowing the creator from the beauty, order, and purposes of nature the sweetest comfort, the most refreshing consolation, as well as the very fire and animation of knowledge that transfers into the capacity to desire and occasions decisions that break out into actions. One should, therefore, grant each sort of knowledge its value and not object to either the most rigorous conviction, proud of its subtleties, or the most ardent persuasion, even if the latter could not contend with all the devices of an adversary. In the contemplation of divine properties one should only guard against the sort of reasons that can be harmful to the noble subject matter. I have in mind the proofs of the existence of a higher being, which are probably based upon our ignorance, and may vanish with a more exact study of and deeper insight into the workings of nature. Whenever someone draws an inference from extraordinary natural events, the subordinate causes of which he cannot establish, to the immediate working of some higher power, he builds on a weak foundation. For all natural events, outside of miracles, probably have their subordinate causes.

Heathens had the misfortune that their religion rested on such weak supports. Their priests wanted to ascribe each extraordinary natural event to the immediate working of some higher power.* To hold a raw and uncultivated people in check, nothing is easier and more convenient than a system of religion that completely surrounds us with divinities and teaches us to recognized the immediate working of a higher power in the rustling of every waterfall, in the voice of thunder or the stormy wind, in everything that stirs the senses. But such a system could not last long. With the emergence of philosophy and the knowledge of nature, one also saw the emergence of atheists and those who scoff at religion, individuals who, by their discoveries, exposed the weak foundations of superstition and fancied that they had overthrown all religion and all possible grounds for the existence of God and his properties. At that time every student of nature had to be an atheist or at least be regarded as one. How was it in Epicurus' case? In order to overturn the reigning superstition he took the trouble of explaining all natural events on mechanical grounds and liberating the gods from the tedious tasks that the priests of that era had imposed upon them.[7] Excellent! If only he had not gone too far on the other side and endeavored to introduce the absurdest disbelief. But the familiar proofs for the existence of the divinity and its immediate effects were now destroyed, and the shortest path available to him was to deny either both or at least the latter. In an enlightened age Epicurus would probably have recognized the invalidity of the inference: "all natural events have their natural causes; therefore, there is no providence or even, as some want to say, no divinity" – so great is the influence of the age in which we live on our opinions and so closely related to one another are superstition and disbelief.

---

* Lucretius, *De Rerum Natura*, VI:
  Ignoratio causarum conferre Deorum
  Cogit ad imperium res, et concedere regnum: et
  Quorum operum causas nulla ratione videre
  Possunt haec fieri divino numine rentur.[8]

[7] See Epicurus "Letter to Herodotus" in Diogenes Lucretius, *Lives of Eminent Philosophers*, Bk. X: "Epicurus," tr. R. D. Hicks (London, Heinemann, 1958), pp. 564–613.

[8] *De rerum natura*, VI. 54–9: "Ignorance of causes forces them to refer/ Things and submit kingdoms to the rule of the gods/ Not seeing any causes of these works or reasons for them,/ They think that these things must be done by divine power." Cf. Lucretius, *De rerum natura*, tr. W. H. D. Rouse, rev. Martin Ferguson Smith, 2nd edn. (Cambridge, Mass., Harvard University Press, 1982).

Mendelssohn's *Philosophische Schriften*

Fourth section
On the evidence in the first principles of ethics

In every legitimate action that a human being undertakes, he silently makes the following rational inference:

> Wherever the property A is encountered, my duty requires me to do B.
> The present case has the property A; therefore, and so on.

The major premise of this rational inference is a maxim, a general rule of life, which we adopted at some earlier time and which must naturally come to mind on the occasion of the present case. The minor premise is based on a precise observation of the present circumstances and on the conviction that they agree fully with the subject of the major premise, that is to say, with the requisite property A.

Here, as in mathematics, there is a distinction between the theoretical and the practical and thus a division of ethics into two parts, instructional and applied ethics. The former expounds the general rules of life which serve as major premises in particular cases that crop up, and the latter teaches the application and exercise of the general rules in a present case. Hence, I have to investigate how far the evidence extends in these sciences and how they relate to the evidence in the first principles of geometry.

It is not difficult to prove that the general principles of ethics can be proven with geometric rigorousness and validity. "If as human beings we have the capacity to know in common with one another," Marcus Aurelius says, "then as rational creatures we also have in common the rational foundations which prescribe to us what is to be done and left undone, and, consequently, we have a *common law.*"[9] Nothing, in my opinion, is more distinct and more valid than this inference. If different things have a similar determination, then they must also have in common the consequences that flow from this determination. Human beings have in common a power of judging diverse subjects, that differs

---

[9] Marcus Aurelius, *Ad Se Ipsum Libri XII* [*Twelve Books to Himself*], ed. Joachim Dalfen (Leipzig, Teubner, 1979), pp. 25–6.

only by degree. Hence, all their concepts and judgments of good and evil also rest upon the same foundation and deviate from one another only as a matter of the degree of their insight. But if this is so, then there are also general, fundamental rules by which they are to decide what is to be done and left undone. These are the laws of nature.

The same perspective also shows us a convenient way of arriving at this general law of nature. Simply consider human beings' actions and omissions, their diverse inclinations and passions, amusements and worries and abstract the one thing on which they all ultimately agree, that determination that is to be found everywhere in this great multiplicity. This *summum bonum, quo tendimus omnes* [highest good to which we all tend], for which all human desires and wishes ultimately aim, this is the standard we must never lose sight of, the guiding thread that safely leads us through the labyrinth of human actions.

What do the thousandfold desires and wishes, passions and inclinations of human beings have in common? This, that they all aim at the preservation or betterment of the intrinsic or extrinsic condition of ourselves or another creature. Even the wickedest inclinations, the vilest desires have no other final purpose. The difference is that they substitute illusory goods for their genuine welfare, or they lack the proper proportion because they prefer their selfish ego to every other purpose or seek to improve their extrinsic condition at the cost of their intrinsic one. The ambitious and avaricious are corrupt only because they prefer the improvement of a condition extrinsic to them, their honor or their wealth, to all other purposes and frequently sacrifice body and soul, friends and fatherland for this vile desire. The libertine has the same makeup. He wrongfully prefers sensuous pleasures to the perfections of his soul or the welfare of his extrinsic condition. Hence, in the final analysis, all the vile as well as virtuous desires of human beings aim solely at the true or apparent perfection (preservation and betterment) of their intrinsic or extrinsic condition or that of their fellow human beings. Flowing from this conclusion is the general practical maxim, the first law of nature: *make your intrinsic and extrinsic condition and that of your fellow human being, in the proper proportion, as perfect as you can.* If one has discovered this general source, then one can derive from it the duties towards oneself, towards one's neighbor, and even towards God. For it is quite easy to prove that the observation of duties towards God is the most direct, secure, indeed, – what am I saying? – the only way of making our soul more perfect. Here one sees ways to the particular divisions of practical philosophy which can be demonstrated with geometrical rigor from this general law of nature.

The same natural law can be proven a priori from the mere definition of a being with free will. A being endowed with freedom can choose what pleases him from various objects or representations of objects. The basis of this satisfaction is the perfection, beauty, and order that he perceives or believes that he perceives in the preferred object. By "perfection" I understand also the utility and sensuous pleasure that the object promises us since both belong to the perfections of our intrinsic or extrinsic condition. – The contemplation of perfection, beauty, and order affords us pleasure, the contemplation of imperfection, ugliness, and disorder affords us displeasure. Hence, order, beauty, and perfection can yield compelling reasons by which a free being is determined in his choice. These compelling reasons do not impose any physical coercion on a free being because the latter chooses in terms of what he finds satisfying and on the basis of an inner energy. At the same time, however, they bring with them a moral necessity by virtue of which it becomes impossible for the free spirit to find satisfaction in imperfections, in the ugly and disorderly.

An obligation is nothing other than a moral necessity to act, that is, to do something or leave it undone. Since a free person is not physically coerced, I can only be bound to will or not will something by being given compelling reasons for it. The compelling reasons produce, however, a moral necessity; hence, each obligation is a moral necessity to do something or leave it undone. Since each free being is ethically compelled to determine himself in his choice according to the most trenchant motives, then he is also obligated to orient his choice to the rule of perfection, beauty, and order, or, what is the same, the free being is obligated to bring about as much perfection, beauty, and order in the world as is possible for him. From this there immediately follows the natural obligation or the natural law previously derived on another basis: *make your intrinsic and extrinsic condition and that of your fellow human being, in the proper proportion, as perfect as you can.*

It can be demonstrated in another way, by the most irrefutable reasons, that this general law of nature is in keeping with God's aims and that I conform to the great final purpose of creation and become an imitator of the divinity whenever I render a creature, myself or another, more perfect. As soon as one assumes that a God, who cannot act without the wisest of intentions, has produced the world, no proposition in Euclid can be proven with more rigor than this one, that the cited law of nature must be the will of God. Can the wisest and most benevolent being have any other intention than the perfection of creatures? Can he accordingly want something other than that we should orient our free actions in conformity with this intention? It is as impossible for him to want this as it is for the tangent to touch the circle at more than one point.

Yet am I obliged to comply with the will of the creator? – Yes, our philosophers reply. God is the complete proprietor of everything that he has produced out of nothing. We are his property, his slaves. Hence, he has the incontestable right of imposing laws on us, prescribing what pleases him and punishing transgressors as rebels. We must obey, fully submitting ourselves and completely annihilating our will in the face of his. – This answer is humbling but does not fit the question. The inference from power to right may not be made so directly. God can, in a physical sense, do what he wants with his creation. How does it follow from this that he can also do so morally, that it is permissible for him, that he has a right to this? I still do not understand how these concepts are connected. – The creation is his property? – Well, yes, but the only thing that can be inferred from this is that someone else, if he also had the power, nevertheless would not have the right of prescribing to him what kind of use to make of his creation. But where is the mathematical proof that he himself has a right, a moral authority to do with his property as he pleases? What no one else can prevent us from is still not, for that reason, permissible. No one can rightly prevent me from strangling the bird who sings here in the cage; but would it be, for that reason, allowed?

The little step that still needs to be taken consists in the following reasoning. One proves that God cannot want anything but the best and that a right is nothing else but a moral capacity to do something that is in keeping with the rule of perfection. Now the inference is as cogent as any geometrical proof. We are God's creatures, hence, his property. If we are his property, then he has the right to make any use of our power that he finds to be good, for what he finds to be good is indisputably the best. He has, therefore, the right, the moral capacity, to prescribe laws to us. For the laws that he prescribes to us, his property, are in keeping with the rule of perfection. He has a right, furthermore, to punish trangressors of these laws if this punishment itself contributes something to perfection, and so on.

A twofold moral necessity (obligation) is incumbent upon us, the property of God, to submit ourselves to the will of our proprietor and to live according to his laws. This is necessary, in the first place, because those laws are, in and for themselves, the best since otherwise God could not possibly prescribe them. How an obligation springs from this concept, has already been shown above. In the second place, the punishments and rewards linked by God to the transgression and observation of his laws provide us with compelling reasons to consider obedience better and thus to submit ourselves to his reign. The compelling reasons are the only impulses by means of which a being with free will can be set into motion, and the wisest Legislator himself has no other means of introducing his laws and making them obligatory than to link them to compelling reasons which incline the being endowed with free will to accept them. Thus, nothing can bind us to assume natural or divine laws but their intrinsic splendidness and the deliberate punishments and rewards which the Supreme Being has found it in our best interest to link to those laws.

The system of practical philosophy can be erected on this foundation without any particular difficulty. Our actions are good or evil insofar as they agree with the rule of perfection or, what is the same, with God's intentions. We are, therefore, obligated to do certain things and leave others undone. Virtue is a proficiency in performing good actions and vice a proficiency in performing evil actions. – Strive for virtue and shun vice! – The obligatory nature of good actions gives us a right to the means necessary to carry out those actions. If all other human beings had an equal right to the same means, then the law of nature would contradict itself, as has been distinctly outlined by Cumberland.[10] There is, then, necessarily a place for privilege, and this privilege can be decided on rational grounds. These rational grounds, insofar as they can be applied to an array of individual cases, constitute the laws of natural right, and the core concept of these laws is called

---

[10] Richard Cumberland's *De legibus naturae* (London, 1672) was published in English as *A Treatise of the Laws of Nature* (London, 1727; reissued New York, Garland, 1978) and *Traité philosophique des loix de la nature*, tr. Jean Barbeyrac (Amsterdam, 1744; Lausanne and Geneva, 1744).

"natural right." It is to be shown on the basis of the universal law of nature that we are obliged to recognize these privileges and to permit those who have these privileges coming to them to enjoy them. We are accordingly bound to natural justice, that is to say, we must allow each person the right coming to him. If one wants to explain justice, as noted above, through a wisely administered benevolence, then the obligation to be just can also be demonstrated on other grounds. For we are obliged to make our intrinsic condition more perfect and, therefore, to be wise and benevolent.

One sees here an example once again of the astonishing fruitfulness of our concepts. From the single definition of a being endowed with free will, the entire system of our duties, rights, and responsibilities can be unpacked; all our inclinations, desires, and passions flow from this general source, and our actions and omissions are legitimate if they conform to this basic concept as a geometrical demonstration does to its presupposition. Yet the splendid harmony of truths is also cause for wonder! We have laid three different maxims as the foundation: first, consider the one thing on which the inclinations of all human beings agree; second, recognize that you are a being endowed with free will; three, recognize that you are God's property. All three basic maxims lead to the common conclusion: make yourself and others perfect. Infinitely many additional basic definitions, or even the right sorts of experiences, can be premised in this way, leading us all on a sometimes shorter, sometimes longer route to the same result. In this wonderful harmony one recognizes the truth! It shows how nature presents infinitely many outlooks, infinitely many perspectives, but all concur in the great painting within which nature depicts the whole. For the all-seeing eye, the whole of nature is *one* painting, the sum total of all possible knowledge is *one* truth.

The concepts of moral philosophy are, therefore, fruitful and coherent enough to be a theoretical system, and, in this theory, we can unpack all our particular duties, rights, and responsibilities from a single, universal law of nature. This certainty will be the same as is promised in the first principles of metaphysics. If philosophy mainly is a science of the constitution of things in general, then moral philosophy in particular is nothing else but the science of the constitution of a being with free will insofar as it has a free will. As we have seen, however, freedom is a fruitful concept, the unpacking of which can lead us to knowledge of all our duties and responsibilities. Hence, the doctrines of theoretical moral philosophy can be demonstrated irrefutably on the basis of sure foundations, and the certainty that reigns in it is the same certainty as that possessed by metaphysics as it unpacks the constitution of things in general. – On the other hand, the proofs in this science can still be less illuminating, less perspicuous than those in the first principles of metaphysics or natural theology. Along with the difficulties that, in every philosophical discipline, being completely convinced necessarily involves (as was shown in the foregoing sections), in moral philosophy there is the additional difficulty of building this science on the foundations of metaphysics. One must have comprehended theology, cosmology, and psychology and have been convinced of them before one can promise oneself some light in moral philosophy. How can I comprehend what I owe God, myself, and my neighbor, if I do not have true and correct concepts of God, my neighbor, myself, and the moral bond which, as creature and fellow creature, I have with the latter? Hence, since practical philosophy places the truths of metaphysics at its foundation, it is easy to understand that the evidence in practical philosophy must be much more difficult to sustain.

The relations in applied ethics are the same as in every other practical science. Each practical rational inference lays the makeup of a present case in the minor premise as a foundation, a makeup which can only be known to us by experience. The truth of the conclusion thus depends upon the certainty of the experience that places the minor premise beyond doubt. If the experience does not contain sufficient grounds to convince us perfectly of the correctness of the minor premise, then the conclusion will follow the weaker part and can appear no more than probable.

The same situation obtains in practical ethics. It is necessary to lay as the foundation experiences which cannot always have the desired degree of certainty. Yet, in this regard, the following considerations are not to be ignored. There are universal laws of nature which flow immediately from the first source. These apply more to the inclinations of our heart than to our external actions. They prescribe to us what we should love and what we should shun, and they leave it to the subordinate law of nature to direct our actions and omissions. The universal laws of nature have this makeup: Revere the creator! Love virtue, flee vice! Control your passions, submit your desires to reason! All these precepts of reason can be transformed into inferences of application, inferences which entail the utmost conviction. I am a rational creature; therefore, I must revere my creator, love virtue, despise vice. My desires can detour me from the path of happiness, my passions can overstep the goal; hence, I must submit them to the rule of reason. All these practical rational inferences can be proven with geometrical rigor. The major premises of them are so universal that no exception to them occurs. It is not possible for their application to stand in the way of any higher duty, for they actually are the source from which all our duties are derived. At all times and in every possible circumstance I am bound to revere my creator, to love virtue, and so forth, and nothing that happens in the world can free me from this responsibility. – The minor premises of this rational inference are grounded on the experiences of an inner sense, experiences which entail conviction. I am a rational creature; I long for happiness; my desires and passions, left to themselves, are able to make me unhappy. To be sure, all these propositions are ultimately grounded on experiences, but on experiences that leave no room for doubt, experiences that are as certain as the most valid rational inference.

However, if one descends to the derivative laws of nature which prescribe to us what we are to do and leave undone in particular cases, then the degree of certainty gradually decreases in practice and climbs down all stages of probability to doubtfulness. For, in the first place, the makeup of the present case everywhere depends upon experiences which seldom contain enough reasons for the truth of the premises. The moral goodness of an action, the value or lack of value of our actions and omissions, depends not only on countless accompanying circumstances and contingencies but also on consequences and effects of these deeds, which cannot possibly be foreseen with certainty. The slightest unexpected accident can dash all our hopes and leave the best intentions with the most damaging effects. One circumstance which we have not noticed – and how seldom are we in a position to weigh all circumstances precisely! – can give a completely different form to the makeup of the present case. Only an all-seeing eye can see the causes, consequences, proportions, and contingencies of an actual event with perfect certainty. In such a case mortals must leave the direction to a mere probability. In addition, higher duties can at times stand in the way of the major premise or the general rules of life that are to be applied in cases at hand, in which case the obligatoriness of those rules ceases. We are bound to do a, not the good, but the best, and a derivative natural law that stands in the way of a higher natural law must give way to the latter. This conflict of higher and lower duties is of all the more concern, the more particular the rule of life is which constitutes the major premise of our practical inference. Occasionally this conflict can be occasioned by circumstances which escape the acutest attentiveness. The most praiseworthy action, the most deserving work can become sinful if we simultaneously neglect a higher duty whose obligatoriness is more important. For each external action, by occurring, excludes all other actions which could have happened at the same time, and each law commanding us to do something must be understood under the condition that our duty does not at the same time require something more important from us that would be neglected by doing this. What mortal can boast of seeing with certainty what the best action is that he can perform as far as the occasion, time, and circumstances are concerned? In such cases, to wait for certainty means to stand there in a state of eternal indecision, never wanting to come to the point of application. Indeed, frequently the occasion is so pressing, the moment so decisive, that there is not even time left to us to weigh the grounds of probability by distinct concepts. *Conscience* and a good *sense for the truth* (*bon sens*), if I may be permitted this expression, must represent the place of reason in most situations, if the opportunity is not to elude us before we seize it. Conscience is a proficiency at correctly distinguishing good from evil by means of indistinct inferences, and the sense for the truth is a proficiency in distinguishing good from evil by similar means. They are in their sphere what taste is in the domain of the beautiful and the ugly. A refined taste in no time finds what sluggish criticism only gradually casts light upon. Just as quickly, conscience decides and the sense for the truth judges what reason does not reduce to distinct inferences without tedious reflection.

The inner feeling, this sentiment of good and evil, true and false, works according to inalterable rules, according to correct principles, but principles which have been incorporated into our temperament by constant practice and, as it were, transformed into our sweat and blood. Although they are founded upon indistinct knowledge and frequently upon mere probabilities, their influence upon the capacity to desire is nonetheless far more passionate and intense than that of the most distinct rational inferences which, without the perfected habit, convince but do not stir, instruct but do not move the mind. – In order to cast some light on this, allow me to consider more precisely the distinction between practical and theoretical conviction (of which I made mention at the end of the previous section).

We give *approval* to a proposition as soon as we see reasons for its truth. The more these reasons approach a complete demonstration and the more distinctly we know them, the more reliable our approval is. Finally, if we see the proof of a proposition so distinctly that we can no longer doubt its truth, then we are completely convinced. This is *theoretical approval*, the conviction of the *intellect*.

The *mind* or the conceptual center of our capacity to desire recognizes a kind of approval which is quite distinct from that and deserves to be called *practical approval*. Whoever is convinced of a truth cannot at the same time doubt it; but one can be theoretically convinced of an obligation and nevertheless act contrary to it. Descartes seems, indeed, not without reason to maintain: "A person sins rarely through a defectiveness in the *theoretical* knowledge of his duty, but instead through a defectiveness in the *practical* knowledge; this is through a defectiveness in the firm habit of assenting to his duty."[11]

Not all demonstrative truths have an equally strong effect on our capacity to desire. Many convince the intellect without moving the mind, afford distinct knowledge but without force, life, and effectiveness, while other truths, on the other hand, move the mind more with less certainty and produce an effective and lively knowledge which passes over into the capacity to desire and incites us to practical decisions. The cause of this is well-known. We human beings possess, in addition to reason, sense and imagination, inclinations and passions, which are of extreme importance in determining what we do and leave undone. The judgment of our reason does not always concur with the judgment of the lower powers of our soul, and if they contend with one

---

[11] "Raro peccatur defectu *theoreticae* cognitionis officii sui, sed defectu *practicae*, hoc est defectu firmi habitus assentiendi officio suo." This appears to be a rough Latin translation of a passage from a letter from Descartes to Princess Elizabeth, 15 September 1645. Cf. Descartes, *Correspondance, July 1643 – April 1647* in *Philosophical Writings*, vol. 3 "Et en ce sens on a raison, dans l'Eschole, de dire que les vertus sont des habitudes; car, en effet, on ne manque guères, faute d'avoir, en théorie, la connoissance de ce qu'on doit faire, mais seulement faute de l'avoir en pratique, c'est-à-dire faute d'avoir une ferme habitude de la croyre." ["And in that sense one has reason, in the schools, to say that virtues are habits, because one does not have, in fact, any theoretical lack of knowledge of what one should, but only a practical lack, that is to say, a lack of firm habit of belief."]

another, then each necessarily weakens the other's influence on the will. The approval of a truth will be practical, then, only if the rational grounds either subdue the lower powers of the soul, or also include them to their advantage. It is easy to see that in the latter case the mind must be far more resolute. For reason and imagination, spirit and heart then harmonize in spurring us to actions. But even in the former case, namely, if the rational grounds suppress all the imagination's representations to the contrary, knowledge is energetic and breaks out into action.

Ethics puts into our hands the means of maintaining the harmony of the lower powers of the soul with reason. These means can be reduced to the following four major parts.

First, there is the *accumulation of compelling reasons.* Many persuasive reasons can have more weight, move the heart more easily, than a single convincing reason. If the former are united with the latter, then they produce the happy agreement of the heart with the intellect, a source of the sweetest satisfaction. The mathematician is content with a single proof since he has only to convince the intellect and to wrest a merely speculative approval. The orator, on the other hand, heaps reason on top of reason, storms the mind from every side, and seeks to use every probable reason to his advantage. For he wants to move the heart and engage the capacity to desire, and he must have an effect not merely on the intellect, but on the senses and the imagination at the same time.

Second, there is *practice.* The more we reflect on certain reasons and the more we derive motives for our actions from them, the livelier the impression is which they leave on the mind and the easier it is for them to include the lower powers of the soul as well. If this practice is continued long enough for the action to become easy for us, we then say that we have acquired a proficiency in doing something. Habit and practice rule despotically in our hearts, and by their help one can subdue the most obstinate inclinations and bring the most stubborn passions under the yoke of reason; or, rather, by their help one can produce inclinations and passions that have the same ultimate purpose as the precepts of reason.

Third, there is the *pleasant sentiment.* If rational grounds are supported by beauty and grace, then the imagination is easily lured into agreement. Perfection is the mainspring of reason, and pleasant sentiment the bait of the imagination. On this is founded the utility of fine arts and sciences for ethics. Rational grounds convince the intellect of the splendidness of virtue, and the fine arts wrest the imagination's approval. The former make it honorable, the latter pleasant. The former show the way to happiness, while the latter strew the path with flowers. How great the virtuoso is in the eyes of the philosopher if he remains true to his vocation and actually procures for virtue the advantages which it can expect from him!

The fourth and final chief means of bringing the imagination in accord with reason is *intuitive knowledge*, if, namely, the universal rational grounds are, as it were, transformed by examples into sensuous concepts. In each theory an example serves merely to illuminate and becomes superficial as soon as we grasp the universal theorem distinctly. In practice, however, an example is always more useful than the maxim. It has a stronger influence on the mind's approval because it stirs the senses and jostles the imagination. The utility of history and Aesop's fables are based on this point.

One sees, then, what is involved if the principles of practical ethics are to have the proper effect on what we do and leave undone and if they are to bring about an enduring and constant readiness for virtue. They must be enlivened by *examples*, supported by the force of *pleasant sentiment*, kept constantly effective by *practice*, and finally transformed into a *proficiency*. Then there emerges the conviction of the heart that is our ultimate and most eminent purpose in ethics. It may be the case that the spirit always sees only probable proofs before it; indeed, it may have never analyzed this probability distinctly and instead merely grasped the probability by virtue of having a sense for the truth. This is not always an obstacle to the life of knowledge. The senses can still be stirred in a lively way, the imagination aroused, and the mind compelled by habit, example, grace, and so on to give the most steadfast and unalterable approval. A sweeter peace of mind and satisfaction springs from this sort of approval than from some cold conviction of spirit.

By no means do these considerations have the purpose of creating doubts about the utility of an ethics that is demonstrated logically. Rather, what was recalled at the end of the previous section in regard to theology and the doctrine of divine properties is also valid here. Each kind of knowledge has its value.

On the ability to know, the ability to feel, and the ability to desire

On the ability to know, the ability to feel, and the ability to desire

Between the ability to know and the ability to desire lies the ability to feel, by means of which we feel pleasure or displeasure in some subject matter, approve of it, deem it good, and find it pleasant or disapprove of it, find fault with it, and find it unpleasant. There are thoughts and representations in which we take no part and which are not connected with any sentiments. There are also sentiments that do not pass over into desires. We can find a piece of music, a painting beautiful and be moved by it without desiring anything.

The goal of the ability to know is the true. That is, insofar as we possess a ability to know, we strive to make the concepts in our soul agree with the properties of their objects.

The goal of the ability to feel is the good. That is, insofar as we possess an ability to feel, we strive to make the objective properties agree with our concepts of goodness, order, and beauty. This object is occasionally in us ourselves if we endeavor to alter our thoughts and sentiments themselves in keeping with the rule of goodness, beauty, and so forth.

Thus, within the human being, there are apparently contrasting inclinations to truth and to fiction: to truth as soon as the ability to know is supposed to be engaged, to fiction, on the other hand, as soon as we intend merely to sustain our ability to feel. In the first case, it does not matter to us what kind of predicates the objects have as long as we simply know them just as they actually are and not otherwise; such as mathematics, natural history. In the second case, on the other hand, our comprehension and knowledge does not mean as much to us as the objective makeup of some matter which we endeavor to arrange according to our concept of order, beauty, and perfection. Not the true, but rather the good is then our goal. In all the affairs of the heart, our wishes and desires are directed at the constitution of the objects, not at our representations. We wish our friends to be happy, not merely in order not to know their misfortune, but in order to deflect any such misfortune.

In the investigation of truth we must have no other interest than the truth. As soon as inclinations come into play and interest us in one part or another, we do not look for our concepts to conform to things but rather, where possible, for things to conform to our inclinations. That is to say, we let the ability to feel work alongside where the ability to know should be at work completely alone and unmixed.

Whoever looks too much to the true in the representation of the beautiful, likewise commits the mistake of letting his ability to know have influence where the ability to feel, the capacity for sentiments, alone is supposed to have influence, and, by this means, he makes himself incapable of any deception.

Each sentiment is combined with a desire to place the properties of the object in harmony with our concepts. This desiring is the element of striving. The moment of its effectiveness stands in composite proportion to its (1) recognized goodness (in terms of its extension and intension), (2) possibility (inner and outer), (3) difficulty.

The very moment which is the greatest at this instant passes over from, as it were, the dead force of desiring into the living force of activity which is either merely internal, that is, if merely the alertness and attentiveness of the soul is governed, or external, if limbs are moved, depending upon whether its goal is to alter thoughts or things.

Wishing extends to the impossible. We wish to be able to fly, to be lords of the entire surface of the earth, never to die, to be able to be at different places at the same time, and the like. – But such a wish never becomes a maximum in the soul of a rational human being, and it produces no activity. A variable of the mentioned proportion is also the possibility of being able to alter the constitution of objects according to our sentiment. Where this becomes $= 0$, the moment itself is $= 0$, and things remain at the level of the dead force of a wish.

On the question: what does "to enlighten" mean?

On the question: what does "to enlighten" mean?

The words "enlightenment," "culture," "education" are still new-comers to our language. At the present time they belong merely to the language of books. The common masses scarcely understand them. Should this be a proof that the theme is also novel to us? I do not believe so. One says of a certain people that they do not have a definite word for virtue or for superstition, although one may correctly ascribe a considerable measure of both to them.

Linguistic usage, meanwhile, appears to want to make a distinction among these words which have similar meanings, but it has not yet had time to establish their borders. Education, culture, and enlightenment are modifications of social life, effects of the hard work and efforts of human beings to improve their social condition.

The more that art and hard work have brought the social condition of a people into harmony with the vocation of a human being, the more educated this people is.

Education breaks down into culture and enlightenment. The former seems to apply more to the practical dimension, that means – objectively – to excellence, finesse, and beauty in trades, arts, and society's mores, and – subjectively – to proficiency, hard work, and skill at those trades, arts, and mores as well as to inclinations, drives, and habits making up that proficiency, hard work, and skill. The more these dimensions within a people correspond to the vocation of a human being, the more culture is ascribed to it, just as a plot of land is said to be cultivated and cared for, to the degree that people's hard work has put it into the position of producing things useful to human beings. – Enlightenment seems, by contrast, to refer more to the theoretical dimension. It seems to refer – objectively – to rational knowledge and – subjectively – to proficiency at rationally reflecting upon things of human life, in terms of their importance and influence on the vocation of the human being.

I always set up the vocation of a human being as the measure and goal of every striving and effort, as the point at which we must direct our eyes, if we do not want to lose our way.

A language attains enlightenment through sciences and culture through social interaction, poetry, and oratory. Through the former, it becomes more fit for theoretical use; through the latter for practical use. Both together make a language educated.

Culture in an external sense is called "refinement." Hail to the nation whose refinement is the effect of culture and enlightenment, whose external splendor and elegance is based upon an internal, solid genuineness.

Enlightenment is related to culture as, generally, theory is related to practice, knowledge to ethics, criticism to virtuosity. Considered in and for itself (objectively), they are connected with one another in the most precise manner, although they can very often be separated subjectively.

One can say: the Nurembergers have more culture, the Berliners more enlightenment, the French more culture, the English more enlightenment, the Chinese much culture and little enlightenment. The Greeks had both culture and enlightenment. They were an educated nation just as their language is an educated language. – Generally, the language of a people is the best indication of its education, of its culture as well as its enlightenment, in terms of both its extent and its strength.

The vocation of a human being can be further divided into, first, the vocation of a human being as a human being and, second, the vocation of a human being as a citizen.

In regard to culture, these considerations collapse into one another since all practical perfections have value merely in relation to the life of society. Hence, they must correspond solely and singularly to a human being's vocation as a member of society. The human being as a human being is not in need of a culture, but is in need of enlightenment.

Standing and profession in civil life determine each individual member's duties and rights, and they demand different skills and proficiency, different inclinations, drives, and habits, a different social sense, culture, and refinement, all in accordance with those duties and rights. The more these requirements of individuals harmonize in all classes with their profession, that is, with their respective vocations as members of the society, the more culture the nation has.

But they also demand of each individual, in keeping with his standing and profession, different theoretical insights and a different proficiency at attaining this, a different degree of enlightenment. The enlightenment that interests the human being as a human being is universal, devoid of any class distinction; the enlightenment of the human being, considered as a citizen, is modified, based upon standing and profession. Here the vocation of the human being again sets the measure and goal of his striving.

Given all this, the enlightenment of a nation is proportional to:

first, the degree of knowledge,
second, its importance, that is, its relation to the vocation of (a) the
human being and (b) the citizen,
third, its dissemination through all classes, and
fourth, the standards of their professions.

The level of enlightenment of a people should, therefore, be determined according to a proportion composed of at least four variables, some of which are in turn themselves proportions composed of simpler variables.

The enlightenment of human beings can come into conflict with the enlightenment of citizens. Certain truths which are useful to the human being as a human being, can at times be harmful to him as a citizen. In this regard, the following should be considered. The collision can arise between, first, essential or, second, contingent vocations of the human being, and third, essential or, fourth, extra-essential, contingent vocations of the citizen.

Without their essential vocations as human beings, humans sink down to the level of cattle; without extra-essential vocations, a human being is not so fine and splendid a creature. Without human beings' essential vocations as citizens, the state constitution ceases to exist; without extra-essential vocations, it no longer remains the same in some accompanying relations.

Unhappy is the state that must confess that a human being's essential vocation cannot harmonize in it with a citizen's essential vocation, that the enlightenment which is indispensable to humanity cannot extend to all classes in the realm without the constitution being in danger of perishing. Here philosophy remains silent! Necessity may prescribe laws or, rather, forge chains that are to be laid upon humanity in order to humiliate it and keep it constantly stifled.

But if the extra-essential vocations of the human being come into conflict with the essential or extra-essential vocations of the citizen, then rules must be established, on the basis of which exceptions ought to occur and cases of collision decided.

If human beings' essential vocations have been brought into conflict with their extra-essential vocations, if one is not permitted to disseminate certain useful truths that embellish humanity without thereby in any way tearing down the principles of religion and ethics inherent in human beings, then the virtue-loving man of enlightenment will proceed with caution and discretion, and prefer to indulge prejudice than drive away the truth that is so wound up with that prejudice. This maxim has, to be sure, always been the bulwark of hypocrisy, and we have it to thank for so many centuries of barbarism and superstition. Whenever one tried to grab hold of the crime, it escaped into the sanctuary. But in spite of this, the friend of humanity himself will have to have recourse to this consideration in the most enlightened times. It is difficult but not impossible, even here, to find the borderline that separates use from misuse.

The nobler a thing's perfection, says a Hebrew writer, the ghastlier is its decomposition.[1] A rotted tree is not as hideous as a decomposed flower, the latter not as repugnant as a putrefied animal, and the latter not as ghastly as a decomposing human being. So, too, with culture and enlightenment. The nobler they are in their blossoming, the more abominable they are when they deteriorate and decompose.

Misuse of enlightenment enfeebles moral feeling and leads to hardheartedness, egoism, irreligion, and anarchy. Misuse of culture engenders lasciviousness, hypocrisy, flaccidity, superstition, and slavery.

Where enlightenment and culture proceed at the same tempo, they are together the best means of defense against corruption. To ruin the likes of one of them is to be in direct conflict with the other.

Hence, the education of a nation, which, given the earlier definition of the words, is composed of culture and enlightenment, will be far less subject to corruption.

---

[1] In his edition of the essay, Alexander Altmann suggests that Mendelssohn is referring to *Mischna Judajim*, IV. 6 (*Kleinere Schriften*, [Stuttgart and Bad Cannstatt, Frommann-Holzboog, 1981], p. 240).

An educated nation knows in itself no danger other than excess of national prosperity which, in and of itself, like the most perfect health of the human body, can already be called a sickness. A nation which has come through education to the highest pinnacle of national prosperity is, precisely because of that, in danger of falling since it can climb no higher. – Yet this leads us too far from the question before us!

Index

318

Cambridge texts in the history of philosophy

Titles published in the series thus far

Antoine Arnauld and Pierre Nicole *Logic or the Art of Thinking* (edited by Jill Vance Buroker)

Boyle *A Free Enquiry into the Vulgarly Received Notion of Nature* (edited by Edward B. Davis and Michael Hunter)

Conway *The Principles of the Most Ancient and Modern Philosophy* (edited by Allison P. Coudert and Taylor Corse)

Cudworth *A Treatise Concerning Eternal and Immutable Morality* and *A Treatise of Freewill* (edited by Sarah Hutton)

Descartes *Meditations on First Philosophy*, with selections from the *Objections and Replies* (edited with an introduction by John Cottingham)

Kant *The Metaphysics of Morals* (edited by Mary Gregor with an introduction by Roger Sullivan)

Kant *Prolegomena to any Future Metaphysics* (edited by Gary Hatfield)

La Mettrie *Machine Man and Other Writings* (edited by Ann Thomson)

Leibniz *New Essays on Human Understanding* (edited by Peter Remnant and Jonathan Bennett)

Malebranche *Dialogues on Metaphysics and on Religion* (edited by Nicholas Jolley and David Scott)

Malebranche *The Search after Truth* (edited by Thomas M. Lennon and Paul J. Olscamp)

Mendelssohn *Philosophical Writings* (edited by Daniel O. Dahlstrom)

Nietzsche *Human, all too Human* (translated by R. J. Hollingdale with an introduction by Richard Schacht)

Schleiermacher *On Religion: Speeches to its Cultured Despisers* (edited by Richard Crouter)